Information Efficiency in Financial and Betting Markets

Betting markets offer economists a fascinating case study of how information efficiency operates in a market. They incorporate features highly appropriate to a study of information efficiency, as each bet has a well-defined end point at which its value becomes certain. Using international examples, this is the first book to review and analyse the issue of information efficiency in financial and betting markets. Part I is an extensive survey of the existing literature, while Part II presents a range of new readings by leading academics. Insights gained from betting interest a wide community: governments, who like to tax betting; financial market analysts, who bet on the financial markets themselves; and, lastly, mathematicians, who bring their particular skills to the great mathematical puzzle of betting. All of these will want to read this topical survey of theory and practice in financial and betting markets.

PROFESSOR LEIGHTON VAUGHAN WILLIAMS is Professor of Economics and Finance and Director of the Betting Research Unit at Nottingham Business School, Nottingham Trent University.

T0312225

Information Efficiency in Financial and Betting Markets

edited by

LEIGHTON VAUGHAN WILLIAMS

CAMBRIDGE
UNIVERSITY PRESS

CAMBRIDGE UNIVERSITY PRESS
Cambridge, New York, Melbourne, Madrid, Cape Town, Singapore, São Paulo, Delhi

Cambridge University Press
The Edinburgh Building, Cambridge CB2 8RU, UK

Published in the United States of America by Cambridge University Press, New York

www.cambridge.org
Information on this title: www.cambridge.org/9780521108171

First published 2005
This digitally printed version 2009

A catalogue record for this publication is available from the British Library

ISBN 978-0-521-81603-8 hardback
ISBN 978-0-521-10817-1 paperback

To my family and friends

Contents

Figures

Tables

Contributors

ALISTAIR C. BRUCE is Director of Nottingham University Business School and Professor of Decision and Risk Analysis. He has published widely in economics, management and psychology journals in the area of decision making under uncertainty, with particular reference to horse-race betting markets.

LES COLEMAN lectures in Finance at the University of Melbourne, and is a member of the Investment Policy Committee of United Funds Management. He has over twenty years' experience in senior management positions with resources, manufacturing and finance companies in Australia and overseas. Les trained originally as an engineer and holds a PhD in Management.

WILLIAM COLLIER is Lecturer in Economics at the University of Kent. His main research interests are in the fields of applied microeconometrics, labour economics and the economics of migration.

DAVID EDELMAN is currently at University College Dublin (Banking and Finance), having had previous posts at Columbia University and Sydney University. He completed his Undergraduate/Masters degrees at MIT, and his PhD at Columbia. He has published widely in Statistics, Mathematical Statistics, Finance, Computer Science, Medicine and Law and is author of a popular book on horse-race betting. David has consulted widely in the areas of derivatives, racing and electricity markets.

DAVID FORREST is Senior Lecturer in Economics in the University of Salford where he teaches on Europe's only gambling studies degree programme. He has published extensively on the economics of lotteries and of betting markets and also in the area of sports economics.

KENT R. GROTE is an assistant professor in the Department of Economics and Business at Lake Forest College near Chicago, IL. He earned his PhD in economics from George Mason University. His research on the economics of lotteries has been published in *Public Finance Review* and *Economics Letters*.

PATRICK J. HARVEY is Adjunct Associate Professor of Accounting at the Hong Kong University of Science and Technology. He has also held positions at the University of Hong Kong, where he began his academic career, and the University of Nevada at Las Vegas.

WILLIAM HURLEY is a Professor in the Department of Business Administration at the Royal Military College of Canada. His research interests are military operations research, operations research in sport, game theory and decision analysis.

JOHNNIE E. V. JOHNSON is Professor of Decision and Risk Analysis and Director of the Centre for Risk Research in the School of Management at the University of Southampton. He has published widely in the areas of risk perception, risk management and decision making under uncertainty, particularly in relation to decisions in betting markets.

DAVID LAW lectures in economics at the University of Wales, Bangor. His research interests are in financial and gambling markets and economic development. He has published articles in *Economica*, the *Journal of Forecasting* and the *Journal of Risk and Uncertainty*.

VICTOR A. MATHESON is an assistant professor in the Department of Economics at the College of the Holy Cross in Worcester, MA. He earned his PhD in economics from the University of Minnesota. Despite his extensive research on the economics of lotteries, which has been published in the *Eastern Economic Journal*, *Public Finance Review* and *Economics Letters*, he has still not won the lottery.

LAWRENCE MCDONOUGH is a Professor in the Department of Politics and Economics at the Royal Military College of Canada in Kingston Ontario. In addition to a body of research related to the observed bias in betting, he has published in the economics of education financing, child care mechanisms and defence economics. His current research is focused on the valuation of the environmental benefits of 'green roofs' in urban centres.

MARTIN MCGRATH is an IT Consultant running his own business. He has over fifteen years' experience working with large organisations developing complex IT solutions, including four years with Microsoft as their specialist data warehousing consultant. He maintains his own database storing large volumes of wagering and form information permitting the performance of complex trend analysis.

IAN MCHALE is Lecturer in Applied Statistics in the University of Salford. Current research interests include statistics in sport and extreme value statistics. He recently developed the new Actim Index, the official player rating system of the FA Premier League.

DAVID PATON is Professor of Industrial Economics at Nottingham University Business School. He has published widely on subjects as diverse as the economics of county cricket, teenage pregnancy and betting markets and has also acted as an advisor on gambling policy for several government departments.

IVAN A. PAYA is Assistant Professor at the Department of Fundamentos Analisis Economico, University of Alicante, Spain. He obtained his PhD from the Cardiff Business School, Cardiff University. His research interests are in the field of macroeconomics, applied econometrics, forecasting and time series analysis. He has published in a variety of international journals.

DAVID A. PEEL is a Professor of Economics at Lancaster University Management School. He was educated at the University of Warwick and has held posts at the University of Liverpool, Aberystwyth and Cardiff University. He has published widely on empirical and theoretical issues in macroeconomics and the economics of gambling markets.

JOHN PEIRSON is the Director of the Energy Economics Research Group at the University of Kent. He has other research interests in the efficiency of betting markets, the efficiency of financial markets and the economics of uncertainty.

ADI SCHNYTZER is an Associate Professor of Economics in the Department of Economics at Bar-Ilan University in Israel. He is a comparative economist who has an extensive research background in the analysis of socialist economic systems and sports betting markets.

YUVAL SHILONY is in the Department of Economics at Bar-Ilan University in Israel. His areas of research are theoretical and applied microeconomics, economics of insurance, markets of contingent claims and industrial organisation.

ROBERT SIMMONS is Senior Lecturer in Economics at the Lancaster University Management School. He has published extensively in the fields of sports economics, the economics of gambling and labour economics. Outside the classroom, he is a qualified FA referee.

MICHAEL A. SMITH has taught extensively in Economics and Business Studies at a range of higher education institutions including the University of York. He is currently Senior Lecturer in Economics at Canterbury Christ Church University College. Michael's research activities are concerned with the informational efficiency of markets for state contingent claims.

ERIK SNOWBERG is an economist currently completing his PhD at the Stanford Graduate School of Business. His interests include political, behavioural and developmental economics.

MING-CHIEN SUNG is a PhD student in the Centre for Risk Research, School of Management at the University of Southampton. She is currently employing both parametric and non-parametric methods to explore the degree to which UK racetrack betting markets are informationally efficient with respect to a range of publicly available information.

PAUL M. TWOMEY returned to the University of Sussex to study for a mathematics DPhil in 2001 after spending two years working in the City documenting equity derivatives. He is close to completing his thesis, on market efficiency of horse-racing markets with applications to spread betting.

LEIGHTON VAUGHAN WILLIAMS is Professor of Economics and Finance and Director of the Betting Research Unit at Nottingham Business School, Nottingham Trent University. He advises the UK government on the taxation and regulation of betting and gaming, and has published extensively in the fields of risk, asymmetric information, financial and betting markets.

W. DAVID WALLS is Professor of Economics and Academic Director of the Van Horne Institute at the University of Calgary. In addition to gambling markets, his research focuses on pirate goods markets, the motion picture industry, transportation and energy economics.

JUSTIN WOLFERS is an Assistant Professor of Business and Public Policy at the Wharton School of the University of Pennsylvania, and a faculty research fellow of the National Bureau of Economic Research. His research focuses on labour economics, macroeconomics, political economy and behavioural finance. He has worked in and around betting markets in both his native Australia and his new home in the United States for fifteen years.

ERIC ZITZEWITZ has been an Assistant Professor of Economics at Stanford Business School since 2001. He received a PhD in Economics from MIT in 2001 and an AB in Economics from Harvard College in 1993. His research interests involve competitive strategy and agency issues, particularly in financial and information industries. He has studied stale pricing and late trading in mutual funds, the economic impact of the Iraq war, the effects of fair disclosure regulation and bias and related distortions in opinions from equity analysts, financial journalists and Olympic judges.

Introduction

A central issue in the analysis of markets is the degree to which they are *efficient*. Although 'efficiency' has a variety of meanings in different contexts, a situation is sometimes termed 'efficient' if it is not possible to increase the well-being (utility) of any one person without reducing the utility of another. This is usually referred to as Pareto efficiency. An implication of Pareto efficiency is *productive efficiency*, a situation which exists when it is not possible to increase the quantity produced of any one good without reducing the quantity produced of another.

In the analysis of betting markets – and, indeed, financial markets more generally – however, the examination of efficiency assumes an informational dimension, the existence of which may well be related to that of Pareto or productive efficiency, but the meaning of which is quite distinct. It is this form of efficiency which is the subject of investigation in this volume. This book traces the development of the idea of informationally efficient markets, and identifies the various precise definitions and variations of the concept extant in the literature on financial markets. The theoretical background is clarified, and empirical tests of information efficiency are reviewed and evaluated.

While most studies of information efficiency are conducted within the framework of conventional financial markets, there are a number of special features of betting markets which warrant particular attention and make them of unique relevance to a study of market efficiency. In particular, these markets not only possess many of the usual attributes of financial markets – notably a large number of investors (or bettors) with potential access to widely available rich information sets – but also the important additional property that each asset (or bet) possesses a well-defined end point at which its value becomes certain. This contrasts with most financial markets, where the value of an asset in the present is dependent both on the present value of future cash flows and also on the uncertain price at which it can be sold at some future point in time.

The defined termination point of betting markets is of particular appeal, therefore, in that it allows researchers employing empirical techniques to avoid many of the difficulties associated with indefinite expected future outcomes. Moreover, by enabling a more productive and clearer learning process, a delineated end point might be expected in particular to promote information efficiency. Evidence of inefficiency in such markets is therefore of special significance. The possibility of insider information and consequent opportunities for insider trading in betting markets is also somewhat analogous to the operation of conventional financial markets, but in some respects easier to measure and assess. For these reasons, the information provided by an examination of betting markets is a convenient and useful perspective from which to consider the evidence and interpretations of consumer and investor behaviour in conventional financial markets, as well as the operation of these markets.

This volume has a two-tiered structure. Part I consists of three chapters. Chapter 1 reviews the academic literature which has investigated the issue of information efficiency in conventional financial markets. The development of the idea of an informationally efficient market is explored, and the various classifications of this issue are identified. Empirical tests of information efficiency in these markets are assessed and evaluated. Chapters 2 and 3 review the academic literature which has investigated the issue of information efficiency in betting markets. The various empirical tests which have been applied in this area are assessed and evaluated. Part II is a collection of hitherto unpublished readings which draws on expertise across the spectrum of research into the issue of information efficiency in betting markets. Each of the contributions is novel and original, but set within the existing framework of literature. As such, this volume will serve as a valuable asset for those who are coming fresh to the subject, as well as for those who are more familiar with the subject matter.

I have greatly enjoyed writing this book, and editing the collection of readings. In great part, this is due to the kindness, support and generosity of family, friends and of colleagues from across the global village of academic research. Special thanks also to all who have contributed to this book. In every case, the contribution offers a new and valuable insight into this fascinating subject.

Welcome to the wonderful world of information efficiency!

Part I
The concept of information efficiency

1   Information efficiency in financial markets

Leighton Vaughan Williams

1.1 Introduction

This chapter examines some of the basic issues relating to the theory of information efficiency in financial markets and, in particular, some of the definitions and distinctions which have influenced the academic literature to date. Various empirical tests of information efficiency are then reviewed and assessed.

Section 1.2 outlines the concept of information efficiency and traces the development of the terms, definitions and meanings associated with this idea. Sections 1.3, 1.4 and 1.5 review the methods which have been applied to test for the existence of information efficiency, as variously defined, in financial markets.

1.2 The 'efficient markets hypothesis'

In this section, a review is undertaken of the literature which has investigated the concept and existence of information efficiency in financial markets, and in particular the role and relevance of the 'efficient markets hypothesis' in our understanding of the operation of these markets.

1.2.1 The efficient markets hypothesis: reviewing the development of an idea

The concept of information efficiency in a market is contained in the so-called 'efficient markets hypothesis', a standard definition of which can be found in Fama (1991): 'I take the market efficiency hypothesis to be the simple statement that security prices fully reflect all available information' (1991: 1575).

The origin of the ideas central to this hypothesis can be traced back to pioneering work undertaken by Bachelier (1900) into the dynamics of stock price behaviour. His examination of the behaviour of securities prices on La Bourse (the Paris Stock Exchange) led him to conclude that the price changes were identically and independently distributed, so that the next movement in a particular time series could not be predicted from an examination of previous movements. In particular, the stochastic process employed by Bachelier to describe such stock price changes has the characteristic that increments in the process are the result of independent random variables, are normally distributed with a zero mean, and possess a variance increasing in proportion to time elapsed. The implication is that stock prices have no memory and, having no systematic tendencies, cannot be exploited by arbitrage. This proposition that stock price movements observe a normal distribution, and that the price changes follow a 'random walk', laid the basis of much subsequent work into what has come to be known as 'efficient markets theory'.

Kendall (1953), for example, analysed serial correlations in the behaviour of weekly changes in spot prices for wheat, cotton and nineteen indices of UK industrial share prices. His conclusion was that the series appeared 'wandering', 'Almost as if once a week the Demon of Chance drew a random number from a symmetrical population of fixed dispersion and added it to the current price to determine the next week's price' (1953: 13).

A serious challenge to this orthodoxy can be traced to Mandelbrot (1963), whose analysis of the actual distribution of price changes disclosed evidence of high-tail distributions without a finite variance. This work served to cast doubt on the value of the existing standard statistical techniques such as serial correlation analyses to test for dependence, and generated a whole new literature proposing and applying new techniques to test for such dependence.

Another important development in the literature since the late 1950s has been the clarification of hitherto implicit distinctions. In particular, the concepts of a random walk, a 'fair game' and the various 'martingale'[1] specifications are now clearly contrasted. Basically, if prices follow a stochastic process, then this can be identified as a martingale if the best forecast of tomorrow's prices that can be made, based on present information, is today's price. Likewise, the stochastic process is identified as a fair game if the expected gain from forecasting tomorrow's price based on present information is zero, i.e. there is no systematic difference between actual and expected returns. The implication of the above is that if a variable in an investor's information set can be used to predict future returns, then the martingale model is violated, and returns cannot follow a fair game. The stochastic process is identified as a random walk if it satisfies the martingale conditions and also that there is no dependence involving the higher conditional moments of future prices. The random walk specification is, therefore, more restrictive than the martingale. These issues are addressed in more detail in subsection 1.2.2.

The possibility that market inefficiency can exist independently of price dependence, however categorised, can be traced to definitions originally associated with Roberts (1959, 1967), and popularised by Fama (1970), i.e. 'weak form', 'semi-strong form' and 'strong form' efficiency. The idea is that the existence of market efficiency may best be examined in terms of three distinct types of test, each subjecting the efficient markets hypothesis to different levels of strictness.

Fama (1970) discussed the tests in terms of the information subset relevant to changes in security prices. First, weak form tests which are concerned with the information set of historical prices. Second, semi-strong form tests, which are concerned with 'information that is obviously publicly available' (1970: 383). Third, strong form tests 'concerned with whether given investors or groups have monopolistic access to any information relevant for price formation' (1970: 383). The three tests seek to identify which subset of information is relevant in the formation of expectations, and thereby security prices. Weak form information is limited to the price history of the relevant security; semi-strong information is limited to publicly available information; strong form information includes all known relevant information, including private information. These issues are explored in greater detail in subsection 1.2.3.

1.2.2 Random walks, fair games and martingales

The idea that the absence of a random walk by financial variables is sufficient in itself to reject the existence of information efficiency in the relevant financial markets was challenged by Fama (1965). He produced findings that larger than average daily stock price changes in his dataset tended to be followed by larger than average daily price changes. However, the signs of the successor changes appeared random. He concluded that although this represented a contradiction of a random walk by these variables, it did not contradict the existence of information efficiency in the markets exhibiting these characteristics.

This distinction was developed by Fama (1970), where he differentiated between a random walk and a fair game, arguing that a fair game assumption is sufficient for information efficiency, but that a fair game formulation is not sufficient in itself to lead to a random walk. In so doing, he echoed Alexander's (1961) contention that assuming a 'fair game' would take one 'well on the way to picturing the behaviour of speculative prices as a random walk' (1961: 200).

LeRoy (1989) offered a clear presentation of these sorts of distinctions. Specifically, he identified a stochastic process x_t as a martingale[2] with respect to a sequence of information sets I_t, if x_t has the property

$$E(X_{t+1} \text{given } I_t) = X_t$$

Where E (n) represents the expected value of n.

So, in assuming that x_t is in I_t, then if x_t is a martingale, the best forecast of x_{t+1} based on current information I_t would be x_t. If the process is a fair game, then the expected gain from forecasting x_{t+1} based on current information I_t is zero.

The implication of the above is that if a variable in an investor's information set can be used to predict future returns the martingale model is violated, and returns cannot follow a fair game. A stochastic process is identified as a random walk if it satisfies the martingale conditions and also that there is no dependence involving the higher conditional moments of x_{t+1}. If, for instance, we model security price behaviour in such a way that successive conditional variances of such prices are positively autocorrelated (though not their levels), then this satisfies the martingale conditions, but not the random walk. The existence of risk-neutrality, in which investors are unconcerned about the higher moments of their return distributions, points therefore to a martingale formulation but not a random walk, since investors in such a scenario are not led to bid away serial dependence in these higher conditional moments. The presence of risk aversion, on the other hand, runs contrary to a martingale and a fair game modelling. The reason stems from the fact that risk-averse investors will only hold more risky assets if they are compensated in terms of higher expected returns. As a consequence, knowledge of the riskiness of the current information set implies some knowledge about the level of expected returns. The idea of a submartingale is that expected rates of return (ignoring dividends), conditional on currently available information, are non-negative, *i.e.*

$$E(p_{t+1} \text{given } I_t) > = p_t$$

which implies that no trading rule based on the current information set can outperform a strategy of buy-and-hold.

Granger (1992) pointed out that if stock prices were not a martingale, then ignoring transactions costs 'price changes would be consistently forecastable and so a money machine is created and indefinite wealth is created' (1992: 3). Granger took care to differentiate, therefore, between a martingale process and the various interpretations identified with the efficient market hypothesis, expressing his own preference for Jensen's (1978) definition – i.e. that a market is efficient with respect to a given information set if it is impossible to make economic profits[3] by trading on the basis of this information.[4]

Support for Jensen's definition is offered by Fama (1991), in a follow-up to his original 1970 survey of the literature on efficient capital markets. Fama (1991) noted Grossman and Stiglitz's (1980) finding that for security prices to reflect fully all available information then information and trading costs must be zero. Finding this implausible, he preferred Jensen's 'weaker and more sensible version of the efficiency hypothesis [which] says that prices reflect information to the point where the marginal benefits of acting on information (the profits to be made) do not exceed the marginal costs' (1991: 1575).

A related issue is raised by Keane (1993), who highlighted a distinction between rationality and exploitability as aspects of pricing efficiency. For Keane (1993), the market is rational if prices and market movements reflect the best estimates of intrinsic values. It is fair game efficient or non-exploitable if systematic abnormal returns cannot be earned through an analysis of price behaviour. The distinction is made clear in a situation where the market in aggregate is subject to excessive movements that are difficult to identify or are unpredictable in behaviour. In such a situation, irrational market behaviour can co-exist with fair game efficiency or non-exploitability.

The essential issues can, however, be categorised into two parts. First, is there evidence in financial markets of price change dependence as variously defined? Second, can any such evidence be used to secure systematic abnormal returns?

1.2.3 Weak, semi-strong and strong form efficiency: classifications of information efficiency

The weak form of the efficient markets hypothesis holds that current security prices fully and instantaneously reflect all weak form information, and similarly for the semi-strong and strong forms of the hypothesis. In a weak form market it follows that no patterns can be identified which would allow future price movements to be predicted from past price movements, and no trading rule will produce consistent above-average or abnormal returns except by chance. Prices are influenced solely by new economic events and new information. Fama (1991) has proposed extending the categorisation of research in this area to include such variables as dividend yields, interest rates, earnings/price ratios and other term-structure variables. Fama identifies these as tests for return predictability, a more general category which includes weak form tests. In a semi-strong form market, new public information impacts on security prices instantaneously and in an unbiased fashion. Such prices, therefore, most faithfully reflect the available published information. In a strong form market, share prices reflect all information, including that not publicly available.[5]

Dowie (1976) made a basic distinction between the strong form of inefficiency (as hitherto defined) and the other forms of inefficiency (weak and semi-strong). The former tells us about access to and the availability of information, whereas the latter is concerned with how well the market responds to information. Although related, these are quite separate issues. Since strong inefficiency implies the existence of subsets of investors who possess monopolistic access to information (which can be exploited to earn above-average returns), Dowie uses the term 'equitable' to describe markets which pass the strong test, and 'efficient' to describe those that pass the weak and semi-strong tests.

Keane (1987) also made a clear distinction. Whereas the weak and semi-strong classifications apply to the stock market itself, strong efficiency, he argues, is about a broader concept of capital markets. Specifically, whereas 'semi-strong efficiency is concerned with how well the market processes the information disclosed to it ... strong efficiency is concerned primarily with the adequacy of the information disclosure process' (1987: 6). In this sense, it might be considered misleading to view strong efficiency as a progression from the weak and semi-strong forms, since this confuses the ability of the market to respond to and interpret information with the failure of the market to supply information (what we might call the information production function).

It can be seen that the development of research into information efficiency in recent years has sought to clarify the nature of the distribution of stock price changes, and in this context to develop statistical tests which offer the possibility of testing for dependence between successive price changes. The type and degree of dependence under examination has been clarified, and the concept of information efficiency itself has been broadened and made more explicit.

1.2.4 The efficient markets hypothesis: a summary

An informationally efficient market can in essence be defined as a market which *incorporates all information*. This is a stringent requirement, and so studies of financial markets have also addressed the issue with respect to subsets of the totality of information. The three principal (though not exclusive) levels at which studies of information efficiency have been undertaken are with respect to weak, semi-strong and strong information.

Weak form information is information contained in the set of historical prices. A market is weakly efficient (with respect to information), therefore, if this is fully and (in the strictest form) instantaneously incorporated in present prices. In such a market, present prices reflect all information available in patterns of historical prices, and so future price movements cannot be derived from an examination of past prices.

Semi-strong information is that contained in the set of all public information. A market is semi-strong efficient if this is fully and (in the strictest form) instantaneously incorporated into present prices. In such a market, present prices reflect all available public information, and so future price movements reflect future (and as yet unknown) revelations of publicly available information.

Strong information is that contained in the set of all information, including that privately and monopolistically held. A market is strongly efficient if all information is fully and (in the strictest form) instantaneously incorporated into present prices. In such a market, present prices reflect all information, and so future price movements reflect future (and as yet unknown) revelations of information.

All these definitions of information efficiency require the incorporation of relevant information. In less strict formulations, it is sufficient for efficiency to exist that it is not possible to trade upon this information so as to earn greater than normal profits.

1.3 Empirical tests of weak form information efficiency in financial markets

This section reviews some of the empirical tests which have been proposed and applied in the literature to investigate the existence of weak information efficiency in financial markets.

It has already been shown that in a financial market characterised by strict weak form efficiency, no patterns can be identified from the history of price data which would allow one to predict the future pattern of price changes. In a market which is weakly inefficient as so defined, the pattern of incremental prices is well approximated by a random walk specification. Subsections 1.3.1–1.3.4 review the evidence for such a specification: 1.3.1 assesses serial correlation techniques of price dependence, 1.3.2 variance ratio tests, 1.3.3 cointegration approaches and 1.3.4 looks briefly at how rescaled range analysis and chaos theory have been applied to the theory of financial markets.

A less strict form of weak efficiency holds that no information can be gathered from such price data which would allow one to make abnormal returns except by chance. In subsection 1.3.5, a review is undertaken of attempts in the literature to use price dependence as a means of earning abnormal returns. Finally, subsection 1.3.6 surveys work which assesses the possibility for predicting returns using a range of indicators, such as dividend yields. Tests of this possibility are usually termed 'tests of return predictability'.

1.3.1 Testing for price change dependence using serial correlation techniques

In examining securities markets, the most obvious test of strict weak form efficiency is to test for price change dependence. The idea here is that there should be zero correlation between increments of a random walk (cumulated series of probabilistically independent shocks).

Although Working (1934) contended that random walks generated patterns that appeared similar to those frequently imputed by market analysts to stock prices, the first rigorous empirical backing for Bachelier's (1900) idea of a 'random walk' in share prices (or 'random wander' as Rowley, 1987: 131, terms it) was provided by Kendall's (1953) serial correlation analyses of weekly changes in commodity spot prices and UK industrial share prices. This was extended by Roberts (1959), whose work emphasised the implications of Kendall's findings for financial analysis and stock market research. He compared movements in a variable generated from a random walk process with movements in the Dow Jones (stock market) industrial average over a 52-week period between 30 December 1955 and 28 December 1956, using actual changes in Friday to Friday closing levels. He concluded that the patterns produced by both were so similar as to suggest that there was a random distribution of index changes. He noted that the random walk model, implied by the instantaneous adjustment of prices to new information, would be just what would be expected in an ideal market composed of rational investors.

Another early test of dependence can be found in Moore (1962, 1964), who examined changes in the prices of common US stocks measured over weekly intervals from 1951 to 1958. He reported an average serial correlation coefficient which was not different from zero at any conventional level of statistical significance. Serial correlation and runs tests of dependence by Brealey (1970) for the British equity market, and serial correlation tests by Cunningham (1973) similarly were unable to detect evidence of dependence. Hagerman and Richmond (1973) also established no evidence of substantial direct dependence between lagged price changes in securities which were traded over-the-counter (OTC) (which might therefore be smaller and less well analysed than typical securities), a result supported by Solnik (1973) in a separate analysis of European stock prices.

Cooper (1982) examined world stock markets, calculating the correlation coefficients between successive monthly changes in the stock market indices of thirty-six countries. He reported coefficients ranging from zero in the cases of Lebanon and Mexico to 0.40 in Ireland, concluding that overall there was no evidence of any significant relationship between successive market movements.

In conclusion, serial correlation techniques, each employing different datasets, and conducted in different periods, failed to provide convincing evidence of the existence of any systematic pattern of security price change dependence through time. It is not possible on this basis, therefore, to reject a null hypothesis of weak form information efficiency in the markets studied.

1.3.2 Variance ratio tests

Tests of information efficiency in financial markets based on an examination of the existence of any serial correlation in changes in stock market returns characterise much of the efficient markets literature, and especially the early literature. A significant trend in later research papers has been the application of *variance ratios tests* to the data. Such tests are based on the idea that the variance of a sample of stock price returns should, if these returns are generated by a random walk, increase in proportion to time elapsed. For example, the variance over six months should be six times as great as the variance over one month. Work by Lo and MacKinlay (1988, 1989) and Cochrane (1988) is indicative of the seminal literature in this field. The test is a widespread method of testing for mean-reversion[6] in stock prices, the idea behind such tests being that non-mean-reverting stock prices implies non-predictability in the long run.[7] Evidence of eventual mean-reversion is offered by Cutler, Poterba and Summers (1990, 1991), who found negative serial correlation in returns at a three- to five-year time horizon (although positive correlations at a shorter horizon), and Chopra, Lakonishok and Ritter (1992), who reported negative correlation in the returns of individual stocks and various portfolios over intervals of three to ten years. French and Roll (1986) and Lehmann (1990) also found negative serial correlation in weekly and daily returns of individual securities, while Rosenberg, Reid and Lanstein (1985) reported predictable return reversals on a monthly basis at the level of individual securities. Fama and French (1988a), Cochrane (1991) and Jegadeesh (1990) also found evidence of mean-reversion in their datasets. This was confirmed by Kim, Nelson and Startz (1991), although they argued that the assumption of normally distributed returns tended to overstate the extent of mean-reversion in previous studies.

McQueen (1992) incorporated the findings of Kim, Nelson and Startz to re-examine the existence of mean-reversion in stock returns. For the period from 1926 to 1987, he concluded that the random walk hypothesis could not be rejected for value- or equally-weighted real returns at any of ten return horizons or by joint tests over all ten horizons simultaneously. The conclusions were unaffected by extending the study period to cover the years 1871 to 1987.

Chelley-Steeley (2001) examined mean-reversion in the short horizon returns of UK portfolios. In particular, the aim of the analysis was to discover whether UK short horizon portfolio returns contain rapidly developing mean-reverting predictable components. Only a weak relationship is identified between the size of firms within a portfolio and the extent to which portfolio returns are mean-reverting. To this extent, it represents a significant contrast with results reported for the US by Conrad and Kaul (1989).

In all cases, however, a model which exploited the mean-reversion generated superior forecasts of the monthly returns.

A potential difficulty in interpreting the existence of return autocorrelations generally was raised by Lo and Mackinlay (1988) who, using variance ratio tests, identified positive serial correlation in short horizon stock returns (of the order of 30 per cent for weekly and monthly stock returns). The particular problem they highlighted was their finding that autocorrelation was stronger for the portfolios of small stocks, indicating the possible influence of a non-synchronous trading effect. This 'non-synchronicity problem', which can be traced to work by Fisher (1966),[8] and perhaps more generally to Working (1960),[9] arises because multiple time series are assumed to be sampled simultaneously when they may not occur simultaneously.[10] This has obvious implications for tests of the efficient markets hypothesis which rely on testing for the existence of autocorrelation in a series of returns. Conrad and Kaul (1988) tried to eliminate any non-synchronicity effect by limiting their analysis to the Wednesday-to-Wednesday returns of size-grouped portfolios of stocks that trade on both Wednesdays. However, Fama (1991) demonstrated that their finding of positive autocorrelation was not totally free of such an effect, particularly for small stocks.

Nevertheless, an analysis by Lo and Mackinlay (1990a) indicated that while the non-trading effect may explain some of the time series properties of stock returns, there was 'little support for nonsynchronous trading as an important source of spurious correlation in the returns of common stock' (1990a:203).

The possibility of spurious autocorrelation caused by non-synchronous trading, and the implications of this for random walk analysis are emphasised, however, by Ayadi and Pyun (1994), in particular for the stock markets of the developing world. Applying a variance ratio test to the Korean Stock Exchange they were unable to reject the random walk hypothesis for time horizons of a week or longer. Wider tests of the random walk hypothesis are found in Frennberg and Hansson (1993) and in Huang (1995), both of whom applied variance ratio tests to specified national stock markets. Frennberg and Hansson rejected a random walk formulation for Swedish stock prices, and Huang (1995), in an analysis of a number of Asian stock markets, concluded that the random walk hypothesis was rejected for Korea and Malaysia for all holding periods. Positive serial correlation was also evident in some periods in the Hong Kong, Singapore and Thai markets.

Cheng (2000) uses variance ratio testing to examine random walks in Taiwan's stock prices between 1971 and 1996. The null hypothesis of a random walk is rejected using a weekly value-weighted index, but it could be rejected with monthly, quarterly and yearly value-weighed market indices.

Lee, Chen and Rui (2001) apply variance ratio analysis to test the random walk hypothesis for stock markets in China. This is particularly interesting in light of the establishment of the Shanghai Stock Exchange (1990) and Shenzhen Stock Exchange (1991). They are unable to reject a random walk hypothesis, finding that volatility of returns showed high persistence and predictability.

An examination of the long horizon returns behaviour of the Portuguese stock market by Armada (2002) was similarly unable conclusively to reject a hypothesis of weak form market efficiency in a dataset extending from January 1983 to November 1996.

Abraham, Seyyed and Alsakran (2002) use variance ratio and runs test approaches to test for weak form efficiency in Gulf stock markets, explicitly allowing for the confounding effect of non-synchronous prices on efficiency and random walk tests. Using data from October 1992 to December 1998, they are unable to reject the random walk hypothesis for the Saudi and Bahraini markets, but do so for the case of Kuwait.

Smith and Ryoo (2003) apply variance ratio tests of the random walk hypothesis to five European emerging stock markets, namely Greece, Hungary, Poland, Portugal and Turkey. Although they find a random walk process in the Turkish (Istanbul) market, they reject the hypothesis of a random walk for the other economies examined. Interestingly, the existence of a random walk in the Istanbul market was examined in a contemporaneous paper by Buguk and Brorsen (2003), with contrasting results. Using the composite, industrial and financial index weekly closing prices of the Istanbul Stock Exchange, they provide evidence of a random walk in all three series, although a non-parametric test did provide some evidence against a random walk specification.

Chang (2004) employs a variance ratio test to examine the random walk for the British pound, Canadian dollar, Deutsche mark, French franc, and the Japanese yen. The results of the study provide evidence rejecting the random walk hypothesis for the Japanese yen over the entire sample, ranging from 1974 to 1998. Subperiod analysis indicates that from 1989 onwards, however, the random walk hypothesis cannot be rejected for the British pound, Canadian dollar, French franc and Deutsche mark.

Patro and Wu (2004) examine the predictability of equity index returns for eighteen developed countries. Based on the variance ratio test, they reject the random walk hypothesis at conventional significance levels for eleven countries with daily data and for fifteen countries with weekly data. They find that the excess returns from buying past winners and selling past losers are positive for daily data, although imposing a 'reasonable' transaction cost substantially reduces the profitability.

1.3.3 Cointegration tests of the efficient markets hypothesis

Cointegration studies as a research method are traceable to the seminal work of Granger (1986), Engle and Granger (1987) and Johansen (1988). Basically, they employ the idea that since asset prices in an efficient market cannot be related in the long run, the absence of common stochastic trends in a system of stock prices implies the existence of efficient markets. Tests of cointegration are employed to check for such trends.[11]

In the first paper to apply a cointegration methodology to the examination of stock market efficiency, MacDonald and Power (1991) tested for the existence of market efficiency in the weekly share prices of forty UK companies, over an eight-year period. The prices were grouped into the five major industrial classifications, but no cointegrating relationships could be identified. MacDonald and Power concluded that the UK stock market was a rational processor of information.

Chelley-Steeley and Pentecost (1994) extended the work of MacDonald and Power by using a longer time period in order to improve the reliability of the tests. They also classified the stock prices by firm size. They found no significant evidence of cointegration in the share prices of large firms, conclusions consistent with the existence of stock market efficiency for large firms. They did find, however, considerable evidence of cointegration in the share prices of small firms, suggesting the existence of static inefficiency in the data relating to small firms.

Choudhry (1994) also employed cointegration tests to look for any evidence of common stochastic trends in a system of stock indices from seven Organisation for Economic Co-operation and Development (OECD) countries between 1953 and 1989. Being unable to identify any such trends, the findings were offered as evidence in support of the efficient markets hypothesis.

The application of this approach to test for efficiency in a range of commodity markets was undertaken by Beck (1994), at an eight- and twenty-four-week horizon. His results indicated that while all five of the commodity markets he studied were inefficient sometimes, none was inefficient at all times.

Further tests, which sought to examine the existence of both short-run and long-run efficiency using cointegration (among other) techniques, were developed and applied to the Financial Times Stock Exchange or FTSE-100 stock index futures contract by Antoniou and Holmes (1996). Their results showed that while this market was efficient over short periods (one or two months), this was not the case for longer periods. They concluded that there are consequently opportunities for consistent speculative profits to be made.

Cointegration analysis has also been employed extensively to test for efficiency in the foreign exchange markets. Ukpolo (1995), for example, used such techniques to test for efficiency in the Japanese foreign exchange market, as did Alexander and Johnson (1992) for exchange markets more generally, using London daily closing rates for the six major currencies. The conclusions of these studies were inconsistent with the efficiency hypothesis, a result reproduced by Diamandis and Kouretas (1995) in their time series analysis of the Greek Drachma.

Pan and Liu (1999) examined a system of nominal exchange rates for the existence of fractional cointegration in the period from 1973 to 1992. They found that fractional cointegration existed only in the 1980-4 sample from that period, but not for 1973-9, 1985-92 and 1973-92. Even so, evidence of usual cointegration was obtained for the period 1985-92.

These findings suggest that the fractional cointegration feature of exchange rates, insofar as it exists, may be changing across various time spans.

Tong (2001) looked at the issue from an economic perspective. He showed that the cointegrating relationship in currency markets, whether cointegrated or fractionally cointegrated, was found mainly among the currencies of the European Monetary System (EMS) which are set to fluctuate within a given range. Some evidence is produced that restricting the forecasting model to consist of only cointegrated currencies improves forecasting efficiency.

1.3.4 The application of rescaled range analysis and chaos theory to efficient markets analysis

In addition to the serial correlations, variance ratio and cointegration approaches outlined above, some authors have applied rescaled range analysis and chaos theoretic analyses to the problem of stock returns dynamics.

The idea of rescaled range analysis was first proposed by Hurst (1951), as a result of his observations of natural phenomena. The statistic, since refined by Mandelbrot (1972, 1975), Mandelbrot and Taqqu (1979) and Lo (1991), can be used to test for long-term dependence. Essentially it is a method of measuring how the path of a time series varies over various timescales. Specifically, the rescaled-range statistic is the range (i.e. high minus low) of partial cumulative sums of deviations of a time series from its mean, rescaled by its standard deviation. A convenient way of viewing its application is through an examination of the so-called Hurst exponent. Named after H. E. Hurst, who first developed its use in studies of the Nile river dam project, it is a measure of correlative persistence.

The correlation can be derived from the following equation:

$$C = 2^{(2H-1)} - 1$$

where C is the measure of correlation and H is the Hurst exponent.

Thus, if the Hurst exponent equals 0.5, $C = 0$, and the probability that a move in one direction will be followed by a move in the same direction (e.g. positive followed by positive) is 50 per cent. If the Hurst exponent is less than 0.5 the system can be characterised as mean-reverting (sometimes termed anti-persistent or ergodic), if greater than 0.5 it is correlative or persistent (also sometimes termed trend-reinforcing). The period of time over which H is greater than 0.5 is a measure of the *memory cycle* of the system, and so measures the time period over which information can be used predictively.[12] This approach is particularly useful in the context of non-normal distributions. The reason is that the variance of such distributions may not exist (i.e. the expected value of the variance may be infinite). The essential intuition behind this is that the tails of the distribution decay too slowly. In these cases, variance ratio tests are inappropriate. The only requirement of rescaled range tests is that the mean exists (i.e. the expected value of the mean is less than infinity). In other words, these tests are less demanding about the existence of moments of the distribution. Its importance in this respect is indicated by a rescaled range analysis undertaken by Peters (1989), and quoted in the *Economist* (23 October 1993: 1–24), of monthly data of the Standard and Poor's (S&P) 500 index from January

1950 through July 1988. This study reported evidence that this data followed not a normal but a highly leptokurtic distribution.[13] Peters found, for periods greater than twenty and less than 110 days, evidence that the market revealed an overlong trend in one direction compared with what would be expected from a random walk. In particular, for the S&P 500 prices were found to increase with the 0.78 root of time, in contrast to the square root configuration which would be consistent with a random walk. Moreover, a memory length of about four years was identified, the length proving independent of the resolution of the data. Scrambling the data randomly so as to alter the order of the returns, though not the probability distribution, and re-running the analysis ruined the structure of the original series. This is consistent with the presence of a memory effect as already proposed. Analysis of other capital markets yielded similar results. Applying a variation of rescaled range analysis to measure the shape of the probability density function of the markets, Peters (1989) also found evidence that stock markets display consistent statistical characteristics prior to particular phases or developments – e.g. a downturn or a period of trend reinforcement (see also Peters, 1994). Another study to apply rescaled range statistics was that of Ambrose, Ancel and Griffiths (1992), whose examination of long-term memory in a number of US asset classes concluded that the returns all displayed tendencies consistent with a random walk process. An application of (modified)[14] rescaled range tests was applied by Huang and Yang (1995) to nine Asian stock markets, together with UK and US indices. No evidence of long-term memory was found for the Asian markets studies, except for the Philippines. There was evidence, however, of such an effect in the UK market for various data frequencies and lags.

Howe and Martin (1999) used both classical and modified rescaled range analysis to study the equity markets of Australia, Hong Kong, Japan, Singapore and South Korea. Although there was evidence of a long-range non-linear deterministic structure in some of the return streams, a correction for short-range dependence using Lo's (1991) modified version of rescaled range analysis eliminated all evidence of long-term memory. It is noted that this apparent absence of long-range dependence is consistent with market efficiency.

Mulligan (2000) examined long-term memory for the post-Bretton Woods period, again using Lo's (1991) modified version as well as classical rescaled range analysis. No support was found in this study, however, for the efficient markets hypothesis, with the additional implication noted that traditional technical analysis should be able to achieve systematic positive returns.

McKenzie (2001) applied a rescaled range analysis to Australian Stock Market data, finding evidence of long memory in the returns-generating process and non-periodic cycles of approximately three, six and twelve years in average duration.

The other type of analysis, and one which has been used in particular to explain the frequency of large movements in asset prices compared with what would be expected under a linear modelling or a normal distribution, is chaos theory. Essentially, 'chaos' is a deterministic non-linear process which appears to be random. In chaotic models, external shocks can cause dynamic processes which follow a non-linear path, and which by a process of self-generation (feedback) can create large and volatile movements. In the wake of the stock market crash of 19 October 1987, interest in chaotic and non-linear dynamics as a tool of financial analysis increased sharply.

Although Baumol and Benhabib (1989) offer a useful general survey of economic models which can produce chaotic behaviour and Hsieh (1991) has examined the role of chaotic processes in the specific context of financial markets there is, however, no coherent empirical evidence of chaotic behaviour in financial markets. Indeed, evidence produced by Hsieh (1991) contradicting a null hypothesis of independent and identical distributions in his data was explained in the study as a consequence, not of chaotic dynamics, but of conditional heteroscedasticity – e.g. predictable variance changes. Brock, Hsieh and Le Baron (1991) and Hsieh (1989) also find no evidence of chaotic behaviour. Nevertheless the ideas behind chaos theory continue to motivate some economists, including De Grauwe, Dewachter and Embrechts (1993), and coherent and convenient outlines of chaos theory can be found in Savit (1988, 1992) and Cunningham (1994).

More recently, Gilmore (2001) employed a 'close returns' test to identify the existence of chaotic behaviour in daily exchange rate series. The results of the study do not support the findings of De Grauwe, Dewachter and Embrechts (1993) of possible chaos in the pound sterling and the Japanese yen, instead agreeing with the conclusion of Hsieh (1989) and Brock, Hsieh and Le Baron (1991) that there is no demonstrable chaotic behaviour.

More recently, Chu (2003) investigated the existence of non-random, non-linear and chaotic characteristics in daily return data from the Shanghai Stock Exchange Index and the Shenzhen Stock Exchange Index. Using the Hurst exponent in rescaled range analysis, he rejected the hypothesis that the index return series were random, independent and identically distributed.

It has been seen, therefore, that a success of tests, using various statistical techniques to test for price dependence, and covering a wide array of datasets, thus far fail to reach a simple consensus in terms of validating the efficient markets hypothesis as broadly defined. How far the differences in the conclusions can be attributed to variations in the testing techniques adopted, and how far to variations in the databases under examination, awaits further work.

It is important, however, to make the distinction between the existence of stock price dependence *per se*, and the possibility of using such a configuration, were it to exist, in order to generate abnormal returns. Subsection 1.3.5 develops this thread in the literature.

1.3.5 Price dependence, abnormal returns and information efficiency

Fama (1970) drew a clear distinction between a definition of market efficiency which sees any existence of statistical dependence in successive price changes as refutation, and a less strict interpretation which identifies market efficiency as existing if no profitable trading rules can be based upon such dependence.

The idea of using the past history of security prices, with the object of formulating rules which would permit the generation of abnormal returns, can be traced in the modern literature to Alexander (1961),[15] who advocated a 'filter' system whereby securities are bought or sold according to their patterns of falling and rising prices. The filter (sometimes referred to as the 'k per cent filter rule') is the name given to the percentage change in the security price used to initiate a position.

Using filters of from 1 per cent to 50 per cent for daily data on price indices between 1987 and 1959, Alexander (1961) sought to generate a profitable rule through a process of separating out random from non-random movements. Alexander (1964) concluded that, taking account of transaction costs, 'for any reader who is interested only in practical results, and who is not a floor trader' (1964: 351) the filter strategy could not outperform a simple policy of buy-and-hold.

Fama and Blume (1966), like Alexander, found that if one ignored transactions costs it was possible to formulate a trading strategy which would outperform buy-and-hold, in their case for very small filters based on very short-term trading (i.e. 'at most daily', 1966: 395). Allowing for even minimum trading costs, however, the advantage disappeared. Fama (1970) concluded that although 'the filter tests, like the serial correlations, produce empirically noticeable departures from the strict implications of the efficient markets model' (1970: 396), 'using a less than completely strict interpretation of market efficiency, this positive dependence does not seem of sufficient importance to warrant rejection of the efficient markets model' (1970: 414).

Early research into the consequences of employing buy-or-sell strategies based on deviations from a moving average of their prices over various periods also failed to identify profitable trading rules net of transaction costs. Work by Cootner (1962) and by Van Horne and Parker (1967) is typical of the literature. Nevertheless, an empirical analysis by Stottner (1990) of a simple downward averaging device seems to indicate a significant improvement in returns compared to a buy-and-hold strategy. Such evidence appears at variance with the implications of at least the stricter form of weak efficiency.

Fortune (1991) conducted a time series analysis of daily stock prices in the 1980s (specifically, the daily closing prices of the Standard & Poor's 500 between 2 January 1980 and 21 September 1990). He rejected the random walk hypothesis, finding statistically significant coefficients in a moving average model of stock price behaviour. He calculated that a trading strategy based on these findings would not, however, be sufficient to cover retail transactions costs, although it could cover institutional transactions costs.

Brock, Lakonishok and Le Baron (1992) used data from the Dow Jones Index from 1897 to 1986 to test specified trading rules, based on a moving average and a trading range break. In particular, they explored twenty versions of the moving average rule (i.e. buy when a short-term moving average exceeds a long-term one), and six versions of the trading range break rule (i.e. buy when the index exceeds its last peak, sell when it falls below its last trough). They found that 'buy' signals consistently outperformed 'sell' signals in terms of returns, and that these returns were less volatile than those following 'sell' signals. Specifically, 'buy' signals produced an average annual return of 12 per cent, whereas sell signals produced an annual average loss of 7 per cent. Gencay (1996) offered further evidence of weak form inefficiency in applying a moving average rule to the Dow Jones Industrial Average Index between January 1963 and June 1988. By employing the past buy-and-sell signals of these rules, Gencay (1996) provided convincing evidence of non-linear predictability in these stock market returns.

The profitability of technical trading systems when applied to futures markets was the subject of a study by Lukac and Brorsen (1990). Applying a trading simulation to twenty-three trading systems on thirty futures markets for eleven years, they found that all but two yielded significant positive gross returns, contrary to the implications of a random walk model. Raj and Thurston (1996) also applied technical trading strategies to a futures market, notably the (Hong Kong) Hang Seng Futures Index. They found that while their moving average strategy failed to produce significant excess returns, the majority of their trading range break rules were able to do so. This is in clear conflict with a weak form efficiency specification for this market.

The existence of a systematic link between trends in past exchange rates and subsequent returns in foreign exchange markets was proposed by Taylor, quoted in the *Economist* (5 December 1992: 23–6).[16] Employing data from a ten-year period to December 1991, Taylor demonstrated the availability on this basis of particular trading rules which could produce above-average returns. Using a 'double moving average' rule, for example, Taylor found average annual returns of 14.2 per cent, compared with an average annual return on US Treasury bills of 8 per cent. Specifically, this rule entailed the trader using a short and a long moving average, selling when the shorter average falls below the long, and buying when the reverse occurs.

Froot, also quoted in the *Economist* (5 December 1992: 23–6), devised a trading rule on the basis of his conclusion that short-term interest rates can be used successfully to forecast returns in foreign exchange stock, bonds and commodity markets at the same time. According to the rule, a fall of 1 per cent in (annualised) short rates is usually associated with an extra 3 percentage points in (annualised) excess returns to those investors who trade on the basis of that change in the interest rates.

Hunter (1998) applied a so-called 'x per cent' filter rule to the daily closing prices of the twenty-six most actively traded stocks listed on the Jamaican Stock Exchange between January 1989 and December 1994. The trading rule, based on Fama and Blume (1966: 227), is described thus:

if the daily closing price of a stock moves up x per cent from a previous low then the investor goes long and holds the stock until the price falls x per cent from a subsequent high, at which point the stock is sold. The investor remains short until the price goes x per cent above a new low at which point he goes long again. (1998: 297)

In other words, the trading strategy is based on buying at the threshold of an expected bull market, and selling on the verge of an anticipated downturn.

The study concludes, however, that a naïve 'buy-and-hold' strategy generally outperformed an active trading strategy, to that extent indicating that the market was efficient.

A slightly different conclusion was reached by Szakmary, Davidson and Schwarz (1999) in their study of the performance of filter and moving average trading rules when applied to 149 Nasdaq stocks between 1 January 1973 and 31 December 1991.

While trading rules that were conditional on a stock's past price history performed poorly, those based on past movements in the overall Nasdaq index appeared to provide excess returns for many specifications. These excess returns diminished in the latter half of the period, consistent with increasing market efficiency over time. Allowing for transactions costs, however, it was not possible to conclude that the returns generally were economically significant. Even so, Szakmary, Davidson and Schwarz do find evidence that some of the strategies could be successful in carefully selected subsets of stocks, such as those with relatively high average prices or range of annual price movement.

Some other studies where the usefulness of technical trading rules has been empirically demonstrated include Gencay (1998a, 1998b) and Ratner and Leal (1999) (equities); Gencay (1999), Le Baron (1999) (currencies); and Kho (1996) (derivatives and futures markets).

Pesaran and Timmerman (2000) simulated real-time search by investors for a model that can forecast stock returns. They found evidence of predictability in UK stock returns which could have been exploited by investors to improve on the risk–return trade-off offered by a passive portfolio strategy.

There is, therefore, supporting evidence for the view that trading rules can in certain circumstances produce excess returns. The methodological soundness of such studies should perhaps be placed, however, in the context of an early investigation by Levy (1967) into 200 stocks listed on the New York Stock Exchange (NYSE). Levy (1967) claimed significant abnormal returns for a trading rule which bought stocks with substantially higher current prices than their average over the previous twenty-seven weeks. The problem came when trying to replicate these findings. A basic criticism of Levy's work, highlighted by Jensen and Bennington (1970) was that it produced a rule from existing data, rather than seeking to test such a rule against new data. In particular, Jensen and Bennington noted that Levy arrived at the successful rule only after a separate examination of sixty-eight other possible trading rules which failed. In consequence, Levy's (1967) findings were, they suggested, due to a form of selection bias.

A more general discussion of the problems for empirical work of data-instigated pre-test biases was presented by Leamer (1978), and this issue of 'data snooping' was taken up by Lakonishok and Smidt (1988), Lo and MacKinlay (1990b) and Brock, Lakonishok and LeBaron (1992). Merton (1987) presented the same issue in the context of cognitive psychology, noting unintended selection biases resulting from what he proposed is a natural predilection for individuals to focus, often disproportionately, on the unusual.

The *Economist* (5 December 1992: 23–6) highlighted a similar point made by Black and Scholes[17] in an attack on data-snooping (or data-mining).

Criticising the claim from data analysis that shares of smaller firms out-perform those of larger firms, Black claims that:

it sounds like people searched over thousands of rules till they found one that worked in the past. Then they reported it, as if past performance was indicative of future performance. As we might expect, in real life the rule did not work any more. (1992: 22)[18]

Nelson and Kim (1990) made a related point, showing that overly encouraging results can result from small-sample in-sample biases of coefficients.

Sullivan, Timmerman and White (1999) employ a methodology subsequently published in White (2000), termed 'White's Reality Check bootstrap methodology', to quantify the data-snooping biases in some simple technical trading rules, notably those considered in Brock, Lakonishok and Le Baron (1992).

The White methodology is designed to allow researchers to control for data-snooping biases in order to calculate the statistical significance of investment performance while accounting for the dependencies resulting from investigating several investment rules. Basically, a single summary statistic is generated to identify the significance of the best-performing model after allowing for data-snooping effects.

On this basis, Sullivan, Timmerman and White (1999) confirm the conclusion of Brock, Lakonishok and Le Baron (1992) that the best-performing technical trading rule was capable of generating significant profits when applied to the Dow Jones Industrial Average. Even so, this superior performance was not reported in an out-of-sample experiment on a later period.

Mirroring the conclusion of Szakmary, Davidson and Schwarz (1999) for NASDAQ stocks, they suggest the possibility that 'historically, the best technical trading rule did indeed produce superior performance, but that, more recently, the markets have become more efficient and hence such opportunities have disappeared' (1999: 1684). Supporting reasons for this apparent trend toward efficiency include cheaper computing power, lower transactions costs and increased stock market liquidity.

In summary, early work suggesting that no profitable trading rules could be devised so as to generate abnormal returns, particularly net of transaction costs, has been challenged by more recent strategies of greater sophistication. The possibility modern computer power offers to generate large numbers of rules has, however, led some writers to challenge the predictive as opposed to the descriptive value of these findings. More work is needed to test proposed new trading rules on future data, and to allow for the possibility of various potential selection biases.

1.3.6 Tests of return predictability

A growing field of literature in recent years has focused on forecasting returns using variables such as dividend yields, interest rates, earnings/price ratios and other term-structure variables. Fama (1991) calls this area of research 'tests for return predictability', identifying it as a more general category which includes the weak form tests identified above. Work in this field can be traced to Bodie (1976), Jaffe and Mandelkar (1976), Nelson (1976) and Fama (1981) on the negative relationship between monthly stock returns and expected inflation, and also (Fama and Schwert, 1977) on a similar relationship between monthly stock returns and the level of short-term interest rates. Later work by Shiller (1984) and by Rozeff (1984) found that dividend yields could be used to forecast short-horizon stock returns.

Fama and French (1988b) used dividend yields to forecast the portfolio returns of NYSE stocks for horizons from one month to five years, finding that such yields served to explain small fractions of monthly and quarterly return variances. Other evidence of the forecasting power of the aggregate equity market dividend yield for US equity returns has been provided by Campbell and Hamao (1989), Attanasio and Wadhwani (1990) and Shah and Wadhwani (1990), although Shah and Wadhwani called into question the general applicability of these results for other countries. Later work by Clare and Thomas (1992), using German, Japanese, UK, and US equity and government bond markets in the 1980s, found clear evidence of the forecasting power of assorted yield spreads. Other findings for the US are offered by Campbell and Shiller (1988), who reported evidence of reliable forecasting power by earnings/price ratios which increased with the return horizon, and by Campbell (1987) and Keim and Stambaugh (1986), who found that a common set of stock market and term-structure variables could be used to predict stock and bond returns. Harvey (1991) reported that the returns on portfolios of foreign common stocks could be forecast from US term-structure variables and from the dividend yield on the Standard & Poor's 500 portfolio. Evidence that such financial variables as the short rate, changes in the short rate and the term structure of interest rates can in some measure predict US equity returns is offered by Fama and Schwert (1977), Keim and Stambaugh (1986), Campbell (1987), Campbell and Hamao (1989), Fama and French (1989), Attanasio and Wadhwani (1990) and Shah and Wadhwani (1990).

Tests for a relationship between average return and specific market variables are found in Banz (1981) – i.e. a strong negative relationship between average return and firm size; Bhandari (1988) – i.e. a positive relationship between average return and leverage; Basu (1983) – i.e. a positive relationship between average return and the earnings/price ratio; Stattman (1980) and Rosenberg, Reid and Lanstein (1985) – i.e. a positive relationship between return and book-to-market equity (BE/ME) for US stocks; and Chan, Hamao and Lakonishok (1991) – i.e. a strong predictive power for BE/ME in explaining average returns on Japanese stocks.

A study which seeks to address the issue of robustness in the predictability of US stock returns in terms of a range of economic factors was presented by Pesaran and Timmerman (1995). They found that the strength of any such relationships can be linked to the volatility of the markets. In this context, they identified clear evidence of past predictability, predictability which was sufficient at certain times to yield excess returns.

Subsequent work by Pesaran and Timmerman (2000) simulated investors' search in real time for a model that can forecast stock returns. They identified evidence of predictability in UK stock returns which could have been exploited by investors to improve on the risk–return trade-off offered by a passive strategy in the market portfolio.

However, Clare, Priestley and Thomas (1997), in an investigation of some previously documented predictable component of excess returns in German, Japanese, UK and US aggregate stock indices, found evidence to suggest that this component was due to a failure of that research to properly consider risk – i.e. there was no evidence of true predictability because of the absence from previous analyses of a suitable proxy for risk.

Tests for weak efficiency have thus taken the form of tests of price dependence through time; of tests which seek to determine the predictability of prices in terms of identifiable trading rules or economic variables; and also of the possibility of earning abnormal returns. Tests of price dependence have progressed from simple serial correlation tests of short-term dependence to variance ratio and mean-reversion tests of long-run patterns in the data. Cointegration tests have played an increasing role in the literature. Trading rules based on postulated strategies linked to price movements and/or to the performance of individual economic variables have been and are being tested for evidence of systematic predictive validity. Any such patterns provide indicative evidence of weak efficiency. At another level, weak form inefficiency is assessed in terms of the possibilities such patterns provide for earning abnormal returns.

Although many studies have failed to identify evidence of weak form inefficiency, there are others which provide strong evidence of dependence and predictability, at least in past datasets and over specified time periods. There is much less compelling evidence, however, that these 'inefficiencies' are sufficient to provide investors with abnormal returns after the fact of their identification.

1.3.7 Empirical tests of weak form information efficiency
in financial markets: a summary

A standard test for the existence of weak information efficiency in financial markets is to test for the existence of *unpredictability* in the movements of security prices. A standard specification of unpredictability is the random walk. In a random walk process, price changes are identically and independently distributed, so that the next movement in a particular time series cannot be predicted from an examination of previous movements. Less strict formulations, such as a fair game or a martingale process, require only that there is no dependence between the means of the series, so that the best forecast of tomorrow's price is today's. A stochastic process is identified as a random walk if it satisfies these conditions and also that there is no dependence through time involving the higher conditional moments of the distributions. Tests of a less strict formulation of weak form efficiency investigate the existence of trading rules, based on information contained in historical prices, which can be used to earn abnormal profits.

Early analysis of price dependence concentrated on testing for *serial correlation* in the behaviour of security price movements through time. Most of the empirical work was unable to reject the hypothesis of independence, although there was some evidence of correlation in the size (but not the sign) of price changes. A general consensus of such studies is that no clear trading rule can be identified, based on historical prices, which can be employed to produce abnormal profits. There was also broad support for the idea of a martingale specification (sometimes adjusted for a gradual upward drift). Evidence for a random walk was more mixed, but still substantial. Later empirical work applied variance ratio tests to the question of price dependence. The idea of these tests is to check for evidence of mean-reversion in the whole dataset. If a system is mean-reverting, there is the implication that if it has moved up from a number of observations, it is more likely to move down than up over subsequent observations, and vice versa. Such a specification is contrary to a random walk model, and implies some sort of predictability in the data. Since variance ratio tests are applied to the whole dataset, they are very useful in detecting any long-term trends in the data which might otherwise have been missed. The basic idea behind these tests is that, in a random walk, the variance of the returns is proportional to time elapsed. If the actual variance is less than this, evidence exists of mean-reversion. Although most studies have found evidence of mean-reversion in their datasets, some investigators have explained this as an effect of the test specification rather than as genuine inefficiency. The sample size and period, the assumption of normality in the distribution and the possibility for spurious autocorrelation (arising from non-synchronous trading) have been cited as reasons. A number of studies have now addressed these problems, but there still remains some evidence of apparently genuine mean-reversion in a number of datasets. A potential weakness of variance ratio tests is the requirement of a finite variance in the distribution of price changes. Some evidence exists, however, that stock returns may follow a leptokurtic (fat-tailed) distribution, and typically a Cauchy distribution, characterised by an infinite variance. Analysis of such distributions requires a different type of approach. Rescaled-range analysis is an approach which can be employed to test for long-term dependence in these cases. Specifically, the rescaled-range statistic is the range of partial cumulative sums of deviations of a time series from its mean, rescaled by its standard deviation. The only requirement of rescaled range tests is that the mean exists (i.e. the expected value of the mean is less than infinity). There are a very limited number of studies which have applied this analysis to financial markets, some markets displaying results consistent with a random walk formulation, others demonstrating evidence of a memory effect in the data.

Another technique comparatively new to the literature is the application of *cointegration methodology* to stock market analysis. The basic idea behind these tests is to check for a long-run relationship between the prices of various assets. Any evidence of such cointegration is evidence of predictability and information inefficiency. On the basis of a small number of studies, there is some evidence of cointegration in share prices, particularly for small firms and over longer periods, which might be employable in order to make consistent speculative profits. *Chaos theory* offers another potential avenue for future research, the essential idea being that non-linear processes can cause large, volatile movements in asset prices which appear random but are in fact determinate. There is, however, to date no coherent empirical evidence of chaotic behaviour in financial markets, and the practical value of this approach has yet to be demonstrated.

A succession of tests, therefore, using various statistical techniques, over a wide range of datasets, has failed to reach a consensus on the validity of the efficient markets hypothesis. There does seem substantial evidence, however, that some markets do diverge, at least in defined circumstances, from a random walk specification. Whether any price dependence through time can be used to secure abnormal returns depends on the reason for the dependence, and the costs of implementing a trading strategy based on evidence of return predictability.

A number of such strategies have been advocated. In 'filter' systems, securities are bought or sold according to their patterns of falling and rising prices. The 'filter' is the name given to the percentage change in the security price used to initiate a position. A number of studies of filter strategies produced empirically discernible deviations from what would be expected in markets which were strictly weak form efficient. There was a lack of evidence, however, that these deviations could be used to make above-average returns net of transaction costs. In this sense, the efficient markets hypothesis was not rejected. Early research into the consequences of employing buy-or-sell strategies based on deviations from a moving average of their prices over various periods similarly failed to identify profitable trading rules net of transaction costs. Some more recent studies of these 'moving average' rules, and also of the 'trading range break' rule (buy when the index exceeds its last peak, sell when it falls below its last trough), have demonstrated some support for the view that they can be effective. Similar success has been claimed by authors of other specified technical trading rules. The problem of data-mining and other testing biases has to be considered, however, in evaluating the conclusions of these studies, as well as making allowance for all the risks and costs of implementation.

There is, therefore, some evidence of predictability and dependence in stock price movements through time, which constitutes *prima facie* evidence of information inefficiency as strictly defined. There is less compelling evidence that this information can be utilised in the market so as to earn abnormal returns. To this extent, the case for the existence of information inefficiency is less strong.

1.4 Empirical tests of semi-strong form information efficiency in financial markets

This section reviews the empirical tests which have been proposed and applied in the literature to investigate the existence of semi-strong information efficiency in financial markets.

In a financial market characterised by strict semi-strong efficiency, prices reflect all publicly available information as soon as it becomes available. In a less strict form of semi-strong efficiency, it is not possible to make above-average or abnormal returns from any divergences between actual security prices and the prices which would obtain if all publicly available information were incorporated into the prices instantaneously and in an unbiased fashion.

Two main approaches have been adopted in the literature as a means of evaluating the extent of semi-strong form efficiency in financial markets. These are addressed in two subsections. In subsection 1.4.1 the impact of new public information on prices is assessed, whereas subsection 1.4.2 investigates opportunities for identifying particular conditions which might systematically produce the possibility of earning above-average or abnormal returns (so-called market 'anomalies'). Subsection 1.4.3 presents a summary and conclusions.

1.4.1 The impact of new public information on security prices

Standard economic theory indicates that asset price changes are caused by unanticipated events which influence the fundamental value of that asset. To that extent, we should be able in theory to explain previous price movements insofar as we are able to identify and control for such events *ex post*. This assumes that asset prices fully reflect available information.

Early contributions to the literature, designed to establish whether share prices in fact fully reflect all available public information, concentrated on the phenomenon of 'stock splits' (otherwise termed stock dividends, scrip issues or (in the UK) capitalisation issues).

A pioneering study of this type was undertaken by Fama, Fisher, Jensen and Roll (1969), who examined the market's reaction to 940 such stock splits, and found no evidence which could be used to yield a profitable trading strategy by or consequent upon the time of the stock split. Studies by Pettit (1972) and Charest (1978) of the market reaction to dividend announcements also found generally quick adjustment to the new information. Pettit (1972) examined abnormal daily price behaviour in 135 stocks on the NYSE during the days surrounding a dividend announcement, concluding that it would not have been possible to make an abnormal profit by buying or selling after the announcement date. Expanding the sample to include 18,000 announcements between 1964 and 1968 (in order to examine the relative performance of stocks during the months surrounding dividend announcements) gave broad, though not total, support to the hypothesis that abnormal profits could not be made by buying or selling after the announcement month.

Asquith (1983), however, produced evidence that although the stock prices of acquiring firms in a merger barely move in response to the announcement, they subsequently exhibit evidence of a slow drift downwards. Fama (1991) identified three distinct explanations already extant in the literature for these findings. First, that acquiring firms pay too much for target firms, but that an inefficient market responds to this information rather slowly (Roll, 1986); second, that there is a measurement bias in calculating the abnormal returns (Franks, Harris and Titman, 1991); and, third, that Asquith's (1983) findings are sample-specific (Mitchell and Lehn, 1990).

Residual analysis of the effect of various other items of information on share prices provides a broad consensus in favour of the semi-strong form of market efficiency. Research along these lines includes work by Kraus and Stoll (1972) on block trading in the New York Stock Exchange; by Foster (1973) on estimates of earnings per share by company officials; by Waud (1970) on Federal Reserve Discount Rate changes; by Scholes (1972) on secondary market issues; by Brown and Kennelly (1972) on quarterly earnings announcements; by Firth (1976) on earnings of similar-type companies in the UK; by Foster (1973) on earnings by similar-type companies in the US; and by Kaplan and Roll (1972), Ball (1972) and Sunder (1973) on various changes in accounting procedures.

These early studies taken as a whole thus seem to suggest that market prices broadly reflect and adjust to new and existing published information, and that there is little evidence that a trading rule based on the available public information can be devised so as to provide superior profit performance.

Subsequent investigations also indicate that share prices move rapidly to a new equilibrium value consequent upon the announcement of new information (Patel and Wolfson, 1984; Brown and Warner, 1985).[19] A survey of daily data studies by Fama (1991) suggests that stock prices seem to adjust within a day to specific event announcements, although the dispersion of returns increases around information events. Direct tests by Colling and Irwin (1990) of the efficient markets hypothesis, undertaken in the US using market survey data in the living hog futures market, provided evidence that futures prices reacted to new information in the way which would be expected if the market were efficient. The weight of evidence thus seems to suggest that markets succeed in reflecting most or all obviously available public information, and to do so quite quickly. Evidence to the contrary is limited, and of reduced significance if account is taken of the transactions costs involved in any attempt to profit from it. However, the findings are not unanimous. In particular, Bernard and Thomas (1990) produced evidence consistent with a failure of stock prices to reflect fully the implications of current earnings for future earnings. It is as if, they argue, stock prices fail to reflect the extent to which the earnings series of each firm differs from that of a seasonal random walk; specifically, that the market fails to understand the autocorrelation of quarterly earnings, and is, therefore, inefficient.

A somewhat different means of addressing this issue is to link regularities in financial markets with the frequency at which news is reported. Studies by Atkins and Basu (1991) and by Berry and Howe (1994) adopt this method. A parallel approach is to relate market volatility to the timing of the release of public announcements, such as macroeconomic data and government policy declarations. This is a technique employed by Harvey and Huang (1991) and by Ederington and Lee (1993). Similar work was undertaken by Mitchell and Mulherin (1994), who related aggregate measures of securities market activity, such as trading volume and market returns, to the news announcements of Dow Jones and Co. At the same time, they attempted to tackle potential estimation problems identified in earlier research, such as the variation in the importance of news and the endogeneity of news reporting. They found a direct relation between market activity and the number of Dow Jones announcements. Furthermore, their results appear robust to the addition of other factors previously identified as influential on financial markets – e.g. day-of-the-week dummy variables. While there is evidence from these studies that some identifiable relationships existed between public announcements and subsequent market indicators, these relationships did not, however, appear to be very strong. In other cases the relationship did not appear to exist at all. Mitchell and Mulherin (1994), for example, found difficulty in confirming any link between volume and volatility and observed measures of information. Mackinlay (1997) provides a valuable survey of the use of event studies in economics and finance.

A subsequent study by Lamb (1998) is a particularly interesting application of the use of event studies. Lamb investigated the impacts of Hurricane Hugo, which struck North and South Carolina in 1989, and Hurricane Andrew, which struck South Florida and Louisiana in 1991. The former caused an estimated $7 billion in property damage, the latter $21.5 billion. Lamb found that the market demonstrated a good ability to discriminate by the magnitude of the hurricane and, in the case of Andrew, by the degree of loss exposure borne by firms in the sample. Moreover, the significant negative response generated by Andrew was focused in the two days following the impact, consistent with a hypothesis that information is rapidly incorporated into the market.

Brown (1999) seeks to add to that existing literature by controlling for the influence of the private information component of all available information. To do this the Security and Exchange Commission (SEC) 'Official Summary' is used (in a sample from January 1990 to December 1997) to identify days where corporate insiders complete transactions in a company's common stock. The *Wall Street Journal* index is used to identify the news days for each firm.

Brown's results are similar to earlier findings by Roll (1986, 1988), Cornell (1990) and Mitchell and Mulherin (1994), in that the majority of asset price movements are unexplained after controlling for proxies of information flow, including private information.

In summary, while evidence does exist to suggest that the market tends to adjust quite promptly to new public information, the exact causation of asset price movements is still unclear, as is a methodology for exploiting public information flows so as to earn abnormal returns.

1.4.2 Reconciling market 'anomalies' with information efficiency

This section examines whether it is possible to identify particular conditions in a financial market which might systematically offer the opportunity of earning above-average or abnormal returns. Such possibilities are generally termed 'market anomalies'.

Some studies appear to suggest that stocks perform better at particular times of the year – e.g. Bonin and Moses (1974), Rozeff and Kinney (1976), Keim (1983), Reinganum (1983), Tinic and West (1984); or at particular times of the week – e.g. Cross (1973), French (1980), Gibbons and Hess (1981), Rogalski (1984); or that the shares of smaller companies seem to earn a greater amount on average than those of larger companies, even allowing for differences in their risk profiles – e.g. Reinganum (1982), Ibbotson (1990). However, there is less evidence that such information can be turned into profitable trading rules – or, where there is evidence, it tends to suggest that the possibility soon disappears. Even so, a review of the field by Fortune (1991) concludes that empirical analysis provides an 'overwhelming case against the efficient market hypothesis' (1991: 34). He cites as evidence such 'well-established' anomalies as the 'small firm' effect, the 'January' and 'weekend' effects, the 'winner's curse', 'loser's blessing' and the 'closed-end fund puzzle' (see below).

Krueger and Kennedy (1990) cite a 'Superbowl effect' and a 'mid-term-election-year' effect to add to this list. The so-called 'Superbowl effect' – i.e. an above-chance link between a team from the National Football Conference (NFC) winning the Superbowl and an improvement in the following year's market – would seem to be a classic example of chance correlation. For the record, the 'Superbowl indicator', after twenty-three consecutive forecasting successes between 1967 and 1989, failed in 1990 (along with the Denver Broncos).

Another interesting relationship is a 'local weather' effect (Saunders, 1993), significant at the 0.0001 level for a correlation between the local weather and listed stock prices in New York City! Some confirmation is provided by Hirshleifer and Shumway (2003), who find in a study of twenty-six countries from 1982 to 1997 a significant (though not clearly exploitable) correlation between morning sunshine in the city of a country's leading stock exchange and daily market returns. In contrast, a study by Pardo and Valor (2003) of the relationship between sunshine hours and humidity on Spanish stock returns offers no evidence of a weather effect.

The more standard 'anomalies' discussed by Fortune (1991) are considered below in greater detail.

The 'small firm' effect

The 'small firm' effect refers to the tendency displayed by the common stocks of small-capitalisation companies to show unusually high rates of return for much of the twentieth century.

Banz (1981) identified a negative correlation between the average returns to stocks and the market value of the stocks. Controlling for risk, he found that small firms appeared to exhibit greater returns than was consistent with their riskiness. In particular, the statistical association between the size of the firm and the average stock return was comparable to that identified by Fama and MacBeth (1973) between average return and risk. Supporting evidence for the existence of this 'small-firm' effect was offered by Fortune (1991). Using data in Ibbotson (1990), Fortune calculated and compared the accumulated values of two investments notionally made in January 1926, the first in a portfolio represented by the Standard & Poor's 500 and the second in a portfolio of small-firm stocks. He reported that the latter portfolio, in the years following the Great Depression, significantly outperformed the former. Hulbert, too, quoted in *Euromoney* (17 August 1992),[20] concluded on the basis of documented research into 'small-cap' stocks (defined as the 20 per cent of companies with the lowest market capitalisation) that such companies showed evidence of outperforming companies with larger capitalisations – the 'small cap' effect. Yet any possibility of outperforming the market is, he argues, limited in this small-cap sector to a small portfolio turnover, owing to the relatively high transactions costs associated with these kinds of stocks.

Nathan (1996) provides a test of a differential information hypothesis to explain the 'small-firm' effect. The hypothesis is based on the theoretical construct that firms for which relatively less information is available should, other things equal, earn relatively higher returns to compensate for estimation risk. Since less information is available, on average, for small firms, this is therefore a possible explanation for the 'small-firm' effect. Using the number of articles in the *Wall Street Journal* as a measure of information availability, Nathan concludes that differential information availability can indeed explain the whole of the small firm effect.

The study builds upon pioneering work by Barry and Brown (1984), who tested for the existence of an explanation based on the 'small-firm' effect by using a period of listing on the Stock Exchange as a proxy for information availability. Barry and Brown concluded that a period of listing could explain some, but not all, of the size effect.

An interesting more recent perspective on the 'small-firm' effect is found in Kim and Burnie (2002). They present an analysis of the link between the 'firm-size' effect and the economic cycle, based on the premise that small firms (which tend to have low productivity and high financial leverage) are more vulnerable to adverse changes in economic conditions. Therefore, they argue, any abnormal returns which small firms earn should be earned in the expansion phase of the economic cycle. In general, their findings confirm this hypothesis. Indeed, they observe no significant 'small-firm' effect in the contraction phase.

The 'January' effect

Another 'anomaly', arguably related to the size effect, is the 'January' effect – i.e. that stock performance improves or is unusually good in January. The literature on this can be traced to work on the seasonality of returns by Bonin and Moses (1974) and Rozeff and Kinney (1976). Rozeff and Kinney (1976) reported a 3.5 per cent stock return average in January, compared with 0.5 per cent in other months, a configuration incompatible with a martingale specification.

Supporting evidence was offered by Keim (1983), who calculated an average risk-adjusted return to a portfolio of stocks of small firms in various months, concluding that it was significantly larger in January than the rest of the year. Specifically, about half of the size effect occurred in January, about one-quarter of the annual size effect occurring during the first five trading days of that month. Supporting evidence is reported in Guletkin and Guletkin (1987) and Lakonishok and Smidt (1988).

On the basis of his own findings, Keim (1983) argued that the 'January' and the 'small-firm' effect might be one and the same thing, the 'January' effect appearing only in samples which weighted small and large firms equally, rather than weighting firms in terms of their value. Reinganum (1983) also noted that the 'January' effect seemed to occur predominantly to smaller firms – and moreover, that much of the 'small-firm' effect occurred in January. Tinic and West (1984, 1986), Keim and Stambaugh (1986) and Rogalski and Tinic (1986) all linked the 'January' returns to seasonality in the risk–return relationship. In particular, Rogalski and Tinic (1986) showed that the risk, as measured by Capital Asset Pricing Model (CAPM) betas, associated with small firms is greater in January than in any other month. In consequence, 'the 'abnormal' return on these stocks may not, after all be abnormal' (Rogalski and Tinic, 1986: 63). Tinic and West (1984), re-examining Fama and MacBeth's (1973) findings that riskier stock earn higher average returns for monthly data, concluded that the trade-off was limited to January. Incidentally, Tinic and West (1984) found that this US phenomenon translated into an 'April' effect when applied to UK data. The idea that this 'small-firm' effect can essentially be redefined as a 'losing-firm' effect is a conclusion supported by De Bondt and Thaler (1985), whose results suggest that 'losers' earn exceptionally large January returns while 'winners' do not. Keim (1989a) found an average return of 7.46 in January for a portfolio which used the highest earnings/price ratios and the smallest size, but only 1.39 in other months. Moreover, the bottom 20 per cent of companies in terms of the market value of their equity outperformed the Standard & Poor's index by 5.5 per cent for January from 1926 through 1986, underperforming in only seven of these years. Similar findings are reported in Ikenberry and Lakonishok (1989). A test of the 'January' effect, quoted in the *Wall Street Journal* (1992),[21] lends support to the hypothesis. In that report, an examination of the industrial average in the eleven years from 1980 to 1990 (inclusive) indicated an improvement in seven of them, an effect particularly marked in the case of the US Nasdaq Composite Index of small stocks, which outperformed the Dow industrials in five of the seven 'up' Januaries. In the years in which the Dow industrials showed a January downturn (1981, 1982, 1984), the small stocks declined further. Taken in aggregate over the eleven-year period studied, the industrials showed a 27 per cent rise, and the Nasdaq Composite Index a 38 per cent improvement.

One explanation of the 'January' effect, common in the literature, centres on the existence of tax-loss selling at year end – e.g. Branch (1977), Dyl (1977), Reinganum (1983), Roll (1983), Rozeff (1985), Chan (1986), Griffiths and White (1993) and Chen and Singal (2003). The idea is that some investors will sell securities at year end in order to institute short-term capital losses for tax purposes.

Reinganum (1983) and Roll (1983) both find a positive correlation between the size of the price increase in the first week of January and the size of short-term capital losses that were realisable at the preceding year end. Both suggest that the effect is greatest for small firms because the stock returns of such firms are more volatile, because such tax-exempt investors as pension funds possess relatively minor holdings of the stocks of small firms, and because of the relatively high transactions costs incurred by trading in such stocks compared with those of larger firms. After isolating those stocks which showed capital gains over the previous year, however, Reinganum (1983) concluded that tax-loss selling could constitute only a partial explanation of the 'January' size effect phenomenon.

The theoretical problem is that in an efficient market, one might expect that any such selling at year end would be offset by other investors with no such tax liabilities taking advantage of the abnormally low December prices – i.e. the tax structure should affect the distribution of share ownership rather than share price.

Berges, McConnell and Schlarbaum (1984) found higher average returns in January, especially of small-firm stock, in their analysis of

Canadian stock between 1951 and 1980. Significantly, however, the results were the same after as before the imposition of a capital gains tax in 1973, indicating the weakness of an explanation of the 'January' size effect couched wholly in terms of tax-loss selling.

Griffiths and White (1993) built upon work by Lakonishok and Smidt (1984) and by Keim (1989b), which reported indirect evidence that the effective end of the tax year coincides with a shift from bid price transactions to transactions at the ask price. They also recognised the finding by Badrinath and Lewellen (1991) of seasonality in the trading of those securities which experienced capital gains and losses, as well as Tinic, Barone-Adesi and West's (1987) evidence of turn-of-the-year seasonality in Canadian data antecedent to the introduction of a capital gains tax in 1972.

Noting the fact that whereas the Canadian tax year precedes the calendar year end by five business days, but that they are coincident in the US, Griffiths and White (1993) sought to discriminate between tax-motivated and other possible year end effects. Using Canadian and US intraday data for comparison purposes, they held that the turn-of-the-year anomaly is linked to the degree of seller- and buyer-initiated trading and is related to the incidence of the taxation (and not the calendar) year end. Like Bhardwaj and Brooks (1992) and Booth and Keim (1999), however, they found no evidence that abnormal returns could be earned from the 'January' anomaly.

Cheung and Coutts (1999) find no evidence of any monthly seasonality effect in daily returns from the Hong Kong Stock Exchange, a conclusion replicated by Coutts and Sheikh (2000) for All-Gold index on the Johannesburg Stock Exchange, and echoed in Hasan and Raj (2001) for New Zealand. However, Ahmad and Hussain (2001) do find evidence of a seasonality effect in the Kuala Lumpur Stock Exchange, linked to the first month of the Chinese New Year (usually February). Because of the nature of the tax regime in Malaysia, Ahmad and Hussain argue that a tax-loss selling hypothesis cannot be used to explain this seasonality at least.

Dimson and Marsh (2001) found that the 'small-firm' effect, which in the US has been concentrated at the turn of the year, behaves quite differently in the UK, again casting doubt on the generality of the January 'small-firm' effect. The tax year ends in April in the UK, but they find that any effect is actually negative in the UK in that month.

However, studies by Al-Khazali (2001) and Smith (2002) of US bond market seasonality find support for the existence of a 'January' effect, although Smith cannot confirm this when using non-parametric tests. Gu and Simon (2003) explore the trend of the 'January' effect of two major stock indices in the UK between 1976 and 2000, finding a significant negative relationship between the effect and market volatility. They also find a weaker 'January' effect during periods of higher real gross domestic product (GDP) growth and a stronger effect during periods of lower GDP growth. Gu (2003) confirms for the US a negative relationship between the 'January' effect and actual and expected real GDP growth and inflation, and a positive relationship between the 'January' effect and volatility.

Chen and Singal (2003) tackle the question of why the 'January' effect persists in the face of the fact that it has been known to academics, practitioners and investors for decades. They argue that its persistence is due to the fact that it is in fact difficult to find a practical method of exploiting its existence profitably. Chen and Singal (2004) try to disentangle explicitly different explanations of the 'January' effect, to identify its primary cause. They conclude that tax-related (tax-loss and tax-gain) selling is the most important cause, overshadowing other explanations.

A brief recent analysis of the literature can be found in Pietranico and Riepe (2004).

Day-of-the-week effects

The original day-of-the-week effect, traceable to findings by Cross (1973), is the proposition that large stock market decreases tend to occur between the Friday close and the Monday close. Since Cross's seminal findings, French (1980), Lakonishok and Levi (1982), Keim and Stambaugh (1984), Jaffe and Westerfield (1985) and Harris (1986) all found evidence that US stock returns are, on average, negative from the close of Friday trading to the opening of Monday trading, findings noted also for bonds by Gibbons and Hess (1981).

A negative effect on Monday returns is also found in Australian, Canadian and Japanese equity markets, the latter two countries displaying a similar effect on Tuesdays (see Alexakis and Xanthakis, 1995). Results for European markets have been more mixed (Hawawini, 1984; Jaffe and Westerfield, 1985; Solnik and Bousquet, 1990). A study of the Greek stock market by Alexakis and Xanthakis (1995) also found a 'Monday' effect and something of a 'Tuesday' effect, but only in data since 1988. Prior data revealed no such biases. This may be related to major structural changes in the Greek market over this period as its characteristics have changed in line with that found in most developed countries.

Subsequent work by Dubois and Louvet (1996) indicates that Cross's (1973) day-of-the-week effect had disappeared in the US, and elsewhere was behaving inconsistently across countries (Agrawal and Tandon, 1994) and over time (Wang, Li and Eriksson, 1997). In particular, Wang, Li and Eriksson (1997) indicate that the traditional 'weekend effect' for the NASDAQ index (which is dominated by smaller firms) is stronger then the weekend effect for the NYSE–AMEX index (dominated by larger firms). Their finding that the 'weekend effect' is stronger for small than large firms is consistent with studies by Gibbons and Hess (1981), Keim and Stambaugh (1984) and Brusa, Liu and Schulman (2000). However, their detection of a 'reverse weekend effect', confirmed for the portfolios of the largest firms, was totally novel. Brusa, Liu and Schulman (2003) claim that the 'reverse weekend effect' is a uniquely US phenomenon, and is not duplicated in any of the foreign markets they study. Instead the foreign markets showed either a traditional or else no 'weekend' effect at all.

Harris (1986) found that most of the average daily return occurs at the beginning and end of the day, while Ariel (1987) identified a systematic pattern of higher average returns on the last day of a month, and in the first half of a month (Ariel, 1987). Lakonishok and Smidt (1988) performed out-of-sample analysis on the 'January' and 'Monday' effects and also tested for a 'holiday' (higher average returns the day before a holiday) and 'end-of-month' seasonal effects. They concluded that all these effects held and did so equally well for data prior to that on which the original tests were undertaken. They were unable, however, to replicate Ariel's finding of a differential return in the first half of a month. Ariel (1990) subsequently confirmed the finding of higher average returns the day before a holiday.

Ariel's (1987) 'turn-of-the-month' effect was also confirmed out-of-sample (Hensel, Sick and Ziemba, 1999), albeit the days on which the effect occurs seemed to have shifted in the meantime.

Fortune (1991) analysed the daily closing prices of the S&P 500 for each of the 2,713 trading days between 2 January 1980 and 21 September 1990. In addition to testing the hypothesis of a random walk in stock prices, which he rejected, Fortune re-estimated the model to test for the existence of a 'weekend', a 'holiday' a 'January' and an 'early January' effect. Specifically he added four dummy variables to test for a 'weekend' effect, a 'holiday' effect, a 'January' effect and an 'early January' (first five days in January) effect. The dummy variable turned out to be insignificant for all but the 'weekend' effect. He failed to distinguish, however, between small and large firms in testing for the 'January' effect, a possibly important omission if any 'small-firm' effect exists.

A conventional 'holiday' effect was, however, found by Liano, Marchand and Huang, 1992; Wilson and Jones, 1993; Liano and White, 1994)[22] in defined samples, and subsequent work has sought to extend the testing to different arenas and datasets. Smit and Smit (1998), for example, in an examination of South African near futures contracts, concluded that any 'holiday' effect was not large enough to be exploited on an on-going basis. Brockman and Michayluk (1998), on the other hand, did find a robust 'holiday' effect in equities traded on the NYSE, AMEX and NASDAQ exchanges for the 1987–93 period. They also found that the 'holiday' effect existed in all size and price categories and across market types. Mookerjee and Yu (1999) tested for market efficiency in the relatively recently established stock markets in Shanghai and Shenzhen, using daily stock price data. They identified a significant negative 'weekend' and positive 'holiday' effect, but no evidence of a 'January' or 'early January' effect.

Vergin and McGinnis (1999) looked at the eight annual US holidays in which the market closes, between 1987 and 1996. First, they compared preholiday returns with those found by other researchers for time periods before 1987. Second, pre-holiday returns were compared with those found by others for periods before 1987. Vergin and McGinnis concluded on the basis of both types of comparison that the 'holiday' effect had disappeared for large corporations, and that the effect had so diminished for small companies that any strategy based on the effect was unlikely to be profitable net of transactions costs.

Abeysekera (2001) finds no evidence of any 'day-of-the-week' effect or indeed a 'month-of-the-year' effect in the Colombo (Sri Lanka) Stock Exchange, although Aggarwal and Rivoli (1989), Martikainen and Puttonen (1996) and Wang, Li and Erickson (1997) do find a 'day-of-the-week' effect in their respective studies of other Asian markets. Abeysekera (2001) is able, however, to reject a hypothesis of serial independence in returns on the Colombo Stock Exchange. Ahmad and Hussain (2001) found a monthly seasonality effect in Kuala Lumpur Stock Exchange (KLSE) returns.

Most recently, Johnson and Cheng (2002), in an examination of the returns from trading Australian Share Price Index futures, demonstrate higher returns for the day preceding holidays, but no evidence of higher returns on exchange-open holidays or on the day following either an exchange-open or exchange-closed holiday.

Lin and Lim (2004) identify a clear 'Tuesday' effect in Australian financial markets. They conclude that this 'Tuesday' effect is caused by the 'weekend' effect in the US conditional on 'weekend' effects in the Japanese and UK markets.

Ajayi, Mehdian and Perry (2004) extend the study of 'day-of-the-week' effects to encompass major stock indices in eleven Eastern European emerging markets. Their empirical results indicate negative 'Monday' returns in six of the emerging markets and positive 'Monday' returns in the remaining five. Two of the six negative 'Monday' returns, and only one of the five positive 'Monday' returns are statistically significant. These findings, they conclude, provide no consistent evidence to support the presence of any significant daily patterns in the stock markets of the Eastern European emerging markets under study.

The 'winner's curse' and 'loser's blessing' (overreaction)

The so-called 'winner's blessing' and 'loser's curse' (overreaction) anomalies were first developed by De Bondt and Thaler (1985, 1987). The basis of these ideas can be found in seminal work by Kahneman and Tversky (1973), which reported that individuals, in revising their beliefs, tend to overweight fresh information and underweight prior data. To test this hypothesis for those active in financial markets, De Bondt and Thaler (1985) used monthly return data for NYSE common stocks for the period between January 1926 and December 1982. They concluded that a stock selection strategy based on this hypothesis could yield large abnormal returns. Specifically, they found that thirty-six months after portfolio formation, portfolios of prior 'losers' (i.e. stocks that have experienced a recent reduction in their price/earning ratios) had earned about 25 per cent more than those of prior 'winners'. Over five-year test periods the portfolio of losers outperformed the portfolios of winners by an average of 31.9 per cent. Moreover, since the strategy is based on past returns only, it also contradicts the weak form of market efficiency.

Bernstein (1985), in a Discussion of De Bondt and Thaler's (1985) paper, explained the anomaly in terms of a quite different behavioural assumption – i.e. that investors, in seeking to reduce the complexity of their decisions, extrapolate historical earnings trends into the future, thereby causing long-term winners and losers to deviate from their fundamental values. Yet even in the face of such behaviour it is not certain that rational traders can gain from this mispricing, because even if the mispricing disappeared eventually, in the short run (see De Long, Shleifer, Summers and Waldmann, 1987, 1990) it could become even more extreme. A strategy based on this anomaly might, therefore, require a longer time horizon or greater resources than the rational arbitrageur possesses.

Nevertheless, support for De Bondt and Thaler was offered by Dark and Kato (1986) in their analysis of the Japanese stock market for the years 1964 to 1980, which revealed that the three-year returns for portfolios of extreme previous losers outperformed those of extreme previous winners by an average of 70 per cent. Dyl and Maxfield (1987), using a random sample of 200 trading days between January 1974 and January 1984 for NYSE and AMEX stocks, offered further support. In particular, they found that the three biggest losers in any particular day experienced an average risk-adjusted return of + 3.6 per cent over the following ten days, whereas the three biggest gainers experienced an average loss of 1.8 per cent over a comparable period.

Using data from the German Stock Exchange market for a period from 1973 to 1989, Stock (1990) also reported evidence of long-term overreaction, although he noted that in the short run the extreme stocks in his dataset showed a strong tendency to continue their initial performance. Jegadeesh (1990) and Lehmann (1990) both found significant abnormal returns resulting from contrarian strategies which selected stocks on the basis of returns in the previous week or month. Brown and Harlow (1988) also identified a 'magnitude' effect – i.e. a tendency for the most extreme initial winners and losers to show the most extreme ensuing price reversals. Lee, Chan, Faff and Kalev (2003) find significantly significant short-term profits to contrarian investment strategies in the Australian stock market using weekly data between 1994 and 2001. However, when allowance was made for 'reasonable' transactions costs, these profits disappeared.

An explanation of the winner–loser 'anomaly', offered by Vermaelen and Verstringe (1986), along with Chan (1986), is that it is no more than a rational response to changes in risk. In particular, Chan (1986) argues that a fall in stock prices leads to an increase in debt–equity ratios and risk (as measured by CAPM betas), and vice versa. In consequence, a higher return is required to compensate for the higher risk incurred in buying losers compared with winners. De Bondt and Thaler (1987), contend, however, that risk is insufficient, in their study, to explain the average annual return over the test period.

Immediate subsequent work was divided. Chan (1988) and Ball and Kothari (1989), for example, attributed the winner–loser results to a failure to properly adjust returns for risk, whereas Zarowin (1989) explained the phenomenon in terms of a size effect – i.e. that small stocks (biased toward losers) exhibit greater returns than large stocks.

Stock (1990) undertook empirical tests of the overreaction hypothesis for the German stock market, analysing the returns behaviour of those stocks accepted for option trading in Germany in 1983. He found evidence of long-term investor overreaction, although 'the most extreme short-term winners and losers both have a strong tendency to continue their initial price movements' (1990: 518). This evidence implies a clear violation of the weak form of the efficient markets hypothesis.

The case for an efficient market explanation was re-stated by Chan and Chen (1991), who proposed the existence of a risk factor associated with the relative economic performance of firms. This view was challenged by Chopra, Lakonishok and Ritter (1992). Using the Center for Research in Security Prices (CRSP) monthly tape of NYSE issues from 1926 to 1986, they report the existence of an occasionally important overreaction effect even after adjusting for size and betas, although the effect was substantially stronger for smaller than for larger firms. However, Dissanaike

(1997) confirmed an overreaction effect in an analysis of larger, better-known listed companies in the US.

Jegadeesh and Titman (1993) contend that long-term losers outperform long-term winners only in January, which if true would question the general validity of overreaction as the explanation of De Bondt and Thaler's (1987) results.

Studies of overreaction have in recent years been extended to consider a variety of countries and circumstances. Fung (1999) looks, for example, for an overreaction effect in the Hong Kong stock market, finding that the 'loser' portfolios of the thirty-three stocks in the Hang Seng Index out-performed, on average, the 'winner' portfolios by 9.9 per cent one year after the formation periods. This reflected earlier equity market studies of Spain and Brazil by Alonso and Rubio (1990) and da Costa (1994), respectively. Again, Mun, Vasconcellos and Kish (1999) found that a strategy based on a short-term contrarian portfolio worked best in the French and German stock markets. Higher returns in this study were not correlated with an increase in risk coefficients, consistent with an explanation couched in terms of investor overreaction.

Other studies have attempted to examine consistency over time and in different circumstances of an overreaction effect. Chen and Sauer (1997), in particular, find that returns obtained from a contrarian investment strategy are not time-stationary. In a study of US stock market returns which ranged from 1926 to 1992, they demonstrate big profits from following a contrarian investment strategy in the years following the Great Depression, negative profits during the Great Depression and in the 1980s, and no abnormal profits at all in the mid-1940s to mid-1950s. If consistent performance is a prerequisite for the contrarian strategy to work well, they say, the strategy fails its first test. On this basis, they argue that the viability of a trading strategy based upon the overreaction hypothesis is somewhat questionable.

Studies by Larsen and Madura (2001) and Schnusenberg and Madura (2001) produce evidence for overreaction and underreaction in different circumstances. Larsen and Madura (2001) examine exchange rate changes following extreme one-day fluctuations for currencies in industrialised and emerging markets. They find evidence of overreaction for currencies in emerging markets, but underreaction in industrialised markets. Events for which no associated announcement was identified ('undefined events') were found to have a stronger tendency toward overreaction than those for which a clear explanation was identified ('defined events'). The implication is that investors overreact more when the source of the extreme fluctuation is unknown. Political events tended to be associated with a stronger tendency to overreaction than did economic events.

Schnusenberg and Madura (2001), in an examination of six US stock market indices, identified evidence of a one-day stock market underreaction to both highly positive and highly negative news releases. The implication is that investors interpret extremely positive news releases pessimistically and extremely negative news releases optimistically. There is some consistency here with Fama's (1998) conclusion that, for individual firms, overreaction to information is about as common as underreaction. Over a sixty-day interval, they also found strong support for stock market underreaction in the case of winners but overreaction for losers, which they argue is consistent with Brown, Harlow and Tinic's (1988) uncertain information hypothesis – i.e. that investors tend (simply put) to err on the side of caution. There is also evidence of a reversal, which implies a correction to overreaction for each index, when the subsequent period is extended to sixty days. Such a reversal may be viewed as consistent with Daniel, Hirshleifer and Subrahmanyam's (1998) argument that investors are overconfident in their ability to value securities.

Cooper, Gutierrez and Hameed (2004) test overreaction theories of short-run momentum and long-run reversal in a cross-section of stock returns. In a data sample ranging from 1929 to 1995, they find that the mean monthly momentum profit following positive market returns is 0.93 per cent, whereas the mean profit following negative market returns is − 0.37 per cent. The up-market momentum, however, reverses in the long-run.

Kadiyala and Rau (2004) find, across four corporate events, that long-run abnormal returns exhibit a pattern that is most consistent with investor underreaction to short-term information available prior to the event and to the information conveyed by the event itself.

Lesmond, Schill and Zhou (2004) examine the profitability of momentum trading strategies – i.e. buying past strong performers and selling past weak performers. They find that those stocks that generate large momentum returns are precisely those stocks with high trading costs. On this basis, they conclude that the magnitude of the seemingly abnormal returns associated with these trading strategies creates an illusion of profit opportunity when, in fact, none exists.

The 'closed-end fund' puzzle

Closed-end mutual funds are distinguished from the more common open-end funds in that a fixed number of shares are issued, trading in which is between investors who already have shares – i.e. a shareholder must sell his shares to someone else in order to liquidate a holding. Closed-end funds thus trade in secondary markets. The net asset value (NAV) of these funds is the market value of the securities portfolio, net of liabilities.

Unlike open-end mutual funds, which sell and redeem shares on the basis of this prevailing net asset value, both the market value of these funds' assets and the market price of their shares are observable and can differ from one another. In an 'efficient market', one might expect this market price to equal the net asset value. In fact, empirical evidence indicates otherwise (see, for example, Weiss, 1989; Peavy, 1990) – i.e. that short of jettisoning the efficient markets hypothesis an explanation is needed in terms of characteristics unique to the fund. Otherwise the opportunity exists for arbitrage which would eliminate the difference. The term commonly used to describe this 'anomaly', first coined by Lee, Shleifer and Thaler (1990), is the 'closed-end fund puzzle'. Other evidence of a 'closed-end fund' effect can be found in Pontiff (1995).

Leonard and Shull (1996) used evidence of a 'January' effect in the returns of closed-end funds (as well as small firms) to suggest that the 'anomaly' has its origins in tax motivations possessed by individual investors who operate in this market. However, as Lofthouse (1999) points out, UK investment trusts are exempt from capital gains tax on gains made within their investment portfolio, so tax liabilities do not explain the observed discount in the UK.

Arak and Taylor (1996) addressed the separate issue of the gain to be made from a strategy of switching from equities into closed-end funds at times of a large discount and reversing the process when the discount reduces. Using Monte Carlo simulations, they found that the returns to this strategy were large, even after allowing for the systematic risk of closed-end country funds. This abnormal return, they conclude, is further to that which may be earned (by holding the fund) on the stock portfolio itself.

Thus it would appear that a wide body of *prima facie* evidence exists to support a contention that assets perform (in the sense of offering a return to a given outlay), or at least have at some time performed, systematically better at particular clearly defined times, and that certain types of particular clearly defined assets perform systematically better than others. Some evidence suggests that profitable trading rules can, or once could, be constructed on the basis of such information so as to yield systemically abnormal returns. Others, while less convinced or unconvinced about this possibility, offer the 'existence' of the 'anomalies' as evidence of market inefficiency.

The relevance of these findings for the efficiency debate turns ultimately on three questions – i.e. are the findings statistically significant, are they statistically valid and do they simply compensate for systematic biases elsewhere?

The breadth and depth of the evidence would seem to offer overwhelming support for its statistical significance. The justification for its statistical validity is less clear-cut, involving judgements of whether, for example, sufficient explanatory variables have been used, and whether any selection bias has occurred. Yet the most wide-ranging criticisms of the orthodox anti-efficiency case centre on the last issue. Does a systematically higher return by certain stocks or at certain times simply compensate, for instance, for greater risk, or less information, or the necessity for making more complex or more time-consuming decisions? Apart from the difficulties of identifying and measuring these factors, there is the problem of assessing the appropriate balance to be applied to the trade-offs.

1.4.3 Summary of empirical tests of semi-strong form information efficiency in financial markets

Two main approaches have been adopted in the literature as a means of evaluating the extent of semi-strong form efficiency in financial markets – i.e. efficiency with respect to available public information. One is to assess the impact of new public information on prices. The other is an exploration of opportunities for earning systematic abnormal returns on the basis of identifiable circumstances (so-called 'market anomalies').

Semi-strong form tests have tended to focus on market reaction to fresh public announcements. While evidence does exist that the market does not always adjust fully and instantaneously to new public information, there is very limited evidence that it is possible to exploit this so as to earn abnormal returns. This is particularly true without a capacity to react very quickly in real time to the publication of such information, and especially so net of transaction costs.

The other method of testing for semi-strong efficiency is to examine whether it is possible to identify particular conditions in a financial market which might systematically offer the opportunity of earning above-average or abnormal returns. Such possibilities are generally termed 'market anomalies'. For instance, do stocks perform systematically better at particular times of the year, or at particular times of the week, or is the market return linked in any systematic way to the size of the company? A number of these 'anomalies' have been identified, some of which have not been replicated, some of which have not been confirmed out-of-sample and some of which are found in a number of studies but rejected in others. There remains a general consensus that there exists or has existed a 'January' effect (shares perform systematically better on average in January) and a 'small-firm' effect (the shares of smaller companies perform systematically better on average than do those of large firms). Other interesting 'anomalies', both of them supported by a weight of empirical evidence, are the 'winner's blessing/loser's curse', and the 'closed-end fund puzzle'. The basis of the 'winner's curse/loser's blessing' anomaly lies in the idea that individuals, in revising their beliefs, tend to overweight fresh information and underweight prior data, so that investors who act in a contrary fashion to this prevailing psychology can on average earn an above-average returns. Closed-end mutual funds are distinguished from the more common open-end funds in that a fixed number of shares are issues, trading in which is between investors. Both the market value of these funds' assets and the market price of its shares are observable, and in an efficient market one might expect these to converge. The 'closed-end fund puzzle' is the finding that these not only can but do differ systematically from one another.

The issue has developed into the question of whether the identified possibility of earning above-average returns from systematic exploitation of genuine 'anomalies' implies the opportunity to earn abnormal returns. Ultimately, the question is not simply empirical, but turns on the weight attached to the costs of purchasing and trading in one set of stocks compared to another. Market efficiency would imply that any empirically observed systematic divergences between the returns to stocks or portfolios of stocks is fair recompense for additional observed or unobserved costs of trading in these particular assets compared to others. Until and unless a general method of evaluating these costs can be agreed and implemented, the issue is ultimately not resolvable.

1.5 Empirical tests of strong form information efficiency in financial markets

This section reviews the empirical tests which have been proposed and applied in the literature to investigate the existence of strong information efficiency in financial markets.

In a financial market characterised by strict strong form efficiency, security prices reflect *all* available information, public and private, as soon as it becomes available. In a less strict form, it is not possible to make above-average or abnormal returns from any divergences between actual security prices and the prices which would obtain if all available information were incorporated into the prices instantaneously and in an unbiased fashion.

Two main approaches have been adopted in the literature in an attempt to measure the extent of strong form efficiency in financial markets. The first is to assess the impact of identifiable monopolistic access to information and assess the impact of this insider knowledge on profitability. Because of the legal implications of overt trading on the basis of insider information, there are of course inherent difficulties in identifying such trading for purposes of evaluation. These studies will be examined in subsection 1.5.1. Following on from this, a second approach will be considered (subsection 1.5.2) which involves assessing the performance of individuals and organisations – in particular, professional forecasting services – in order to assess whether they have access to private information not reflected in stock prices.

1.5.1 The effect of insider information on expected returns

Niederhoffer and Osborne (1966) proposed that specialists on major security exchanges in the US have monopolistic access to information which could be used to derive profitable trading rules, a state of affairs which they explain in terms of the market structure of the NYSE. Any use of this informational monopoly power to make a systematic abnormal return is evidence of strong form market inefficiency. Scholes (1972) presented other evidence of monopolistic access to information by corporate insiders about their firms, information which was reportedly not reflected in prices. Similar work was conducted by Finnerty (1976). Collins (1975) looked at Securities and Exchange Commission (SEC) product-line reporting, concluding that information available privately, though not publicly, on historical segment prices in his data could be used to yield above-average returns.

An examination by Lorie and Niederhoffer (1968) of 'insider trades' reported in the official summary of stock reports of the SEC also produced evidence of performance superior to the market average, conclusions in line with work by Pratt and de Vere (1968) and by Jaffe (1974). Jaffe found that outsiders can also profit from information publicly available about insider behaviour for up to eight months after the information becomes public. If true, this would indicate semi-strong form inefficiency. Seyhun (1986), however, offered an explanation of Jaffe's findings in terms of a size effect, smaller firms (exhibiting relatively higher returns – see Banz, 1981) displaying a bias to 'insider buying' compared to larger firms (which favour 'insider selling'). Rozeff and Zaman (1988) suggested that these studies are in any case flawed, by failing to take account of biases in the calculations which could be caused by size and earning/price ratio effects. Controlling for these variables, they found, on the basis of a data sample of NYSE issues between 1973 and 1982, a zero or negative return to outsiders (net of transactions costs), and only a small return to insiders in the aggregate (3 per cent per annum, after deducting an assumed 2 per cent transaction cost). An examination of OTC/NASDAQ securities by Lin and Howe (1990) found that transaction costs could reduce or even eliminate the possibility for insiders to earn excess risk-adjusted returns from an active trading strategy, while Jarrell and Poulsen (1989) suggested that much of the evidence adduced to demonstrate insider trading is in reality simply evidence of the legitimate influence on the market of pre-bid media rumours. Other work has asked how far insiders possess valuable information, unknown to outsiders, which would cause any of their actions, where publicly known, to signal information about their company. Grammatikos and Saunders (1990) is an example of this approach, reporting a positive effect in the banking sector. These findings are supported, albeit subject to identified qualifications by Madura and Wiant (1995): 'insider buy transactions appear to contain favourable information for banks that did not recently experience adverse valuation effect' (1995: 227). The use of such information early so as to earn abnormal profits has been reported in Damodaran and Liu (1993) who found, in a study of real estate investment trusts, that insiders traded on internal appraisal information in the time between the appraisal and its public announcement, sufficient to elicit significant abnormal returns. Sivakumar and Wagmire (1994) also offered evidence, based on an identification of the relationship between insider trades and quarterly earnings announcements, of abnormal profits to insider trading. Lustgarten and Mande (1995) produced results indicating increased insider purchases (sales) prior to the announcement of good (bad) earnings news. This is consistent with Pettit and Venkatesh's (1995) finding of anticipatory insider trading and annual earnings figures for a large sample of firms (1978–87). Detta and Iskandardatton (1996), by investigating price reactions in response to the publication by the *Wall Street Journal* of insider transactions, also document the existence of significant information content in trading by registered corporate insiders, for the bond and stock markets.

Conventional wisdom suggests that the sale of stock by insiders reveals negative information. Livingston (2002), however, presents evidence, albeit on a small sample, which suggests that sales by controlling insiders should not be considered bad news. In fact, the study finds that firm value is just as likely to rise on the news of large insider sales as it is to fall, so that significant selling activity need not imply negative information. One possible explanation for a positive response to a controlling blockholder's sale, advanced by Livingston, is that such a sale in fact makes the insider vulnerable to meaningful oversight by external shareholders. In this sense, a large sale may be a signal of insiders' willingness to expose themselves to shareholder discipline and monitoring.

Finally, an interesting perspective on the issue of semi-strong form information efficiency in the context of insider activity is provided in Ferreira and Brooks (2000). The authors look at 'stale' information published in the weekly 'Insider Trading Spotlight' of the *Wall Street Journal* – i.e. information that had already been released publicly but not published in the profile column. They identified abnormal share price movements consequent upon the publication which had not occurred when the information was originally disseminated. This result, they argue, is clearly inconsistent with a hypothesis of semi-strong form efficiency. Although trading costs might prohibit the average individual investor from profiting from the inefficiency, this does not apply, they contend, to 'specialists, floor traders and dealers' (2000: 33).

In summary, there is some evidence that insiders can earn abnormal returns, but these returns may be somewhat limited net of operating costs. Similarly, the information which can be gleaned by outsiders from the public behaviour of insiders may be somewhat restricted, in both scope and value. Even so, none of these studies serves to contradict the presumption that individual cases of trading on the basis of inside information can and do yield large abnormal returns to such individuals, nor that some returns may have escaped analysis:

Some insider trades may be hidden from the SEC and not reported. Some profits may go undetected, namely those from trading in shares of other companies or those garnered through arrangements in which inside information is shared with others. In other words, it is possible that, even though corporate insider trading profits net of transactions and other costs appear to be zero based on the reported trades of corporate insiders, they are really not zero. (Rozeff and Zaman, 1988: 39–40)

1.5.2 The performance of professional forecasting services

The idea of using trading rules in order to generate abnormal returns can be traced in the academic literature to work by Wyckoff (1910), Gartley (1930) Schabacker (1930) and Neill (1931).[23]

The first major study to analyse the performance of professional forecasters *per se*, however, was published by Cowles (1933), who concluded that the recommendations of major brokerage houses failed to outperform the market. Much more extensive studies by Ambachtsheer (1972, 1974) of the forecasting ability of market analysts concentrated on comparing rankings of stock in terms of prospective performance by professional analysts with the actual outcome some time later. In each case, they found evidence of a significant, albeit small, degree of forecasting ability. A later study by Ambachtsheer and Farrell (1979) into the performance of investment advisory services produced similar results.

An important contribution to the literature is associated with Dimson and Marsh (1984) who, in an analysis of brokers' and analysts' unpublished forecasts of UK stock returns, undertook a survey of thirty published studies, involving 47,053 'investment tips' by over 200 advisory firms over a fifty-year period (1933–84). They found an average gain of 1.5 per cent by the day after publication, the longer term averaging 0.6 per cent (over periods typically between a quarter and a year). Although statistically significant, thereby providing evidence of at least a small degree of forecasting skill, most of the information content appeared to be impounded into share prices by the end of the publication day. Moreover, such returns did not take account of dealing costs, these returns working out to be less, they calculated, than the round trip costs incurred.[24]

Dimson and Fraletti (1986) focused on the value of verbal recommendations made prior to, or in the absence of, publication. Specifically, they investigated the profitability of following the telephone recommendations given daily during 1983 by a leading UK stockbroker (1,649 recommendations for ninety different companies). They concluded that these verbal recommendations were of similar value to written advice:

Neither the freedom given to the brokers to choose their own time to favour a stock, nor the focus on unpublished advice, led to any proof of marked outperformance. (1986: 157)

A report by *Insurance Age* (1988)[25] is also not encouraging, concluding that only one in three UK equity fund managers were able to match the return of the Financial Times (FT) All-Share Index over a five-year period. Studies such as those of Grinblatt and Titman (1992), Brown, Draper and Mackenzie (1993) and Goetzmann and Ibbotson (1994), however, are able to identify consistency in the performance of managed funds. Indeed, Hendricks, Patel and Zeckhauser (1993) concluded that some American mutual fund managers were able to successfully outperform the market (possessing what the authors term 'hot hands'), at least for a limited period. Specifically they examined quarterly returns between 1974 and 1988 inclusive, from a sample of open-end, no load, growth-oriented equity funds. They found that those funds which performed relatively well (compared to other similar funds) in the most recent years, also exhibited superior performance in the near term thereafter, the 'near term' being identified as one–eight quarters. Moreover, those funds which underperformed in this regard continued to underperform in both the short term and in the longer term. They concluded that the 'icy hand' is more sustained than the 'hot hand'. To counter the possibility that the results are due to known anomalies in the sample, they constructed a sample specifically to avoid problems of survivorship bias (a potential problem identified by Brown, Goetzmann, Ibbotson and Ross, 1992), and tested for other possible influences. They concluded that 'superior performance is also achieved relative to an eight-portfolio benchmark that accounts for effects of firm size, dividend yields, and reversion in returns' (1992: 122). Their finding of 'hot hands' benefits confirmed results they reported for a different sample covering mutual fund performance for the eight quarters during 1989 and 1990.[26] However, Malkiel (1995) conducted an examination of all equity mutual funds between 1971 and 1991 and found substantial evidence of hitherto unreported survivorship bias. He claimed that statistical evidence that mutual fund returns are predictable on a period-to-period basis was not robust. Moreover, they did not outperform the market.

Lakonishok, Shleifer and Vishny (1992) offered ambivalent backing for the idea of persistent overperformance. They found that in the period from 1983 to 1989, managers running equity portfolios for a sample of 769 American pension funds underperformed the Standard and Poor's 500 index, even before subtracting their fees, by 2.6 per cent after weighting by size (1.3 per cent using unweighted figures). Even so, those pension fund managers who performed relatively well in one three-year period had a better probability of performing relatively well in the next period, although they did not do well enough to score above-average returns after allowing the fees. Restricting the analysis to those managers whose performances over the previous three years placed them in the top quartile of all pension funds, they found a performance of 2.1 per cent superior to that by managers in the bottom quartile. These results are broadly comparable with the results of a twelve-year study published in the *Hulbert Financial Digest* into the performance of investment advisory letters.[27] Letters outperforming the market over one three-year period achieved better results in the following three-year period than those underperforming the market in the same initial term, by an average of 2.8 per cent per year. Applying the test to six-year periods yielded even more significant differences, letters outperforming the market over this expanded time scale making 5.1 per cent more in the subsequent six-year period than those underperforming the market. Overall, of sixty-seven investment advisory letters tracked over the six-year period from mid-1986, fifteen outperformed the market on average.

An extended examination by Sirri and Tufano (1993a, 1993b) of a large sample of equity mutual funds reported evidence that although funds and management houses which performed relatively well did tend to attract more assets, the relationship was asymmetric. In other words, good performance was rewarded to a greater degree than bad performance was punished.

A smaller scale test of forecasting performance was offered by Allen and Taylor (1989, 1990), in a Bank of England study of a select group of twenty foreign exchange chartists between June 1988 and March 1989.[28] The authors found 50 per cent accuracy in predictions of the direction of currency movements over a one-week period, and between 46 and 49 per cent accuracy over a four-week period. In particular, the 'experts' tended to miss turning points. Moreover, a rise in one period led them on average to expect a smaller rise in the next, while a fall led them to expect a smaller fall. They concluded that, taken as a whole, these currency forecasts were no better than a random walk.[29] They noted, however, evidence of variations around this average, concluding that in terms of forecasting the direction of future rates the best among those studied outperformed a wide range of exchange forecasting methods. In terms of forecasting actual rates, however, only one of the chartists consistently outperformed a random walk. Even so, an analysis of 200 questionnaires returned by foreign exchange dealers revealed that 90 per cent claimed to pay attention to chartists in predicting up to one week ahead. More than 60 per cent viewed charts as at least as useful as fundamentals.[30]

In a London School of Economics (LSE) laboratory study, conducted by Curcio and Goodhart, quoted in the *Economist* (5 October: 1991: 84), sixty LSE students took part in an experiment in which they traded (hypothetically) in one or more of nine assets, ranging from the FTSE-100 Index to US bonds. Half the students were in possession of a chartist package from the London firm of Fiamss, the others were limited to information on the price history of each asset. Actual reward was linked to hypothetical returns. There was no evidence of a significant difference in the performance of the two groups, a result repeated when the experiment was re-run using twenty-four foreign exchange dealers. Moreover, the foreign exchange dealers performed barely any better than the students. Even so, the authors did find evidence that those who used charts to 'trade' performed more similarly as a group than the rest of the sample.[31] A report on this study, in the *Economist* (5 October: 1991: 84) concluded thus:

So charts may be worthwhile for cautious firms, which do not pine for the profits of a trading ace so long as they never have to suffer the losses of a trading fool. Either that, or Chartism thrives because there's one born every minute.

De Bondt and Thaler (1990) tested whether the experimental 'overreaction' noted by Kahneman and Tversky (1973) for student subjects applied also to stock market professionals. Using analysts' earnings forecasts taken from the Institutional Brokers-Estimate-System tapes between 1976 and 1984, they concluded that 'the same pattern of overreaction found in the predictions of naïve undergraduates is replicated in the predictions of stock market professionals. Forecasted changes are simply too extreme to be considered rational' (1990: 57).

Evidence supporting the view that particular identified fund managers can outperform a *prima facie* random walk interpretation is, however, offered in a report in the *Economist* (8 August 1992: 67–8),[32] of the performance of the Boston-based fund management firm, Fidelity. In particular, in an analysis undertaken by Lipper Analytical Services, Fidelity's Magellan equity fund outperformed the Standard and Poor's 500 by 27 per cent in the year to June 1978, 21 per cent in 1979, 26 per cent in 1980, 51 per cent in 1981 and 53 per cent in 1983, though its subsequent performances waned, in later years barely outperforming the S&P 500. One explanation offered to explain the earlier success centres on the riskiness of Magellan's investments. An analysis by Rekenthaler of specialist research firm Morningstar, quoted in the same report, found a significantly higher variation in the month-on-month returns of Magellan investments in the period 1977–83, compared with both the Standard and Poor's 500 and other funds possessing a similar profile of small-firm investment.

The excess returns documented by, for example, Bjerring, Lakonishok and Vermaelen (1983), Copeland and Mayers (1982), Stickel (1985) and Huberman and Kandel (1987, 1990) for US investment advisory service Value Line seem somewhat more difficult to explain away. The Value Line Investment Survey[33] produces reports on 1,700 publicly traded firms, ranking their stocks on a scale from one to five in order of their desirability of purchase (their 'timeliness'). Studies dating back to Black (1973) reported that the higher-ranked stocks generated significantly higher returns than those lower ranked, a conclusion which, if not produced by chance, might most obviously be explained in an efficient market by variations in other costs, such as the level of risk associated with different rankings. However, Black found that the mean beta coefficients (i.e. measures or risk) were the same for all rankings, concluding that the service provided genuine predictive value. Holloway (1981) compared the results of active and passive trading strategies based on the Value Line rankings, an active strategy being defined as one of changing stocks before a year end if and when it is downgraded in rank, a passive strategy being one of buy-and-hold. Although the active strategy produced higher returns than the passive approach, the advantage was reversed net of associated transaction costs. Even so, the Value Line Ranking system provided profitable information, even allowing for transactions costs and risk. Stickel (1985) also identified information contained in the Value Line rankings not reflected in prices, although the information in Value Line rank changes was stronger for smaller stocks.

Fama (1991) placed such findings within a more general theoretical perspective, proposing that they were compatible with Grossman and

Stiglitz's (1980) 'noisy rational expectations' model of competitive equilibrium. Fama argued that:

because generating information has costs, informed investors are compensated for the costs they incur to ensure that prices adjust to information. The market is then less than fully efficient (there can be private information not fully reflected in prices), but in a way that is consistent with rational behaviour by all investors. (1980: 1605)

An explanation offered by Lee and Park (1987) contradicted earlier findings by Black (1973), in reporting evidence that the beta (risk) coefficients of stock were after all inversely related to their Value Line rank – i.e. higher-ranking stocks tending to be associated with higher-risk profiles. Affleck-Graves and Mendenhall (1992) offered an alternative explanation of the 'abnormal' returns generated by the Value Line ranking system as no more than the post-earnings announcement drift already documented by, for example, Ball and Brown (1968), Bernard and Thomas (1989) and Abarbanell and Bernard (1992). The reason, they suggest, is that Value Line rank changes follow closely upon recent earnings surprises. After controlling for earnings surprises, they found no significant abnormal returns associated with the Value Line rank. Peterson (1995) acknowledged the presence of post-earnings announcement drift, but contended that it was too small to explain the short-term abnormal returns which can be made from the Value Line announcements.

Not all studies, however, have supported the persistence or even existence of a genuine Value Line 'anomaly'. Hulbert (1990), for example, found a weakening of Value Line's Group 1 stocks after 1983. Keane (1991) made the more general assertion that the significance of the 'Value Line enigma' has diminished over time as the research methodology applied to it has become increasingly more refined. These conclusions are supported by Chandy, Peavy and Reichenstein (1993), who reported that a significant three-day return which they found to a weekly Value Line 'highlights' announcement, was largely reversed over a short subsequent period.

More recent analysis has tended to generate mixed evidence for the Value Line anomaly, however. Porras and Griswold (2000), for example, extend Copeland and Mayers' (1982) study to confirm that the Value Line effect continued to exist through 1995. Consistent with Copeland and Mayers (1982), they also find that this is due to Value Line's ability to identify poor performing firms rather than its ability to pick winners. The latter findings mirrors an analysis of Value Line's convertible bond recommendations by Lewis and Rogalski (1997), who demonstrate that while Value Line's convertible recommendations earn significant returns over time, once these are risk-adjusted they are successful only in identifying losers.

On the other hand, Choi (2000) dismisses his initial finding that Value Line outperforms the market even after controlling for size, book-to-market, momentum and earning surprise effects, when he allows for transaction costs. He concludes that Value Line can no longer stand independently of other market anomalies as an enigma' (2000: 496).

An interesting perspective on this whole issue is associated with the empirical studies of, for example, Stael von Holstein (1972) and Yates, McDaniel and Brown (1991), which suggest that so-called 'experts' are not in fact able to outperform a random dart-throwing approach to stock-picking. The view was given some additional support by a *Wall Street Journal* (1989)[34] analysis of stocks recommended by investment professionals in its column's stock-picking contest over a period of a year. This indicated a worse performance in four of the twelve months examined compared with a random 'dart-tossing' approach. Any boost to the professionals' fortunes from a publicity effect is more difficult to assess. In an assessment of investment dartboard columns since new and still current rules were adopted in 1990, and taking account of price changes only (i.e. ignoring dividends), Dorfman (1993) produced evidence that the professionals outperformed the darts on twenty-four occasions, compared to seventeen successes for the darts. The average six-month gain for the professionals was 8.4 per cent compared to 3.3 per cent for the darts.

Barber and Loeffler (1993) used a sample of ninety-five expert selections in the dartboard column and found a two-day announcement effect of an excess return of 4.06, which falls by 2.08 per cent over the next twenty-five trading days, to an excess return of 1.98 per cent. They attribute the 2.08 per cent to an announcement effect, and the 1.98 per cent that remained after the twenty-five trading days to actual information contained in the professionals' recommendations.

In an analysis of dartboard contests surveyed between January 1990 and December 1992, Metcalf and Malkiel (1994) reported that the experts beat the market eighteen times out of thirty (yielding a total return of 9.5 per cent), while the darts beat the market fifteen times (yielding a total return of 6.9 per cent). The stock chosen by the professionals also outperformed the market, as proxied by the S&P 500 stock index. Even so, Metcalf and Malkiel (1994) failed to reject the hypothesis that the experts won by chance at conventional levels of significance. The 'superior performance' by the professionals is in any case explained by Metcalf and Malkiel (1994) as a consequence of the tendency of the 'experts' to choose riskier, more volatile stock than would a random approach, and to a favourable publicity or announcement effect. The stock chosen by the professionals was in fact 40 per cent more volatile than the market, compared to a 6 per cent greater volatility displayed by the darts. Adjusting for risk, they concluded that the margin of superiority exhibited by the professionals fell to the statistically insignificant figure of 0.4 per cent, and disappeared altogether when allowance is made for any announcement effect. Critics of this approach claim that the professionals are given an unfair task in the rules of the contest, in particular the stipulation that the base line is taken at 4 p.m., when most of the gains from professional tipping will already have been realised. Moreover, the six-month contest period is sufficient time, it is argued, to obviate any persisting announcement effect. More recent support for Metcalf and Malkiel (1994) has been offered by Dickens and Shelor (2003) using stochastic dominance to analyse the contest. They find for total returns (including dividends) no difference between the performance of the professionals and the darts.

An earlier study by Sundali and Atkins (1994), however, produced evidence that the 'experts' in their study sample did outperform both darts and market averages. They found, however, that no particular class of expert was able to consistently outperform any other.

Atkins and Sundali (1997) divided their sample into one- and six-month returns to control for an announcement effect. They found that during twenty one-month contests, the professionals earned abnormal returns of around 3.0 per cent, beating the market around 60 per cent of the time. For their twenty-seven six-month contests, the professionals earned abnormal returns of − 0.4 per cent, however, beating the market only about 50 per cent of the time.

Atkins and Sundali conclude that 'Whether it is a publicity effect, compensation for acquiring costly information, superior information or just dumb luck, the financial markets can breathe a sigh of relief' (1997: 637). The return to following the advice of 'experts' was also examined by Zivney, Bertin and Torabzedeh (1996). They highlighted evidence of different reactions to different pieces of professional advice, even on the same page of the *Wall Street Journal*. However, their most interesting conclusion is that the market appears to overreact to 'rumours' published in the *Journal*'s 'Abreast of the Market' column, at least in their dataset taken from 1985 to 1988. Indeed, trading on these overreactions would, they report, have permitted a 20 per cent annual excess return. Other evidence on the issue has been produced by Sant and Zaman (1996) and by Womack (1996). In a study of stocks mentioned in the columns of *BusinessWeek* magazine, Sant and Zaman (1996) identified short-term positive abnormal returns for stocks tipped by a limited number of analysts (less than twenty, and the less the better), although a subsequent negative bias in the returns was sufficient to offset any positive effect by the end of a six-month period.

Womack (1996), however, used a new data source (created by First Call Corporation of Boston) which is able to provide (at a cost) the exact date and approximate time that information is made available to investors. This study concluded that both buy-and-sell recommendations have a substantial (and, for the period studied, non-reverting) impact on stock prices, an effect which continues to influence prices (at least for sell recommendations) for a period of months.

Supporting evidence for the value of professional investment advice is offered by Adrangi, Chatrath and Shank (2002), who conducted another dartboard analysis, using the Dow Jones Industrial Average (DJIA) and the S&P 500 to proxy for the market portfolio. On this basis, they compared randomly selected portfolios with the overall market and with professionally managed portfolios. They found that the short-term (six month) performance of the dart-throwing portfolio was consistently poorer than the market and the professionally selected portfolio. Moreover, the portfolio selected by the professionals surpassed that of the both market indices, findings which they report as robust to adjustment for risk.

In light of this evidence, it is questionable how far can one take literally Malkiel's (1973) assertion that a 'blindfolded monkey' throwing darts at a newspaper's financial pages could select a portfolio that would do just as well as one carefully selected by experts. Indeed, unless one ascribes the differential performance to additional risk or costs or an announcement effect, it is difficult to accept the statement in its starkest form. Perhaps Grossman and Stiglitz's (1976) analysis is nearer the mark. First, they propose that some investors choose to become informed, while others do not. Since the acquisition of information can be costly, those who choose to become informed are rewarded for their extra costs. In equilibrium, their compensation will be just sufficient to offset their costs: 'Thus, an individual who throws darts at a dartboard to allocate his portfolio will not do as well as the informed individual' (Grossman and Stiglitz, 1976: 248).

1.5.3 A summary of empirical tests of strong form information efficiency in financial markets

In a financial market characterised by strict strong form efficiency security prices reflect *all* available information, public and private, as soon as it becomes available. In a less strict form, it is not possible to make abnormal returns from any divergences between actual security prices and the prices which would obtain if all available information were incorporated into the prices instantaneously and in an unbiased fashion.

One way of measuring the extent of strong form efficiency in financial markets is to assess the impact of insider knowledge on profitability. The second approach is to assess the performance of professional forecasters, as a method of indicating whether they have access to private information not reflected in stock prices.

Because genuine insider activity is illegal it is, of course, difficult to measure directly. Most studies examine reportable insider trades, or else adopt an indirect approach – for example, by seeking to identify unusual trading patterns prior to the announcement of new information. Although there is evidence that above-average returns can be earned by insiders, there is only limited support for the view that, net of operating costs, these are sufficient to constitute serious abnormal profits. Similarly, the evidence tends to suggest that the information which can be gleaned by outsiders from the public behaviour of insiders is positive but somewhat restricted, in both scope and value. It is, nevertheless, very possible that the most successful insider trades escape detection altogether.

Examination of the performance of professional forecasters has taken the form of empirical tests which are applied to a sample of forecasts. The results are examined for evidence of significant above-average returns, and these findings are interpreted for the light they throw upon the possibility for identified groups or individuals to earn abnormal returns. Early studies of the forecasting ability of market analysts concentrated on comparing rankings of stock, as judged by the analysts, with the performance of the stock, actually ranked, some time later. These studies produced evidence of some, albeit a small, degree of forecasting ability, as did some analyses of the professional buy-and-sell recommendations. Allowing for risk, transactions costs (including bid–ask spreads), management salaries, etc., other studies revealed evidence of underperformance by 'experts' relative to the market. There was a general consensus, in any case, that most of the information content in the recommendations of professional advisors was rapidly impounded into share prices, and any gain was often less than the costs involved. Evidence has been provided, however, of a 'hot hand' effect – i.e. advisors who performed relatively well (compared to other similar funds) in the most recent years, also exhibited superior performance in the near term thereafter, and vice versa (an 'icy hand').

Smaller scale tests of forecasting performance have also been undertaken at experimental level. In these laboratory studies, the forecasts of experts were compared with those of non-specialists, the results showing no significant differences. Indeed, evidence of identical 'anomalous' behaviour, in particular overreaction to recent data, was found in both groups.

Excess returns have, however, been recorded in some cases on a systematic basis. The most well documented is the forecasting performance of the US investment advisory service, Value Line. A number of studies have reported that their higher-ranked stocks generated significantly higher returns than those lower ranked. The implications of these findings have to be judged in the context of other studies which ascribe the performance to variations in other costs, such as the level of risk associated with different rankings.

One other challenging and radical approach to the question of forecasting ability has been proposed by some advocates of the efficient markets hypothesis. It is based on the idea that, in a truly information-efficient market, so-called 'experts' should not be able to outperform a random dart-throwing approach, and this has served to popularise the debate. A number of empirical studies and challenges have developed from this, some of which have shown an underperformance by the 'experts' in individual periods, though not overall. This evidence of superior performance by professional forecasters over a sustained period has, however, been rejected by some economists as either not significant, or else simply a far higher return for the higher-risk profiles of the stocks compared to a random approach. There is also the suggestion of a boost to the professionals' performance in the form of an announcement effect.

A compromise position to all such studies of information efficiency is perhaps offered by Womack (1996):

The [positive] returns I document [to prior recommendations] ... are consistent with the expanded view of market efficiency suggested by Grossman and Stiglitz (1980), that there must be returns to information search costs. These information search costs are often assumed to be zero when considering the efficient market hypothesis. The nontrivial magnitude of the returns reported here challenges the innocence of that assumption. (1996: 165)

Notes

1 'The French word martingale refers to Martigues, a city in Provence. Inhabitants of Martigues were reputed to favour a betting strategy consisting of doubling the stakes after each loss so as to assure a favourable outcome with arbitrarily high probability' (LeRoy, 1989: 1588).
2 The link between capital market efficiency and martingales can be traced to work by Samuelson (1965). Samuelson held that the martingale model is satisfied if agents have common and constant time preferences, have common probabilities, and are risk-neutral.
3 By 'economic profits' is meant the risk-adjusted returns net of all costs.
4 LeRoy (1989) proposed that a market is efficient if, given transaction costs, no agent is able to earn returns in excess of the opportunity cost.
5 Fama (1991) also proposed replacing the traditional terminology – i.e. 'semi-strong' and 'strong' form tests of efficiency – with new terms – i.e. 'event studies' and 'tests for private information'.

6 Mean-reversion in stock prices is the tendency for these prices always to revert to some fundamental level. A useful survey of the literature on mean-reversion can be found in Forbes (1996).

7 A useful and more detailed review of this issue can be found in Engel and Morris (1991).

8 Fisher (1966) argued that spurious positive serial correlation in portfolio returns, caused by non-synchronous closing trades for the portfolio securities, was especially significant in portfolios weighted toward small stock.

9 Working (1960) identified potential problems in using serial correlation analyses on indices. In particular, he demonstrated that in a random chain the correlations of first differences of averages can lead to correlations which do not exist in the original data. A further discussion of issues related to non-synchronous trading can be found in Cohen, Hawawini, Maier, Schwartz and Whitcomb (1980).

10 The idea is that if two stocks X and Y have independent returns, but X trades less often than Y, then the price of Y will react more swiftly to news affecting both, the result of which being that the return to X will seem to react with a time delay to the return of Y. These positive serial correlations measured across a number of stocks will show up as positive autocorrelation in an index of such stocks. Such positive autocorrelation in the index may even mask negative autocorrelation in the returns to an individual stock.

11 See also Granger (1992).

12 A convenient outline of these issues can be found in Cunningham (1994).

13 The Cauchy distribution is an example of a highly leptokurtic distribution. It is characterised by an expected value of the variance of infinity, and an expected value of the mean of less than infinity.

14 This modification was developed by Lo (1991) to allow for short-term dependency.

15 Even so, examples of the use of trading rules can be found as early as the work of Wyckoff (1910), such techniques being commonly accepted as originating in the work of Charles Dow (an editor of the *Wall Street Journal*) around the turn of the century. Other references are found in Neill (1931) and Schabacker (1930), while Gartley (1930) discusses the use of a moving average trading rule. Coslow and Schultz (1966) provide a useful survey of the early work.

16 *Economist*, 5 December 1992: 23–6, 'Beating the Market: Yes, It Can be Done'.

17 *Economist*, 5 December 1992: 23–6, 'Beating the Market: Yes, It Can be Done'.

18 *Economist*, 5 December 1992: 23–6, 'Beating the Market: Yes It Can be Done'.

19 Froot and Perold (1990) suggest that the spread of stock index futures and portfolio trading has made the short-term adjustment of share prices to market-wide information very efficient albeit slowing, they suspect, the reflections of stock-specific information.

20 Mark Hulbert, editor of the Alexandra, VA-based *Hulbert Financial Digest*, quoted in *Euromoney: Forbes*, 17 August 1992: 135.

21 *Wall Street Journal*, March 1992, quoted in Reuters Textline service as 'Wall Street Journal C/C 3/92'.

22 Earlier studies of the influence of business cycles on calendar effects can be found in Liano and Gup (1989), Liano (1992), Liano, Manakyan and Marchand (1992) and Liano, Huang and Gup (1993).

23 Coslow and Schultz (1966) survey this work.

24 The estimates of the 'round-trip' dealing spread – i.e. the difference between the bid and offer price of the securities, are taken from unpublished research by Dimson and Marsh, quoted in Dimson and Fraletti (1986: 45).

25 *Insurance Age*, October 1988: 10–11.

26 In Patel, Zeckhauser and Hendricks (1992).

27 Mark Hulbert, *The Hulbert Guide to Financial Newsletters*, New York Institute of Finance, quoted in *Euromoney*: *Forbes*, 17 August 1992: 135.

28 See *Financial Times*, 1 September 1989: 10.

29 The *Bank of England Quarterly Bulletin* (1989) provides a survey of technical analysis used in the foreign exchange markets.

30 See *Economist*, 23 September 1989: 135.

31 Allen Taylor (1990) shows that if Chartists in the foreign exchange market have bandwagon expectations, excess volatility in exchange rates will result from the destabilising influence of these expectations on the market.

32 'Fidelity Changes Tack', *Economist*, 8 August 1992: 67–8.

33 See Bernard (1984) for a useful guide to the Value Line investment survey.

34 *Wall Street Journal*, 3 October 1989. 'USA: Pros Outperform Investment Dartboard in Stock Picking'.

References

Abarbanell, J. S. and Bernard, V. L. (1992) 'Test of Analysts' Over-Reaction/Under-Reaction to Earnings Information as an Explanation for Anomalous Stock Price Behaviour', *Journal of Finance*, 47, pp. 1181–1207

Abeysekera, S. P. (2001) 'Efficient Markets Hypothesis and the Emerging Capital Market in Sri Lanka: Evidence from the Colombo Stock Exchange A Note', *Journal of Business Finance & Accounting*, 28(1), pp. 249–61

Abraham, A., Seyyed, F. J. and Alsakran, S. A. (2002) 'Testing the Random Walk Behaviour and Efficiency of the Gulf Stock Markets', *The Financial Review*, 37(3), pp. 469–80

Adrangi, B., Chatrath, A. and Shank, T. M. (2002) 'A Comparison of the Risk-Adjusted Portfolio Performance: The Dartboard versus Professionals and Major Indices', *American Business Review*, January, pp. 82–90

Affleck-Graves, J. and Mendenhall, R. R. (1992) 'The Relation Between the Value Line Enigma and Post-Earnings-Announcement Drift', *Journal of Financial Economics*, 31, pp. 75–96

Aggarwal, P. and Rivoli, P. (1989) 'Seasonal and Day-of-the-Week Effects in Four Emerging Markets', *The Financial Review*, 24, pp. 541–50

Agrawal, A. and Tandon, K. (1994) 'Anomalies or Illusions? Evidence from Stock Markets in Eighteen Countries', *Journal of International Money and Finance* 13, pp. 83–106

Ahmad, Z. and Hussain, S. (2001) 'KLSE Long Run Overreaction and the Chinese New Year Effect', *Journal of Business Finance and Accounting*, 28(1), (2), pp. 63–105

Ajayi, R. A., Mehdian, S. and Perry, M. J. (2004) 'The Day-of-the-Week Effect in Stock Returns', *Emerging Markets Finance and Trade*, 40(4), pp. 53–62

Al-Khazali, O. M. (2001) 'Does the January Effect Exist in High-Yield Bond Markets?', *Review of Financial Economics*, 10, pp. 71–80

Alexakis, P. and Xanthakis, M. (1995) 'Day of the Week Effect on the Greek Stock Market', *Applied Financial Economics*, 5, pp. 43–50

Alexander, C. O. and Johnson, A. (1992) 'Are Foreign Exchange Markets Really Efficient?', *Economics Letters*, 40(4), pp. 449–53

Alexander, S. S. (1961) 'Price Movements in Speculative Markets: Trends or Random Walks', *Industrial Management Review*, 2, pp. 7–26; reprinted in P. Cootner (ed.) (1964), *The Random Character of Stock Market Prices*, Cambridge, MA: MIT Press, 199–218

   (1964) 'Price Movements in Speculative Markets: Trends or Random Walks No 2', *Industrial Management Review*, 5, Spring, pp. 25–46; reprinted in P. Cootner (ed.) (1964), *The Random Character of Stock Market Prices*, Cambridge, MA: MIT Press, pp. 338–72

Allen, H. C. and Taylor, M. P. (1989) 'Chartists and Fundamentals in the Foreign Exchange Market', *Bank of England Discussion Paper*, 40

   (1990) 'Charts, Noise and Fundamentals in the London Foreign Exchange Market', *Economic Journal*, 100, pp. 49–59

Alonso, A. and Rubio, G. (1990) 'Overreaction in the Spanish Equity Market', *Journal of Banking and Finance*, 14, pp. 469–81

Ambachtsheer, K. P. (1972) 'Portfolio Theory and the Security Analyst', *Financial Analysts Journal*, 28, pp. 53–7

   (1974) 'Profit Potential in an "Almost Efficient" Market', *Journal of Portfolio Management*, 1, pp. 84–7

Ambachtsheer, K. P. and Farrell, J. L. (1979) 'Can Active Management Add Value?', *Financial Analysts Journal*, 35, pp. 39–48

Ambrose, B. W., Ancel, E. and Griffiths, M. D. (1992) 'The Fractal Structure of Real Investment Trust Returns: The Search for Evidence of Market Segmentation and Non-linear Dependency', *American Real Estate and Urban Economics Association Journal*, 20(1), pp. 25–54

Antoniou, A. and Holmes, P. (1996) 'Futures Market Efficiency, the Unbiasedness Hypothesis and Variance-Bounds Tests: the Case of the FTSE 100 Futures Contract', *Bulletin of Economic Research*, 48(2), pp. 115–28

Arak, M. and Taylor, D. (1996) 'Risk and Return in Trading Closed-End Country Funds: Can Trading Beat Holding Foreign Stocks?', *Quarterly Review of Economics and Finance*, 36(2), pp. 219–31

Ariel, R. A. (1987) 'A Monthly Effect in Stock Returns', *Journal of Financial Economics*, 18(1), pp. 161–74

—— (1990) 'High Stock Returns Before Holidays: Existence and Evidence on Possible Causes', *Journal of Finance*, 45, pp. 1611–26

Armada, M. J. D. (2002) 'The Long-Horizon Returns Behaviour of the Portuguese Stock Market', *European Journal of Finance*, March, 8(1), pp. 93–122

Asch, P. and Quandt, R. E. (1988) 'Betting Bias in Exotic Bets', *Economic Letters*, 28, pp. 215–19

Asquith, P. (1983) 'Merger Bids, Uncertainty and Stock Holder Returns', *Journal of Financial Economics*, 11, pp. 51–83

Atkins, A. B. and Basu, S. (1991) 'The Impact of Public Announcements Made After the Stock Market Closes', University of Arizona and University of Denver, unpublished manuscript

Atkins, A. B. and Sundali, J. A. (1997) 'Portfolio Managers Versus the Darts: Evidence from the Wall Street Journal's Dartboard Column', *Applied Economics Letters*, October, 4(10), pp. 635–7

Attanasio, O. and Wadhwani, S. (1990) 'Does the CAPM Explain Why the Dividend Yield Helps Predict Returns?', Discussion Paper, LSE Financial Markets Group

Ayadi, O. F. and Pyun, C. S. (1994) 'An Application of Variance Ratio Tests to the Korean Securities Market', *Journal of Banking and Finance*, 18(4), pp. 643–58

Bachelier, L. (1900) *Théorie de la speculation*, Paris: Gautier-Villars, reprinted in English in P. Cootner (ed.) (1964) *The Random Character of Stock Market Prices*, Cambridge, MA: MIT Press

Badrinath, S. G. and Lewellen, W. (1991) 'Evidence on Tax-Motivated Securities Trading Behaviour', *Journal of Finance*, 46, pp. 369–82

Ball, R. (1972) 'Changes in Accounting Techniques and Stock Prices, Empirical Research in Accounting: Selected Studies', *Journal of Accounting Research*, 10, supplement, pp. 1–38

Ball, R. and Brown, P. (1968) 'An Empirical Evaluation of Accounting Income Numbers', *Journal of Accounting Research*, 6, pp. 159–78

Ball, R. and Kothari, S. P. (1989) 'Nonstationary Expected Returns: Implications for Tests of Market Efficiency and Serial Correlation in Returns', *Journal of Financial Economics*, 25, pp. 51–74

Bank of England Quarterly Bulletin (1989) 'Chart Analysis and the Foreign Exchange Market', November, pp. 548–51

Banz, R. W. (1981) 'The Relationship Between Return and Market Value of Common Stocks', *Journal of Financial Economics*, 9(1), pp. 3–18

Barber, B. M. and Loeffler, D. (1993) 'The Dartboard Column: Second-Hand Information and Price Pressure', *Journal of Financial and Quantitative Analysis*, 28(2), pp. 273–84

Barry, C. B. and Brown, S. J. (1984) 'Differential Information and the Small Firm Effect', *Journal of Financial Economics*, 13(3), pp. 283–94

Basu, S. (1983) 'The Relationship Between Earnings' Yield Market Value and Returns for NYSE Common Stocks: Further Evidence', *Journal of Financial Economics*, 21(1), pp. 129–56

Baumol, W. J. and Benhabib, J. (1989) 'Chaos: Significance, Mechanism and Economic Applications', *Journal of Economic Perspectives*, 3(1), pp. 77–105

Beck, S. E. (1994) 'Cointegration and Market Efficiency in Commodities Futures Markets', *Applied Economics*, 26(3), pp. 249–57

Berges, A., McConnell, J. J. and Schlarbaum, G. G. (1984) 'The Turn of the Year in Canada', *Journal of Finance*, 39(1), pp. 185–92

Bernard, A. (1984) *How to Use the Value Line Investment Survey: A Subscriber's Guide*, New York: Value Line

Bernard, V. L. and Thomas, J. K. (1989) 'Post-Earnings Announcement Drift: Delayed Price Response or Risk Premium?', *Journal of Accounting Research*, 27, supplement, pp. 1–36

(1990) 'Evidence that Stock Prices Do Not Fully Reflect the Implications of Current Earnings for Future Earnings', *Journal of Accounting and Economics*, 13(4), pp. 305–40

Bernstein, P. L. (1985) 'Does the Stock Market Overreact? Discussion', *Journal of Finance*, 40(3), Papers and Proceedings, 43rd Annual Meeting, American Finance Association, Dallas, December 28–30 1984, July, pp. 806–8

Berry, T. D. and Howe, K. M. (1994) 'Public Information Arrival', *Journal of Finance*, 49(4), pp. 1331–46

Bhandari, L. C. (1988) 'Debt/Equity Ratio and Expected Common Stock Returns: Empirical Evidence', *Journal of Finance*, 43, pp. 507–28

Bhardwaj, R. and Brooks, L. (1992) 'The January Anomaly: Effects of Low Share Price, Transaction Costs and Bid–Ask Bias', *Journal of Finance*, 47(2), pp. 553–75

Bjerring, J. H., Lakonishok, J. and Vermaelen, T. (1983) 'Stock Market Prices and Financial Analysts' Recommendations', *Journal of Finance*, 38, pp. 187–204

Black, F. (1973) 'Yes Virginia, There is Hope: Tests of the Value Line Ranking System', *Financial Analysts Journal*, 28, pp. 10–14

Bodie, Z. (1976) 'Common Stocks as a Hedge Against Inflation', *Journal of Finance*, 41, pp. 529–43

Bonin, J. M. and Moses, E. A. (1974) 'Seasonal Variation in Prices of Individual Dow Jones Industrial Stocks', *Journal of Financial and Quantitative Analysis*, 9, pp. 963–91

Booth, D. and Keim, D. (1999) 'Is There Still a January Effect?', in D. Keim and W. Ziemba (eds.), *Security Market Imperfections in World Wide Equity Markets*, Cambridge: Cambridge University Press

Branch, B. (1977) 'A Tax Loss Trading Rule', *Journal of Business*, April, pp. 198–207

Brealey, R. A. (1970) 'The Distribution and Independence of Successive Rates of Return from the British Equity Market', *Journal of Business Finance*, Summer, pp. 29–40

Brock, W. A., Hsieh, D. A. and LeBaron, B. (1991), *Non-linear Dynamics, Chaos and Instability: Statistical Theory and Economic Evidence*, Cambridge, MA: MIT Press

Brock. W., Lakonishok, J. and Le Baron, B. (1992) 'Simple Technical Trading Rules and the Stochastic Properties of Stock Returns', *Journal of Finance*, 47(5), pp. 1731–64

Brockman, P. and Michayluk, D. (1998) 'The Persistent Holiday Effect: Additional Evidence', *Applied Economics Letters*, 5, pp. 205–9

Brown, G., Draper, P. and MacKenzie, E. (1993) 'Consistency of UK Pension Fund Investment Performance', Strathclyde University, Unpublished Paper

Brown, K. C. and Harlow. W. V. (1988) 'Market Overreaction: Magnitude and Intensity', *Journal of Portfolio Management*, 14, pp. 6–13

Brown, K. C., Harlow, W. V. and Tinic, M. S. (1988) 'Risk Aversion, Uncertain Information and Market Efficiency', *Journal of Financial Economics*, 22, pp. 355–85

Brown, P. and Kennelly, J. W. (1972) 'The Informational Content of Quarterly Earnings: An Extension and Some Further Evidence', *Journal of Business*, 45, pp. 403–15

Brown, S. J., Goetzmann, W., Ibbotson, R. and Ross. S. (1992) 'Survivorship Bias in Performance Studies', *Review of Financial Studies*, 5, pp. 553–80

Brown, S. J. and Warner, J. B. (1985) 'Using Daily Stock Returns: The Case of Event Studies', *Journal of Financial Economics*, 14, pp. 3–32

Brown, W. O. (1999) 'Inside Information and Public News: R2 and Beyond', *Applied Economics Letters*, 6(10), pp. 633–6

Brusa, J., Liu, P. and Schulman, C. (2000) 'The Weekend Effect, "Reverse" Weekend Effect, and Firm Size', *Journal of Business Finance and Accounting*, 27(5), (6), pp. 555–74

(2003) 'The "Reverse" Weekend Effect: The US Market Versus International Markets', *International Review of Financial Analysis*, 12(3), pp. 267–86

Buguk, C. and Brorsen, B. (2003) 'Testing Weak-Form Market Efficiency: Evidence from the Istanbul Stock Exchange', *International Review of Financial Analysis*, 12(5), pp. 579–90

Campbell, J. Y. (1987) 'Stock Returns and the Term Structure', *Journal of Financial Economics*, 18, pp. 373–99

Campbell, J. Y. and Hamao, Y. (1989) 'Predictable Stock Returns in the United States and Japan: A Study of Long-Term Capital Market Integration', LSE Financial Markets Group Discussion Paper

Campbell, J. Y. and Shiller, R. (1988) 'The Dividend-Price Ratio and Expectations of Future Dividends and Discount Factors', *Review of Financial Studies*, 1, pp. 195–228

Chan, K. C. (1986) 'Can Tax-Loss Selling Explain the January Seasonal Effect in Stock Returns?', *Journal of Finance*, December, pp. 1115–28

(1988) 'On the Contrarian Investment Strategy', *Journal of Business*, 61, pp. 147–63

Chan, L. K. C., Hamao, Y. and Lakonishok, J. (1991) 'Fundamentals and Stock Returns in Japan', *Journal of Finance*, 46, pp. 1739–89

Chan, L. K. C. and Chen, N.-F. (1991) 'Structural and Return characteristics of Small and Large Firms', *Journal of Finance*, 46, pp. 1467–84

Chandy, P. R., Peavy, J. W. and Reichenstein, W. (1993) 'A Note on the Value Line Stock Highlight Effect', *Journal of Financial Research*, 16(2), pp. 171–9

Charest, G. (1978) 'Dividend Information, Stock Returns and Market Efficiency – II', *Journal of Financial Economics*, 6, pp. 297–330

Chelley-Steeley, P. L. (2001) 'Mean-Reversion in the Short Horizon Returns of UK Portfolios', *Journal of Business Finance and Accounting*, 28(1), (2), pp. 107–26

Chelley-Steeley, P. L. and Pentecost, E. J. (1994) 'Stock Market Efficiency, the Small Firm Effect and Co-Integration', *Applied Financial Economics*, 4, pp. 405–11

Chen, C. R. and Sauer, D. A. (1997) 'Is Stock Market Overreaction Persistent Over Time?', *Journal of Business Finance and Accounting*, 24(1), pp. 51–66

Chen, H. and Singal, V. (2003) 'A December Effect with Tax-Gain Selling?', *Financial Analysts Journal*, 59(4), pp. 78–90

(2004) 'All Things Considered, Taxes Drive the January Effect', *Journal of Financial Research*, 27(3), pp. 351–72

Cheng, K. (2000) 'A Variance Ratio Test of the Random Walk Hypothesis for Taiwan's Stock Market', *Applied Financial Economics*, 10(5), pp. 525–32

Cheung, K. C. and Coutts, J. A. (1999) 'The January Effect and Monthly Seasonality in the Hang Seng Index: 1985–97', *Applied Economics Letters*, 6(2), pp. 121–3

Choi, J. J. (2000) 'The Value Line Enigma: The Sum of Known Parts?', *Journal of Financial and Quantitative Analysis*, 35(3), pp. 485–98

Chopra, N., Lakonishok, J. and Ritter, J. (1992) 'Measuring Abnormal Returns: Do Stocks Over-React?', *Journal of Financial Economics*, 31, pp. 235–68

Choudhry, T. (1994) 'Stochastic Trends and Stock Prices: An International Inquiry', *Applied Financial Economics*, 4(6)

Chu, P. K. K. (2003) 'Study on the Non-Random and Chaotic Behaviour of the Chinese Equities Market', *Review of Pacific Basin Financial Markets and Policies*, 6(2), pp. 199–223

Clare, A. D. and Thomas, S. H. (1992) 'International Evidence for the Predictability of Stock and Bond Returns', *Economic Letters*, 40, pp. 105–12

Clare, A. D., Priestley, R. and Thomas, S. H. (1997) 'Stock Return Predictability or Mismeasured Risk?', *Applied Financial Economics*, 7, pp. 679–87

Cochrane, J. H. (1988) 'How Big is the Random Walk in GNP?', *Journal of Political Economy*, 96(5), pp. 893–920

(1991) 'Production-Based Asset Pricing and the Link Between Stock Returns and Economic Fluctuations', *Journal of Finance*, 46, pp. 209–38

Cohen, K. J., Hawawini, G. A., Maier, S. F., Schwartz, R. A. and Whitcomb, D. K. (1980) 'Implications of Microstructure Theory for Empirical Research on Stock Price Behaviour', *Journal of Finance*, 35(2), pp. 249–57

Colling, P. L. and Irwin, S. H. (1990) 'The Reaction of Live Hog Future Prices to USDA Hogs and Pigs Reports', *American Journal of Agricultural Economics*, 72(1), pp. 84–94

Collins, D. (1975) 'SEC Product-Line Reporting and Market Efficiency', *Journal of Financial Economics*, 2, pp. 125–64

Conrad, J. and Kaul, G. (1988) 'Time-Variation in Expected Returns', *Journal of Business*, 61, 409–25

(1989) 'Mean-Reversion in Short Horizon Expected Returns', *Review of Financial Studies*, 2, pp. 225–40

Cooper, J. C. B. (1982) 'World Stockmarkets: Some Random Walk Tests', *Applied Economics*, pp. 515–31

Cooper, M. J., Gutierrez, R. C. and Hammed, A. (2004), 'Market States and Momentum', *Journal of Finance*, 59(3), pp. 1345–65

Cootner, P. (1962) 'Stock Prices: Random vs. Systematic Changes', *Industrial Management Review*, 3, Spring, pp. 24–45; reprinted in P. Cootner (ed) (1964), *The Random Character of Stock Market Prices*, Cambridge, MA: MIT Press

Copeland, T. and Mayers, D. (1982) 'The Value Line Enigma (1965–1978): A Case Study of Performance Evaluation Issues', *Journal of Financial Economics*, 10, pp. 289–321

Cornell, B. (1990) 'Volume and R2: A First Look', *Journal of Financial Research*, 13, pp. 1–6

Coslow, S. and Schultz, H. D. (1966) *A Treasury of Wall Street Wisdom*, Pallisades Park, NY: Investors Press Inc.

Coutts, J. A. and Sheikh, M. A. (2000) 'The January Effect and Monthly Seasonality in the All Gold Index on the Johannesburg Stock Exchange, 1987–1997', *Applied Economics Letters*, 7(8), pp. 489–92

Cowles, A. (1933) 'Can Stock Market Forecasters Forecast?', *Econometrica*, 1(4), pp. 309–24

Cross, F. (1973) 'The Behaviour of Stock Prices on Fridays and Mondays', *Financial Analysts Journal*, 29(6), pp. 2–69

Cunningham, L. A. (1994) 'From Random Walks to Chaotic Crashes: The Linear Genealogy of the Efficient Capital Market Hypothesis', *George Washington Law Review*, 64(4), pp. 546–73

Cunningham, S. W. (1973) 'The Predictability of British Stock Market Prices', *Applied Statistics*, 22(3), pp. 315–31

Cutler, D. M., Poterba, J. M. and Summers, L. H. (1990) 'Speculative Dynamics and the Role of Feedback Traders', *American Economic Review*, 80, pp. 63–8

(1991) 'Speculative Dynamics', *Review of Economic Studies*, 58, pp. 529–46

da Costa, M. C. A (1994) 'Overreaction in the Brazilian Stock Market', *Journal of Banking and Finance*, 18, pp. 633–42

Damodaran, A. and Lin, C. H. (1993) 'Insider Trading as a Signal of Private Information', *Review of Financial Studies*, 6, pp. 79–120

Daniel, K., Hirshleifer, D. and Subrahmanyam, A. (1998) 'Investor Psychology and Security Market Under- and Overreaction', *Journal of Finance*, 53(6), pp. 1839–85

Dark, F. H. and Kato, K. (1986) 'Stock Market Over-Reaction in the Japanese Stock Market', Iowa State University, Working Paper

De Bondt, W. and Thaler, R. (1985) 'Does the Stock Market Over-React?', *Journal of Finance*, 40(3), pp. 793–805

(1987) 'Further Evidence on Investor Over-Reaction and Stock Market Seasonality', *Journal of Finance*, July, 42(3), pp. 557–81

(1990) 'Do Security Analysts Over-React?', *American Economic Review*, 80, Papers and Proceedings, pp. 52–7

De Grauwe, P., Dewachter, H. and Embrechts, M. (1993) *Exchange Rate Theory: Chaotic Models of Foreign Exchange Markets*, Oxford: Blackwell

De Long, J. B., Shleifer, A., Summers, L. H. and Waldmann, R. J. (1987) 'The Economic Consequences of Noise Traders', NBER Working Paper, W2395, October

(1990) 'Positive Feedback Investment Strategies and Destabilising Rational Speculation', *Journal of Finance*, 45, pp. 379–96

Detta, S. and Iskandardatton, M. E. (1996) 'Does Insider Trading have Information Content for the Bond Market?', *Journal of Banking and Finance*, 20(3), pp. 555–75

Diamandis, P. F. and Kouretas, G. P. (1995) 'Cointegration and Market Efficiency: A Time-Series Analysis of the Greek Drachma', *Applied Economics Letters*, 1955, 2(8), pp. 271–7

Dickens, R. N. and Shelor, R. M. (2003) 'Pros Win! Pros Win! ... Or Do They?: An Analysis of the "Dartboard" Contest Using Stochastic Dominance', *Applied Financial Economics*, 13(8), pp. 573–9

Dimson, E. and Fraletti, P. (1986) 'Brokers Recommendations: The Value of a Telephone Tip', *Economic Journal*, 96, pp. 139–59

Dimson, E. and Marsh, P. (1984) 'An Analysis of Brokers' and Analysts' Unpublished Forecasts of UK Stock Returns', *Journal of Finance* 39(5), pp. 1257–92

(2001) 'UK Financial Market Returns, 1955–2000', *Journal of Business*, 74(1), pp. 1–30

Dissanaike, G. (1997) 'Do Stock Market Investors Overreact?', *Journal of Business Finance and Accounting*, 24(1), pp. 27–49

Dorfman, J. R. (1993), 'Luck or Logic? Debate Rages on over Efficient Market Theory', in *Wall Street Journal*, 4 November, p. C1

Dowie, J. (1976) 'On the Efficiency and Equity of Betting Markets', *Economica*, 43(170), pp. 139–50

Dubois, M. and Louvet, P. (1996) 'The Day-of-the-Week Effect: The International Evidence', *Journal of Banking and Finance*, 20, pp. 1463–84

Dyl, E. A. (1977) 'Capital Gains Taxation and Year-End Stock Market Behaviour', *Journal of Finance*, March, pp. 165–75

Dyl, E. A. and Maxfield, K. (1987) 'Does the Stock Market Over-React?', University of Arizona, Working Paper

Economist (1989), 'Chartism: An M That Works', 23 September, p. 135

(1992a), 'Fidelity Changes Track', 8 August, pp. 67–72

(1992b), 'UK Special: Beating the Market: Yes, It Can Be Done', 5 December, pp. 23–6

Ederington, L. H. and Lee, J. H. (1993) 'How Markets Process Information: News Releases and Volatility', *Journal of Finance*, 48, pp. 1161–91

Engel, C. and Morris, C. S. (1991) *Attitudes and Decisions*, London: Routledge

Engle, R. F. and Granger, C. W. J. (1987) 'Cointegration and Error Correction: Representation, Estimation and Testing', *Econometrica*, 55, pp. 987–1007

Fama, E. F. (1965) 'The Behaviour of Stock Market Prices', *Journal of Business*, 38, pp. 34–105

(1970) 'Efficient Capital Markets: A Review of Theory and Empirical Work', *Journal of Finance*, 25(2), pp. 383–417

(1981) 'Stock Returns, Real Activity, Inflation and Money', *American Economic Review*, 71, pp. 545–65

(1991) 'Efficient Capital Markets, II', *Journal of Finance*, 46(5), pp. 1575–1617

(1998) 'Market Efficiency, Long-Term Returns and Behavioural Finance', *Journal of Financial Economics*, 49, pp. 283–306

Fama, E. and Blume, M. (1966) 'Filter Rules and Stock Market Trading Profits', *Journal of Business*, 39(1), special supplement, pp. 226–41

Fama, E. and French, K. (1988a) 'Permanent and Temporary Components of Stock Prices', *Journal of Political Economy*, 96(2), pp. 246–73

(1988b) 'Dividend Yields and Expected Stock Returns', *Journal of Financial Economics*, 22(1), pp. 3–25

(1989) 'Business Conditions and Expected Returns on Stocks and Bonds', *Journal of Financial Economics*, 25, pp. 23–49

Fama, E. F. and MacBeth, J. D. (1973) 'Risk, Return and Equilibrium: Empirical Tests', *Journal of Political Economy*, 81(3), pp. 607–36

Fama, E. F. and Schwert, G. W. (1977) 'Asset Returns and Inflation', *Journal of Financial Economics*, 5, pp. 115–46

Fama, E. F., Fisher, L., Jensen, M. C. and Roll, R. (1969) 'The Adjustment of Stock Prices to New Information', *International Economic Review*, 10(2), February, pp. 1–21

Ferreira, E. J. and Brooks, L. D. (2000) 'Re-Released Information in the *Wall Street Journal's* "Insider Trading Spotlight" Column', *Quarterly Journal of Business and Economics*, 39(1), pp. 22–33

Financial Times (1989) 'Chartists with a Hot Line on Currency', 1 September, p. 10

Finnerty, J. E. (1976) 'Insiders and Market Efficiency', *Journal of Finance*, 16 September, pp. 1141–8

Firth, M. A. (1976) 'The Impact of Earnings Announcements on the Behaviour of Similar Type Firms', *Economic Journal*, 86, pp. 296–306

Fisher, L. (1966) 'Some New Stock Market Indexes', *Journal of Business*, 39, pp. 191–225

Forbes, W. P. (1996) 'Picking Winners? A Survey of the Mean-Reversion and Over-Reaction of Stock Prices Literature', *Journal of Economic Surveys*, 10(2), pp. 123–58

Fortune, P. (1991) 'Stock Market Efficiency: An Autopsy?', *New England Economic Review*, March, pp. 17–40

Foster, G. (1973) 'Stock Market Reaction to Estimates of Earnings per Share by Company Officials', *Journal of Accounting Research*, 11, pp. 25–37

Franks, J., Harris, R. S and Titman, S. (1991) 'The Postmerger Share Price Performance of Acquiring Firms', *Journal of Financial Economics*, 29, pp. 81–96

French, K. R. (1980) 'Stock Returns and the Weekend Effect', *Journal of Financial Economics*, 8(1), pp. 55–70

French, K. R. and Roll, R. W. (1986) 'Stock Return Variances: The Arrival of Information and the Reaction of Traders', *Journal of Financial Economics*, 17(1), pp. 5–26

Frennberg, P. and Hansson, B. (1993) 'Testing the Random Walk Hypothesis on Swedish Stock Prices: 1919–1990', *Journal of Banking and Finance*, 17, pp. 175–91

Froot, K. and Perold, A. (1990) 'New Trading Practices and Short-Run Market Efficiency', National Bureau of Economic Research, Working Paper, 3498

Fung, A. (1999) 'Overreaction in the Hong Kong Stock Market', *Global Finance Journal*, 10(2), pp. 223–30

Gartley, H. M. (1930) *Profits in the Stock Market*, New York: H. M. Gartley Inc.

Gencay, R. (1996) 'Non-linear Prediction of Security Returns with Moving Average Rules', *Journal of Forecasting*, 15(3), pp. 165–74

(1998a) 'Optimisation of Technical Trading Strategies and Profitability in Security Markets', *Economics Letters*, 59(2), pp. 249–54

(1998b) 'The Predictability of Security Returns with Simple Technical Trading Rules', *Journal of Empirical Finance*, 5(4), pp. 347–59

(1999) 'Linear, Non-Linear and Essential Foreign Exchange Prediction with Simple Technical Trading Rules', *Journal of International Economics*, 47(1), pp. 91–107

Gibbons, M. R. and Hess, P. J. (1981) 'Day of the Week Effects and Asset Returns', *Journal of Business*, 54(4), pp. 579–96

Gilmore, C. G. (2001) 'An Examination of Non-linear Dependence in Exchange Rates, using Recent Methods from Chaos Theory', *Global Finance Journal*, 12(1), pp. 139–51

Goetzmann, W. and Ibbotson, R. (1994) 'Do Winners Repeat?', *Journal of Portfolio Management*, 20, pp. 9–18

Grammatikos, T. and Saunders, A. (1990) 'Additions to Loan-Loss Reserves', *Journal of Monetary Economics*, 22, pp. 289–304

Granger, C. W. J. (1986) 'Developments in the Study of Cointegrated Variables', *Oxford Bulletin of Economics and Statistics*, 48, pp. 213–28

(1992) 'Forecasting Stock Market Prices: Lessons for Forecasters', *International Journal of Forecasting*, 8(1), pp. 3–13

Griffiths, M. D. and White, R. W. (1993) 'Tax-Induced Trading and the Turn-of-the-Year Anomaly: An Intraday Study', *Journal of Finance*, 48(2), pp. 575–98

Grinblatt, M. and Titman, S. (1992) 'The Persistence of Mutual Fund Performance', *Journal of Finance*, 47, pp. 1977–84

Grossman, S. J. and Stiglitz, J. (1976) 'Information and Competitive Price Systems', *American Economic Review*, 66(2), pp. 246–53

(1980) 'On the Impossibility of Informationally Efficient Markets', *American Economic Review*, 70(3), pp. 393–408

Gu, A. Y. (2003) 'The Declining January Effect: Evidence from the US Equity Markets', *Quarterly Review of Economics and Finance*, 43(2), pp. 395–404

Gu, A. Y. and Simon, J. T. (2003) 'Declining January Effect – Experience in the United Kingdom', *American Business Review*, 21(2), pp. 117–21

Guletkin, M. N. and Guletkin, N. B. (1987) 'Stock Return Anomalies and the Tests of the APT', *Journal of Finance*, 42(5), pp. 1213–24

Hagerman, R. L. and Richmond, R. D. (1973) 'Random Walks, Martingales and the OTC', *Journal of Finance*, 28, pp. 897–909

Harris, L. (1986) 'A Transaction Data Study of Weekly and Intradaily Patterns in Stock Returns', *Journal of Financial Economics*, 16(1), pp. 99–117

Harvey, C. R. (1991) 'The World Price of Covariance Risk', *Journal of Finance*, 46, pp. 111–57

Harvey, C. R. and Huang, R. D. (1991) 'Volatility in the Foreign Currency Futures Market', *Review of Financial Studies*, 4, pp. 543–69

Hasan, T. and Raj, M. (2001) 'An Examination of the Tax Loss Selling Behaviour in a Deregulated Pacific Financial Market', *American Business Review*, 19(2), pp. 100–5

Hawawini, G. (ed.) (1984) 'European Equity Markets: Price Behaviour and Efficiency', Salomon Brothers Centre/NYU Monograph, 4/5

Hendricks. D., Patel, J. and Zeckhauser, R. (1993) 'Hot Hands in Mutual Funds', *Journal of Finance*, 48, pp. 3–130

Hensel, C., Sick, G. and Ziemba, W. (1999) 'A Long-Term Examination of the Turn-of-the-Month Effect in the S&P 500', in D. Keim and W. Ziemba (eds.), *Security Market Imperfections in World Wide Equity Markets*, Cambridge: Cambridge University Press

Hirshleifer, D. and Shumway, T. (2003) 'Good Day Sunshine: Stock Returns and the Weather', *Journal of Finance*, 58(3), pp. 1009–32

Holloway, C. (1981) 'A Note on Testing on Aggressive Investment Strategy Using Value Line Ranks', *Journal of Finance*, 36, pp. 711–19

Howe, J. S. and Martin, D. W. (1999) 'Much Ado About Nothing: Long-Term Memory in Pacific Rim Equity Markets', 8(2), pp. 139–51

Hsieh, D. A. (1989) 'Testing for Non-linearity in Daily Foreign-Exchange Rates', *Journal of Business*, 62, pp. 329–68

(1991) 'Chaos and Non-Linear Dynamics: Applications to Financial Markets', *Journal of Finance*, 46, pp. 1839–77

Huang, B. (1995) 'Do Asian Stock Market Prices Follow Random Walks? Evidence from the Variance Ratio Test', *Applied Financial Economics*, 4, pp. 251–6

Huang, B. and Yang, C. W. (1995) 'The Fractal Structure in Multinational Stock Returns', *Applied Economics Letters*, 2, pp. 67–71

Huberman, G. and Kandel, S. (1987) 'Value Line Rank and Firm Size', *Journal of Business*, 60, pp. 577–89

Hulbert, M. (1990) 'Proof of Pudding', *Forbes*, 10, p. 316

Humberna, G. and Kandel, S. (1990) 'Market Efficiency and Value Line's Record', *Journal of Business*, 63, pp. 197–216

Hunter, D. (1998) 'The Performance of Filter Rules on the Jamaican Stock Exchange', *Applied Economics Letters*, 5, pp. 297–300

Hurst, H. (1951) 'Long Term Storage Capacity of Reservoirs', *Transactions of the American Society of Civil Engineers*, 116, pp. 770–99

Ibbotson Associates (1990) *Stocks, Bonds, Bills and Inflation: 1990 Yearbook*, Chicago, IL: Ibbotson Associates

Ikenberry, D. and Lakonishok, J. (1989) 'Seasonal Anomalies in Financial Markets: A Survey', in R. M. C. Guimaraes, B. G. Kingsman and S. J. Taylor (eds.), *A Reappraisal of the Efficiency of Financial Markets*, Berlin: Springer-Verlag

Insurance Age (1988), 10, pp. 10–11

Jaffe, J. F. (1974) 'Special Information and Insider Trading', *Journal of Business*, 47, pp. 410–29

Jaffe, J. F. and Mandelkar, G. (1976) 'The "Fisher Effect" for Risky Assets: An Empirical Investigation', *Journal of Finance*, 31, pp. 447–58

Jaffe, J. F. and Westerfield, R. (1985) 'The Week-End Effect in Common Stock Returns: The International Evidence', *Journal of Finance*, 40(2), pp. 433–54

Jarrell, G. A. and Poulsen, A. B. (1989) 'Stock Trading Before the Announcement of Tender Offers: Insider Trading or Market Anticipation?', *Journal of Law, Economics and Organisation*, 5(2), pp. 225–48

Jegadeesh, N. (1990) 'Evidence of Predictable Behaviour of Security Returns', *Journal of Finance*, 45, pp. 881–98

Jegadeesh, N. and Titman, S. (1993) 'Returns to Buying Winners and Selling Losers: Implications for Stock Market Efficiency', *Journal of Finance*, 48(1), pp. 65–91

Jensen, M. C. (1978) 'Some Anomalous Evidence Regarding Market Efficiency', *Journal of Financial Economics*, 6, pp. 95–101

Jensen, M. C. and Bennington, G. A. (1970) 'Random Walks and Technical Theories: Some Additional Evidence', *Journal of Finance*, 25, pp. 469–82

Johansen, S. (1988) 'Statistical Analysis of Cointegration Vectors', *Journal of Economic Dynamics and Control*, 12, pp. 231–54

Johnson, J. and Cheng, S. W. (2002) 'Holidays and Trading and Return Patterns of Australian SPI Futures', *Journal of Derivatives*, 9(4), pp. 56–67

Kadiyala, P. and Rau, P. R. (2004) 'Investor Reaction to Corporate Event Anouncements: Underreaxction or Overreaction?', *Journal of Business*, 77(2), pp. 357–86

Kahneman, D. and Tversky, A. (1973) 'On the Psychology of Prediction', *Psychological Review*, 80, pp. 237–51

Kaplan, R. and Roll, R. (1972) 'Investor Evaluation of Accounting Information: Some Empirical Evidence', *Journal of Business*, 45, pp. 225–57

Keane, S. M. (1987) *Efficient Markets and Financial Reporting*, Edinburgh: Institute of Chartered Accountants of Scotland

(1991) 'Paradox in the Current Crisis in Efficient Market Theory', *Journal of Portfolio Management*, Winter

(1993) 'Emerging Markets – The Relevance of Efficient Market Theory', Occasional Research Paper, 15, Glasgow University

Keim, D. B. (1983) 'Size-Related Anomalies and Stock Return Seasonality: Further Empirical Evidence', *Journal of Financial Economics*, 12(1), pp. 13–32

(1989a) 'Earnings Yield and Size Effects: Unconditional and Conditional Estimates', in R. M. C. Guimaraes, B. G. Kingsman and S. J. Taylor, *A Reappraisal of the Efficiency of Financial Markets*, Berlin: Springer-Verlag

(1989b) 'Trading Patterns, Bid–Ask Spreads and Estimated Security Returns: The Case of Common Stocks at Calendar Turning Points', *Journal of Financial Economics*, 25, pp. 75–97

Keim, D. B. and Stambaugh, R. F. (1984) 'A Further Investigation of the Weekend Effect in Stock Returns', *Journal of Finance*, 39(3), pp. 819–40

(1986) 'Predicting Returns in the Stock and Bond Markets', *Journal of Financial Economics*, 17, pp. 357–90

Kendall, M. G. (1953) 'The Analysis of Economic Time Series Part 1: Prices', *Journal of Royal Statistical Society*, 96, pp. 11–25; reprinted in P. Cootner, (ed.) (1964), *The Random Character of Stock Market Prices*, Cambridge, MA: MIT Press

Kho, B. (1996) 'Time-Varying Risk Premia, Volatility, and Technical Trading Rule Profits: Evidence from Foreign Currency Futures Markets', *Journal of Financial Economics*, 41(2), pp. 249–90

Kim, M. J., Nelson, C. R. and Startz, R. (1991) 'Mean-Reversion in Stock Prices? A Reappraisal of the Empirical Evidence', *Review of Economic Studies*, 58, pp. 515–28

Kim, M. K. and Burnie, D. A. (2002) 'The Firm Size Effect and the Economic Cycle', *Journal of Financial Research*, 25(1), pp. 111–24

Kraus, A. and Stoll, H. (1972) 'Price Impacts of Block Trading on the New York Stock Exchange', *Journal of Finance*, 27, pp. 569–88

Krueger, T. and Kennedy, W. (1990) 'An Examination of the Super Bowl Stock Market Predictor', *Journal of Finance*, 45(2), pp. 691–7

Lakonishok, J. and Levi, M. (1982) 'Weekend Effects on Stock Returns: A Note', *Journal of Finance*, 37(3), pp. 883–9

Lakonishok, J. and Smidt, S. (1984) 'Volume and Turn-of-the-Year Behaviour', *Journal of Financial Economics*, 13, pp. 435–55

(1988) 'Are Seasonal Anomalies Real? A Ninety-Year Perspective', *Review of Financial Studies*, 1(4), pp. 403–25

Lakonishok, J., Shleifer, A. and Vishny, R. (1992) 'The Structure and Performance of the Money Management Industry', *Brookings Papers on Economic Activity*, pp. 339–91

Lamb, R. P. (1998) 'An Examination of Market Efficiency Around Hurricanes', *Financial Review*, 33(1), pp. 163–72

Larsen, S. J. and Madura, J. (2001) 'Overreaction and Underreaction in the Foreign Exchange Market', *Global Finance Journal*, 12, pp. 153–77

Leamer, E. (1978) *Specification Searches*, New York: Wiley

Le Baron, B. (1999) 'Technical Trading Rule Profitability and Foreign Exchange Intervention', *Journal of International Economics*, 49(1), pp. 125–43

Lee, C. F. and Park. H. Y. (1987) 'Value Line Investment Survey Rank Changes and Bets Coefficients', *Financial Analysts Journal*, September–October, pp. 70–2

Lee, C. F., Chen, G.-M. and Rui, O. M. (2001) 'Stock Returns and Volatility on China's Stock Markets', *Journal of Financial Research*, 24(4), pp. 523–43

Lee, C. F., Shleifer, A. and Thaler, R. (1990a) 'Closed-End Mutual Funds', *Journal of Economic Perspectives*, Fall, pp. 153–164

(1990b) 'Invester Sentiment and the Closed End-Fund Puzzle', *Journal of Finance*, 46, pp. 75–109

Lee, D. D., Chan, H., Faff, R. W. and Kalev, P. S. (2003) 'Short-Term Contrarian Investing – Is It Profitable? ... Yes and No', *Journal of Multinational Financial Management*, 13(4/5), pp. 385–404

Lehmann, B. (1990) 'Fads, Martingales and Market Efficiency', *Quarterly Journal of Economics*, 105(1), pp. 1–28

Leonard, D. C. and Shull, D. M. (1996) 'Investor Sentiment and the Closed-End Fund Evidence: Impact of the January Effect', *Quarterly Review of Economics and Finance*, 36(1), pp. 117–26

LeRoy, S. F. (1976) 'Efficient Capital Markets: Comments', *Journal of Finance*, 3, pp. 139–41

(1989) 'Efficient Capital Markets and Martingales', *Journal of Economic Literature*, 27(4), pp. 1583–1621

Lesmond, D. A., Schill, M. J. and Zhou, C. (2004) 'The Illusory Nature of Momentum Profits', *Journal of Financial Economics*, 71(2), pp. 349–70

Levy, R. (1967) 'Relative Strength as a Criterion for Investment Selection', *Journal of Finance*, 22, pp. 595–610

Lewis, C. M. and Rogalski, R. J. (1997) 'The Information Content of Value Line Convertible Bond Rankings', *Journal of Portfolio Management*, 24(1), pp. 42–52

Liano, K. (1992) 'Macroeconomic Events and Seasonality of Risk and Return', *Applied Financial Economics*, 2, pp. 205–9

Liano, K. and Gup, B. E. (1989) 'The Day-of-the-Week Effect in Stock Returns over Business Cycles', *Financial Analysts Journal*, 45, pp. 74–7

Liano, K., Huang, G. C. and Gup, B. E. (1993) 'A Twist on the Monday Effect in Stock Returns: A Note', *Journal of Economics and Business*, 45, pp. 61–7

Liano, K., Manakyan, H. and Marchand, P. H. (1992) 'Economic Cycles and the Monthly Effect in the OTC Market', *Quarterly Journal of Business and Economics*, 31, pp. 41–50

Liano, K., Marchand, P. H. and Huang, G. C. (1992) 'The Holiday Effect in Stock Returns: Evidence from the OTC Market', *Review of Financial Economics*, 2(1), pp. 45–54

Liano, K. and White, L. R. (1994) 'Business Cycles and the Pre-Holiday Effect in Stock Returns', *Applied Financial Economics*, 4, pp. 171–4

Lin, J. C. and Howe, J. S. (1990) 'Insider Trading in the OTC Market', *Journal of Finance*, 45, pp. 1273–84

Livingston, L. S. (2002) 'Are Insider Sales Always Bad News? Evidence on Large Sales to Key Insiders', *Journal of Applied Business Research*, 18(1), pp. 23–36

Lo, A. W. (1990a) 'An Econometric Analysis of Nonsynchronous Trading' *Journal of Econometrics*, 45(1–2), pp. 181–211

(1990b) 'Data-Snooping Biases in Tests of Financial Asset Pricing Models', *Review of Financial Studies*, 3, pp. 431–68

(1991) 'Long-Term Memory in Stock Market Prices', *Econometrica*, 59, pp. 1279–1313

Lo, A. W. and MacKinlay, A. C. (1988) 'Stock Market Prices do not Follow Random Walks: Evidence from a Simple Specification Test', *Review of Financial Studies* 1(1), pp. 41–66

(1989) 'The Size and Power of the Variance Ratio Test in Finite Samples: a Monte Carlo Investigation', *Journal of Econometrics*, 22(7), pp. 27–59

Lofthouse, S. (1999) 'Closed-End Fund and Investment Trust Discounts', *Journal of Investing*, Spring, 8(1), pp. 27–37

Lorie, J. H. and Niederhoffer, V. (1968) 'Predictive and Statistical Properties of Insider Trading', *Journal of Law and Economics*, 11, pp. 35–53

Lukac, L. P. and Brorsen, B. W. (1990) 'A Comprehensive Test of Futures Market Disequilibrium', *Financial Review*, 25(4), pp. 593–622

Lustgarten, S. and Mande, V. (1995) 'Financial Analysts' Earnings Forecasts and Insider Trading', *Journal of Accounting and Public Policy*, 14(3), pp. 233–61

MacDonald, R. and Power, D. (1991) 'Stock Prices, Efficiency and Cointegration', Working Paper, Department of Economics, Dundee University, August

Mackinlay, A. C. (1997) 'Event Studies in Economics and Finance', *Journal of Economic Literature*, 35, pp. 13–39

Madura, J. and Wiant, K. J. (1995) 'Information Content of Bank Insider Trading', *Applied Financial Economics*, 5, pp. 219–27

Malkiel, B. G. (1973) 'A Random Walk Down Wall Street', 7th edn., New York: W. W Norton, p. 2

(1995) 'Returns from Investing in Equity Mutual Funds 1971–1991', *Journal of Finance*, 50, pp. 549–72

Mandelbrot, B. (1963) 'The Variation of Certain Speculative Prices', *Journal of Business*, 36, pp. 394–419

(1972) 'Statistical Methodology for Non-Periodic Cycles: From the Covariance to R/S Analysts', *Annals of Economic and Social Measurement*, 1, pp. 259–90

(1975) 'Limit Theorems on the Self-Normalized Range for Weakly and Strongly Dependent Processes', *Zeitschrift für Wahrscheinlichkeitstheorie verw. Gebiete*, 31, pp. 271–85

Mandelbrot, B. and Takku, M. (1979) 'Robust R/S Analysis of Long-Run Serial Correlation', *Bulletin of the International Statistical Institute*, 48(2), pp. 59–104

Martikainen, T. and Puttonen, V. (1996) 'Finnish Day-of-the-Week Effects', *Journal of Business Finance and Accounting*, 23(7), pp. 1019–32

McKenzie, M. D. (2001) 'Non-Periodic Australian Stock Market Cycles: Evidence from Rescaled Range Analysis', *Economic Record*, 77(239), pp. 393–406

McQueen, G. R. (1992) 'Long-Horizon Mean-Reverting Stock Prices Revisited', *Journal of Financial and Quantitative Analysis*, 27(1), pp. 1–18

Merton, R. C. (1987) 'On the Current State of the Stock Market Rationality Hypothesis', in R. Dornbusch, S. Fischer and J. Bossons, (ed.), *Macroeconomics and Finance: Essays in Honor of Franco Modigliiani*, Cambridge MA: MIT Press

Metcalf, G. E. and Malkiel, B. G. (1994) 'The *Wall Street Journal* Contests: The Experts, the Darts, and the Efficient Market Hypothesis', *Applied Financial Economics*, 4, pp. 371–4

Mitchell, M. L. and Lehn, K. (1990) 'Do Bad Bidders Become Good Targets?', *Journal of Political Economy*, 98, pp. 372–8

Mitchell, M. L. and Mulherin, J. H. (1994) 'The Impact of Public Information on the Stock Market', *Journal of Finance*, 49, pp. 923–50

Mookerjee, R. and Yu, Q. (1999) 'An Empirical Analysis of the Equity Markets in China', *Review of Financial Economics*, 8, pp. 41–60

Moore, A. B. (1962) 'A Statistical Analysis of Common Stock Prices', Graduate School of Business, University of Chicago, Unpublished PhD thesis
    (1964) 'Some Characteristics of Changes in Common Stock Prices', in P. H. Cootner (ed.), *The Random Character of Stock Market Prices*, Cambridge, MA: MIT Press, pp. 262–96

Mulligan, R. F. (2000) 'A Fractal Analysis of Foreign Exchange Markets', *International Advances in Economic Research*, 6(1), pp. 33–49

Mun, J. C., Vasconcellos, G. M. and Kish, R. (1999) 'Tests of the Contrarian Investment Strategy: Evidence from the French and German Stock Markets', *International Review of Financial Analysis*, 8(3), pp. 215–34

Nathan, S. (1996) 'A Test of the Differential Information Hypothesis Explaining the Small Firm Effect', *Journal of Applied Business Research*, 13(1), pp. 115–20

Neill, H. B. (1931) *Tape Reading and Market Tactics*, New York: Forbes Publishing

Nelson, C. R. (1976) 'Inflation and Rates of Return on Common Stocks', *Journal of Finance*, 31, pp. 471–83

Nelson, C. R. and Kim, M. J. (1990) 'Predictable Stock Returns: Reality or Statistical Illusion?', Working Paper, Economics Department, University of Washington, Seattle

Niederhoffer, V. and Osborne, M. F. M. (1966) 'Market Making and Reversal on the Stock Exchange', *Journal of the American Statistical Association*, 61, pp. 897–916

Pan, M. and Liu, Y. A. (1999) 'Fractional Cointegration, Long Memory, and Exchange Rate Dynamics', *International Review of Economics and Finance*, 8, pp. 305–16

Pardo, A. and Valor, E. (2003) 'Spanish Stock Returns: Where is the Weather Effect?', *European Financial Management*, 9(1), pp. 117–26

Patel, J. M. and Wolfson, M. A. (1984) 'The Intraday Speed of Adjustment of Stock Prices to Earnings and Dividend Announcements', *Journal of Financial Economics*, 13, pp. 223–52

Patel, J. M., Zeckhauser, R. and Hendricks, D. (1992) 'Investment Flows and Performance: Evidence from Mutual Funds, Cross-Border Investments and New Issues', in R. Sato, R. Levich and R. Ramachandran (eds.), *Japan and International Financial Markets: Analytical and Empirical Perspectives*, Cambridge: Cambridge University Press

Patro, D. K. and Wu, Y. (2004) 'Predictability of Short-Horizon Returns in International Equity Markets', *Journal of Empirical Finance*, 11(4), pp. 553–84

Peavy, (1990)

Pesaran, M. H. and Timmerman, A. (1995) 'Predictability of Stock Returns: Robustness and Economic Significance', *Journal of Finance*, 50(4), pp. 1201–28

(2000) 'A Recursive Modelling Approach to Predicting US Stock Returns', *Economic Journal*, 110, pp. 159–91

Peters, E. E. (1989) 'Fractal Structure in the Capital Markets', *Financial Analysts Journal*, July–August, pp. 32–7

(1994) *Fractal Market Analysis: Applying Chaos Theory to Investment and Economics*, New York: John Wiley

Peterson, D. R. (1995) 'The Informative Role of the Value Line Investment Survey – Evidence From Stock Highlights', *Journal of Financial and Quantitative Analysis*, 30(4), pp. 607–18

Pettit, R. R. (1972) 'Dividend Announcements, Security Performance and Capital Market Efficiency', *Journal of Finance*, 27, pp. 993–1007

Pettit, R. R. and Venkatesh, P. C. (1995) 'Insider Trading and Long-Run Return Performance', *Financial Management*, 24(2), pp. 88–103

Pietranico, P. and Riepe, M. W. (2004) 'The January Effect Revisited', *Journal of Financial Planning*, 17(4), pp. 26–7

Pontiff, J. (1995) 'Closed-End Fund Premia and Returns – Implications for Financial Market Equilibrium', *Journal of Financial Economics*, 37(3), pp. 341–70

Porras, D. and Griswold, M. (2000) 'The Value Line Enigma Revisited', *Quarterly Journal of Business and Economics*, 39(4), pp. 39–50

Pratt, S. P. and De Vere, C. W. (1968) 'Relationship Between Insider Trading and Rates of Return for N. Y. S. E. Common Stocks 1960–1966', Paper presented for the Seminar on the Analysis of Security Prices, University of Chicago, May; reprinted in J. H. Lorie and R. A. Brealey, (eds.) (1978) *Modern Developments in Investment Management*, 2nd edn., Hinsdale, IL: Dryden Press

Raj, M. and Thurston, D. (1996) 'Effectiveness of Simple Technical Trading Rules in the Hong Kong Futures Market', *Applied Economics Letters*, 3(1), pp. 33–6

Ratner, M. and Leal, R. P. C. (1999) 'Tests of Technical Trading Strategies in the Emerging Equity Markets of Latin America and Asia', *Journal of Banking and Finance*, 23(12), pp. 1887–1905

Reinganum, M. R. (1982) 'A Direct Test of Roll's Conjecture on the Firm Size Effect', *Journal of Finance*, 37(1), pp. 27–35

(1983) 'The Anomalous Stock Market Behaviour of Small Firms in January: Empirical Tests for Tax-Loss Selling Effects', *Journal of Financial Economics*, 12(1), pp. 89–104

Roberts, H. V. (1959) 'Stock Market "Patterns" and Financial Analysis: Methodological Suggestions', *Journal of Finance*, 14(1), pp. 1–10; reprinted in P. H. Cootner (ed.) (1964), *The Random Character of Stock Market Prices*, Cambridge, MA: MIT Press

(1967) 'Statistical Versus Clinical Prediction of the Stock Market', Unpublished paper presented to the Seminar on the Analysis of Security Prices, University of Chicago, May

Rogalski, R. (1984) 'New Findings Regarding Day-of-the-Week Returns over Trading and Non-Treading Periods: A Note', *Journal of Finance*, 39(5), pp. 1603–14

Rogalski, R. J. and Tinic, S. M. (1986) 'The January Size Effect: Anomaly or Risk Measurement?', *Financial Analysts Journal*, November–December, pp. 63–70

Roll, R. (1983) 'Vas ist das? The Turn-of-the-Year Effect and the Return Premia of Small Firms', *Journal of Portfolio Management*, 9(2), pp. 18–28

(1986) 'The Hubris Hypothesis of Corporate Takeovers', *Journal of Business*, 59, pp. 197–216

(1988) 'R2', *Journal of Finance*, 43, pp. 541–66

Rosenberg, B., Reid, K. and Lanstein, R. (1985) 'Persuasive Evidence of Market Inefficiency', *Journal of Portfolio Management*, 11, pp. 9–16

Rowley, E. E. (1987) *The Financial System Today*, Manchester: Manchester University Press

Rozeff, M. S. (1974) 'Money and Stock Prices: Market Efficiency and the Lag in Effect of Monetary Policy', *Journal of Financial Economics*, 1, pp. 245–302

(1984) 'Dividend Yields are Equity Risk Premiums', *Journal of Portfolio Management*, 11, pp. 68–75

(1985) 'The December Effect in Stock Returns and the Tax-Loss Selling Hypothesis', Working Paper, 85–18, College of Business Administration, University of Iowa, May

Rozeff, M. S. and Kinney, W. (1976) 'Capital Market Seasonality: The Case of Stock Returns', *Journal of Financial Economics*, 3, pp. 374–402

Rozeff, M. S. and Zaman, M. A. (1988) 'Market Efficiency and Insider Trading: New Evidence', *Journal of Business*, 61, pp. 25–44

Samuelson, P. A. (1965) 'Proof That Properly Anticipated Prices Fluctuate Randomly', *Industrial Management Review*, 6, pp. 1–49

Sant, R. and Zaman, M. A. (1996) 'Market Reaction to Business Week Inside Wall Street Column – A Self-Fulfilling Prophecy', *Journal of Banking and Finance*, 20(4), pp. 617–43

Saunders, E. M. Jr. (1993) 'Stock Prices and Wall Street Weather', *American Economic Review*, pp. 1337–45

Savit, R. A. (1988) 'When Random is not Random: An Introduction to Chaos in Market Prices', *The Journal of Futures Markets*, 8(3), pp. 271–89

(1992) 'Chaos on the Trading Floor', in N. H. Hall (ed.), *The New Scientist Guide to Chaos*, London: Penguin

Schabacker, R. (1930) *Stock Market Theory and Practice*, New York: Forbes Publishing

Schnusenberg, O. and Madura, J. (2001), 'Do US Stock Market Indexes Over-or Underreact?', *Journal of Financial Research*, 24(2), pp. 179–204

Scholes, M. S. (1972) 'The Market for Securities: Substitution versus Price Pressure and the Effects of Information on Share Prices', *Journal of Business*, 45, pp. 179–211

Seyhun, H. N. (1986) 'Insiders' Profits, Costs of Trading, and Market Efficiency', *Journal of Financial Economics*, 16, pp. 189–212

Shah, M. and Wadhwani, S. B. (1990) 'The Effect of the Term Spread, Dividend Yield and Real Activity on Stock Returns: Evidence From 15 Countries', LSE Financial Markets Group Discussion Paper, 98

Shiller, R. J. (1984) 'Stock Prices and Social Dynamics', *Brookings Papers on Economic Activity*, 2, pp. 457–510

Sirri, E. and Tufano, P. (1993a) 'Competition and Change in the Mutual Fund Industry', in S. Hayes (ed.), *Financial Services: Perspectives and Challenges*, Cambridge, MA: Harvard Business School Press

(1993b) 'Buying and Selling Mutual Funds: Flows, Performance, Fees and Services', Working Paper, Harvard Business School

Sivakumar, K. and Wagmire, G. (1994) 'Insider Trading Following Material News Events – Evidence from Earnings', *Financial Management*, 23(1), pp. 23–32

Smit, C. F. and Smit, E. (1998) 'Holiday Effects in the South African Futures Market', *South African Journal of Business Management*, 29(3), pp. 119–33

Smith, G. and Ryoo, H.-J. (2003) 'Variance Ratio Tests of the Random Walk Hypothesis for European Emerging Stock Markets', *European Journal of Finance*, 9(3), pp. 290–300

Smith, K. L. (2002) 'Government Bond Market Seasonality, Diversification, and Cointegration: International Evidence, *Journal of Financial Research*, 25(2), pp. 203–21

Solnik, B. H. (1973) 'Note on the Validity of the Random Walk for European Stock Prices', *Journal of Finance*, 28, pp. 1151–9

Solnik, B. H. and Bousquet, L. (1990) 'Day-of-the-Week Effect on the Paris Bourse', *Journal of Banking and Finance*, 14, pp. 461–8

Stael von Holstein, C. A. S. (1972) 'Probabilistic Forecasting: An Experiment Related to the Stock Market', *Organisational Behaviour and Human Performance*, 30, pp. 132–56

Stattman, D. (1980) 'Book Values and Stock Returns', *The Chicago MBA: A Journal of Selected Papers*, 4, pp. 25–45

Stickel, S. E. (1985) 'The Effect of Value Line Investment Survey Rank Changes on Common Stock Prices', *Journal of Financial Economics*, 14, pp. 121–44

Stock, D. (1990) 'Winner and Loser Anomalies in the German Stock Market', *Journal of Institutional and Theoretical Economics*, 146(3), pp. 518–29

Stottner, R. (1990) 'P & F Filteranalyse, Averaging Strategie und Buy & Hold-Anlageregel-Ein Beitrag zur Efficient market Hypothese' (Point & Figure Analysis, Averaging and Buy & Hold Strategies – Challenging the Efficient Market Hypothesis, with English summary), *Jahrbucher für Nationalökonomie und Statistik*, 207(4), pp. 374–90

Sullivan, R., Timmerman, A. and White, H. (1999) 'Data-Snooping, Technical Trading Rule Performance, and the Bootstrap', *Journal of Finance*, 54(8), pp. 1647–91

Sundali, J. A. and Atkins, A. B. (1994) 'Expertise in Investment Analysis – Fact or Fiction?', *Organisational Behaviour and Human Decision Processes*, 59(2), pp. 223–41

Szakmary, A., Davidson, W. N., III and Schwarz, T. V. (1999) 'Filter Tests in Nasdaq Stocks', *The Financial Review*, 34(1), pp. 45–70

Tinic, S. M. and West, R. R. (1984) 'Risk and Return: January vs the Rest of the Year', *Journal of Financial Economics*, 13(4), pp. 561–74

(1986) 'Risk, Return and Equilibrium: A Revisit', *Journal of Political Economy*, 94(1), pp. 126–47

Tinic, S., Barone-Adesi, G. and West, R. R. (1987) 'Seasonality in Canadian Stock Prices: A Test of the Tax-Loss Selling Hypothesis', *Journal of Financial and Quantitative Analysis*, 22, pp. 51–63

Tong, W. H. S. (2001) 'Cointegration, Efficiency and Forecasting in the Currency Market', *Journal of Business Finance and Accounting*, 28(1), (2), pp. 127–50

Ukpolo, V. (1995) 'Exchange Rate Market Efficiency – Further Evidence From Cointegration Tests', *Applied Economics Letters*, 2(6), pp. 196–8

Van Horne, J. C. and Parker, G. G. C. (1967) 'The Random Walk Theory: An Empirical Test', *Financial Analysts Journal*, 23, pp. 87–94

Vergin, R. C. and McGinnis, J. (1999) 'Revisiting the Holiday Effect: Is it a Holiday?', *Applied Financial Economics*, 9, pp. 477–82

Vermaelen, T. and Verstringe, M. (1986) 'Do Belgians Over-React?', Working Paper, Catholic University of Louvain, November

Wall Street Journal (1989) 'Pros Out-perform Investment Dartboard in Stock Picking', October 3

(1992) quoted in Reuters Textline service, as 'Wall Street Journal' March

(1993) 11 April, 'Luck or Logic? Debate Rages on over Efficient Market Theory', April 11

Wang, K., Li, Y. and Erickson, J. (1997) 'A New Look at the Monday Effect', *Journal of Finance*, 52(5), pp. 2171–86

Waud, R. (1970) 'Public Interpretation of Federal Reserve Discount Rate Changes: Evidence on the Announcement Effect', *Econometrica*, 38, pp. 231–50

White, H. (2000) 'A Reality Check for Data Snooping', *Econometrica*, 68(5), pp. 1097–1126

Wilson, J. W. and Jones, C. P. (1993) 'Comparison of Seasonal Anomalies Across Major Equity Markets: A Note', *Financial Review*, 28, pp. 107–15

Womack, K. L. (1996) 'Do Brokerage Analysts' Recommendations Have Investment Value?', *Journal of Finance*, 51(1), pp. 137–67

Working, H. (1934) 'A Random Difference Series for Use in the Analysis of Time Series', *Journal of the American Statistical Association*, 29, pp. 11–24

    (1960) 'Note on the Correlation of First Differences of Averages in a Random Chain', *Econometrica*, 28, October, pp. 916–18; reprinted in P. Cootner (ed.) (1964), *The Random Character of Stock Market Prices*, Cambridge, MA: MIT Press, 129–31

Wyckoff, R. (1910) *Studies in Tape Reading*, Burlington, VT: Fraser Publishing Co.

Yates, J. F., McDaniel, L. S. and Brown, E. S. (1991) 'Probabilistic Forecasts of Stock Prices and Earnings: The Hazards of Nascent Expertise', *Organisational Behaviour and Human Decision Processes*, 49, pp. 60–79

Zarowin, P. (1989) 'Does the Stock Market Over-React to Corporate Earnings Information?', *Journal of Finance*, 44, pp. 1385–99

Zivney, T. L., Bertin, W. J. and Torabzadeh, K. M. (1996) 'Over-Reaction to Takeover Speculation', *Quarterly Review of Economics and Finance*, 36(1), pp. 89–115

2 Weak form information efficiency in betting markets

Leighton Vaughan Williams

2.1 Introduction

This chapter examines the idea of weak form information efficiency as it has been applied to betting markets, and reviews the concepts, distinctions and tests which are associated with this concept.

It has been shown in chapter 1 that weak form information efficiency is the notion that current prices incorporate all the information available from a study of past prices and price movements. In consequence, in a financial market which is weakly efficient it should not be possible to earn abnormal returns through a strategy of predicting future prices from past information on prices. Indeed, any such strategy should on average yield the same return.

Many studies of weak form information in betting markets have adapted this idea to examine the possibility for earning differential (or even abnormal) returns in the future, from betting on the basis of past information about the yield to bets at identified prices. In a betting market, these prices take the form of 'odds'. Odds of 3 to 1 laid against an outcome, for example, imply a return to a successful bet of three times the initial stake, plus the initial stake returned. An unsuccessful bet loses the entire stake. The theoretical point is that in a betting market which is weak form efficient the expected return to betting at any identified odds or odds grouping should be identical, unless there are differential costs or risks associated with betting at the various prices. Indeed, Snyder (1978a) argues that if horse-race betting markets are weakly efficient, 'then the expected rate of return for all types of bets would be identical' (1978a: 1110). Section 2.2 of this chapter contains a review of studies which have investigated the expected returns to bets at differing odds, identifies systematic biases in these returns, and considers various explanations for these biases. An assessment is made of the implications of these findings for the existence of weak form efficiency in betting markets. Sections

2.3–2.6 investigate an explanation of the observed biases framed in terms of the rational behaviour of profit-maximizing odds-setters who face bettors who possess potentially superior information. Section 2.7 reviews the literature on 'technical systems' of betting. These systems employ and utilise the information contained in current odds and the pattern in such odds, with the purpose of identifying and exploiting market inefficiencies so as to make above-average or abnormal returns. Section 2.8 summarises the chapter and draws some conclusions.

2.2 Measuring the expected returns to bets at differing odds

This section reviews studies which have investigated systematic patterns in the expected return to bets placed at various odds levels and ranges of odds.

Tests for the potential existence of a differential return at different odds can be traced to laboratory experiments by Preston and Baratta (1948), Yaari (1965) and Rosett (1971). They each found evidence of a systematic tendency by subjects (under controlled conditions) to underbet or undervalue events characterised by high probability, and to overbet or overvalue those with low probability. Preston and Baratta calculated an indifference point below which subjective probabilities are objectively too large, and above which they are too small. They found this indifference point to lie close to the geometric mean of their series. These findings, if reproduced among real bettors, would imply that at lower odds the subjective probabilities attached by such bettors to a successful outcome would tend to understate the objective probabilities, while the reverse would be true at higher odds. Such an effect has come to be known in the literature as the 'favourite-longshot bias'[1] or simply the 'longshot bias'.

Tests for the existence of this bias in non-laboratory conditions can be traced to Griffith (1949),[2] who investigated the pool ('parimutuel') betting markets characteristic of US racetracks. In these markets, winning bets share the pool of all bets. The objective probability, in the sense of the percentage of winners, was calculated for each odds grouping and compared with the subjective probability implicit in the established odds. Griffith found that the subjective probabilities were close to the objective probabilities of winning. This point was developed and clarified by Hoerl and Fallin (1974), who ranked horses within a race by their track odds (for races categorised by the number of runners), and compared the average subjective probability implied in the odds with the actual finishing positions. They found a close correspondence between the subjective and objective probabilities, and that the average finishing position fell monotonically in the direction predicted by the odds. They concluded that bettors were able on average to 'discriminate small differences' (1974: 230) in the probability of events occurring. Griffith (1949) also confirmed a tendency for bettors to undervalue events characterised by high probability, and to overvalue those with low probability, an effect which is consistent with higher expected returns at lower odds than at higher odds. Like Preston and Baratta, he calculated an indifference point below which subjective probabilities were objectively too large, and vice versa, reaching broadly similar conclusions. Moreover, it was almost invariant as between samples taken from years with widely differing economic conditions,[3] suggesting that the point of indifference is stable and independent of both the geometric means and the amount of money available to bettors. Griffith (1961) extended the analysis to cover 'show' betting – i.e. betting on horses to finish third or better,[4] for horses offering odds to win of less than 2 to 1, in the months of May 1949 and August 1960. For these data he was able not only to confirm the existence of a longshot bias, but also to demonstrate that a strategy of betting on all horses to show which started at odds to win of less than 1.4 to 1 would have yielded a profit net of all deductions. 'As was to be expected, the tendency, which had been demonstrated with win betting, for horse race bettors to place too little money on the horses most likely to win is magnified in their even more conservative bets on the same horses to show' (1961: 81). Since then, others have identified evidence of mispricing in the place and show pools; for example, Hausch, Ziemba and Rubinstein (1981), Tuckwell (1981) and Swidler and Shaw (1995).

McGlothlin (1956) used betting patterns and outcomes associated with a series of horse-races[5] in order to determine the expected value of constant-size bets over a range of probabilities of success. Odds below 3 to 1 (against) yielded a positive expected value[6] after correcting for track deductions, odds above 8 to 1 a negative expected value[7] and odds of 3 to 1 to 6 to 1 yielded an expected value approximately equal to zero.[8] McGlothlin located the indifference point at a value between 0.15 and 0.22 (i.e. between 3.5 and 5.5 to 1 against), findings which are consistent with those of Griffith (1949).

Performing the same analysis on subsamples of the data corresponding to races classified by their position in the eight-race order yielded no surprises for the first six races on the cards. The patterns found were not significantly different from those established for the whole sample. Significant differences were, however, identified for the final two races of the day. Uniquely, the relatively high expected values displayed by the shortest odds groupings was not reproduced for the seventh (i.e. penultimate, usually feature) races on the card, although a significantly higher than expected return appeared in the 6 to 7.95 odds classification,[9] and the horses in the odds range from 16 to 25.95 displayed an exceptionally low expected return. For the eighth (i.e. last) races of the day, the expected return to betting on horses in the very shortest odds category chosen by McGlothlin – i.e. 0.5 to 1.95 – was particularly high,[10] dropping sharply for odds in the 3 to 3.95 category.[11]

Snyder (1978a, 1978b) provided surveys of the published evidence. On the basis of the existing literature[12] and his own data on the US horse-race betting markets, he concluded that lower odds tend to be associated with higher returns, and vice versa. Indeed, all of the studies indicated that bets placed at odds below 5 to 1 would have yielded above-average returns. However, the returns were not large enough to yield a profit after allowing for standard deductions from the pool.

Snyder (1978a) concluded that 'the evidence collected for the weak form test shows that the public has a clear and strong bias which substantially affects the expected rate of return for various odds-groups, but that bias is not large enough to overcome track takes of nearly 20 per cent' (1978a: 1114).[13] Of the authors surveyed by Snyder (1978a), McGlothlin (1956)[14] and Fabricand (1965)[15] also found evidence of monotonically decreasing rates of return from the lowest odds to the highest, while Ali (1977)[16] offered evidence of a greater bias at smaller tracks. McGlothlin (1956) reported a systematically lower bias in the feature race of the day.

Snyder (1978a, 1978b) found the same bias in the predicted odds of various track experts. Using data gathered about 7,657 horses running in 1975 at Arlington Park racetrack, Chicago, together with the predicted odds of the official track handicapper, of the *Daily Racing Form* and of three major Chicago newspapers, he found that each of the 'experts' exhibited this same bias. However, he ascribed this to perceived constraints on the range at which the 'experts' quoted the horses rather than to any inherent preference for longer odds. Another explanation is that the 'experts' are simply trying to predict the odds rather than what they perceive to be the actual winning chances, and so will reproduce any such bias. Snyder noted, however, that this in itself does not explain his finding that the degree of bias exhibited by the experts is greater in every instance than that demonstrated by the public, as indicated in the final track odds.

Asch, Malkiel and Quandt (1982) examined the relationship between the subjective and objective probabilities of a horse winning a race, as evidenced by the parimutuel odds[17] and actual outcomes, respectively.[18] Although they found a close relationship between a horse's place in the order of favouritism and the likelihood of it winning, they also found that bettors tend to overbet horses offered at particular odds and to underbet others. In particular, whereas the objective probability of a horse winning was significantly greater[19] than the subjective probability for the favourites examined, the bias was gradually reversed until the subjective probability was significantly greater than the objective probability for the ninth horse in the order of favouritism. The implication is that betting on shorter-priced horses would tend to produce a higher rate of return than those on offer at higher odds, and this was borne out by an analysis they undertook. Specifically, they calculated the rates of return for bets at odds groupings varying from 0 to 2 to 1 against at one extreme, and of odds ranging from 25 to 1 upwards at the other. They also derived results employing the same odds groupings, but limiting the sample to the last two races of the day. Their findings for the total dataset are consistent with the existence of the longshot bias already noted by Griffith (1949), while their analysis of the later races confirmed an earlier finding of McGlothlin (1956), Ali (1977) and Kahneman and Tversky (1979) that the bias toward underbetting short odds and overbetting long odds is particularly strong in such races. In contrast, Metzger's (1985) analysis[20] of the betting public's first and second favourites revealed virtually identical patterns of betting in the first and last races of the day, these patterns being different from all other races. Omitting the first races of the day, however, Metzger identified a significant underestimation of the true probabilities of favourites winning the last two races as compared with earlier races.

A survey of the overall picture, by Thaler and Ziemba (1988),[21] assessed the evidence from a wide range of previously published studies to calculate the expected market return at various odds. Net of deductions from the pool, expected returns confirmed the conventional bias, turning positive at a cut-off point of about 4.5 to 1. At odds of below 0.3 to 1, they even report a positive expected return gross of deductions – i.e. an expected profit.[22] This direction of bias is also documented in Hausch and Ziemba (1990), and has been confirmed for Australian data (Bird, McCrae and Beggs, 1987) and for New Zealand data (van Zijl, 1984).

Even so, there is not universal consistency in the published studies. A notable exception to these findings is reported by Busche and Hall (1988), for Hong Kong racetrack betting markets, and by Busche (1994) for Hong Kong and Japanese racetracks. In these markets they found no evidence of a positive bias, if anything the bias operated in the opposite direction. This sort of effect was also reported by Swidler and Shaw (1995) for a small US racetrack. More recently, Gandar, Zuber and Johnson (2001) also found no evidence of a systematic favourite-longshot bias in the parimutuel betting markets characteristic of New Zealand, at least at the close of the market. Although there is evidence that such a bias exists in early trading, the authors conclude that late bettors tend to be more informed and that this informed money acts so as to eliminate any mispricing created by early uninformed off-course bettors.

Busche and Hall's (1988) study used data gathered from 2,653 races at Hong Kong racecourses between 1981–2 and 1986–7. In line with earlier studies, such as Hausch, Ziemba and Rubinstein (1981), Busche and Hall's methodology involved asking how far the returns to random bets across differing odds categories were equal. Their logic is that if those placing bets are risk-neutral and also make accurate and unbiased predictions, then the returns should be equated across horses characterised by differing win odds (to reflect the winning proportions).[23] In other words, if a regression line is drawn through the scatter of points generated on a graph described by observed win odds on the horizontal axis and the actual available betting odds on the vertical axis, then risk-neutrality is consistent with a regression line demonstrating a slope of one. Similarly, a slope of greater than one is consistent with risk-aversion, and a slope of less than one with risk-preference. Their actual results are (standard errors in brackets):

$$\text{Betting odds} = -2.908 + 1.251 \text{ win odds}, R^2 = 0.99$$
$$(1.40) \quad (0.036)$$

The slope estimate was significant beyond the 0.001 level, indicating evidence in this sense of risk aversion.[24]

Allowing for the existence and structure of measurement errors Busche and Hall were unable, however, to reject a hypothesis of equal average returns across groups of horses. They concluded that there was no evidence that Hong Kong bettors underbet favourites and overbet longshots.

Busche (1994) reported analogous results from a later sample of 2,690 new Hong Kong races (1987–92), by pooling the new and original data into a total sample of 5,343 Hong Kong races (i.e. 1981–92), and separately for 1,738 Japanese races from 1990.

Swidler and Shaw (1995), as noted above, also found no evidence of a favourite-longshot bias in their study of a small US racetrack. The track, Trinity Meadows Raceway, was selected for study precisely because it is small ('a second tier Texas track', 1995: 306). In this context, the small pool and the cost of obtaining accurate information might be expected to produce a population of relatively 'uninformed' bettors. Their dataset covered 2,946 horses, running in 288 races between June and December 1991. Although the subjective and objective win probabilities were highly correlated, the application of a Spearman rank correlation coefficient to the returns in different odds groups revealed no significant bias (at the 5 per cent level). At less strict levels of significance, there was a reverse bias – i.e. bettors tending to overbet the favourite and vice versa.

Common to the studies of Busche and Hall (1988), Busche (1994), and Swidler and Shaw (1995) is that they examine behaviour in parimutuel markets. An investigation of the US baseball betting market by Woodland and Woodland (1994) is distinguished by the fact that this is a fixed-odds betting market, in the sense that the odds can be agreed with odds-setters (bookmakers) at the time a bet is placed. As such, a bettor is able to ascertain in advance the eventual payoff to a successful bet. It is also equivalent to a set of two-horse races, inasmuch as bets are either on one team or its unique opponent. In this sense, bettors are in effect buying or selling an asset. The dataset consisted of 24,603 major league baseball games for the 1979–89 seasons. Woodland and Woodland (1994) tested for efficiency by applying z tests and regressions (after Asch and Quandt, 1987, 1988) to ascertain whether there were systematic differences in the subjective and objective probabilities of the longshot ('underdog') winning. Their methodology is based on the premise that there should not be any significant differences if the market is weak form efficient. Their results suggest some evidence of market inefficiency (at the 10 per cent level of significance) with baseball bettors tending to overbet the favourites relative to the longshots. A strategy of betting only on the longshot produced a higher average return than would be consistent with this definition of efficiency, at the 5 per cent level of significance. Any ineffi-ciencies were not great enough, however, to yield a positive return net of deductions. Woodland and Woodland (2003) update their original study with ten years of additional data for the 1990–9 season, finding an almost identical reverse favourite-longshot bias to the earlier study. The validity of the conclusion of the Woodland and Woodland studies, notably their finding of a reverse bias, has since been questioned in a penetrating critique of their methodology by Gandar, Zuber, Johnson and Dare (2002).

Most studies of betting with bookmakers have, however, been con-ducted using British racetrack betting data. In the markets from which this information is derived, bettors can take posted odds or else, in horse and greyhound racing, sometimes take the 'Starting Price'. The Starting Price here is the independently determined assessment of the general price at which a significant bet could have been placed about any particular outcome with bookmakers on the course at the start of the race (see Paton and Vaughan Williams, 2002, for evidence of the integrity of this process). This option is often, even usually, taken by off-course bettors. Bettors taking posted odds (or 'board prices') are unaffected, however, by any subsequent odds movements.

These studies are traceable to studies of betting patterns undertaken by Figgis (1951, 1974a, 1974b, 1976) and quoted in part in the report of the Royal Commission on Gambling (1978), and point in the same direction as most of the US parimutuel data. Figgis' evidence for 1950, 1965 and 1973, using starting prices, demonstrates that for the shortest odds examined – i.e.

0.4 to 1 (5 to 2 on) or less – the average pre-tax return varied from 97.2 per cent in 1950 to 108.1 per cent in 1965 and to 108.5 per cent in 1973.[25] Calculations of the returns in 1975 and 1976, performed for the Royal Commission on Gambling, found rates of return of 112.1 per cent and 107 per cent, respectively. Figgis' calculations for the longest odds range – i.e. 20 to 1 and over – on the other hand, demonstrate much lower average returns, varying from 23.8 per cent in 1950 to 37.3 per cent in 1965 and to 23.2 per cent in 1973. These returns to extreme longshots are qualitatively in line with the US findings reported by Snyder, although much more pronounced in extent. Although not a monotonic relationship, Figgis produced evidence of persistence in this tendency over the intervening odds ranges. Over all odds ranges, the average return was about 80 per cent.

Dowie (1976) calculated the expected return at each of a wide variety of starting prices for the 1973 flat season, and derived the expected rate of return to a pattern of betting a unit stake on each and every horse at the starting price. He also derived the expected rate of return to a policy of betting on every horse so that the return at its starting price would yield a constant return. Whereas he calculated that the first approach would have yielded a pre-tax loss of 39.4 per cent, the second approach would have yielded a loss of 20 per cent, although most of the disparity occurred when examining odds in excess of 20 to 1 against. His sample of 2,777 races also revealed evidence of a significant longshot bias, which he examined by subdividing the results into actual returns and cumulative returns to a policy of level staking, and also to a policy of staking to yield a constant return. He noted a profit even after tax at odds up to 4 to 6 (often termed 6 to 4 on). An examination of his figures reveals a cumulative profit before tax for all wagers struck at less than evens (odds of 1 to 1), given either of the two staking methods he explores. Again, the return to longshots (especially extreme longshots) was far worse in extent than that reported by Snyder for US parimutuel markets.

Henery (1985) examined later evidence from the UK flat racing season, selecting 883 races in 1979 and 1980. The average return to a unit stake was calculated over various odds ranges, showing a similar bias to that offered by Figgis (1976) – i.e. ranging from 97.9 per cent in the odds range 0 to 0.396 to 1, to 10 per cent in the odds range 38.12 to 1 and above. This inverse tendency, though not systematic through all odds ranges, was preserved as a general trend over all intervening odds classifications.

The *Ladbrokes Pocket Companion, Flat Edition* (1990) provides findings for the flat racing seasons from 1985 to 1989, showing evidence again of a systematic bias against the expected return at long odds, a result even more clearly illustrated by grouping the odds. The results suggest that a positive rate of return was available at strategies involving the consistent placing of bets at odds of 1 to 2 (2 to 1 on) or shorter. In particular, betting at odds of 1 to 5 (5 to 1 on) to 1 to 15 (15 to 1 on) would have yielded a 6.5 per cent profit, and at 1 to 8 (8 to 1 on) or shorter a positive return every time.

Cain, Law and Peel (1992) examined the evidence for the existence of a favourite-longshot bias in UK greyhound racing betting markets. They compared the probability of winning implied by the starting prices, standardised to deduct the (*ex post*) bookmakers' margin, with the realised win probabilities. The average returns were calculated using the returns to a unit stake on every greyhound at the starting price, and also by the average return from placing a stake to win a unit return at each starting price – i.e. the reciprocal of the starting price. While they offer no conclusions supporting a positive linkage between expected returns and shorter odds, they did find that the realised win probabilities exceeded the win probabilities implied by their standardised starting prices at all odds up to 1.5 to 1 (6 to 4 against). This is evidence of a favourite-longshot bias. They were unable, however, to translate any such inefficiencies into a strategy capable of yielding abnormal returns.

An analysis of English Premier League soccer, by Cain, Law and Peel (2000), confirmed the existence of the traditional bias for soccer. They found, in a sample of 2,855 matches played in the UK during the 1991–2 season, evidence of the traditional favourite-longshot bias, notably that the odds offered by bookmakers for very strong favourites seemed to provide a better expected return than bets on longshots. Moreover, low scores (favourites) were better bets than high scores (longshots). Among correct score odds, incidentally, the best value lay in backing very strong favourites to win by a scoreline of 1–0, 2–0, 2–1 or 3–2.

The finding of a conventional bias for soccer confirms the outcome of an empirical study of bets placed with traditional fixed-odds bookmakers on Premier League soccer games (Paton and Vaughan Williams, 1998). These studies are quite different in nature to other recent studies (Dixon and Coles, 1997; Dixon and Robinson, 1998; Kuypers 2000) which develop a prediction model for English League soccer based on form attributes, which are then contrasted with actual results and bookmakers' odds.

Cain, Peel and Law (2003) verify the existence of the favourite-longshot bias for a variety of sports betting markets where odds are set by bookmakers.

The weight of the evidence, at least in the UK and the US (Sauer 1998; Vaughan Williams 1999), is thus broadly in favour of the existence of some positive relationship between the expected rate of return to betting and the placing of bets on the most likely outcome in a range of environments. The implication is that higher average returns can be earned by betting on horses offered at particular identified odds (generally lower) than others (generally higher), and particularly so by betting at extremely short odds. As such, this not only violates one definition of weak form efficiency, but also requires explanation in terms of rational economic behaviour.

2.3 Risk, return and favourite-longshot bias

In this section various ideas are advanced to explain the existence of a favourite-longshot bias in racetrack betting data. In the context of these proposed explanations, the significance of the existence of this bias for weak form market efficiency is evaluated.

Much of conventional capital market theory assumes that a higher return is required to compensate investors for the incurrence of higher risk. 'Higher risk' in the context of horse-race betting may be associated with betting at higher odds, inasmuch as such odds are usually associated with lower probabilities of winning and a higher variance of return.

Specifically, assuming a probability of winning, p, and fair odds, $(1 - p)/p$, the variance of returns can be given as:

$$\text{Variance (returns)} = [(1 - p)/p]^2 p + (-1)^2 (1 - p) = 1/p - 1$$

An implication of the theory, therefore, is that a higher expected return would be required to compensate for greater risk, implied by the greater odds. Evidence from the behaviour of bettors in horse-racing markets in the UK and the US suggest the opposite.

Attempts to provide an explanation founded in economic theory (for this apparent incongruity) can be traced to work by Rosett (1965) and Weitzman (1965). Rosett asked whether such observed behaviour was reconcilable with the existence of a sophisticated rational betting public. A 'sophisticated bettor' in this sense is one who satisfies three conditions. First, if the probabilities of winning are equal, he will choose that with the greater return to winning; second, if the returns to winning are equal, he will choose the one with the greater probability of winning; and third, in a choice of bets, he will always prefer a bet which exhibits both superior returns and a higher probability of winning than the alternatives. These conditions are referred to by Rosett as the 'rationality hypothesis' (1965: 596). To test this rationality hypothesis, Rosett examined and compared the distinct risk/return profiles associated with different types of bets. He concluded from an empirical examination of the evidence from actual betting behaviour that bettors are sophisticated and rational, but that in their choice of betting strategies they displayed a strong preference for low-probability, high-return bets.

Weitzman (1965), using the same data and assuming that a proposed representative bettor[26] obeys the expected utility hypothesis, constructed a representative utility of wealth function from the relationship between the subjective and objective probabilities implied by the odds and the results, employing a weighted least-squares method that corrects for heteroscedasticity. For the sums of money examined, he found a range of values which implied increasing marginal utility (convexity in the utility function), signifying that bettors exhibit risk-loving behaviour. The implication of this convexity is that expected utility maximisation would generate the observed longshot bias. Weitzman suggests that these findings coincide with the range of increasing marginal utility proposed on theoretical grounds by Markowitz (1952) as an amendment to the utility of money curve offered by Friedman and Savage (1948).[27]

Quandt (1986) demonstrates the favourite-longshot bias as an equilibrium outcome of an assumption of risk-loving preferences in an environment in which bettors choose among alternative gambles simply on the basis of the expected payoff and the variance of the payoff distribution. Asch and Quandt (1986) adhere to a similar conception of betting behaviour – i.e. that the utility function of horse-race bettors may well be convex above the current level of wealth and concave below it.

Of course, motivations derived from totally different utility functions could explain the same result, among which may be a preference for positive skewness in the payoff distribution. Some more recent contributions to the literature have attempted to distinguish between these motivations, with contrasting conclusions. e.g. Hamid, Prakash and Smyser (1996) in support of bettors as risk-lovers, and Golec and Tamarkin (1998) in support of bettors as skewness-lovers.

Walls and Busche (2003) demonstrate a more complex set of preferences, based on evidence from Japanese horsetracks distinguished by level of turnover. First, they find that tracks with higher turnover are more informationally efficient than those with lower turnover. Second, utility estimates at tracks with low bet turnover showed evidence of risk aversion and skewness preference, while bettors at high-turnover tracks were found to display a preference for variance and an aversion to skew.

Cain, Law and Peel (2002) provide a counter-example which questions the view that risk-averse agents desire positive skewness and are prepared to trade off a lower mean return for more skewness. Coleman (2004) argues that there are, in fact, two quite different bettor populations. One of these is risk-averse, knowledgeable about winners, backs favourites and has a positive expected return. The other, larger group, is risk-loving, backs longshots and has a significant negative return.

An obvious problem about the different available theories of betting behaviour, as Thaler and Ziemba (1988) note, is whether they explain behaviour displayed by bettors in other contexts:

We venture a guess that when it comes to retirement saving, Professors Asch and Quandt would not be willing to accept a lower mean return in order to obtain a higher level of risk. (1998: 170)

An approach favoured in a number of studies of risk-taking behaviour is indeed to propose such behaviour to be very context-specific (see Slovic, 1972). In particular, Thaler and Ziemba employ a concept of 'mental accounting' (see Kahneman and Tversky, 1984; Thaler, 1985), whereby 'people adopt mental accounts and act as if the money in these accounts is not fungible' (1985: 171) in order to demonstrate how one may be risk-seeking at the racecourse, but risk-averse with respect, for example, to one's pension provisions.

Other studies, however, frame the issue of variations in attitude to risk in terms of the availability of ready capital to the bettor, or changes in such over the course of the betting period. A seminal study along these lines was undertaken by Ali (1977), who estimated subjective and objective winning probabilities from a database of 20,247 harness horse-races at three tracks between 1970 and 1974. He confirmed the tendency for the odds to understate the likelihood of outcomes with a high probability (the subjective probability understates the objective probability), and to overstate those with a low probability. Employing Weitzman's concept of the 'representative bettor', Ali found that such bettors did exhibit behaviour consistent with adopting a riskier approach at the smallest of the three tracks – i.e. at Saratoga. Ali offered this in support of the view that the more capital the representative has, the less he tends to be a risk lover' (1977: 185). The implication is that bettors possess an increasing marginal utility of money function,[28] gambling being explained in terms of reallocating consumption possibilities in response to this. Ali also reported risk acceptability in the last race of the day compared to the first two races of the day (an effect first suggested by McGlothlin, 1956), a result he interprets as due to the influence of a change (decrease) in capital, as the day progresses, on attitude to risk (increasing risk-loving behaviour).

Two other studies, one by Kahneman and Tversky (1979) and the other by Asch, Malkiel and Quandt (1982), also identified greater apparent risk acceptability in races occurring later on the racecard, in the form of a greater longshot bias. Asch, Malkiel and Quandt explained this, like Ali, in terms of a proposed change in the risk attitude of bettors with respect to variations over the course of the day in their available betting capital. Their explanation is couched in terms of the fact that bettors are seeking to recoup their overall losses on the day. This conclusion should be examined in the context of the findings of a study by Hamid, Prakash and Smyser (1996) of Florida greyhound races. That study supported the view that bettors' aversion to risk declined as their losses increased during a racing session, causing an increase in the favourite-longshot bias in later races.

Although Metzger (1985) was unable to confirm any significant differences in risk acceptability between the last and first races on the card (possibly due to special features in these races), there was evidence that bettors' first choices were under-estimated in races 8 and 9 (overall mean of 94) compared to races 2 through 7 (overall mean of 105). No significant pattern was detected, however, for the sample of second choices. Metzger offered these results as evidence in support of Tversky and Kahneman's (1981) proposition that variations in reference points for the framing of outcomes produce variations in the acceptability of risk.

In particular, given that the reference point is the status quo at the beginning of the racing day and that the public expectation is negative, outcomes are framed increasingly in terms of getting-even versus loss rather than gain versus loss, producing fewer bets on favourites over the day. The public should increasingly underestimate the chances of favourites in later races. (Metzger, 1985: 883)

If true, this tendency by bettors produces a clear implication, and one lent empirical support in parimutuel markets by Kopelman and Minkin (1991), that 'The Best Time to Bet the Favourite is in the Last Race' (1991: 701), known as Gluck's Second Law. A study of behaviour by bettors in the fixed-odds arena of UK off-course bookmakers by Johnson and Bruce (1993) offers quite different conclusions. Employing a random sample of 1,212 real bets, placed at betting offices throughout the UK between 12 March and 18 April 1987, they found a tendency for bets on races later in the day to be placed on horses at shorter odds, even allowing for disparities in field size (and therefore mean odds size). Moreover, there was a tendency for the mean stake size to increase in later (the last three) races compared with bets on the first two and first three races. The expected return to bets placed on later races also tended to exceed that to bets on earlier races, although only one of the early/late race comparisons was significant at the 5 per cent level. These results are consistent with the suggestions of empirical work by Thaler and Johnson (1990) and Garling, Romanus and Selart (1994, see above) that prior losses tend to produce less risk-seeking/more loss-aversive behaviour. Even so, any interpretation of these findings should, as Johnson and Bruce point out, take account of potential differences in off-course behaviour (studied here) and on-course behaviour. It may well be that two separate influences are at work; a tendency for prior losses to increase risk aversion, but also an overimportance placed by on-course bettors on the need to at least break even on the day.

Hamid, Prakash and Smyser (1996), using their Florida greyhound data, sought more basically to distinguish in bettors' utility functions between preference for variance and preference for skewness (i.e. preference for non-symmetry in the distribution of payoffs implied by a sample of par-imutuel odds). Employing a standard von Neumann–Morgenstern expected utility of wealth function, they concluded, on the basis of their observation of the relevant payoffs, that the representative bettor exhibited behaviour which demonstrated a preference for variance and an aversion to positive skewness. This is consistent with the conclusions of a study by Quandt (1986), which showed how a favourite-longshot bias could arise as a natural and necessary consequence of equilibrium in a market characterised by risk-loving bettors, with homogeneous beliefs, in the context of a mean–variance framework.

Chadha and Quandt (1996) demonstrate an alternative scenario in which a favourite-longshot bias can arise in the context of risk-neutral bettors, each of whom optimises given the bets of all other bettors. Simplifying (though not necessarily realistic) assumptions are that the aggregate of bettors arrives simultaneously at a Nash equilibrium, and that there are no arbitrage opportunities between parimutuel betting and betting with bookmakers. In this model, the bias is a consequence of random, rather than systematic, errors by bettors in their perception of the true underlying probabilities.

There are also other explanations which do not require any assumption of risk-loving behaviour. One such explanation is offered by Golec and Tamarkin (1995), who ask simply whether bettors prefer longshots because they are risk-lovers or because they are overconfident. In order to compare the validity of these hypotheses, they identify a dataset which is able to distinguish, it is claimed, the influence of overconfidence from that of risk-loving behaviour. The dataset is composed of so-called 'teaser' bets. These bets are a variation on a normal point-spread bet, in which the bookmaker sets the margin of victory (the spread) of one team over another. In normal point-spread bets, the bettor chooses whether the spread will be greater or less than this. If the actual margin of victory equals the spread, the bet is void. Otherwise, winning bets earn 10/11 of their stake (plus stake returned), while losing bets lose the whole stake. In 'teaser' bets, on the other hand, the bettor can be wrong by a given number of points ('teaser points') and yet still win. For instance, if the spread of team A over team B is 8 points, and team A actually win by 12 points, a bet on B would lose (4 points out) without any 'teaser' adjustment. With 5 'teaser' points, the bet is clearly a winning one. Bookmakers may adjust the agreed payout to the bettor downwards to compensate for the higher probability of winning. In order to win an n-team teaser bet, all of the bets (adjusted by the teaser points) must win in order to earn the agreed payoff. A losing bet loses the entire stake. In order to win a standard multiple (or 'exotic') bet, all of the bets (unadjusted) must win. The bettor choosing the 'teaser' bet has a higher objective probability of winning (and lower risks), but will usually receive a lower payoff to a winning bet. If bettors underestimate the likelihood of making larger errors (as suggested by Tversky and Kahneman, 1974; Tversky, Slovic and Kahneman, 1990; De Long, Shleifer, Summers and Waldman, 1991), they will overvalue the 'teaser' points. Since 'teaser' bets reduce risk (return variance), however, risk-loving bettors should require an additional return in order to bet on 'teasers'.

Golec and Tamarkin (1995) tested this empirically by comparing a given 'teaser''s expected return with the expected return to other bets that have similar or greater objective win probabilities. They found that the 'teaser' bets had larger win probabilities but much smaller returns. These findings are consistent, they argue, with the hypothesis of overconfident bettors, but not with risk-loving bettors.

Golec and Tamarkin (1998) provide evidence in favour of another hypothesis, that bettors in US horse-race betting markets are in fact averse to risk but display a strong preference for skew.

In contrast, Hurley and McDonough (1995) and Terrell and Farmer (1996) propose explanations of the favourite-longshot bias which require neither a hypothesis of overconfidence nor of risk or skewness-loving behaviour. Instead, the bias can arise in a risk-neutral, confidence-neutral environment, as a consequence of positive transactions/information costs.

Hurley and McDonough (1995) consider the case of two types of risk-neutral bettor occupying a parimutuel betting market – 'informed handicappers', who know the 'true' probabilities, and 'uninformed handicappers', who do not. Since the uninformed bettors are unable to distinguish good bets from bad they will, in the simplest case of a two-horse-race, bet a roughly equal amount on a favourite as on a longshot. If there are no transactions/information costs, the informed bettors should take advantage of this mispricing in the pool to bet on the horse with the highest objective probability of winning (defined as the favourite). In the model, it is assumed that there are a large number of informed bettors, and that the objective probability, net of track deductions, is greater than the probability implicit in the bets of the uninformed. The expected profit from this strategy is positive so long as the advantage of being informed is not outweighed by the costs of betting. The presence of transactions and information costs, however, cause the subjective probability that the 'favourite' (the horse with the highest objective probability) wins to diverge systematically below the objective probability. This systematic divergence produces a favourite-longshot bias, and the bias increases as the costs increase. Nevertheless, laboratory evidence using groups of students, some of whom were exposed to betting costs and some of whom were not, was unable to confirm the theory at an experimental level. On this basis Hurley and McDonough conclude that 'the bias on the favourite is not explained by costly information and transaction costs' (1995: 953).

Terrell and Farmer (1996) employ a similar formulation, composed of informed bettors (who, in their case, purchase the true probabilities of events), and uninformed bettors (who do not). They model the decision as to whether to become informed explicitly, in terms of the costs of becoming informed, and the wagers of other informed bettors. In this model, if all bettors are uninformed, then the expected loss to any random betting pattern is equal to the track take-out. There is no favourite-longshot bias. The addition of informed bettors complicates the issue, however, as these bettors will bet on horses whose true probabilities of winning exceed the probabilities implicit in the wagers of the uninformed bettors, so long as the net expected return to a bet is greater than one. The size of the bet (and therefore the net expected return) will depend on the size of bets in the uninformed pool, the extent of the divergence of initial market odds from the true probabilities and the number of other informed bettors in the pool. Informed bettors will therefore act so as to lower the odds on events with high expected returns and increase the odds on events with low expected returns. In consequence, low-odds events will tend to be associated with higher expected returns than high-odds events. This is the favourite-longshot bias. As transactions and information costs fall, however, the number of informed bettors rises, the expected profit on each bet tends to zero and subjective probabilities (implicit in market odds) converge to the objective probabilities. At this point the observed favourite-longshot bias disappears. The bias is, therefore, a consequence of costs involved in the betting process, such as the track take-out. Terrell and Farmer tested their hypothesis using a sample of 4,121 races at a Kansas City greyhound racetrack[29] in the 1989–90 season, and also data from the 1993–4 season. Calculating the return to a random betting strategy revealed an expected payout of 78.3 per cent, compared with a track deduction of 18 per cent. They explain the shortfall from 100 per cent (3.7 per cent) as income to informed bettors. They also found evidence of the traditional longshot bias. The empirical evidence is offered in support of their model of betting behaviour.

Sobel and Raines (2003) also propose an explanation for the existence of a favourite-longshot bias which requires no assumption of risk-loving behaviour, but is in their case based instead on bet complexity and the information possessed by bettors.

Paton and Vaughan Williams (1998) seek to test the hypothesis that costs explain the favourite-longshot bias by considering two parallel betting markets for soccer bets, distinguished by different levels of transactions costs. The first market is the conventional fixed-odds market and the second is the relatively new option of 'spread' (index) betting.

Unlike fixed-odds betting, spread betting (which is not in any way related to US point spread betting) is regulated in the UK in the same way as traditional financial markets. Indeed, it is derived from those markets. It operates through the quotation by the bookmaker of a 'spread' on an uncertain future outcome. Bettors are not offered odds but are instead invited to buy or sell notional assets associated with an event (for example, goals in a soccer match or the price of gold), based on a 'spread' set by market-makers (bookmakers). If the market-maker, for example, expects a team to score 3 goals, a typical spread may be set between 2.9 and 3.2. Bettors who expect the number of goals to exceed the top end of the spread (3.2) are invited to buy at this level. Similarly, bettors who expect the number of goals to fall short of the bottom end of the spread (2.9) are invited to sell at this level. The spread may move upwards or downwards before or during the course of the game until the value of the asset is known with certainty. At this point a bettor who bought (sold) the asset will win or lose the difference between the *ex post* value of the asset and the bid price, multiplied by their original stake. The bettor may 'close' the trade at any time.

For illustrative purposes, let us look specifically at a derivative of the total goals market, the time-of-first-goal market – i.e. a market based on the time (in minutes) when the first match goal is scored. Say, for example, the bookmaker's best estimate of the time that the first goal will be scored is 35 minutes. In this case, the spread may be quoted at, say, 34–36. The bettor may now *buy* at the higher end of the spread (36) or *sell* at the lower end (34), for a given stake. If the bettor *buys* at 36 and the first goal is scored in, say, 44 minutes, the bettor wins 8 (the difference between 44 and 36) times the stake. If, on the other hand, the first goal was scored in 24 minutes, the bettor would lose 12 (the difference between 24 and 36) times the stake. The same logic applies to a *sell*, so that the bettor wins (or loses) in proportion to how right (or wrong) the original bet turned out to be. The size of the spread is an indicator of the bookmaker's implied profit margin.

A common bet is on the number of goals (quoted in tenths) by which one team will beat another. Say, for example, that team A is given a goal supremacy quote of 1.2 over team B. This means that the bookmaker estimates that team A is likely to score, on average, 1.2 more goals than team B, so that if they played team B ten times, say, they would score a total of 12 more goals than team *B*. The bookmaker might quote a supremacy spread of 1.1–1.3 in this case, inviting bettors to *buy* at 1.3 or to *sell* at 1.1. More usually, the spread size in these markets is three-tenths of a goal.

The costs facing the bettor differ between the fixed-odds and spread markets. Spread betting markets have historically been characterised by a low level of transaction costs, at least relative to traditional betting markets, partly because of their relatively favourable tax treatment. They have therefore offered an attractive option both to small traders, motivated primarily by wealth considerations, and to larger traders, using financial spread betting markets as part of a more general risk management strategy. In particular, spread betting is often used to hedge against, for example, a potential short-term fall in the market. The low transactions costs have also made it possible for potential arbitrageurs to profit from relatively small mispricings in the market.

If a cost-based explanation of the favourite-longshot bias is correct, we would expect the bias to be lower, therefore, where costs are lower – i.e. in the spread markets.

To test this, Paton and Vaughan Williams (1998) examined the fixed-odds and spread prices for 265 matches from the 1996–7 English Premier League soccer season. If the traditional favourite-longshot bias applies in the spread markets, it might be expected that the average return to a *buy* of the supremacy of the favourite team (team *A* in the example above) would be greater than the average return to a *sell* of their supremacy. In fact, no evidence of any bias at all is found in the spread markets, but the traditional favourite-longshot bias was confirmed in the fixed-odds market.

These findings are consistent with a hypothesis that costs are at least a contributory factor in establishing the bias.

It should be noted that the tax structure has altered in the UK since October 2001, moving from a tax on the turnover of bookmakers to a tax on their gross profits (see Paton, Siegel and Vaughan Williams, 2000, 2001, 2002, 2003, 2004; Vaughan Williams, 2004a, 2004b, 2005). The introduction of the new tax was coincident with a substantial effective reduction in the tax burden on fixed-odds bookmakers, and an effective increase in the tax burden on spread bookmakers, though the tax on the gross profits of spread bookmakers is still levied at a lower rate (10 per cent of gross profits for sports spread bookmakers and 3 per cent for financial spread bookmakers) than it is for fixed-odds bookmakers (15 per cent of gross profits).

Supporting evidence for the explanatory influence of costs on the existence and size of a favourite-longshot bias is offered in a study of the modern phenomenon of person-to-person betting exchanges (Smith, Paton and Vaughan Williams, 2004, 2005). Betting exchanges exist to match people who want to bet on a future outcome at a given price with others who are willing to offer that price. The person who bets on the event happening at a given price is the *backer*. The person who offers the price is known as the *layer*, and is essentially acting in the same way as a bookmaker. The advantage of this form of betting for the bettor is that, by allowing anyone with access to a betting exchange to offer or lay odds, it serves to reduce margins in the odds compared to the best odds on offer with traditional bookmakers. Exchanges allow clients to act as a bettor (backer) or bookmaker (layer) at will, and indeed to back and lay the same event at different times during the course of the market.

The way in which this operates is that the major betting exchanges present clients with the three best odds and stakes which other members of the exchange are offering or asking for. For example, for England to beat Brazil at football the best odds on offer might be 4 to 1, to a maximum stake of £80, 3.5 to 1 to a further stake of £100 and 3 to 1 to a further stake of £500. This means that potential backers can stake up to a maximum of £80 on England to beat Brazil at odds of 4 to 1, a further £100 at 3.5 to 1 and a further £500 at 3 to 1. These odds, and the staking levels available, may have been offered by one or more other clients who believe that the true odds were longer than they offered.

An alternative option available to potential backers is to enter the odds at which they would be willing to place a bet, together with the stake they are willing to wager at that odds level. This request (say £50 at 4 to 1) will then be shown on the request side of the exchange, and may be accommodated by a layer at any time until the event is over.

The margin between the best odds on offer and the best odds sought tends to narrow as more clients offer and lay bets, so that in popular markets the real margin against the bettor (or layer) tends towards the commission levied (normally on winning bets) by the exchange. This commission normally varies from about 2 per cent to 5 per cent. As such, this is considerably less than the notional profit margin of bookmakers implied in the 'over-round' – i.e. the sum of probabilities implied in the odds minus 1, which averages at 25.63 per cent in our 700-race sample (based on mean bookmaker prices). If the costs-based explanation of the bias is correct, therefore, we should expect the favourite-longshot bias to be more pronounced in the bookmaker data.

Smith, Paton and Vaughan Williams (2004) – see also Paton, Smith and Vaughan Williams (2005) – in a study of 799 races run in the UK during 2002, find that the bias is indeed demonstrably higher in traditional betting markets than in the lower-cost environment characteristic of person-to-person (exchange) markets. As exchange betting markets are characterised by relatively low transactions costs, the findings are consistent with models in which such costs can help to explain the favourite-longshot bias. They further find that in both exchange and traditional betting markets the level of bias is lower the greater the amount of public information that is available to traders, a finding consistent with models in which information costs help to explain the favourite-longshot bias. This is consistent also with Sobel and Raines (2003), who identify a lower bias in high-volume betting markets, assumed to be better informed, than in low-volume markets, assumed to be proportionately more heavily populated by casual bettors.

2.4 Explaining the favourite-longshot bias in terms of utility maximisation

All the above explanations are couched within a financial framework. There is, however, no general agreement that bettors' motivations are best addressed from this perspective. Competing explanations of the favourite-longshot bias seek rather to distinguish bettors as utility-maximisers rather than profit-maximisers (although financial considerations may enter as an element into the utility function). For instance, bettors may derive utility specifically from selecting longshots. Snyder (1978a: 1113), for example, notes that 'the main reward of horse betting comes from the thrill of successfully detecting a moderately long-odds winner and thus confirming one's ability to outperform everyone else', a motivation linked perhaps to what Bruce and Johnson (1992: 205) identify as the 'peer-group esteem associated with perceived "skill"'. Thaler and Ziemba (1988) suggest that bettors may even derive utility just from holding a ticket on a longshot, while the tendency among a section of the betting public to bet for reasons totally unconnected with any serious assessment of the objective probabilities – for example, because they like a horse's name, may contribute to a cut in the odds offered against longshots. Vaughan Williams and Paton (1998) propose a quite different model of betting behaviour, in which bettors derive specific utility from placing winning bets, additional to the net financial return on the bets.

Letarte, Ladouceur and Mayrand (1986) examined the behaviour of forty-five subjects who had never played roulette, selected from the general public via advertisements, in the context of a simulated roulette playing exercise.[30] They found that the amount of money bet increased as a function of the number of trials, that the type of bets became more risky as the game went on and that subjects having frequent wins took significantly more risk than individuals having infrequent wins. They explained their findings in terms of the acquisition by gamblers of a sense of personal, albeit illusory, control which increases in line with increased familiarity with the gambling process and with increased frequency in success (see Langer, 1975; Langer and Roth, 1975; Langer, 1983).[31] One possible

implication of their findings is a tendency for bettors who win disproportionately – i.e. those who bet at short odds, to follow this trend toward risk
by switching gradually to longer odds. So long as this tendency is not
compensated fully by a movement in the opposite direction by other
bettors, a 'longshot bias' will result.

An approach favoured by Bruce and Johnson (1992) is to examine the
motivations which cause people to bet at all. One such motivation which
they specify is *excitement*. In this context, they comment that:

The excitement experienced by bettors with an interest in the race is naturally
heightened by the risk to which they have exposed their stakes and the anticipation
of possible success. (1992: 204)

As noted earlier, Bruce and Johnson also identify how 'the successful
bettor who makes known this success may expect to receive ... peer-group
esteem associated with perceived "skill"' (1992: 205). This effect may be
more pronounced in the case of successful prediction of a longshot, there no
doubt being some asymmetry in the reporting of failures to successes. It is,
on the other hand, possible to argue that more excitement and peer-group
esteem is furnished by a succession of successful, if more predictable, short-
priced winners.

The desire for excitement, heightened pleasure and social esteem may
thus on certain, though not all, interpretations offer explanations of a
longshot bias in terms of the maximisation of expected utility as opposed
to expected profit. A further possibility is that bettors are confused in their
assessment of the expected returns. Bruce and Johnson tested both these
types of explanations. By dividing bets into categories based on the
timing of the bet, they sought to distinguish inputs into a non-monetary
utility function, broadly classified as excitement, social interaction and
intellectual challenge, from inputs into a predominantly monetary utility
function – i.e. maximisation of financial gain; and offered the possibility of
assessing the influence of confusion or 'non-cognitive constraints' on the
ability to make effective decisions.[32] Specifically, they argue that bets
placed early in the day contain a disproportionate number of bets placed
to meet a need for intellectual challenge. Those placed later contain a
disproportionate number of bets designed to meet a need for social interaction; those placed later still tend to satisfy a need for excitement; and
those placed latest contain a disproportionate number of bets placed for
the specific purpose of maximising financial gain. Of these, those in the
third subset are likely to contain the largest ratio of those subject to some
form of cognitive overload or 'decision paralysis', because these bettors
are, Bruce and Johnson observe, 'subject to rapid and continual changes in
the information sets (e.g. prices of horses, horses' pre-race behaviour)',

which 'may tend to distort the meaning of information, suspend vigilant search and be characterised by selective inattention' (1992: 211).[33] On the basis of a random selection of 1,200 bets placed throughout the UK between March and April 1987, they concluded that according to a variety of measures of actual financial return, the third subset performed worst and the fourth subset – i.e. the very late bettors – best. The group of bettors best identified as profit-maximisers (i.e. the very late bettors) displayed the highest propensity to bet on favourites, and the lowest propensity to bet on longshots (i.e. the lowest longshot bias).

The implication of this sort of approach is that one cannot fully explain betting behaviour within the framework of a totally rational and unconfused cognitive process which strictly adheres to the goal of maximising financial return. Any understanding of longshot bias must allow for this.

An alternative possibility is to explain the phenomenon in terms of differences in the staking patterns. Findings offered by Filby and Harvey (1988),[34] for example, on the link between amounts staked and other variables provide some interesting support for the idea of a longshot bias linked to staking levels. In particular, they identified a clear relationship between the size of stake and the type of bet, larger bets being associated with lower-risk bets such as singles. An examination of the relationship between the probability of a positive return and the size of stakes revealed that their largest bets (over £20) were more than three times as likely to yield a positive return as bets under 50 pence (36.8 per cent to 12.1 per cent). Higher stakes were also associated with the pre-payment of betting tax,[35] notable inasmuch as it can be shown that for any given total stake the expected return to a bet is greater if tax is pre-paid rather than paid on the winnings.

A compromise position between explanations which are proposed in the context of assumed profit-maximising behaviour and those drawing upon a broader utility-maximising approach is offered by Busche (1994). This explanation, which seeks to reconcile the absence of a longshot bias in Hong Kong data (see pp. 88–9) with its prevalence elsewhere, is formulated in terms of two distinct types of bettors, those who bet to maximise their money and those who bet as a consumption activity. Since expected returns are limited by the size of the betting pool, Busche proposes that money-maximisers may in consequence dominate tracks offering large pools, whereas betting as a consumption activity may dominate the market at smaller tracks. In this context, it should be noted that average stakes in a day at Hong Kong racetracks is several times greater than that at the leading US racetracks. Significantly perhaps, Ali (1977: 813) also observed a much greater bias at the smallest of the racetracks he examined. This sort of approach is echoed in Walls and Busche (1996), who provide empirical evidence that, within a given race, the volume of betting causes the track odds to converge towards to the odds implied by optimal betting. Busche and Walls (2000) and Walls and Busche (2003) also provide empirical evidence in support of a hypothesis that market efficiency across racetracks is systematically related to the volume of betting, which appears consistent with Smith and Walker's (1993a, 1993b) hypothesis that non-optimal (inefficient) betting behaviour occurs only where the costs of non-optimal behaviour are low – i.e. where betting volumes are small. 'At race tracks with low bet volumes the potential gains to a professional bettor are proportionally small, so that deviations from the predictions of optimization theory – that returns be equalized across horses – reflect the risk preferences of recreational bettors' (Busche and Walls, 2000: 487).

Adams, Rusco and Walls (2002) draw upon Busche and Walls (2000) to develop a model in which well-informed profit-maximizing professional bettors engage in arbitrage when faced with sufficiently profitable betting opportunities. On the basis of their model they show how professional bettors, attracted by high betting volumes and hence expected profits, serve to drive final track odds towards the levels implied by the true win probabilities.

2.5 The implications of systematic underestimation by bettors of their losses for understanding favourite-longshot bias

One of the simplest explanations of the favourite-longshot bias can be found in Henery (1985). Henery argues that a favourite-longshot bias can arise as a consequence of bettors discounting a fixed fraction of their losses – i.e. they underweight their losses compared to their gains. This argument also explains in a clear manner an observed link between the sum of bookmakers' prices and the number of runners in a race. The prices being summed here are simply the odds. If, for example, odds of 3 to 1 (against) are offered about each of the five horses in a race, the implied probability of winning for each horse is 1/4 and the sum of prices is 5/4. In this context, an 'over-round' is defined as the excess of the sum of prices over unity, in this case 1/4.

The rationale for Henery's hypothesis is that punters will tend to explain away and therefore discount losses as atypical, or unrelated to the judgement of the bettor. This is an explanation which is consistent with work on the psychology of gambling, such as Gilovich (1983) and Gilovich and Douglas (1986). These studies demonstrate how gamblers tend to discount their losses, often as 'near wins' or the outcome of 'fluke' events, while bolstering their wins.

Table 2.1. *Objective and subjective odds*

Objective odds	Subjective odds
Evens	3 to 5 against
4 to 1 against	6 to 4 against
Infinity to 1 against	3 to 1 against
0 to 1 against	0 to 1 against

The consequence of Henery's hypothesis is that if the true probability of a horse losing a race is q, so that the true odds against winning are $q/(1-q)$, then the bettor will assess the chance of losing not as q, but as Q which is equal to fq,[36] where f is the fixed fraction of losses undiscounted by the bettor. If f, for example, is 3/4, and the true chance of a horse losing is 1/2 (i.e. $q = 1/2$), then the bettor will rate subjectively the chance of the horse losing as $Q = fq$ – i.e. $Q = 3/4$. $1/2 = 3/8$.

Another way of looking at this approach is in terms of a £100 wager placed on a horse to win a race. If the true chance of this occurring is 1 in 2, the bettor can expect to lose £50 – i.e. £100 one time in two (we are here ignoring any compensatory returns to a winning outcome). The objective odds against him are therefore evens – i.e. a 0.5 chance of losing divided by a $1-0.5$ chance of winning.

The subjective assessment of the expected loss, following Henery's logic, with $f = 3/4$, is $3/4 \times £50$, i.e. £37.50, or 0.375 of the stake (£100). The subjective odds against the bettor are therefore 0.375 (the subjective probability of losing) divided by $1-0.375$ (the subjective probability of winning) – i.e. 3 to 5 against (or 5 to 3 on). This means that he will be just indifferent (if he is risk-neutral, and is motivated solely by profit maximisation) at odds of 0.375 to 0.625 – i.e. 0.6. In general terms, the bettor facing true odds of $q/(1-q)$ will evaluate the true odds as $fq/(1-fq)$.

Listing, for purposes of exposition, some objective odds, together with their subjective counterparts, on the basis of $f = 3/4$ reveals the position in table 2.1.

The implication of the above is that, for instance, for a given f of 3/4, 3 to 5 is perceived as fair odds for a horse with a 1 in 2 chance of winning. In fact, however, £100 wagered at 3 to 5 yields £160 ($3/5 \times £100$, plus the stake back) half of the time – i.e. an expected return of £80 (or 0.8 times the stake). £100 wagered at 6 to 4 yields £250 ($6/4 \times £100$, plus the stake back) one-fifth of the time – i.e. an expected return of £50 (or 0.5 times the stake). In fact, the higher the odds the lower is the expected rate of return on the stake, although the relationship between the subjective and objective probabilities remains at a fixed fraction throughout.

The same simple assumption about bettors' behaviour can explain in a simple manner (see Vaughan Williams, 1997) the observed relationship between the over-round (sum of bookmakers' prices minus 1) and the number of runners in a race. If only a fixed fraction of losses, f, is counted by bettors, the subjective probability of losing on any horse is $f(qi)$, where qi is the objective probability of losing for horse i. The winning probabilities implied by the equilibrium odds are now $1 - f(qi)$.

OR (the over-round) may thus be derived as follows:

$$OR = \sum_{i=1}^{n} (1 - fq_i) - 1 \tag{2.1}$$

$$OR = n - f. \sum_{i=1}^{n} q_i - 1 \tag{2.2}$$

$$OR = n - 1 - f. \sum_{i=1}^{n} q_i - 1 \tag{2.3}$$

$$OR = (n - 1) - f(n - 1) \tag{2.4}$$

$$OR = (n - 1). (1 - f) \tag{2.5}$$

Hence the over-round is linearly related to the number of runners.

Henery did in fact use data from the 1979–80 flat racing seasons to plot the average over-round against the number of runners in these races. He found a good fit for the aggregate of races, although consistent aberrations were produced by some, notably prestige, races.

There are, therefore, a number of explanations of the favourite-longshot bias, linked by the common thread that they explain the data solely in terms of the demand side of the market. The bias is explained, therefore, as the natural outcome of bettors' pre-existing perceptions and preferences. This is quite consistent with a market efficiently processing the information available to it. Moreover, there is little evidence that the market offers opportunities for market players to earn abnormal returns or positive profits. Thus although possibilities clearly exist for earning above-average returns on the basis of weak form information, there is no convincing evidence that this contradicts a wider conceptualisation of this type of information efficiency.

2.6 The favourite-longshot bias as a supply-side phenomenon

The idea motivating the supply-side explanation of the bias is that odds-setters (bookmakers) face an adverse selection problem when they are faced by bettors who know more than they do ('insiders'), the extent and identity of whom are unknown. The bookmakers' optimal pricing strategy in this environment is to contract odds, particularly where potential losses are greatest – i.e. at higher odds. The consequent differential contraction at different odds levels leads to a favourite-longshot bias.

The debate about the contribution of this supply-side theory will be considered more fully in chapter 3.

2.7 Technical systems of betting

'Technical systems' of betting employ information contained in the odds and odds movements in an attempt to earn above-average or abnormal returns. If successful, they constitute evidence of weak form inefficiency in these markets.

Attempts to exploit any favourite-longshot bias in order to secure systematic profits constitute an example of what is termed a 'technical system' of betting. Most of the evidence from studies of win betting suggests that while the longshot bias does usually exist (at least outside of Hong Kong and Japan), it is not sufficiently strong to permit systematic abnormal profits after allowing for track or bookmaker deductions (see, for example, Hausch and Ziemba, 1990).

Research traceable to Griffith (1961) has, however, tended to show evidence of inefficiency in the US place and show bet markets, with some evidence that this can be translated into systematic abnormal profits. Subsequent work along these lines was surveyed by Hausch, Ziemba and Rubinstein (1981), in an article which, supported by an analysis of their own data, concluded that there existed evidence of inefficiency in a weak form sense in the place and show markets, and thus the possibility of using technical analysis to make substantial positive profits from these pools. The analysis assumes, however, that the bettor is able to bet after the final odds are set – i.e. after all other bets have been made. In practice, the bettor has to balance the advantages of betting as late as possible so as to minimise inaccuracies with being able to perform all the necessary calculations on a given dataset. In fact, though, an examination they undertook of odds changes in the last two minutes before the off found that although expected returns did change, profitable bets based on the odds displayed two minutes before the close of betting tended to stay profitable based on the final odds.

Nevertheless, their model in its precise form is a complex non-linear optimisation problem that may be difficult if not impossible to solve quickly. As such, they propose approximate solutions using regression procedures which, by limiting the data input, make the system operational in real time. Their approximations, developed for a range of constrained initial wealth levels and a given track take, were able to yield profits of about 11 per cent in the place and show markets. They also developed a model to show that the abnormal profits were due to the proper identification of market inefficiencies rather than pure chance.

Hausch, Ziemba and Rubinstein's (1981) analysis was developed by Ziemba and Hausch (1984, 1987) and Hausch and Ziemba (1985) into a system known as the 'Dr Z' system for exploiting inefficiencies in place and show betting. Ziemba and Hausch (1994) present a modified version of the Dr Z system for place betting at British racetracks. In the British context, place betting is normally on a horse to finish in the first three. They reported the possibility of earning a positive profit from the application of their system, although in light of the higher track take in Britain compared to the US, most notably in the Tote place pool (26.5 per cent in Britain compared to less than 20 per cent in the US), they were unable to state how often profitable bets would exist or to assess the likely long-run scenario. Incidentally, this deduction from the UK Tote place pool is somewhat higher than the deduction from the UK Tote win pool (the regressive impacts of which are considered by Dowie, 1992a, 1992b).

Swidler and Shaw (1995) also employed an analysis following Hausch, Ziemba and Rubinstein (1981) to identify mispricings in the place and show betting pools. They found evidence of opportunities for a positive expected return on sixty-one occasions (out of 288 races) in which there were disparities between the place and win pool payouts, allowing a positive net expected return. The value of this strategy was, however, limited by the high operational costs (in terms of time), the risk of last-minute odds adjustments, and the deflating effect of a large bet on the pool payout.

Tuckwell (1981) used data from the win and place betting markets at Melbourne and Sydney racetracks in order to examine the relationship between win odds and place odds. He observed that the relationship was inconsistent – i.e. horses with given win odds did not consistently possess the same place odds. In order to assess whether this reflected genuine differences in the actual probabilities of the various possible outcomes, he used the bookmakers' starting price odds to estimate the true win probabilities, and on the basis of these win probabilities to estimate the probabilities of being placed. His results indicated that a strategy of betting on horses to place in the totalisator (parimutuel) pool when the actual place odds exceed the implied place odds was capable in theory of generating positive profits. However, two practical difficulties were noted. First, the effect of the bet may be to depress the relevant odds, and so reduce or eliminate the profitability. Second, the calculations assume that the bets can be and are taken at the starting price – i.e. the bettor can lay the final bet. The finite time it takes to perform the relevant calculations render this unlikely.

Cain, Law and Peel (2000) looked at place ('each way') betting in the UK. In the UK, bettors can bet on a horse to win and place (normally to finish in the first three) but the stake on the place element (which normally pays a fifth the odds) cannot be larger than the stake on the win portion of the bet. Cain, Law and Peel asked whether this 'product bundling' was sufficient to negate a betting strategy designed to exploit any inefficiency in the pricing of the place component of the bet. On the basis of certain reasonable assumptions, they found evidence in favour of a rule of thumb which generated each way bets with expected positive returns, although this applied to only 0.0145 per cent of runners. The actual percentage return in sample to betting on these runners was 6 per cent, which they interpret as too low (given the costs of implementation) to describe as evidence in favour of a market inefficiency.

Even so, there is one anomaly, available for a period of time in the UK and Irish Tote pools, which is identified by Jackson and Waldron (2003). Because of the way in which place dividends were calculated when large amounts were bet on the favourite, they are able to describe a simple overall betting strategy which gave bettors in these pools a substantial positive expected return. In a best-case scenario from the bettors' point of view, the operator could have expected to lose over 50 per cent of the total place pool in certain races. This loophole has now been closed.

The results of these studies taken in aggregate are consistent, therefore, with the existence of some form of weak efficiency in the market for win bets, and of mispricing in the place and show betting pools. There has been less success in utilising this information so as to make significant abnormal profits from a 'technical' approach to betting. Although some success has been reported in generating such rules in the market for place and show bets, some of this has disappeared under close re-examination. Indeed, most systems based on the identification of win/place/show mispricings depend on an ability to perform difficult calculations (see Thaler, 1992), and to make operational complex decision making procedures in limited real time. The size of any positive return is also limited by the size of the pool, and may offer only a small return to time invested.

Finally, let us turn to the UK spread betting markets for a novel technical trading system, based on identifying and trading upon prices offered by the bookmaker offering outlying odds.

There are a number of different spread betting companies operating in the UK, and these companies may offer different quotes about the same market, in the form of a spread. For example, a company may offer a spread of 10–11 about the number of corners in a soccer match. The bettor can now *buy* at the top end of the spread (11) or *sell* at the bottom end of the spread (10). A *buy* at 11 would yield a profit if there were more than 11 corners, of that number of corners by which it exceeds 11 multiplied by whatever unit stake the bettor specifies. Any number of corners below 11 would yield a corresponding loss, however. Similarly, a *sell* of corners at 10 would yield a profit if there were fewer than 10 corners, but a corresponding loss if there were more.

Assume now that company *A* offers a quote of 10–11 and company *B* a quote of 12–13. In this case, it is possible to make a risk-free profit through a *buy* of corners at 11 with company *A* and a *sell* of corners at 12 with company *B*. In such a scenario, the bettor wins regardless of the outcome. This is an 'arbitrage' position.

Two examples will illustrate:

(a) If the outcome is 15 corners, then a *buy* at 11 and *sell* at 12 would yield a profit of 4 times the unit stake (with company *A*) but a loss of 3 times the unit stake (with company *B*). The net profit is one times the unit stake.

(b) If the outcome is 8 corners, then a *buy* at 11 and *sell* at 12 would yield a loss of 3 times the unit stake (with company *A*) but a profit of 3 times the unit stake (with company *B*). The net profit is again one times the unit stake.

This is general, regardless of the outcome. Indeed, the riskless profit is always equal to the gap between the spreads times the unit stake.

More commonly, the top end of the spread offered by one company coincides with the bottom end of the spread offered by another. This is a sort of quasi-arbitrage (what might be called a 'Quarb' – Vaughan Williams (2000a, 2001a, 2004c). If the top end of one spread coincides with the bottom end of another we have what is termed in Vaughan Williams (2000a) a 'Simple Quarb'. In such a circumstance, it is possible to *buy* with one company and *sell* with the other, for a sure profit/loss of zero.

The term 'quasi-arbitrage' may, however, be used in another sense to represent a situation where the top (or bottom) end of the spread quoted by at least one market-maker lies outside the average mid-point of all the spreads quoted by all the market-makers. This is termed (Vaughan Williams, 2000a) a 'Full Quarb'.

There may be good news in these 'Quarbs' for those of a practical turn of mind. In particular, these is evidence that those seeking to exploit price differentials offered by different market-makers (a 'Quarb' strategy – Vaughan Williams, 2000a, 2002; Paton and Vaughan Williams, 2005) have historically been able to earn significant profits in spread betting markets, at least in the market available about the number of disciplinary cards issued in Premiership football matches in the UK – i.e. the 'bookings' market. In this market, 10 points are awarded for a yellow and 25 for a red card.

The logic underpinning the 'Quarb strategy' is straightforward. In the absence of other information, the mid-point of all spreads provides us with an obvious point estimate of the expected value of the asset. On this basis, we can expect positive returns as long as this value is greater (less) than the price at which we buy (sell). Take the case of the bookings market in a game between Arsenal and Manchester United. Suppose three of the market-makers offer a spread of 46–50 bookings points, while the fourth market-maker offers a spread of 50–54 bookings points. Now, the mean mid-point of all spreads in the market is $(48 + 48 + 48 + 52)/4$, i.e. 49, which is below the spread offered by the 'maverick' market-maker of 50–54. The strategy would be to *sell* bookings with this outlying market-maker at 50. If the outlying spread was 40–48, with a mean of 49, on the other hand, the strategy would be to *buy* bookings at 48. If no market-maker offered a spread everywhere outside the mean of the mid-points of all the spreads, this would imply no trade.

Using this framework, Paton and Vaughan Williams (2005) test for the existence of an exploitable market inefficiency, asking whether it is the average (mean) market position or the outlying market position which provides most information. The average market position is determined by the average of the mid-point of all the spreads on offer, while the outlying position is taken as the mid-point of the spread offered by the market-maker who is most out of line with the average market position.

In a study of 207 matches played in the English Premier League in 1999–2000 and 240 matches in 2000–1, Paton and Vaughan Williams find that the average mid-point of all spreads provides a better forecast of the actual outcome in the bookings market than does the mid-point of the spread offered by the market outlier (the 'maverick' market-maker).

This finding casts doubt on a hypothesis that market-makers who set quotes out of line with the prevailing market view do so because they possess better (even privileged) information, or that they are able to process a given set of information more effectively than the market as a whole.

Further, Paton and Vaughan Williams (2005) find that it is possible to devise a trading strategy on the basis of the outlying spread that yields returns, both within and out of sample, that are consistently positive and superior to those that might be expected from noise trading. Moreover, this result is robust to a variety of checks to control for the possibility that published prices might not be available, and also for differential risk (in terms of potential downside) incurred in *buy* and *sell* bets.

2.8 Weak form information efficiency in betting markets: summary and conclusions

Many studies of weak form information efficiency in betting markets have adapted the idea of *price predictability* to examine the possibility for earning differential (or even abnormal) returns in the future from betting on the basis of past information about the yield to bets at identified prices (odds) or odds groupings. In a betting market which is weak form efficient, the expected return to betting at any identified odds or odds grouping should be identical, unless there are differential costs or risks associated with betting at the various odds. The existence of a differential return at different odds has been identified in a number of laboratory studies, the evidence pointing to a systematic tendency by bettors to underbet events with a high objective probability of occurring relative to those with a low probability of occurring. Many studies of actual betting behaviour at racetracks have confirmed the existence of this bias, the expected return (measured after the event) to bets placed at lower odds tending to exceed that to bets placed at higher odds. The implication of this 'favourite-longshot bias' is that bettors can make above-average (though not usually profitable) returns by betting at lower odds. This dependence of future returns on existing prices (odds), derivable from a study of past patterns of returns and prices, is adduced as evidence of weak form information inefficiency in betting markets displaying it. The existence of a bias in the other direction (a 'longshot-favourite bias') has similar implications, but requires a converse betting strategy. In fact, the usual bias (against higher-odds events) has been found in most (but not all) studies of US parimutuel betting markets (in which winning bettors share some fixed proportion of the pool of all bets), and also in markets characterised by bookmakers, such as can be found in the UK (for horses and greyhounds) and in Australia. Some studies, however, find an absence of bias, notably in Hong Kong parimutuel betting markets, and even evidence – albeit disputed, of a reverse bias, in the US baseball betting market.

Another finding common to a number of studies is that the behaviour of bettors in later races differs significantly from that in earlier races. Explanations have been offered in terms of variations in the amount of capital available to bettors, or a shift in the degree of risk aversion caused by prior losses. Whether these indications of weak inefficiency constitute genuine information inefficiency depends upon the reasons for the observed behaviour, and in particular for the favourite-longshot bias. Some studies explain it as a rational outcome in a market characterised by risk-loving bettors, or else that the market is responding efficiently to bettors who just like longshots. Variations of the latter argument are contained in theories of utility-maximising (rather than profit-maximising) behaviour by bettors. Such explanations can, however, be so broadly drawn that they are as difficult (or impossible) to refute as to prove. A number of other theoretical explanations fall into the same trap, either not being testable or else reliant on very restrictive assumptions. A good explanation of the favourite-longshot bias should perhaps not only explain the bias where it exists, but also the studies where it does not exist, and even other regularities in the data.

In conclusion, while there is an indication of weak form efficiency in the form of systematic biases in the expected returns at different odds, it is important to understand the reason for the biases if we are to draw the correct conclusions about the existence of genuine information inefficiency.

Notes

1 See, for example, Thaler and Ziemba (1988: 164).
2 In a study of 1,386 US horse-races during August 1947, and subsequently of all US horse-races during August 1934.
3 0.18 for the 1934 data as compared with 0.16 for the 1947 data.
4 Betting on horses to finish second or better is known in the US as 'place' betting.
5 The sample used is one of 9,248 races over a period of 1,156 days taken from *The Daily Racing Form Chart Book*, vols. 53–59, 1947–53, Los Angeles: Triangle Publications.
6 The expected value of 0.08 exceeded zero by four standard errors.
7 Of about − 0.1, significant at the 5 per cent level of confidence.
8 Significant at the 5 per cent level of confidence.
9 Significant at the 5 per cent level of confidence.
10 Significantly above zero at the 0.1 per cent level of confidence, and above the first seven races beyond the 2 per cent level of significance.
11 The difference between this expected value and that for the first seven races was not quite significant at the 5 per cent level.
12 Griffith (1949), McGlothlin (1956), See Fabricand (1965), Weitzman (1965) and Seligman (1975).
13 For the record, Ali (1977) for New York data, 1970–4, reported an average track take of 15 per cent; Hausch, Ziemba and Rubinstein (1981), for California data, a take of 16.8 per cent; Asch, Malkiel and Quandt (1982), for Illinois data, a take of 17 per cent; Busche and Hall (1988), for Hong Kong data, a track take of 17 per cent.
14 In a study of 9,248 races, mostly from California tracks, between 1947 and 1953.
15 In an analysis of 10,000 races between 1955 and 1962.
16 In a survey of 20,247 races at three US tracks – i.e. Saratoga, Roosevelt and Yonkers – between 1970 and 1974.
17 The subjective probability may be defined as proportional to the reciprocal of the market return, cf. Griffith (1949), McGlothlin (1956) and Ali (1977).

18 Their dataset is provided by the 729 races making up the 1978 thoroughbred racing season at the Atlantic City, New Jersey racecourse.

19 Significant at the 5 per cent level.

20 For 11,313 races run on nine-race cards at thoroughbred tracks in the US in the months of May, June and December 1978.

21 Using data in Ziemba and Hausch (1986).

22 This finding was first presented in Ziemba and Hausch (1986).

23 The odds must be adjusted so that the fractions of money wagered and the suggested probabilities add up to one.

24 Hausch, Ziemba and Rubinstein (1981), in contrast, for US data, found the following:

$$\text{Betting odds} = -1.144 + 0.747 \text{ win odds}, \ R^2 = 0.993$$
$$(0.403) \quad (0.023)$$

25 The calculation of the return is undertaken on the assumption that horses are backed to return a given pre-tax stake.

26 The idea of proposing a single racetrack bettor, representative of all the bettors at the racetrack (Mr Avmart – i.e. the average man at the racetrack) with a single utility function, can be traced to this article.

27 Friedman and Savage (1948) posited a utility function which is concave at low levels of wealth, convex at intermediate levels and concave again at higher levels, with the first point of inflection coinciding with the current level of wealth. Markowitz (1952) amended this utility function to include a convex portion at low levels of wealth.

28 See also Weitzman (1965: 26).

29 Woodlands Greyhound Park.

30 The subjects were allowed to keep 5 per cent of their final winnings in the interests of realism.

31 Bruce and Johnson (1992) link the 'illusion of control' argument to the idea of an 'intellectual challenge' motivation for gambling.

32 Quoting Eiser and van der Pligt (1988: 100).

33 See Janis and Mann (1977) for more on this. Also Eiser and van der Pligt's (1988: 101) contention that 'Firstly, individuals tend to use simpler and less optimal choice rules as the information load increases. Usually accuracy declines considerably when the number of features or the number of alternatives increases. Secondly, the reliability with which choice rules are used tends to decrease as the decision-maker's information load increases.'

34 In a survey of over 9,000 betting slips collected from three Birmingham betting offices over one week in June 1984.

35 Such payment of tax (termed 'tax on' bets) accounted for 57.8 per cent of all bets, 38.8 per cent of bets under 50 pence and 71.9 per cent of bets over £20.

36 Since in reality the true win probabilities are unknown, the problem is in fact one of estimating the win probabilities from the starting price odds. In effect, then, q should more precisely be identified with the empirical average loss probability for given Starting Price (SP) odds than with the empirical lose

probability itself. See Henery (1985: 347) for a more complete discussion of the issues.

References

Adams, B. R., Rusco, F. W. and Walls, W. D. (2002) 'Professional Bettors, Odds-Arbitrage Competition, and Betting Market Equilibrium', *J Singapore Economic Review*, 47(1), pp. 11–127

Ali, M. M. (1977) 'Probability and Utility Estimates for Racetrack Bettors', *Journal of Political Economy*, 83, pp. 803–15

Asch, P. and Quandt, R. E. (1986) *The Professor's Guide to Strategies*, Dover, MA: Auburn House

(1987) 'Efficiency and Profitability in Exotic Bets', *Economica*, 59, pp. 278–98

(1988) 'Betting Bias in Exotic Bets', *Economic Letters*, 28, pp. 215–19

Asch, P., Malkiel, B. G. and Quandt, R. E. (1982) 'Racetrack Betting and Informed Behaviour', *Journal of Financial Economics*, 10, pp. 187–94

Ball, R. and Brown, P. (1968) 'An Empirical Evaluation of Accounting Income Numbers', *Journal of Accounting Research*, 6, pp. 159–78

Bird, R., McCrae, M. and Beggs, J. (1987) 'Are Gamblers Really Risk Takers?', *Australian Economic Papers*, December, pp. 237–53

Bruce, A. C. and Johnson, J. E. V. (1992) 'Toward an Explanation of Betting as a Leisure Pursuit', *Leisure Studies*, 11, pp. 201–18

Busche, K. (1994) 'Efficient Market Results in an Asian Setting', in Donald B. Hausch, Victor S. Y. Lo and William T. Ziemba (eds.), *Efficiency of Racetrack Betting Markets*, London: Academic Press, pp. 615–16

Busche, K. and Hall, C. D. (1988) 'An Exception to the Risk Preference Anomaly', *Journal of Business*, 61, pp. 337–46

Busche, K. and Walls, W. D. (2000) 'Decision Costs and Betting Market Efficiency', *Rationality and Society*, 12(4), pp. 477–92

Cain, M., Law, D. and Peel, D. A. (1992) 'Greyhound Racing: Further Empirical Evidence on Market Efficiency in a Wagering Market', Aberystwyth Economic Research Papers, March

(2000) 'The Favourite-Longshot Bias and Market Efficiency in UK Football Betting', *Scottish Journal of Political Economy*, 47(1), pp. 25–36

(2002) 'Skewness as an Explanation of Gambling by Locally Risk Averse Agents', *Applied Economics Letters*, 9(15), pp. 1025–8

(2003) 'The Favourite-Longshot Bias, Bookmaker Margins and Insider Trading in a Variety of Betting Markets', *Bulletin of Economic Research*, 55(3), pp. 263–73

Chadha, S. and Quandt, R. E. (1996) 'Betting Bias and Market Equilibrium in Racetrack Betting', *Applied Financial Economics*, 6(3), pp. 287–92

Coleman, L. (2004) 'New Light on the Longshot Bias', *Applied Economics*, 36(4), pp. 315–26

De Long, J. B., Shleifer, A., Summers, L. H. and Waldman, R. J. (1991) 'The Survival of Noise Traders', *Journal of Business*, 64, pp. 1–19

Dixon, M. J. and Coles, S. G. (1997) 'Modelling Association Football Scores and Inefficiencies in the Football Betting Market', *Journal of the Royal Statistical Society: Series C (Applied Statistics)*, 46(2), pp. 265–80

Dixon M. J. and Robinson M. E. (1998) 'A Birth Process Model for Association Football Matches', *The Statistician*, 47(3) 523–38

Dowie, J. (1976) 'On the Efficiency and Equity of Betting Markets', *Economica*, 43(170), pp. 139–50

(1992a) 'The Ethics of Parimutuel Systems', *Journal of Gambling Studies*, 8(4), pp. 371–81

(1992b) 'The Ethics of Parimutuel Systems', in W. R. Eadington (ed.), *Gambling and Commercial Gaming: Essays in Business, Economics, Philosophy and Science*, Reno: University of Nevada, pp. 345–55

Eiser, J. R. and van der Pligt, J. (1988) *Attitudes and Decisions*, London: Routledge

Fabricand, B. P. (1965) *Horse Sense*, New York: David McKay

Figgis, E. L. (1951) *Focus on Gambling*, London: Barker

(1974a) *Sporting Life*, 11 March, quoted in *Royal Commission on Gambling* (1978), *Final Report*, 2, London: HMSO, p. 469

(1974b) *Betting to Win*, London: Playfair

(1976) *Gamblers' Handbook*, London: Hamlyn

Filby, M. P. and Harvey, L. (1988) 'Recreational Betting: Everyday Activity and Strategies', *Leisure Studies*, 7, pp. 159–72

Friedman, M. and Savage, L. J. (1948) 'The Utility Analysis of Choices Involving Risk', *Journal of Political Economy*, August, pp. 279–304

Gandar, J. M., Zuber, R. A. and Johnson, R. S. (2001) 'Searching for the Favourite-Longshot Bias Down Under: An Examination of the New Zealand Pari-Mutuel Betting Market', *Applied Economics*, 33, pp. 1621–9

Gandar, J. M., Zuber, R. A., Johnson, R. S. and Dare, W. (2002) 'Re-Examining the Betting Market on Major League Baseball Games: Is There a Reverse Favourite-Longshot Bias?', *Applied Economics*, 34(10), pp. 1309–17

Gärling, T., Romanus, J. and Selart, M. (1994) 'Betting at the Race-Track: Does Risk Seeking Increase When Losses Accumulate?', *Perceptual and Motor Skills*, 78 1248–50

Gilovich, T. (1983) 'Biased Evaluation and Persistence in Gambling', *Journal of Personality and Social Psychology*, 44, 1110–26

Gilovich, T. and Donglas, C. (1986) 'Biased Evaluations of Randomly Determined Gambling Outcomes', *Journal of Experimental Social Psychology*, 22, pp. 228–41

Golec, J. and Tamarkin, M. (1995) 'Do Bettors Prefer Long Shots Because They Are Risk-Lovers or Are They Just Over-Confident?', *Journal of Risk and Uncertainty*, 11, pp. 51–64

(1998) 'Bettors Love Skewness, Not Risk, at the Horse Track', *Journal of Political Economy*, 106(1), pp. 205–25

Griffith, R. M. (1949) 'Odds Adjustments by American Horse-Race Bettors', *American Journal of Psychology*, 62, pp. 290–4

(1961) 'A Footnote on Horse Race Betting', *Transactions, Kentucky Academy of Science*, 22, pp. 78–81; reprinted in Donald B. Hausch, Victor S. Y. Lo and William T. Ziemba (eds.), *Efficiency of Racetrack Betting Markets* (1994), London: Academic Press, pp. 27–30

Hamid, S., Prakash, A. and Smyser, M. (1996) 'Marginal Risk Aversion and Preferences in a Betting Market', *Applied Economics*, 28, pp. 371–6

Hausch, D. B. and Ziemba, W. T. (1985) 'Transaction Costs, Extent of Inefficients, Entries and Multiple Wagers in a Racetrack Betting Model', *Management Science*, 31, pp. 381–94

(1990) 'Arbitrage Strategies for Cross-Track Betting on Major Horse Races', *Journal of Business*, 33, pp. 61–78

Hausch, Donald B., Ziemba, William T. and Rubinstein, M. (1981) 'Efficiency of the Market for Racetrack Betting', *Management Science*, 27, pp. 1435–52

Henery, R. J. (1985) 'On the Average Probability of Losing Bets on Horses with Given Starting Price Odds', *Journal of the Royal Statistical Society*, 148(4), pp. 342–9

Hoerl, A. E. and Fallin, H. K. (1974) 'Reliability of Subjective Evaluations in a High Incentive Situation', *Journal of the Royal Statistical Society A*, 137, pp. 227–30

Hurley, W. and McDonough, L. (1995) 'A Note on the Hayek Hypothesis and the Favourite-Longshot Bias in Parimutuel Betting', *American Economic Review*, 85, pp. 949–55

Jackson, D. and Waldron, P. (2003) 'Pari-Mutuel Place Betting in Great Britain and Ireland: An Extraordinary Opportunity', in L. Vaughan Williams (ed.), *The Economics of Gambling*, London: Routledge, pp. 18–29

Janis, I. L. and Mann, L. (1977) *Decision Making: A Psychological Analysis of Conflict, Choice and Commitment*, New York: Free Press

Johnson, Johnnie E. V. and Bruce, Alistair C. (1993) 'Gluck's Second Law: An Empirical Investigation of Horse-race Betting in Early and Late Races', *Psychological Reports*, 72, pp. 1251–8

Kahneman, D. and Tversky, A. (1979) 'Prospect Theory: An Analysis of Decision Under Risk', *Econometrica*, 47, pp. 263–91

(1984) 'Choices, Values and Frames', *American Psychologist*, 39, pp. 341–50

Kopelman, R. E. and Minkin, B. L. (1991) 'Toward a Psychology of Parimutuel Behaviour: Test of Gluck's Laws', *Psychological Reports*, 68, pp. 701–2

Kuypers, T. (2000) 'Information and Efficiency: An Empirical Study of a Fixed Odds Betting Market', *Applied Economics*, 32(11), pp. 1353–63

Ladbrokes Pocket Companion 1990 Flat, Oswestry: Aesculus Press

Langer, E. J. (1975) 'The Illusion of Control', *Journal of Personality and Social Psychology*, 32, pp. 311–28

(1983) *The Psychology of Control*, London: Sage

Langer, E. J. and Roth, J. (1975) 'The Effect of Sequence Outcome in a Chance Task on the Illusion of Control', *Journal of Personality and Social Psychology*, 32, pp. 951–55

Letarte, A., Ladouceur, R. and Mayrand, M. (1986) 'Primary and Secondary Illusory Control and Risk Taking in Gambling', *Psychological Reports*, 58, pp. 299–302

Markowitz, H. (1952) 'The Utility of Wealth', *Journal of Political Economy*, 60, pp. 151–8

McGlothlin, W. H. (1956) 'Stability of Choices Among Uncertain Alternatives', *American Journal of Psychology*, 69, pp. 604–19

Metzger, M. A. (1985) 'Biases in Betting: An Application to Laboratory Findings', *Psychological Reports*, 56, pp. 883–8

Paton, D. and Vaughan Williams, L. (1998) 'Do Betting Costs Explain Betting Biases?', *Applied Economics Letters*, 1998, pp. 333–5

(2002) 'Identifying Irregularities in a Financial Market', *Applied Financial Economics*, September, 12(9), pp. 633–7

(2005) 'Forecasting Outcomes in Spread Betting Markets: Can Bettors Use "Quarbs" to Beat the Book?', *Journal of Forecasting*, forthcoming

Paton, D., Siegel, D. and Vaughan Williams, L. (2000) *An Economic Analysis of the Options for Taxing Betting: A Report for HM Customs and Excise*, London: HMCE

(2001) 'Gambling Taxation: A Comment', *Australian Economic Review*, 34(4), pp. 427–40

(2002) 'A Policy Response to the E-Commerce Revolution: The Case of Betting Taxation in the UK', *Economic Journal*, 112, pp. 296–314

(2003) 'The Demand for Gambling. A Review', in L. Vaughan Williams (ed.), *The Demand for Gambling*, London: Routledge

(2004) 'Taxation and the Demand for Gambling: New Evidence from the UK', *National Tax Journal*, 57(4), pp. 847–61

Paton, D., Smith, M. J. and Vaughan Williams, L. (2005) 'Market Efficiency in Person-to-Person Betting', Paper Presented at the Royal Economic Society Conference, Nottingham, March

Preston, M. G. and Baratta, P. (1948) 'An Experimental Study of the Auction-Value of an Uncertain Outcome', *American Journal of Psychology*, 61, pp. 183–93

Quandt, R. E. (1986) 'Betting and Equilibrium', *Quarterly Journal of Economics*, 101, pp. 201–7

Rosett, R. N. (1965) 'Gambling and Rationality', *Journal of Political Economy*, 6, pp. 595–607

(1971) 'Weak Experimental Verification of the Expected Utility Hypothesis', *Review of Economic Studies*, 38(116), pp. 481–92

Royal Commission on Gambling (1978) *Final Report*, 2, London: HMSO

Sauer, R. D. (1998) 'The Economics of Wagering Markets', *Journal of Economic Literature*, 36(4), pp. 2021–64

Seligman, D. (1975) 'A Thinking Man's Guide to Losing at the Track', *Fortune 92*, September, pp. 81–7

Slovic, P. (1972) 'Psychological Study of Human Judgment: Implications for Investment Decision Making', *Journal of Finance*, 27, pp. 779–99

Smith, M. A., Paton, D. and Vaughan Williams, L. (2004) 'Costs, Biases and Betting Markets: New Evidence', Nottingham Trent University Discussion Papers in Applied Economics and Policy, 2004/5

Smith, V. and Walker, J. M. (1993a) 'Monetary Rewards and Decision Costs', *Economic Inquiry*, 31(2), pp. 245–61

(1993b) 'Rewards, Experience and Decision Costs in First Price Auctions', *Economic Inquiry*, 31(2), pp. 237–44

Snyder, W. W. (1978a) 'Horse Racing: Testing the Efficient Markets Model', *Journal of Finance*, 33(4), pp. 1109–18

(1978b) 'Decision-Making with Risk and Uncertainty: The Case of Horse Racing', *American Journal of Psychology*, 91(2), pp. 201–9

Sobel, R. S. and Travis Raines, S. (2003) 'An Examination of the Empirical Derivatives of the Favourite-Longshot Bias in Racetrack Betting', *Applied Economics*, 35(4), pp. 371–85

Swidler, S. and Shaw, R. (1995) 'Racetrack Wagering and the Uninformed Bettor: A Study of Market Efficiency', *Quarterly Review of Economics and Finance*, 35(3), pp. 305–14

Terrell, D. and Farmer, A. (1996) 'Optimal Betting and Efficiency in Parimutuel Betting Markets with Information Costs', *Economic Journal*, 106, pp. 846–68

Thaler, R. (1985) 'Mental Accounting and Consumer Choice', *Marketing Science*, 4, pp. 199–214

(1992) *The Winner's Curse: Paradoxes and Anomalies of Economic Life*, New York: Free Press

Thaler, R. H. and Johnson, E. (1990) 'Gambling with the House Money or Trying to Break Even: The Effects of Prior Outcomes on Risky Choice', *Management Science* 36, 643–60

Thaler, R. and Ziemba, W. (1988) 'Parimutuel Betting Markets: Racetracks and Lotteries', *Journal of Economic Perspectives*, 2, pp. 161–74

Tuckwell, R. (1981) 'Anomalies in the Gambling Market', *Australian Journal of Statistics*, pp. 287–95

Tversky, A. and Kahneman, D. (1974) 'Judgment Under Uncertainty: Heuristics and Biases', *Science*, 185, pp. 1124–31

(1981) 'The Framing of Decisions and the Psychology of Choice', *Science*, 211, pp. 453–8

Tversky, A., Slovic, P. and Kahneman, D. (1990) 'The Causes of Preference Reversal', *American Economic Review*, 80, pp. 205–17

Van Zijl, A. (1984) 'Returns and Weak Form Efficiency: Betting Markets', Victoria University of Wellington, Working Paper

Vaughan Williams, L. (1999) 'Information Efficiency in Betting Markets: A Survey', *Bulletin of Economic Research*, 51(1), pp. 1–30

(2000) 'Index Investment Markets and Information Efficiency: Evidence from the UK', in D. Kantarelis (ed.), *Global Business and Economics Review – Anthology 2000*, Worcester, MA: Business Economics Society International, pp. 24–9

(2001) 'Can Bettors Win? A Perspective on the Economics of Betting', *World Economics*, 2(1), pp. 31–48

(2002) *Betting to Win: A Professional Guide to Profitable Betting*, London: High Stakes Publishing

(2004a) Response to Question 370, Joint Committee on the Draft Gambling Bill, House of Lords, House of Commons, Session 2003–04, II, HL Paper 63-II, EV 98–111

(2004b) 'The Consequences of Gambling Deregulation in the UK: A Critical Review of some Theory and Evidence', Joint Committee on the Draft Gambling Bill, House of Lords, House of Commons, Session 2003–04, III, HL Paper 63-III, HC 139-III, April, EV 739–43

(2004c) 'Decision-Making in Betting Markets', *Significance*, 1(3), pp. 109–12

(2005) 'The Modernisation of the UK Gambling Industry – An Issue of Tax and Regulation', *Royal Economic Society News letter*, 128, pp. 11–12

Vaughan Williams, L. and Paton, D. (1997) 'Why is there a Favourite-Longshot Bias in British Racetrack Betting Markets?', *Economic Journal*, 107(1), pp. 150–8

(1998) 'Why are some Favourite–Longshot Biases Positive and others Negative?', *Applied Economics*, 30, pp. 1505–10

Walls, W. D. and Busche, K. (1996) 'Betting Volume and Market Efficiency in Hong Kong Race Track Betting', *Applied Economics Letters*, 3(12), pp. 783–7

(2003) 'Breakage, Turnover and Betting Market Efficiency: New Evidence From Japanese Horse Tracks', in L. Vaughan Williams (ed.), *The Economics of Gambling*, London: Routledge, pp. 43–66

Weitzman, M. (1965) 'Utility Analysis and Group Behaviour: An Empirical Study', *Journal of Political Economy*, 73(1), pp. 18–26

Woodland, L. M. and Woodland, B. M. (1994) 'Market Efficiency and the Favourite-Longshot Bias: The Baseball Betting Market', *Journal of Finance*, 49(1), pp. 269–79

(2003) 'The Reverse Favourite-Longshot Bias and Market Efficiency in Major League Baseball: An Update', *Bulletin of Economic Research*, 55(2), pp. 113–22

Yaari, M. E. (1965) 'Convexity in the Theory of Choice Under Risk', *Quarterly Journal of Economics*, 79, pp. 278–90

Ziemba, W. T. and Hausch, D. B. (1984) *Beat the Racetrack*, San Diego: Harcourt Brace Jovanovich

(1986) *Betting at the Racetrack*, Vancouver and Los Angeles: Dr Z Investments Ltd

(1987) *Dr Z's Beat the Racetrack*, revised edn., New York: William Morrow & Co.

(1994) 'The Dr. Z Betting System in England', in D. B. Hausch, V. S. Y. Lo and W. T. Ziemba (eds.), *Efficiency of Racetrack Betting Markets*, London: Academic Press, pp. 567–74

3 Semi-strong and strong form information efficiency in betting markets

Leighton Vaughan Williams

3.1 Introduction

So far, our analysis has concentrated on weak form information efficiency in betting markets. In this chapter the focus turns to semi-strong and strong form efficiency. Semi-strong form information efficiency is the notion that current prices incorporate *all publicly available information.* In consequence, in a financial market which is semi-strong efficient it should not be possible to earn above-average or abnormal returns on the basis of information which is publicly available. In a market which is strong form efficient it should not be possible to do so even if given all information, including private information. Indeed, any such strategy should on average yield the same return, unless there are differential costs or risks associated with these strategies.

The existence of semi-strong efficiency in betting markets would imply, therefore, that the expected returns to any bet, or type of bet, placed about identical outcomes on the basis of publicly available information, should be identical (subject to identical costs and risks). The same applies with respect to strong efficiency when assessed in respect of all information. Otherwise bettors could use this information to increase their expected returns. In a semi-strong efficient market, for example, the expected return to a bet placed on a horse on the parimutuel (or 'Tote') should be identical to that available with bookmakers, should both options be available. Similarly, it should not be possible to identify patterns in the returns which can be used to yield above-average or abnormal returns. For example, the expected return to bets on favourites after a preceding losing favourite should be identical to the expected return after a preceding winning favourite. In a strongly efficient market, it should not be possible for those with access to all information, including private, monopolistic information, to secure a higher expected return (at least net of costs and risk) than those with access to all publicly available information. Prices set

123

later in the market, after those trading on the basis of private information might have been active, should not in this type of market incorporate any more information than those set earlier in the market. It is ambiguous whether information contained in forecasting (tipping) services is publicly available or is private information. Whichever is the case the distinction must be borne in mind in assessing the significance of this information for the existence of semi-strong/strong form betting market efficiency.

In section 3.2, the evidence is assessed with respect to the returns about different types of bet. In section 3.3, evidence is considered as to whether there exists an identifiable market anomaly in the form of a 'gambler's fallacy' – i.e. an overreaction to recent information. Section 3.4 reviews the evidence as to the usefulness of betting systems based on a range of published information (fundamental betting strategies). Section 3.5 assesses the value of racetrack forecasts and forecasting services, and what this tells us about the existence in racetrack betting markets of semi-strong and strong form information efficiency. In Section 3.6, a review is undertaken of strong form tests of efficiency. Such tests are based on an evaluation of the extent of insider activity in racetrack betting markets. Section 3.7 presents a summary and conclusions.

3.2 Employing expected returns to different types of bets placed about identical outcomes to test for semi-strong efficiency

In this section, the evidence on the expected returns to different types of bet are considered and assessed. Conclusions are drawn from these findings for the existence of weak form information efficiency in betting markets.

3.2.1 Efficiency and exotic betting markets

Studies of Canadian, Hong Kong, UK and US racetracks have attempted to assess the expected returns to different types of bet, each of which is placed about identical outcomes. In an informationally efficient market, these returns should converge, at least net of differential costs of implementation and risk.

Much of the evidence is based on an analysis of so-called 'exotic bets' – i.e. bets involving two or more horses. Since these bets can be constructed in different ways they offer a convenient test of the hypothesis that the actual returns to bets with identical probabilities of success will themselves be identical. The idea behind these tests is that *differential actual returns* would indicate evidence of market efficiency.

Ali (1979) tested the hypothesis of differential returns to two forms of 'exotic bet', known as the 'daily double' and the 'parlay'. In a win bet 'daily double' (also known as a double) the bettor selects the winner of two consecutive races before the first race is run, securing a return only if both horses win. In the 'parlay', the bettor selects a series of horses, betting the total proceeds of each win on the next, until he has had a pre-determined number of wins, or until one loses. The usefulness of comparing these two types of bet is that one can be constructed from the other. In particular, a parlay can be constructed to duplicate the double by selecting the same two horses as in the double before the first race. The added stipulation is that any return from the first race is bet in full on the pre-specified horse in the second race, to win. In this form, the win probabilities of this daily double and this parlay are identical. However, the market returns will not necessarily be identical. In a parimutuel system, the return to a daily double depends on the amounts bet on all possible daily doubles involving the two races in question. Similarly, the return to a parlay is determined by the returns to win bets in these races, the win bet return in each race being dependent on the relative amounts bet on all possible outcomes in each particular race. Ali's test of market efficiency is based on the idea that in an efficient market bets will be valued according to their probability distributions alone, and so the return to a daily double will be the same as that of the corresponding parlay.

Using data from thirty-four racetracks in Canada and the US between September and December 1975, Ali (1979) compared the return to daily double bets with the corresponding return to equivalent parlays. His results are consistent with the hypothesis that both bets are identically priced and, therefore, that the efficient market hypothesis cannot be rejected.

Asch and Quandt (1987), employing data from 705 races at the US Meadowlands racetrack between May and August 1984, performed a similar exercise to Ali (1979), comparing the returns to winning daily doubles with the returns to the corresponding parlays. They found the daily double bets to be significantly more profitable than the parlays, a difference almost precisely accounted for by the fact that the track take is applied twice to the parlay (since this consists of two separate bets) but only once to the daily double. It is as if daily double bettors did not take into account the lower deductions they faced.

Using data from Meadowlands (1984) and Hong Kong (1981–9), Lo and Busche (1994) compared the mean returns to various types of double bets with those for corresponding parlays. Although they found that the various types of double revealed a higher expected return than the equivalent parlays at conventional levels of statistical significance, the difference disappeared if allowance was made for the differential track takes associated with the different types of bet. Taken as a whole, their findings on the difference in the expected payoffs to doubles and to the corresponding self-constructed parlays are consistent with those of Asch and Quandt (1987). Evidence from the UK tells a different story, and is based upon a comparison of the two types of betting market which co-exist in the UK – i.e. the Tote ('Totalisator') and the bookmakers. This evidence is discussed below.

3.2.2 *Employing expected returns to bets at 'Tote' odds and at starting prices to test for semi-strong form efficiency*

In the Tote system, which is the British version of the parimutuel, winning bets share the pool of a fixed proportion of all bets. The final dividend is not known with certainty until after the race. Bookmakers, on the other hand set fixed odds, although the starting price is often taken off-course, which is the price at which a sizeable bet could have been placed with bookmakers on-course at the start of the race. This division of the market provides a useful test of information efficiency, the expectation being that in an efficient market any differences in Tote and bookmakers' prices should be eliminated by the end of trading (when starting prices are returned). Although there is some evidence that this does occur in Australia, which possesses an off-course Tote monopoly (see Bird and McCrae, 1994), the UK evidence points to a semi-strong form inefficiency. This evidence can be traced to Gabriel and Marsden (1990, 1991), who compared the returns to two types of betting; first, bets struck with bookmakers at the starting price; and, second, bets placed at 'Tote' odds.[1] The starting price was chosen in preference to any other agreed fixed-odds price since it possesses the dual strengths of forming a significant part of the betting market, and also being fully and properly recorded. In particular, the data can be regarded as accurate, widely available and easily accessible. Comparing the odds implied *ex post* in the starting price and in the Tote return, Gabriel and Marsden's (1990) main point is that 'Since the differing bets are two options for purchasing exactly the same item (a bet to win on a specific horse), we would expect the odds to converge' (1990: 877).

Gabriel and Marsden tested this hypothesis using data drawn from the first 1,427 flat races of the 1978 racing season in England. The year 1978 was chosen because the general absence of mechanical or electronic Tote boards in that year limited the information available to bettors on betting patterns or likely final odds. The idea here is that in order to equalise the risk of betting with the Tote or with bookmakers, bettors should be equally uncertain under either betting system of the exact odds until after the race starts: 'Thus a rough test of such [semi-strong] market efficiency is simply to compare the average tote and starting price payoffs after races' (1990: 878). In fact, an examination of the difference in the mean Tote and starting price, employing standard *t*-tests and a Wilcoxon matched-pairs signed-rank test (because it requires no assumption about the shape of the underlying distributions), revealed a significantly greater expected return to the aggregate of bets placed on the Tote.

To test for the possibility that the differences could be explained in terms of a few very large Tote payouts, Gabriel and Marsden deleted Tote payouts above a certain level. Although the average difference fell as the size of the payout decreased, they still found that the difference persisted at a statistically significant level.

To test for a 'learning effect' as the season developed (which would tend to reduce the importance of insider information) Gabriel and Marsden performed the calculations for three successive periods. While they found lower average Tote and starting price payouts as the season progressed, as well as generally lower differences between Tote and starting price payouts in the later periods, these were not sufficient for semi-strong efficiency. Moreover, the differences after excluding higher Tote payoffs (specifically, Tote odds of more than 20 to 1) remained not only statistically significant, but also showed no indication of convergence.

In the presence of insider information, in an efficient market one might expect the market to absorb evidence of such information, and market participants should assimilate this into their choices of how and where to bet. Thus, if starting prices are being artificially depressed relative to Tote odds, rational bettors should switch their bets from bookmakers to the Tote, and vice versa when the opposite occurs. This should lead to convergence. The fact that Gabriel and Marsden's results suggest that it does not lead to such convergence is *prima facie* evidence of some form of market inefficiency. Ultimately though, as Gabriel and Marsden themselves accept, 'is it even possible to ... separate an inefficient market from one in which the participants are pursuing the satisfaction of nonmonetary preferences' (1990: 885).

A further test of inefficiency is included by Gabriel and Marsden, following de Leeuw and McKelvey (1984) and Zuber, Gandar and Bowers (1985). This is an estimation of the parameters of the following equation:

$$TOTE_i = \alpha_0 + \alpha_1 SP_i + \mu_i$$

where $TOTE_i$ is the Tote payment in the *i*th race, SP_i is the starting price payout in the *i*th race, and μ is the error term.

Following Zuber, Gandar and Bowers (1985: 800–1), Gabriel and Marsden use a standard *F*-test to test the null hypothesis that $\alpha_0 = 0$ and $\alpha_1 = 1$ jointly. Applying this test for the whole season, for races through April, through May and through June separately, they found that the null hypothesis is rejected for all these datasets at the 1 per cent level of significance, providing additional evidence of market inefficiency.

Gabriel and Marsden (1991) corrected their 1990 conclusions to rectify an error in calculating the Tote returns in their sample of Irish races, which led to an overstatement of these returns. Allowing for this, and re-calculating their original figures, they reported continued broad support for the proposition that Tote returns are on average significantly better than starting price returns, although they are unable to reproduce the finding at all the original levels of subaggregation. They concluded that 'Simply put, the corrected results are not as strong as those reported earlier' (1991: 564).

Blackburn and Peirson (1995) and Vaughan Williams and Paton (1997b) provide further evidence of significant differences, and show that starting price returns are actually superior to Tote returns at lower odds.

Unless a convincing explanation can be offered for these persisting differences, they constitute evidence in a limited sense of information inefficiency at a semi-strong form level. It is not clear, however, that this information is capable of being traded upon so as to earn abnormal returns or positive profits. To this extent, any rejection of the hypothesis of semi-strong information efficiency in these markets is less satisfactory.

Cain, Law and Peel (2003b) demonstrate that the Tote/starting price differentials do not, in any case, constitute clear evidence of inefficiency. This is so, they argue, only if the representative bettor is assumed to be risk-neutral. In the context of uncertainty in the payout to Tote bets, they show that the findings of a differential return in the two mediums is exactly what be expected (on certain reasonable assumptions) if bettors exhibit risk-loving preferences over favourites, and risk-averse preferences over longshots. They argue indeed that the Gabriel and Marsden analysis would have really been anomalous if mean Tote and starting prices had proved to be equal.

Peirson and Blackburn (2003) also note that the differences between the two markets are compatible with profit maximisation by bookmakers and efficient behaviour by bettors.

Even so, Vaughan Williams (1999, 2001) finds evidence that the differential between Tote and starting price odds is less (or disappears) in samples which might be expected to contain lower levels of insider activity – i.e. high-grade and high-class races.

Paton and Vaughan Williams (2001), however, pose a challenge to this growing orthodoxy in their comparison of the forecast bets offered by bookmakers and the UK Tote, namely the bookmakers' Computer Straight Forecast (CSF), based on correct identification of the first two past the post in the correct order, and the Tote's Dual Forecast bet which existed at the time, based on correct identification of the first two past the post in either order. They show significant differences between the expected returns to the CSF and the Dual Forecast in favour of the Dual Forecast, and that this was immune to an explanation based on differential risk (or, indeed, skewness). They explain the differential in terms of monopoly rents derived from the pricing structure of the CSF bet.

The Australian evidence provides another interesting perspective. Bird and McCrae (1994) found for their Australian data that any difference between bookmaker and parimuteul (Totalisator) odds tended to evaporate as the start of a race approached. Whereas the Totalisator take was about 17 per cent, the bookmaker take, as implied by the market odds (the 'over-round') varied from about 26 per cent at the opening of the market to a level roughly equivalent to the Tote 'take' at the off – i.e. about 17 per cent. Even so, the starting prices laid by bookmakers tended to be lower than those available 'on the Tote' in those cases where the odds lengthened, and tended to be higher in those cases where the odds shortened, although this pattern could not be used to create a profitable betting strategy. Bird and McCrae (1994) also found that most of the odds movement occurred in the first half of the betting fraction, implying perhaps that insiders are not strict monopolists of superior information, and so bet early at advantageous odds before these odds disappear.

3.3 Testing for the existence of a 'gambler's fallacy'

The 'gambler's fallacy' is the proposition that bettors, instead of accepting an actual independence of successive outcomes, are influenced in their perceptions of the next possible outcome by the results of the preceding sequence of outcomes – e.g. throws of a die, or spins of a wheel. Terrell (1994) states it thus:

> The 'gambler's fallacy' is the belief that the probability of an event is decreased when the event has occurred recently, even though the probability of the event is objectively known to be independent across trials. (1994: 309)

This idea is generalised in Kahneman and Tversky (1982). Their notion of a 'winner's curse and loser's blessing', as it is commonly known, is a reported tendency for people, in revising their beliefs, to overweight newer information and underweight older information. Such a hypothesis has been extensively tested in financial markets – e.g. De Bondt and Thaler (1985), Brown and Harlow (1988) and Stock (1990). Each of these studies found evidence of the existence of such an 'anomaly', and has yielded, therefore, the idea of trading upon a contrarian strategy. Insofar as such a strategy is based on the historical pattern of past prices, it provides at least *prima facie* support for a hypothesis of weak form efficiency in these markets. Since it also implies a failure by traders to allow for all public information, it is also indicative of semi-strong form inefficiency. However, some authors (e.g. Chan, 1986) explain any above-average or abnormal returns which can be elicited by acting on the basis of such strategies as simply fair compensation for additional risk or other factors.

The existence of a 'gambler's fallacy' has been documented in laboratory studies (Ordohook and Morrissey, 1984); lottery-type games (Clotfelter and Cook, 1991, 1993); and lotteries (Terrell, 1994). In particular, Clotfelter and Cook (1991, 1993) found (in a study of a Maryland numbers game) a significant fall in the amount of money wagered on winning numbers in the days following the win, an effect which did not disappear entirely until after about sixty days. This particular game was, however, characterised by a fixed-odds payout to a unit bet, and so the gambler's fallacy had no effect on expected returns. In parimutuel games, on the other hand, the return to a winning number is linked to the amount of money bet on that number, and so the operation of a systematic bias against certain numbers will tend to increase the expected return about those numbers. Terrell (1994) investigated one such parimutuel system, the New Jersey state lottery. In a sample of 1,785 daily drawings from 1988 to 1993, he constructed a subsample of 97 winners which repeated as a winner within the sixty day cut-off point suggested by the Clotfelter and Cook (1991) findings. He found that these numbers had a higher payout than when they previously won on 80 of the 97 occasions. In order to determine the relationship more precisely, Terrell also regressed the payout to winning numbers on the number of days since the last win by that number. The expected payout on a number increased by 28 per cent one day after winning, and decreased from this level by about 0.5 per cent each day after the number won, returning to the original level after sixty days or so. The size of the gambler's fallacy observed in New Jersey, while significant, was nevertheless not as great as that found by Clotfelter and Cook (1993) for the fixed-odds Maryland numbers game. It is as if irrational (certainly non-profit-maximising/loss-minimising) behaviour exists, but reduces as the cost of the anomalous behaviour increases.

Two studies of a 'gambler's fallacy' in racetrack betting found the same effect: Metzger (1985) in US horse-race betting and Terrell and Farmer (1996) in US greyhound racing. Metzger (1985) set out to test one prediction consistent with the concept of a gambler's fallacy, specifically that bettors will tend to overestimate the chances of a favourite winning after a series of wins by longshots compared to the situation after a series of wins by favourites. On the basis of an examination of a sample of US horse-races, Metzger concluded that there was indeed such a tendency shown by bettors in the aggregate. In particular, a series of wins by favourites (longshots) made less (more) favourable a bet on a favourite, which in turn produced underbetting (overbetting) of favourites. Terrell and Farmer (1996) calculated the return to a strategy of betting the greyhound in the starting trap occupied by the previous winner. This yielded a 9 per cent profit, and as such constituted 'the only strategy earning positive profits' (1996: 864). The finding is consistent with the hypothesis that bettors were underestimating the probability of a repeated outcome and that as such, they were victims of a gambler's fallacy.

If confirmed, such trends or patterns could be exploited in order to earn above-average or abnormal returns. Indeed, if such configurations can be shown to exist in betting markets at an appropriate level of confidence and to constitute more than fair compensation for other factors, such as changes in the incidence of risk, then this constitutes potential evidence in contradiction of the existence of informationally efficient betting markets.

3.4 Fundamental strategies and tests for semi-strong form efficiency in betting markets

In this section, evidence is derived from racetrack betting markets which addresses the issue of whether bettors can apply decision rules, based on fundamental information, which can be employed to earn above-average or abnormal returns. This evidence is used to draw conclusions as to the existence of semi-strong information efficiency in these markets.

Hausch, Ziemba and Rubinstein (1981) offered a convenient interpretation of 'fundamental strategies' as decision rules which 'utilise past data available from racing forms, special sources, etc. to "handicap" races. The investor then wagers on one or more horses whose probability of winning exceeds that determined by the odds by an amount sufficient to overcome the track take' (1981: 1435).[2] Similarly, Benter (1994) defines the idea of 'fundamentally' handicapping a race as 'to empirically assess each horse's chance of winning and utilise that assessment to find profitable wagering opportunities' (1994: 183). Such strategies are different from the systems based on utilising information contained in the betting odds, and usually more complex to make operational.

Vergin (1977) examined six such strategies, in the form of published betting systems,[3] on the basis of a sample of 102 races run in January and February 1972 at Santa Anita Park, California. Of these, only one – i.e. the McQuaid (1971) 'elimination rule' – produced a profit to level stakes, and that only for win bets. McQuaid's 'elimination rule', reproduced in Vergin (1977) is stated below:

'Eliminate any horse which:

a. has not had one race at today's track;
b. has not run today's distance at today's track (+ 1 furlong);
c. has not raced within one month of today's race;
d. has not won a race;
e. in its last race did not finish in the money;
f. did not finish within eight lengths of the winner in its last race;
g. in its last race lost more than 3/4 lengths in the stretch;
h. has a speed rating at today's distance which is not within five points of the highest speed rating for any of the competing horses for the past four races;
i. has consistency rating which is not within five points of the highest consistency rating for any of the competing horses unless the horse's speed rating is as high or within one point of the highest speed rating'. (Vergin 1977: 43)

McQuaid proposed three ways of improving this rule: eliminating low-odds bets, deleting ineffective individual elimination rules and adding rules drawn from other sources where this would reduce the number of non-winning horses predicted as winners. Although this increased the return on investment from 17 per cent to 78 per cent, this is hardly surprising since the returns were calculated using data from which the modifications were derived. Applying the same system to new data still yielded a return above what could be expected by chance, although less than that yielded by the original data. Nevertheless, even after modifying the amended system in order to generate more bets McQuaid admits that 'this sample is still too small for anything approaching the level of statistical tests of significance' (1971: 44).

Canfield, Fauman and Ziemba (1987) questioned whether trading rules based on a knowledge of one example of a persistent bias in racetrack outcomes could be used to earn abnormal returns. In particular they tested for the existence of a post-position bias, employing a sample of 3,345 races at Exhibition Park, Vancouver, Canada, between 1982 and 1984. As such, they built upon the ideas of Quirin (1979) and Beyer (1983). Beyer noted that 'At tracks less than a mile in circumference, the sharp turns and short stretch almost always work to the advantage of the front runners and the horses on the inside' (1983: 42). An examination of mile racetracks by Quirin (1979) indicated that the inside six positions produced winners more often than would be expected by chance, with the inside under most conditions the most advantageous of all.

Canfield, Fauman and Ziemba examined win bets for the whole sample, and for subsamples comprising fast tracks (which might favour the inside post) and off (wet) tracks (in which the conditions might disadvantage the horse holding the inside position) separately. They also examined a sample of longer races in order to test the hypothesis that the greater number of turns in longer races might make the bias against outside positions particularly pronounced, and assessed the influence of the circumference of the track in eliciting the same bias. Although a strategy of betting on particular post positions, under particular track conditions, could be devised which appeared to offer positive profits, it was not possible to reject a hypothesis of non-positive profits in the long run from any such strategy at conventional levels of significance. Canfield, Fauman and Ziemba's explanation of the inability to translate post position bias into significant net profits rests on the idea that, after allowing for track deductions, bettors overbet the favourable positions to the extent of negating any potential advantage from a betting strategy based on the bias. Applying their data to an examination of the incidence and consequence for expected returns of post-position bias in the market for 'exotic' bets, they reached similar conclusions.

Bolton and Chapman (1986) developed a stochastic utility model, parametrised in the form of a multinomial logit model, employing horse, jockey and various race characteristics (ten basic horse and jockey independent variables in total), to evaluate the worth (or 'utility') of racehorses. Their database consisted of 200 races reported in the *Daily Racing Form*. Finding that the signs of the coefficients on their explanatory variables were consistent with their '*a priori*' theoretical expectations, they tested the usefulness of their model across various alternative betting strategies. By constraining wealth to a level at which bets have negligible influence on the track odds, they were able to obtain expected returns significantly greater than would be generated by a random betting strategy, though not sufficient to enable a positive expected return to be earned across the sample of races.

Applying various side constraints they eventually decided to eliminate those bets for which the logit model provided poor estimates of the winning probabilities – i.e. longshots. In other words, bettors should confine their bets to horses whose estimated probability of winning exceeds some minimum value, which they estimate. They were able to express, subject to further modifications, some optimism that positive returns could be made from a specified betting strategy, although the strength of their conclusions were limited by their small sample size and existence of positive estimation errors.

Chapman (1994) extended this type of analysis, using a much larger database with a larger number of covariates. In particular, he applied a twenty-variable pure fundamental multinomial logit handicapping model to 2,000 races in Hong Kong,[4] which included handicapping variables linked to horse, jockey, situational context (e.g. track and distance conditions) and observable current performance signals (e.g. recent track workouts). There was no evidence of the usual longshot bias, in line with analyses of the Hong Kong market by Busche and Hall (1988) and Busche (1994), and there was a close correspondence between the expected win frequencies and the actual winning frequencies. Chapman tested for the possibility that positive profits could be made on the basis of the sophisticated handicapping model he proposed, concluding that there was a potential to make positive expected returns from such a model. These findings are consistent in principle with the results published by Bolton and Chapman (1986), but much greater in size. Moreover, the returns are found to be higher still if the logarithm[5] of the public's win probabilities, as revealed by their actual win bets, is included as an additional (i.e. 21st) variable in the multinomial horse-race handicapping model. To make the latter operational as an optimal betting system in a practical sense would, nevertheless, require replacing in real time the estimates of the true win probabilities with the final public win bets, and acting upon the final information set.

Employing the same data, Benter (1994) constructed a computer model designed to estimate current performance potential. This involved the investigation of variables and factors with potential predictive significance and the refining of these individually so as to maximise their predictive accuracy. In order to counter any tendency to overfit on the basis of past data, Benter was careful to test his refinements on out-of-sample data. The sole criterion for inclusion of a variable as a predictor of performance was, therefore, improvements in the model's goodness-of-fit at an acceptable degree of statistical significance. This was the paramount consideration even when any theoretical explanation of the variable's effect was either missing or else unconvincing. Implementing a betting strategy based on this model, he reported an overall net profit for five years of large-scale betting, although a loss was reported in one of the five seasons. He concluded that 'at least at some times, at some tracks, a statistically derived fundamental handicapping model can achieve a significant positive expectation' (1994: 196). As such modelling became more widely available, however, he was led to suspect that the market would become efficient to such predictions – i.e. 'The profits have gone, and will go, to those who are "in action" first with sophisticated models' (1994: 196).

Betton (1994), in an analysis based on 1,062 races from the same racetrack as Canfield, Fauman and Ziemba (1987), re-examined the incidence of post-position bias. A t-test was employed to compare the average post position of the first three horses finishing with the average post position expected if no post-position bias existed. The bias was found to be significant for the first two places, but not for the third.

Betton concluded that while 'knowledge of the post position significantly improves the information available from the odds rankings, the relatively low overall explanatory power of these models suggests that more is unknown than known in the determination of racing results' (1994: 520).

Terrell and Farmer (1996) employed a large dataset of 4,121 races (at the Woodlands Greyhound Park, Kansas City) for the 1989–90 season, and follow-up data from 1994, to investigate the post-position 'anomaly'. They found a consistent pattern over time of significant differences in the win rates of starting boxes, and the expected returns to bets on these boxes. The best return was to bets on dog one (the 'inside trap'), the worst to dog seven (the 'outside trap'). The implication is that bettors tended to overbet the outside traps, although this disparity was not sufficiently strong so as to yield a positive return (net of deductions) to bets on the inside traps.

More promising evidence has come from Australia. Edelman (2003) generated probability forecasts for horses in Australian sprint races based on competitive ratings. He demonstrated significant added value to his handicapping system, in both a statistical and financial sense – i.e. a clear out-of-sample profit.

Goddard and Asimakopoulos (2004) focus on the application of forecasting models for projecting football results. In particular, they employ an ordered probit regression model using ten years' data to forecast English league football match results. Significant variables include the relevance of the match for end-of-season league outcomes, the involvement of the teams in cup competition and the geographical distance between the teams' home bases. A strategy of selecting end-of-season bets with a favourable expected return according to the model appears capable, they conclude, of generating a positive return.

Levitt (2004) provides a different perspective on the issue of 'fundamental handicapping' by noting that bookmakers do not simply set prices to match buyers and sellers in the market but, rather, take positions with respect to the outcome of an event. Levitt concludes that bookmakers tend to be more skilled at predicting outcomes than bettors and exploit bettor biases by choosing prices that deviate from the market-clearing price.

In summary, although there is an array of evidence which suggests that forecasting strategies are capable to some degree of forecasting sports market outcomes, less (though some) evidence is available that such an improvement can be used to make abnormal returns. Where such evidence does exist, the strength of the findings is usually either linked to the ability to make operational a model incorporating changing variables in limited real time (more difficult for racetrack than football forecasting), or else subject to variations in the return which may permit extended short-term losses. Even if these models are accepted as *ex post* evidence of the possibility of earning abnormal profits from a fundamental handicapping system, bettors seeking to make use of the model in the future are subject to the risk that the findings have already been incorporated into future odds.

3.5 Racetrack forecasts and betting market efficiency: an appraisal of theory and evidence

The relationship between racetrack forecasting services and the concept of information efficiency in betting markets in which such forecasting services operate is an example of the need for a clear distinction between the semi-strong and strong forms of information efficiency.

This issue is highlighted by Snyder's (1978a, 1978b) tests of five forecasting services, which he termed 'five strong tests of market efficiency' (1978a: 1117). This designation was subsequently disputed by Losey and Talbott (1980), who argued that Snyder's 'experts' are not 'insiders' in the sense of possessing monopolistic access to information. To the extent that the odds which they quote are based on publicly available information, and are published and disseminated widely before each race, Losey and Talbott compare their role to that of advisory service analysts. In this sense, they argue that Snyder's tests may be more accurately viewed as tests of semi-strong efficiency.

It seems that there is a need, therefore, to distinguish between forecasts which are widely available, such as the tips provided in a national daily newspaper, and those which are provided to a small group of clients who normally pay for this service. There is no clear dividing line, however, and the strength of the test for efficiency is inevitably, therefore, a matter of interpretation. In this chapter the tests are of widely available forecasts, and the conclusions, must be interpreted in light of this.

3.5.1 Efficiency and the information content of publicly available racetrack forecasts

Work on the information content of racetrack forecasts can be traced to Snyder's tests of the hypothesis that individuals or groups with special or expert information are able to outperform the general betting public. To do this Snyder compared the performance of 'expert'[6] advice with that of actual bets struck. To do so, he calculated the rate of return to bets placed at parimutuel odds and also at the odds forecast by the 'experts', using these as if they were the real payout odds. He found that the experts' rate of return was both larger at low odds and smaller at high odds than that of the public. Indeed, all of the 'experts' displayed a greater bias than the public.

Losey and Talbott re-examined Snyder's work using a similar dataset. Their objective was to determine whether and to what degree knowledge of the divergences noted by Snyder could be used by bettors to improve their expected return. The point is that if the market imperfectly incorporates all the information supplied by experts, a bettor acting upon such imperfections may be able to make above-average or even abnormal returns. As such, a test for the existence of such an imperfection can be used to test for the existence of market efficiency.

Losey and Talbott identified those cases in which the parimutuel odds exceeded the odds listed by the 'Racing Form' handicapper, the extent of this divergence being calculated as the simple ratio of the final parimutuel odds to the handicappers' odds. This is termed the 'overlay ratio'. The idea behind the Losey and Talbott approach is that if the handicappers do possess superior information, then higher than average expected returns should be derivable from betting on horses with higher than average overlay ratios. In fact, they observed that bettors employing such strategies tended to earn lower than average returns. Paradoxically, it appears that a bettor could have secured an above-average expected return by avoiding the low-return bets as indicated by a high overlay ratio. Losey and Talbott conclude that parimutuel markets are inefficient in the sense of reflecting all available information, but that they have insufficient evidence to claim the existence of inefficiency in the sense of a systematic profit potential.

A different type of analysis of the relationship between expert opinion and betting odds was offered by Figlewski (1979), who employed a multinomial logit probability model to assess the information content of professional handicappers' published forecasts, and related the observed frequency of winning to the handicappers' odds and the final odds. The study is based on an examination of data on win bet odds from 189 thoroughbred races run at Belmont racetrack, New York, in June and July 1977. Figlewski observed that while substantial information was contained within the handicappers' advice, most of this was already incorporated into the betting odds. It could not, therefore, be used to improve significantly the forecast accuracy of the betting odds as determined in the market. While he found that on-track bettors discounted the information in full, this was not true of off-track bettors. The implication is that on-course bettors at least were able to attach the appropriate weight to the handicappers' information in placing their bets.

3.5.2 Relationship between expert opinion and betting odds

Studies of the relationship between expert opinion and betting odds, using Australian data, offer mixed conclusions. The case for semi-strong form inefficiency in Australian racetrack markets can be traced to Tuckwell (1983), who showed in his dataset how a strategy of betting on horses whose market odds deviated significantly from forecast odds could be used to generate positive returns. This finding has not, however, been reproduced in later studies. In particular, Anderson, Clarke and Ziegler (1985), employing a two-stage regression, found that such information was impounded into the market odds at the off, and knowledge of the forecast prices could not be used to generate profitable trading rules. Bird and McCrae (1987) examined 'expert' opinion in the form of the forecasts supplied by ten so-called 'experts' which were published on the morning of each race in a Melbourne newspaper. Since all the newspaper tipsters provide a first, second and third selection in each race, these selections were pooled and aggregated on the basis of three points for a first selection, down to one point for a third selection. The rate of return was calculated for a strategy of placing level stakes on horses ranked on the basis of the poll of these 'experts'. The equivalent level stakes strategy was applied to horses ranked at a particular level of favouritism. No strategy based on the above produced a positive rate of return. Neither were the rates of return from bets placed on horses ranked according to the experts' poll significantly different from those based on the level of favouritism or the odds. Bird and McCrae (1987) concluded that the betting market is efficient with respect to information supplied by the newspaper 'experts', and that this information is incorporated into the bookmakers' odds.

Thus, although there is some evidence that genuine information is contained in forecast prices, there is less evidence that such information is unincorporated into the payout odds available in the market, and even less that this can be systematically exploited so as to yield abnormal returns.

3.6 Inside information, insider trading and tests of strong form efficiency

In this section, betting markets are investigated for the existence of 'inside information' which can be traded upon to earn above-average or abnormal returns. Conclusions are drawn from the evidence for the existence of strong information efficiency in these markets.

3.6.1 Available and predicted odds

In order to test for the existence of strong form efficiency in the Fama (1970) sense[7] – i.e. efficient with respect to all information including private information – Dowie (1976) noted the importance of drawing the distinction between odds available or predicted at differing times. His methodology centres on the fact that the starting price, being determined extremely late in the market, should incorporate more information than any of the various odds generated early, and should include any inside or monopolistically held information. Indeed, since those possessing such information will exploit this continuously up to the point at which the starting price is determined, then the correlation between the starting price returns and the realised probabilities should, in the presence of insider activity, be higher than that between any odds formed earlier in the market and these probabilities. Certainly it should be higher than for any odds assigned before the market is formed. To test this, Dowie used a very large dataset of races, covering the 1973 flat racing season (29,307 horses in 2,777 races). He calculated two relevant correlations. The first was between the realised probabilities and the starting prices, while the second was between the realised probabilities and odds forecast before the formation of the market (the forecasts in the daily racing newspaper, the *Sporting Life*, were chosen). Because the over-round is not standard as between starting prices and forecast prices, Dowie standardised these prices for each race, adjusting the prices by a percentage implied in the respective over-rounds so as to generate hypothetical perfectly round books (i.e. no over-round or under-round). He found no significant difference between the two sets of correlations, and therefore, while acknowledging data deficiencies at the short end of the odds market, concluded that there exist 'serious doubts as to the significance of inside information' (1976: 150).

Crafts (1985) extended Dowie's study to allow for the possibility of profitable arbitrage. Crafts' point is that insiders may take advantage of market dynamics to bet at odds greater than the starting price. Although this is not an option in a parimutuel system, it is in a bookmaking system, where bettors can 'take a price' at any time during the course of the market. To allow for this, Crafts proposed a test based on separating out cases where there is a 'marked' difference between the forecast price and the starting price. He reasoned that a shortening (lengthening) of the odds available about a horse during the course of the market may indicate evidence of insiders who knew the true probabilities of that horse winning were greater (less) than those implied in the odds offered early in the market.

Crafts applied an equivalent test also to marked differences in the prices actually offered on the course during the period of trading. The dataset consisted of 16,769 runners in total, over a period from 11 September 1982 to 8 January 1983, and employed various arbitrary definitions of a marked difference – e.g. forecast price greater than or equal to twice the starting price. In all, he identified 2,280 (13.6 per cent of the total sample) which fell into one of his categories. He also cleaned the data to allow for idiosyn-crasies in the compilation of the forecast prices. For example, he eliminated all observations which did not have either a starting price or a forecast price of 10/1 or more, because of the tendency to collate higher forecast prices into a residual category (the 'bar'), and also cases where the sum of implied probabilities in each of these set of prices did not diverge from each other too greatly.[8]

If insider trading is the cause of these 'marked' price movements, then where these marked differences occur the expected return to bests placed earlier in the market should be significantly different to those placed later in the market. Moreover, this should be even more the case in races which offer particular scope for insider trading.

In order to isolate races which might be the target of above-average levels of insider activity, Crafts divided the sample into handicap and non-handicaps, the idea being that these are distinguished by the amount of established public form available about them. In handicap races horses are weighted by past form (which must be established over a series of races) in an attempt to equalise their chances. Such races are less likely, therefore, to offer as much scope for insiders to trade as non-handicap races, where the form need not be so exposed to public scrutiny.

Crafts' results suggest that horses displaying a marked shortening of the odds between the forecast and starting price stages are indeed characterised by an exceptionally high expected return at forecast prices. Moreover, this is particular strong for non-handicap races. An examination of the scope for profitable arbitrage during the formation of starting price odds in the actual on-course market produced similar findings, although splitting the sample as before (into handicaps and non-handicaps) failed to reproduce the earlier result.

Crafts offered supporting evidence in descriptions of betting patterns, published in the *Sporting Life*, about the previous day's on-course trading. In particular, he identified examples of large sums of money placed on horses with poor previous form, which went on to shorten considerably in the market and to win. On the basis of this evidence, Crafts concluded that British horse-race betting markets do offer insiders the opportunity for profitable exploitation of information not publicly available. As such, it is not strongly efficient.

Crafts (1994) developed this work by identifying a category of horses about which inside information is likely to be particularly useful – i.e. horses which have not run for a long time (the season before last). As in his 1985 paper, he used the existence of a 'marked' shortening of the odds (forecast price/starting price > 1.5) to indicate positive insider trading. Presumably to eliminate the potential negative bias to returns implied by the favourite-longshot bias, all horses starting at odds of 7 to 1 against or greater were eliminated from consideration.

For eighty-eight observations taken over a period between September 1982 and November 1987, the rate of return was 261.9 per cent at forecast prices, and 55.8 per cent at starting prices. The return at forecast prices would appear to contradict strong form efficiency, and the return at starting price to contradict the existence of less strong forms of efficiency. The implication is that a good strategy for outsiders in the British horse-race betting market is to identify and selectively follow information provided by insiders. If Crafts' results are significant and reproducible, then those seeking to continue their advocacy of information efficiency in these markets may do worse than accept Crafts' lifeline – i.e. that there are substantial costs incurred in collecting the data required to make the decision rule operational.

Crafts also examined the existence of market efficiency in British betting markets by analysing the performance of three marketed betting systems. Each of the systems provided special decision making rules based on public information, and were tested on data generated prior to the publication of the systems, and again for data generated after publication. No evidence of significant post-tax profits were revealed either before or after publication, although the return to one of the systems, which showed some evidence of pre-tax profitability, declined markedly after publication. This is indicative, perhaps, of a market response to knowledge contained therein. Further tests of nine racing systems and five ratings services (i.e. services providing tips rather than decision rules), based on results reported in Roberts and Newton (1987), also failed to show profits. These results, Crafts (1994) noted, are consistent with the operation of the efficient markets hypothesis in British betting markets. He concludes: 'The continued sale of these systems suggests that the participants in British horse-race betting include many gullible outsiders' (1994: 547).

A subsequent study of five racetrack forecasting services was undertaken by Vaughan Williams (2000). In selecting the services, two factors were taken into account. First, past success at advised prices as measured by an independent publication, the Racing Information Database; second, a reasonable degree of public awareness of the service, as assessed by their advertising profile.

Based on different trading strategies, all of the services generated a pre-tax profit, and some strategies a post-tax profit, at the starting price, although these profits could not be confirmed at conventional levels of significance. The starting price is, however, in general not the best price at which a bet on a winning horse can be placed, because the weight of money during the course of the market tends to follow the eventual winner (again indicative of the profitable use of inside information). This effect is likely to be particularly strong for horses tipped by professional forecasting services since these are often heavily backed, leading to a shortening of the available odds. For these reasons, it is fair to expect that the profitability of the forecasting services surveyed would, in general, have been higher if odds prevailing earlier in the market had been taken.

Smith (2003) looks specifically at the impact of media tips on price movements and finds evidence to suggest that the identification of key forecasts could be used to predict large contractions in price.

Because in a parimutuel market it is not possible to arbitrage at different prices, it is more difficult to test for the existence of insider trading. However, Asch and Quandt (1986) do offer some evidence. Employing data from 729 races at the Atlantic City racetrack, they report that the final parimutuel odds tended to be lower than the predicted (or 'morning line') odds for winners. Moreover, in the case of winners, the later in the betting period the money was laid, the stronger was this effect. Asch and Quandt proposed an explanation of this finding as the withholding of 'smart money' (money bet by people with superior information) until late in the betting period, in order to avoid giving out market signals which could depress the final payout odds.

The influence of inside information on betting markets was also the subject of an investigation conducted by Schnytzer and Shilony (1995). This approach compared two mutually isolated groups, one of which they propose has access to inside information and one of which does not. The informed group are identified as on-course bettors in Australian (Victoria) racetrack betting markets who are able to detect a significant shortening of the odds offered by on-course bookmakers about particular horses, an effect consistent with a 'plunge' on these horses by insiders. Although they may miss the value with bookmakers by the time they identify the 'plunge' there may still, it is hypothesised, be opportunities to benefit from this second-hand information by betting on the 'Tote'. Off-course bettors, on the other hand, are isolated from the information about the on-course bookmaker market, as the 'Tote' in Australia has a monopoly of off-course betting.

Schnytzer and Shilony found, using a standard and a Spearman rank correlation coefficient, that the betting behaviour (in terms of the proportions bet on given horses) of their two groups was significantly different, the on-course betting population accruing a 13 per cent advantage compared to the off-course bettors, and also tending to bet more on longshots.

In order to distinguish whether this is due to differences in the relative availability of inside information or the differences in the ability of the two populations to understand and process public information, they calculated the predictive power of the two populations, and compared the variance of the predictions. Using a multinomial logit model, they estimated that the variance of the prediction by those with access to both public and private information was less than that by those with access only to public inform-ation. This, they conclude, is consistent with the hypothesis of valuable inside information.

A separate test of the value of inside information was to estimate whether proxies for positive and for negative insider information are statistically predictors of race outcomes. Evidence that a significantly greater proportion of money is bet by on-course bettors on a particular horse is used to proxy for positive inside information, and vice versa. If there is useful positive private information about a horse it might be expected, they argue, that the ensuing 'plunge' would cause a shortening of that horse's odds. This information should constitute a useful predictor of race outcomes. They found that it did. Negative inside information about a horse may also cause a lengthening of its odds, but odds lengthen also as an attempt by bookmakers to attract money away from the 'plunge'. Because of this ambiguity they argue that proxies for negative inside information cannot readily be used to predict race outcomes. They found that this was indeed the case.

This evidence is adduced in further support of the contention that differences in betting behaviour between on-course and off-course bettors is explained by differences in their access to inside information rather than in their capacity to process public information.

Schnytzer and Shilony believe that a judicious use of information con-tained in on-course/off-course betting patterns can be used to secure positive profits net of deductions. One such method they advocate is to 'compare the last off-course Tote odds with the bookmakers' odds a minute or two before the end of betting and back those horses for which the ratio of bookmakers' odds to tote off-course odds is greatest, in proportion to that ratio' (1995: 970). In an exercise they undertook on this basis of hypothetical betting results, they found that betting on horses where there existed a marked difference between the on-course and off-course win bet ratios at the time of the race gave a net profit up to 32.5 per cent. Whatever the difficulties may be of making this operational in real time, this is certainly evidence of inside information in the Australian betting market under consideration.

3.6.2 Measuring the incidence of insider trading in a betting market

An approach which seeks to estimate the actual extent of insider trading can be found in Shin (1993). This analysis models the betting process in a fixed-odds system along the lines of Shin (1991, 1992), and brings the debate full circle, to the earlier consideration of the reasons for a favourite-longshot bias in these markets.

Shin (1991, 1992) first proposed that the bias could be explained not only by the demand-side influences of bettors, but in fixed-odds betting markets also as the result of an optimal pricing strategy by bookmakers who face a number of bettors who possess superior information to that publicly available ('insiders'). Shin assumes that there is perfect competition among risk-neutral bookmakers, no transaction costs and that insiders can identify the outcome with certainty, while the rest of the betting population (outsiders), are simply noise traders.

Assuming that the incidence of insider trading is not larger when a favourite is tipped to win than when a longshot is tipped to win (or more precisely, so long as the ratio of insider trading to the winning probability falls as the probability of winning rises), it is shown that equilibrium prices will exhibit a favourite-longshot bias. The intuition is clear. If insiders (who make up a proportion z of all bettors) know with certainty the outcome of a race, then bookmakers face a greater loss from insiders at higher odds (lower implied winning probabilities) than at lower odds. So long as it is not the case that the proportion of insiders (the value of z) is relatively higher at lower odds, bookmakers will face greater expected losses to insiders at higher odds. A simplifying assumption is that where insiders play no part market prices correspond to the true probabilities, and so any deviation from this can be attributed to insider trading. The consequence of price-setting behaviour by bookmakers facing this uncertain environment is for the normalised betting odds to understate the winning chances of favourites and to overstate the winning chances of longshots. This is the traditional favourite-longshot bias.

Shin (1993) provided an estimate of the extent of insider trading based on a proposed link between the size of the bid–ask spread in the market and the prevalence of insider trading in the market. The key to the analysis lies in the idea that the direct effect of insider trading on the sum of bookmakers' prices will tend to increase as the number of runners (and therefore the size of the odds) increases, and that this regularity can be used to isolate the proportion of insiders in the total betting population. Shin estimated this proportion by applying an iterative estimation procedure of linearised versions of his equations, although Jullien and Salanié (1994) show how this can be achieved using standard non-linear estimation procedures. While Shin's modelling can explain a favourite-longshot bias in betting markets characterised by odds-setters, and also a link between the number of runners and the bookmakers' over-round, it can be shown (see Vaughan Williams and Paton, 1997a: 152) that identical results may result from demand-side explanations, such as the behaviour of bettors who discount a fixed fraction of their losses, a suggestion proposed by Henery (1985). Because of this, Vaughan Williams and Paton (1997a) employ a much larger dataset than that in Shin (1993), and distinguish between two types of race, on the basis of their relative potential for insider trading.

It is shown that in those races in which there might be expected to be very limited opportunity for the non-disclosure of inside information, the link between the number of runners and the over-round disappears. This lends empirical support to Shin's supply-side explanation of the phenomenon.

Thus an estimate (of the extent of inside information) can be derived, from the form of relationship between the sum of bookmakers' prices and the number of runners. Shin (1993), Jullien and Salanié (1994)[9] and Vaughan Williams and Paton (1997a),[10] all calculate a figure of about 2 per cent of all sums staked. Fingleton and Waldron (1996), however, who model the issue on the assumption that bookmakers are risk-averse, engage in anti-competitive behaviour and/or face significant transaction costs, estimate a figure for their Irish data of 3.1 to 3.7 per cent.

Further evidence in support of Shin's approach is provided in Cain, Law and Peel (2001a), who find in a study of the British horse and greyhound betting markets that Crafts' (1985) measure – see above – of insider trading (i.e. marked odds shortening) is positively related to z.

If insider trading has a part to play in the spread of odds offered by bookmakers, one might also expect that the bias against higher odds is greater for bets placed with UK bookmakers than with the UK Tote, since the latter simply responds passively to the weight of bettors' money. Blackburn and Peirson (1995) and Vaughan Williams and Paton (1997b) confirm this pattern for comparisons of the UK bookmaker and Tote returns, while Vaughan Williams (1999, 2001) indicates that the differentially greater bias in bookmaker returns difference is linked to a measure of the likely incidence of insider trading in the races concerned. Cain, Law and Peel (2001b) confirm, using Shin's 'z' as a measure of insider trading, that the higher was the incidence of insider trading in horse races as so measured then the greater was the extent to which Tote returns to winning bets exceeded that of bookmakers. This is consistent, they argue, with the conjecture that, in maximising the benefit of their insider knowledge by striking early fixed-odds bets, insider traders may be responsible for depressing winning payoffs at the closing prices in the market with bookmakers ('Starting Prices') relative to those of the Tote.

A comparison of the bias displayed by UK bookmakers with US pari-mutuel markets shows the same type of differential. A useful comparison is provided by two very large studies which covered roughly similar periods in the 1970s – i.e. Dowie (1976) for the UK and Snyder (1978) for the US. Dowie's study revealed a much greater bias against bets placed at higher odds than did Snyder's.

Cain, Law and Peel (1999) and Paton, Vaughan Williams and Fraser (1999) both use Shin's measure to estimate the degree of insider trading in defined markets. Cain, Law and Peel examine British horse-race betting and betting on the 1997 general election, while Paton, Vaughan Williams and Fraser seek to determine the extent of insider trading in UK fixed-odds and spread betting markets for soccer.

Cain, Law and Peel make race-by-race estimates of insider trading in horse-racing. Their average estimate of the degree of insider trading (0.027) is very similar to that obtained by Shin (1993), although the estimates varied from 0.005 to 0.1762. Interestingly, their estimate of the degree of insider trading in election betting was much higher (0.078), ranging in the thirty-two constituencies analysed from 0.047 to 0.118.

Paton, Vaughan Williams and Fraser apply the 'z' methodology to estimate the degree of insider trading in fixed-odds and spread betting markets for Premier League soccer. Their estimate of 0.032 for fixed-odds betting was significantly higher than their 0.015 for spread betting, which they attribute to the more rigorous regulatory framework pertaining to spread betting in the UK.

Most recently, Schnytzer and Shilony (2003) modify Shin's model to take account of proposed biases in bettors' estimates of horses' winning probabilities. They conclude that although a bias is present even without inside information, the bias is nevertheless exacerbated by insiders.

Cain, Law and Peel (2003a) find evidence in the odds offered by book-makers about a variety of sports in support of a central prediction of the Shin model, which asserts that bookmakers are impelled to create a bias in their odds because of the presence of insider traders – moreover, that margins increase with the number of competitors.

An interesting and complementary perspective is offered by Law and Peel (2002), who seek to distinguish the shortening of odds across a betting market caused by insider activity and that caused by 'herding' behaviour – i.e. uninformed money following a horse shortening in the market simply because of the fact that it is shortening, and thereby causing the odds to contract yet further. To do this, they use Shin's (1993) measure of insider trading at the beginning of the betting period and at the end of the betting period. The idea is that to the extent that the odds about a horse shorten markedly at the same time as the Shin measure of insider trading declines there is evidence of 'herding' behaviour. When the Shin measure increases over the betting period, however, this is evidence of insider activity. They find that significant positive betting returns are achieved when shortening odds are accompanied by a rise in the Shin measure; when they are accompanied by a fall, returns are negative. These results are consistent with at least some measure of 'herding' behaviour in the betting markets considered.

Future research might usefully build further upon the sort of modelling pioneered by Shin (1993), in particular to amend some of the more heroic assumptions, to test different markets for insider activity, and to develop alternative empirical tests which can arbitrate between demand-side and supply-side explanations of the data. It is unlikely that such an approach would affect the qualitative findings, although they may well affect the estimate of the extent of insider trading.

Finally, a more direct test of the extent of insider trading is provided by Terrell and Farmer (1996). They propose a model of a betting market characterised by informed bettors (who purchase the true probabilities) and uninformed bettors (who do not). The presence of these uninformed bettors is sufficient to cause the market odds to diverge from the objective probabilities. Any difference between the return to a random betting strategy based on market odds and the actual return to bettors (the pool minus deductions) is thus interpreted as income to informed bettors. Since the expected return to random bets was calculated to be 78.3 per cent of total stakes, compared to a pool payout of 82 per cent, the difference (3.7 per cent) is classified as the reward to being informed. Extrapolating across all races at the Woodlands track in the 1989 season yielded an estimate of $2.23 million as this reward.

3.7 Semi-strong and strong form information efficiency in betting markets: summary and conclusions

In testing for the existence of semi-strong form efficiency in financial markets, two main approaches have been adopted. One is to assess the impact of new public information on prices. The other is an exploration of opportunities for earning systematic abnormal returns on the basis of identifiable circumstances (so-called 'market anomalies').

Semi-strong form tests of betting market efficiency employ the same methodology, applied to the special circumstances pertaining to betting markets. In a financial market which is semi-strong form efficient, it should not be possible to earn abnormal returns through a strategy of predicting future prices on the basis of information which is currently publicly available. Indeed, any such strategy should on average yield the same return, unless there are differential costs or risks associated with these strategies. Likewise, the existence of semi-strong form efficiency in betting markets would imply that the expected returns to any bet, or type of bet, placed about identical outcomes on the basis of publicly available information, should be identical (subject to identical costs and risks). In a semi-strong efficient market, for example, the expected return to a bet placed on a horse on the parimutuel (or Tote) should be identical to that available with bookmakers, should both options be available, as should the actual return to different bets which have the same expected return. Similarly, it should not be possible to identify patterns on the basis of information publicly available in the returns which can be used to yield above-average or abnormal returns.

A number of studies have sought to identify significant differences in the actual return to different types of bet available in parimutuel markets. To do this, 'exotic bets' (bets involving two or more horses) are used, since they allow a comparison of the actual return to bets characterised by equivalent probabilities of success. Although significant differences in the raw figures have sometimes been found, these tend to disappear when differential costs (e.g. track take) are applied to the bets. On this basis a hypothesis of market efficiency cannot be rejected.

In a semi-strong form market, the expected return to identical bets placed in different arenas (where both are equally available) should also converge, or else there are opportunities for arbitrage. A study of Gabriel and Marsden (1990) purports to show just such a divergence (between Tote odds and bookmaker odds), but the significance of their findings is reduced somewhat when an error in their method was corrected (Gabriel and Marsden, 1991). Further evidence of significant differences in starting price and Tote returns is, however, provided by Blackburn and Peirson (1995) and Vaughan Williams and Paton (1997b).

As part of the more general issue of market 'anomalies', some studies of betting markets have tested for the existence of a 'gambler's fallacy' – i.e. a tendency for bettors to believe that the probability of an event is decreased when the event has occurred recently, e.g. a number drawn in a lottery or a sequence of previous winning favourites. This sort of bias has been observed in lottery play and in studies of the US racetrack.

To summarise, the existence of semi-strong form efficiency in a betting market implies that no patterns in the returns would be identifiable which could indicate the existence of superior returns from betting on the basis of public information under certain clearly defined circumstances. One type of test is to assess whether there exists a differential expected return to events with identical probabilities of success in different identified types of betting medium, another whether there exists any 'anomalous' behaviour in the form of systematic exploitable patterns in the history of publicly available information. Although there is some evidence of unexploited opportunities for arbitrage between different sectors of the betting market, and evidence that bettors tend to underestimate the likelihood of consecutive identical outcomes, there is much less (though there is some) evidence that the use of publicly available information can be used to earn abnormal returns.

A quite different approach to testing for semi-strong form efficiency has been the application of 'fundamental' strategies to racetrack data – i.e. assessing the value of decision rules based on publicly available information. These range from simple policies such as always betting the inside track, to complex handicapping models. While there is evidence that such fundamental strategies are capable to some degree of forecasting racetrack outcomes, there is less evidence available that such an improvement can be used to make abnormal returns. Where such evidence does exist, the strength of the findings is either linked to an ability to make the model operational in limited real time, or else it is subject to variations in the return which may permit extended short-term losses.

It is ambiguous whether information contained in forecasting (tipping) services should be classed as private information. In assessing financial market efficiency, forecasting performance was classified as evidence of strong form inefficiency, albeit loosely defined. Information implicit in the prices forecast about horses in daily publications is, however, clearly publicly available. Studies which have sought to generate rules based on these prices have usually found that any information is impounded into the odds by the off. Even where there is some indication that the use of this early price information could generate above-average returns, there is very little evidence of any opportunity to earn abnormal profits. There has been very little academic work on the performance of private professional forecasting services (tipsters), a study by Crafts (1994) revealing little evidence of inefficiency. Vaughan Williams (2000b) is slightly more positive about the value of following the advice of identified forecasting services.

Studies which investigate the existence of strong form efficiency in race-track betting markets address the issue of the value of inside information in these markets. Three distinct methodologies have been adopted in the literature. One such approach is to compare prices (odds) at different stages in the development of the market (Dowie, 1976; Crafts, 1985). Forecast prices are sometimes used as a convenient representation of pre-market or earliest prices. The idea behind such studies is that, in a fixed-odds market devoid of inside information, there should be no opportunities to earn a higher expected return at earlier prices (before insiders can take the price) than at later prices. If such opportunities can be identified, this is *prima facie* evidence of strong form inefficiency in the market.

There has been some evidence produced (Crafts, 1985) that horses whose odds shorten in the market demonstrate a higher expected return (especially at earlier or forecast prices) than those whose odds do not, and vice versa. Moreover, this effect seems to be greater in races where insider information is likely to be more prevalent. Another approach, identified by Schnytzer and Shilony (1995), compares two mutually isolated groups, one of which it is proposed has access to inside information and one of which does not. Empirical tests of differences in the betting behaviour of these two groups are consistent, they argue, with the presence of inside information which possesses a positive value. In particular, the group with access to the inside information were better (and more consistently) able to predict the outcomes of races than the other group. The third approach (Shin, 1993; Fingleton and Waldron, 1996; Vaughan Williams and Paton, 1996, 1997a,) is to derive or imply the incidence of insider trading indirectly by an analysis of the divergence of the pricing behaviour of bookmakers relative to what would be expected were there no possibility of insider activity. Such studies imply that bookmakers perceive the existence of some positive level of insider trading, estimated to be between about 2 and 4 per cent of all sums staked.

In summary, there is significant evidence for the suggestion that insiders in betting markets possess valuable information unavailable to the public, which they can trade upon so as to earn above-average and even abnormal returns, and to this extent the market may be considered informationally inefficient. It is important, however, not to confuse the ability of the market to process information efficiently with the withholding of information from the market itself.

The case for information efficiency in racetrack betting markets has thus not been disproved (although neither has it been proved), at least in the sense of an opportunity to earn systematic abnormal expected returns, except perhaps at the level of and in the sense of insiders acting upon monopolistically held private information.

Dowie (1976) termed 'a market as efficient to the extent that it passes the weak and semi-strong tests and equitable to the extent that it passes the strong test' (1976: 140). In these terms, the weight of evidence supports the view that betting markets are inequitable, although it is not so clear that they can in every sense be termed inefficient.

Notes

1 Tote odds, as in all parimutuel systems, are not fixed or guaranteed, but depend on the size of the pool and the number of wining ticket holders. A large pool, with few winning tickets, for example, pays higher odds than a small pool with a large number of winning tickets. The odds are displayed as a dividend to a £1 stake, and rounded downwards to the nearest 10 pence. A Tote dividend of £4.50 thus implies odds of 3.5 to 1 against. Such odds are the actual return and are not subject to any further deductions, the deductions being accounted for in the dividend.

2 The same idea can be applied to the British bookmaking system by substituting 'to earn a positive profit' for 'to overcome the track take'.

3 'System 73' by Ainslie, in Ainslie (1973); 'Singularly Best Race and Speed' by Cohen and Stephens, and 'Singularly Easy Win' by Cohen and Stephens, both in Cohen and Stephens (1963); 'An Elimination Rule' by McQuaid and 'The Consistent Horse System' by McQuaid, in McQuaid (1971); and 'A Breaks and Trial System' by Reynolds, in Reynolds (1971).

4 See Benter (1994) for details of the database.

5 The log transformation of the public's win probabilities is used instead of the actual win probabilities because of evidence that it improves the statistical fit. See Asch and Quandt (1986: 123–5) and Benter (1994).

6 The 'experts' chosen were from the *Daily Racing Form* publication, three Chicago newspapers and the track handicapper.

7 Where a section of the population have monopolistic access to information not available to others, Dowie prefers to describe this as inequitable rather than inefficient; 'we will talk of a market as efficient to the extent that it passes the weak and semi-strong tests and equitable to the extent that it passes the strong test' (Dowie, 1976: 140).

8 In cases where starting prices exceeds forecast prices, Crafts includes only those where the sum of the forecast price probabilities were greater than the sum of the starting price probabilities by less than 0.01 per horse after disregarding the residual (or 'bar') category.

9 Using Shin's dataset.

10 Using their own dataset but Shin's estimation procedure.

References

Ali, M. M. (1979) 'Some Evidence on the Efficiency of a Speculative Market', *Econometrica*, 47, pp. 387–92

Anderson, D., Clarke, R. and Ziegler, P. (1985) 'Information, Equilibrium, Efficiency in Betting Markets', University of Queensland, Working Paper

Asch, P. and Quandt, R. E. (1986) *The Professor's Guide to Strategies*, Dover, MA: Auburn House

(1987) 'Efficiency and Profitability in Exotic Bets', *Economica*, 59, pp. 278–98

Benter, W. (1994) 'Computer Based Horse Race Handicapping and Wagering Systems: A Report', in Donald B. Hausch, Victor S. Y. Lo and William T. Ziemba (eds.), *Efficiency of Racetrack Betting Markets*, London: Academic Press, pp. 183–98

Betton, S. (1994) 'Post Position Bias: An Econometric Analysis of the 1987 Season at Exhibition Park', in Donald B. Hausch, Victor S. Y. Lo and William T. Ziemba (eds.), *Efficiency of Racetrack Betting Markets*, London: Academic Press, pp. 511–26

Beyer, A. (1983) *The Winning Horseplayer*, Boston: Houghton-Mifflin

Bird, R. and McCrae, M. (1987) 'Tests of the Efficiency of Racetrack Betting Using Bookmaker Odds', *Management Science*, 33, pp. 1552–62

(1994) 'Efficiency of Racetrack Betting Markets: Australian Evidence', in Donald B. Hausch, Victor S. Y. Lo and William T. Ziemba (eds.),

Efficiency of Racetrack Betting Markets, London: Academic Press, pp. 575–82

Blackburn, P. and Peirson, J. (1995) 'Betting at British Racecourses: An Analysis of Semi-Strong Efficiency between Bookmaker and Tote Odds', *Studies in Economics*, 95/4, University of Kent

Bolton, R. N. and Chapman, R. G. (1986) 'Searching for Positive Returns at the Track: A Multinomial Logit for Handicapping Horse Races', *Management Science*, 32, pp. 1040–59

Brown, K. C. and Harlow. W. V. (1988) 'Market Overreaction: Magnitude and Intensity', *Journal of Portfolio Management*, 14, pp. 6–13

Busche, K. (1994) 'Efficient Market Results in an Asian Setting', in D. B. Hausch, Victor S. Y. Lo and William T. Ziemba, (eds.), *Efficiency of Racetrack Betting Markets*, London: Academic Press, pp. 615–16

Busche, K. and Hall, C. D. (1988) 'An Exception to the Risk Preference Anomaly', *Journal of Business*, 61, pp. 337–46

Cain, M., Law, D. and Peel, D. A. (1999) 'Estimates of the Degree of Insider Trading in Two Disparate Betting Markets', *Applied Economics Letters*, 6(3), pp. 191–3

(2001a) 'The Relationship between Two Indicators of Insider trading in British Racetrack Betting', *Economica*, 68, pp. 97–104

(2001b) 'The Incidence of Insider Trading in Betting Markets and the Gabriel and Marsden Anomaly', *Manchester School*, 69(2), pp. 197–207

(2003a) 'The Favourite-Longshot Bias, Bookmaker Margins and Insider Trading in a Variety of Betting Markets', *Bulletin of Economic Research*, 55(3), pp. 263–73

(2003b) 'The Favourite-Longshot Bias and the Gabriel and Marsden Anomaly: An Explanation Based on Utility Theory', in L. Vaughan Williams (ed.), *The Economics of Gambling*, London: Routledge, pp. 2–13

Canfield, B., Fauman, B. C. and Ziemba, W. T. (1987) 'Efficient Market Adjustment of Odds Prices to Reflect Track Biases', *Management Science*, 33, pp. 1428–39

Chan, K. C. (1986) 'Can Tax-Loss Selling Explain the January Seasonal Effect in Stock Returns?', *Journal of Finance*, December, pp. 1115–28

Chapman, R. G. (1994) 'Still Searching for Positive Returns at the Track: Empirical Results from 2,000 Hong Kong Races', in Donald B. Hausch, Victor S. Y. Lo and William T. Ziemba (eds.), *Efficiency of Racetrack Betting Markets*, London: Academic Press, pp. 173–81

Clotfelter, C. and Cook, P. J. (1991) 'Lotteries in the Real World', *Journal of Risk and Uncertainty*, 4, pp. 227–32

(1993) 'The "Gambler's Fallacy" in Lottery Play', *Management Science*, 39(12), pp. 1521–25

Cohen, I. S. and Stephens, G. D. (1963) *Scientific Handicapping: Tested Ways to Win at the Track*, Englewood Cliffs, NJ: Prentice-Hall

Crafts, N. F. R. (1985) 'Some Evidence of Insider Knowledge in Horse Race Betting in Britain', *Economica*, 52, pp. 295–304

(1994) 'Winning Systems? Some Further Evidence on Insiders and Outsiders in British Horse Race Betting', in Donald B. Hausch, Victor S. Y. Lo and

William T. Ziemba (eds.), *Efficiency of Racetrack Betting Markets*, London: Academic Press, pp. 545–9

De Bondt, W. and Thaler, R. (1985) 'Does the Stock Market Over-React?', *Journal of Finance*, 40(3), pp. 793–805

De Leeuw, F. and McKelvey, M. J. (1984) 'Price Expectations of Business Firms: Bias in the Short and Long Run', *American Economic Review*, 74, pp. 99–100

Dowie, J. (1976) 'On the Efficiency and Equity of Betting Markets', *Economica*, 43(170), pp. 139–50

Edelman, D. (2003) 'A Competitive Horse-Race Handicapping Algorithm Based on an Analysis of Covariance', in L. Vaughan Williams (ed.), *The Economics of Gambling*, London: Routledge, pp. 106–13

Fama, E. F. (1970) 'Efficient Capital Markets: A Review of Theory and Empirical Work', *Journal of Finance*, 25(2), pp. 383–417

Figlewski, S. (1979) 'Subjective Information and Market Efficiency in a Betting Model', *Journal of Political Economy*, 87, pp. 75–88

Fingleton, J. and Waldron, P. (1996) 'Optimal Determination of Bookmakers' Betting Odds: Theory and Tests', *Trinity Economic Papers*, Technical Paper, 9, December

Gabriel, P. E. and Marsden, J. R. (1990) 'An Examination of Market Efficiency in British Racetrack Betting', *Journal of Political Economy*, 98, pp. 874–85

(1991) 'An Examination of Market Efficiency in British Racetrack Betting: Errata and Corrections', *Journal of Political Economy*, 99, pp. 657–9

Goddard, T. J. and Asimakopoulos, I. (2004) 'Forecasting Football Results and the Efficiency of Fixed-Odds Betting', *Journal of Forecasting*, 23(1), pp. 51–66

Hausch, Donald, B., Ziemba, William, T. and Rubinstein, M. (1981) 'Efficiency of the Market for Racetrack Betting,' *Management Science*, 27, pp. 1435–52

Henery, R. J. (1985) 'On the Average Probability of Losing Bets on Horses with Given Starting Price Odds', *Journal of the Royal Statistical Society*, 148(4), pp. 342–9

Jullien, B. and Salanié, B. (1994) 'Measuring the Incidence of Insider Trading: A Comment on Shin', *Economic Journal*, 104, pp. 1418–19

Kahneman, D. and Tversky, A. (1982) 'Intuitive Prediction: Biases and Corrective Procedures', in D. Kahneman, P. Slovic and A. Tversky (eds.), *Judgment under Uncertainty: Heuristics and Biases*, Cambridge: Cambridge University Press, pp. 414–21

Law, D. and Peel, D. A. (2002) 'Insider Trading, Herding Behaviour and Market Plungers in the British Horse-Race Betting Market', *Economica*, 69, pp. 327–38

Levitt, S. D. (2004) 'Why are Gambling Markets Organized so Differently from Financial Markets?', *Economic Journal*, 114(495), pp. 223–46

Lo, V. S. Y. and Busche, K. (1994) 'How Accurately Do Bettors Bet in Doubles?', in Donald B. Hausch, Victor S. Y. Lo and William T. Ziemba (eds.), *Efficiency of Racetrack Betting Markets*, London: Academic Press, pp. 465–8

Losey, R. L. and Talbott, J. C., Jr. (1980) 'Back on the Track with the Efficient Markets Hypothesis', *Journal of Finance*, 35, pp. 1039–43

McQuaid, C. (ed.) (1971) *Gambler's Digest*, Chicago: Follett Publishing Co.

Metzger, M. A. (1985) 'Biases in Betting: An Application to Laboratory Findings', *Psychological Reports*, 56, pp. 883–8

Paton, D. and Vaughan Williams, L. (2001) 'Monopoly Rents and Price Fixing in Betting Markets', *Review of Industrial Organization*, 19(2), pp. 265–78

(2005) 'Forecasting Outcomes in Spread Betting Markets: Can Bettors Use 'Quarbs' to Beat the Book?', *Journal of Forecasting*, 24(2), pp. 139–54

Paton, D., Vaughan Williams, L. and Fraser, S. (1999) 'Regulating Insider Trading in Betting Markets', *Bulletin of Economic Research*, 51(3), pp. 237–41

Peirson, J. and Blackburn, P. (2003) 'Betting at British Racecourses: A Comparison of the Efficiency of Betting with Bookmakers and at the Tote', in L. Vaughan William (ed.), *The Economics of Gambling*, London: Routledge, pp. 30–42.

Quirin, W. L. (1979) *Winning at the Races: Computer Discoveries in Thoroughbred Handicapping*, New York: William Morrow

Reynolds, R. (1971) *Everything You Should Know About Making Money At the Races*, Toronto: Pagurian Press

Roberts, P. M. and Newton, B. A. (1987) *The Intelligent Punter's Survey*, Weymouth: TIPS Publishing

Schnytzer, A. and Shilony, Y. (1995) 'Inside Information in a Betting Market', *Economic Journal*, 105, pp. 963–71

(2003) 'Is the Presence of Inside Traders Necessary to Give Rise to a Favorite-Longshot Bias?', in L. Vaughan Williams (ed.), *The Economics of Gambling*, London: Routledge, pp. 14–17

Shin, H. S. (1991) 'Optimal Betting Odds Against Insider Traders', *Economic Journal*, 101, pp. 1179–85

(1992) 'Prices of State Contingent Claims with Insider Traders and the Favourite-Longshot Bias', *Economic Journal*, 102, pp. 426–35

(1993) 'Measuring the Incidence of Insider Trading in a Market for State-Contingent Claims', *Economic Journal*, 103, pp. 1141–53

Smith, M. A. (2003) 'The Impact of Tipster Information on Bookmakers' Prices in UK Horse-Race Markets', in L. Vaughan Williams (ed.), *The Economics of Gambling*, London: Routledge, pp. 67–79

Snyder, W. W. (1978a) 'Horse Racing: Testing the Efficient Markets Model', *Journal of Finance*, 33(4), pp. 1109–18

(1978b) 'Decision-Making with Risk and Uncertainty: The Case of Horse Racing', *American Journal of Psychology*, 91(2), pp. 201–9

Stock, D. (1990) 'Winner and Loser Anomalies in the German Stock Market', *Journal of Institutional and Theoretical Economics*, 146(3), pp. 518–29

Terrell, D. (1994) 'A Test of the Gambler's Fallacy: Evidence From Pari-Mutuel Games', *Journal of Risk and Uncertainty*, 8, pp. 309–17

Terrell, D. and Farmer, A. (1996) 'Optimal Betting and Efficiency in Parimutuel Betting Markets with Information Costs', *Economic Journal*, 106, pp. 846–68

Tuckwell, R. (1983) 'The Thoroughbred Gambling Market: Efficiency, Equity and Related Issues', *Australian Economic Papers*, 22, pp. 106–8

Vaughan Williams, L. (1999) 'The Costs of Insider Trading: Evidence from Defined Markets', *Economic Issues*, pp. 19–30

(2000) 'Can Forecasters Forecast Successfully? Evidence from UK Betting Markets', *Journal of Forecasting*, 19(6), pp. 505–14

(2001) 'Insiders and International Finance: Evidence from Complementary Markets', *Ekonomia*, 5(2) 2001

Vaughan Williams, L. and Paton, D. (1996) 'Risk, Return and Adverse Selection: A Study of Optimal Behaviour Under Asymmetric Information', *Rivista di Politica Economica*, November–December, pp. 63–81, reprinted in M. Baldasssari, M. Bagella and L. Paganetto (eds.) (2001), *Financial Markets: Imperfect Information and Risk Management*, New York: Palgrave, pp. 63–81

(1997a) 'Why is there a Favourite-Longshot Bias in British Racetrack Betting Markets?', *Economic Journal*, 107(1), pp. 150–8

(1997b) 'Does Information Efficiency Require a Perception of Information Inefficiency?', *Applied Economics Letters*, 4, pp. 615–17

Vergin, R. C. (1977) 'An Investigation of Decision Rules for Thoroughbred Racehorse Wagering', *Interfaces*, 8(1), pp. 34–45

Zuber, R. A., Gandar, J. M. and Bowers, B. D. (1985) 'Beating the Spread: Testing the Efficiency of the Gambling Market for National Football League Games', *Journal of Political Economy*, 93, pp. 800–6

Part II
Selected readings

4 An assessment of quasi-arbitrage opportunities in two fixed-odds horse-race betting markets

Michael A. Smith, David Paton and Leighton Vaughan Williams

4.1 Introduction

In this chapter, we build upon work by Vaughan Williams (2000, 2001) and Paton and Vaughan Williams (2005) who examine the concept of Quasi-Arbitrage Opportunities (Quarbs[1]), a class of weak form market inefficiencies. Quarbs exploit apparent differences in subjective assessments of the value of an asset (in this study the asset is a class of state contingent claims, namely racehorse bets). Such a strategy requires the existence of a number of market-makers contemporaneously offering the same asset at different prices. The assumption underpinning a Quarb strategy is that the consensus market price is a better indicator of the asset's objective value than the outlier price. Further, if we can estimate the true or objective value of the asset from the market mean price, it may be possible to trade the asset profitably at the outlier price (in the case of racehorse bets, by obtaining longer odds than the mean).

Our chapter describes the application of a simple Quarb model to two distinct datasets, one comprising 549 races, the other 700 races, to establish whether or not this type of inefficiency is evident in fixed-odds horse-race betting markets in the UK, and whether it can be exploited with an appropriate betting strategy. Specifically, the initial premise is that the mean morning odds available about a horse are a more accurate reflection of its winning chance than the odds outlier.

4.2 Background

'Weak form' information inefficiencies (Fama, 1970) arise if past price movements or histories hold exploitable information undiscounted in the current price. An example of a weak form inefficiency that has been identified in horse-race betting markets is the 'favourite-longshot bias' (see, for example, Hausch, Ziemba and Rubinstein, 1981; Vaughan Williams and Paton, 1997) – i.e. a tendency for bettors to overvalue (and hence overbet) low-probability outcomes, and to relatively undervalue high-probability outcomes. The bias is a generally accepted feature of many horse-race betting contexts, although there is disagreement as to its cause (Vaughan Williams, 1999, surveys the debate).

The purest form of weak form inefficiency is where price structures permit riskless arbitrage. This is when it is possible to buy an asset at one price and sell the same asset at a guaranteed higher price, such that the price difference exceeds the transactions costs involved. In an informationally efficient market, however, such price anomalies should persist only if the positive returns are smaller than warranted by the outlay of time and capital.

Paton and Vaughan Williams (2005) outline a more indirect, risk bearing Quarb in respect of spread betting markets – i.e. markets in which a 'spread' is quoted about a variable (say, runs in a cricket match), inviting clients to buy at the top end (say, at 260 runs) or sell at the bottom end (say, 240 runs) of the spread. In these markets, the profit (or loss) is equal to the difference between the buy (sell) prices and the actual outcome, multiplied by the unit stake. For example, if 280 runs were scored, then a buy bet at 260 of £10 per run would win £200 (£10 × (280–260)), while if 240 runs were scored the same bet would lose £200 (£10 × (240–260)). The underlying asset in Paton and Vaughan Williams (2005) is a specialised football variable – i.e. the number of disciplinary cards issued in a specified football match (the 'bookings' market). The hypothesis they pose is that an outlying offer will tend to provide a less accurate estimate of the true probability distribution of bookings in a match than the mean of the mid-points of all spreads. If true, this would mean that an outlying spread on the low side of the mean might offer profitable buy opportunities, whereas an outlying spread on the high side of the mean would in a similar way be a signal to sell.

Paton and Vaughan Williams find a *prima facie* case that the probability estimates implied by the mainstream spreads are indeed more accurate than the outliers, and provide a positive return to a wagering strategy based on this. As is often the case with financial assets, however, the returns distribution in the study proves to be non-normal, and the positive returns are only weakly significant using conventional statistical tests. In order to explore this concept in relation to horse-race betting, we use here a simple mean–outlier model with an expected value decision rule to establish a betting strategy to exploit Quarbs. We replace conventional tests of the significance of returns with an expected returns reference measure.

4.3 A model of Quarbs

The underlying assumption of the model is that the consensus market assessment of the chances of a horse winning, as evidenced by the mean price of that horse, is a more accurate estimate than that represented by the outlier odds.

Each horse i in a race, j, has a subjective probability of winning, p_i^s, implied by the mean of bookmaker prices available for that horse on the morning of the race (the study was exclusively concerned with races where early morning fixed odds were available).

p_i^s is not the true probability of winning, as the sum of implied probabilities for the race exceeds one, representing the *over-round*, or the bookmaker's margin. This tends to be true for individual bookmaker prices and also for composite books made up of the best prices taken from the range of competing bookmakers.

Furthermore, the existence of the favourite-longshot bias means that even if the sum of probabilities were to equal one, the prices are still unlikely to represent the true chances of the runners. To establish the true probability of a runner relative to the population as a whole, an adjustment to the nominal odds in respect of the bias must be made:

$$p_{ij}^t = p_{ij}^s + fl_{ij} \tag{4.1}$$

where p_{ij}^t is the true probability of horse i winning, and fl_{ij} is the favourite-longshot bias adjustment in terms of probabilities for the class of horses at that price. Previous studies suggest that the bias (fl_{ij}) will tend to be positive where the nominal probability of winning is high, and negative when it is low. To derive fl_{ij} for horses in our samples, we estimated the favourite-longshot bias from a separate dataset of bookmaker starting prices covering over 12,800 races (see data below). A weighted least squares linear regression was used to estimate a function relating true or objective probabilities of winning to the subjective probabilities implied by the odds corresponding to the different categories, as follows:

$$\ln(p_g^t) = \alpha_1 + \alpha_2 \ln(p_g^s) + \alpha_3 [\ln(p_g^s)]^2 + e_g \tag{4.2}$$

where p_g^t indicates the actual win proportion of all horses in odds grouping, g. In the interests of parsimony, the functional form adopted for this estimated relationship was quadratic; higher-order functions offered no better fit and exhibited significant degrees of heteroscedasticity. The estimated values of the coefficients α_1 and α_2 and α_3, corresponding t-values and White's test statistic against the χ^2 distribution, are summarised in table 4.1 of the results section. The exponent of the fitted value of $ln(p_g^t)$ was used to derive fl for each odds category in (4.1) above.

Table 4.1. *Coefficients for the objective probability function (equation 4.2),
estimated from dataset one (weighted least squares linear regression)*

Coefficient	Estimated value	*t*-value	Significance
α_1	−0.168	−12.465	0.000
α_2	0.742	651.036	0.000
α_3	−0.129	−588.464	0.000
N	22		
R^2	0.996		
White's statistic	7.247		
Critical χ^2 value at $p = 0.05$	9.488		

Having adjusted for the favourite-longshot bias in this way for all
runners, we normalised the p_{ij}^t to sum to one to arrive at an estimate of
the true chance of each runner taking into account the competition in its
specific race:

$$p_{ij}^n = p_{ij}^t / \sum p_{ij}^t \qquad (4.3)$$

where p_{ij}^n is an estimate of the race-specific true probability of horse i
winning race j.

As in previous studies (Bird and McCrae, 1987; Tuckwell, 1983), we
adopted proportional normalisation, as our estimate of the favourite-
longshot bias was derived from industry starting prices reported in aggregate over many races, which therefore yielded no information concerning
price structures of individual races. This is not ideal, as this method of
normalisation meant that our subsequent 'quasi-arbitrage index' (QI) was
to an extent overinflated in fields with many runners due to the disproportionate impact of the favourite-longshot bias in such races (Shin, 1993).
This means that the index is not strictly comparable between individual
races (the derivation of the index is described below).

Next we computed the expected value of each horse, backed at its outlier
odds to a unit stake:

$$EV_{ij} = (p_{ij}^n \times O_{ij}) - (1 - p_{ij}^n) \qquad (4.4)$$

where EV_{ij} is the expected value of horse i, and O_{ij} are the odds represented
by the outlier.

Finally, we converted the expected value of each horse winning to a QI:

$$QI_{ij} = 100(EV_{ij} + 1) \qquad (4.5)$$

where a QI of 100 represents a horse whose outlying odds are a true reflection of its chance of winning that race, an index of 110 suggests an advantage of 10 per cent – i.e. 10 per cent net profit relative to stake, long term, and so on.

Our selected betting strategy was to place a nominal 1-point stake on the horse in each race with the highest value of QI, subject to QI $\geq$ 100, and the condition that there should be no bet if there was more than one horse in a race with an identical top QI.

In order to test the validity of our assumption that the consensus book-maker price is more accurate than the outlier as a predictor of race outcomes, we calculated an expected cumulative return for different filter levels of QI over 100; evidence of convergence between actual and expected returns to top-rated QI horses would support the above assumption, and hence a Quarb-based betting strategy. Although this is primarily a cross-sectional study, we seek to say something about the dynamics of the market by applying the QI as an absolute measure to two sets of data: one drawn from a set of prices available at 9 a.m. each morning (9 a.m. markets), and the other from a set of prices available at 10.30 a.m. (10.30 a.m. markets). If an active Quarb strategy is practised by market participants, we might expect to see lower QI values in the 10.30 data.

4.4 Data

We estimated the favourite-longshot bias from starting price (SP) data (odds obtaining at the start of the race) for 12,800 races (Dataset One) run during two UK flat racing seasons, 2000 and 2001, acquired from Adams (2002). Note that these were available only as the number of winners to runners in various odds categories. It was therefore not possible to use this dataset in our Quarb analysis.

There is no obvious method of odds classification which can accommodate the data with a full range of odds values that are significant when weighted by total runners per class in the SP data. An answer to this problem, traceable to Weitzman (1965), is to classify odds according to a measure of the monetary rate of return to a nominal winner at given odds to a unit bet, including stake. In relation to our bookmaker data used to estimate the favourite-longshot bias, runners were classified by SP according to the closest whole-number rate of return corresponding to their odds. This largely solved the problem of specifying classes having an insignificant number of runners in the SP data, especially in the shortest-odds categories.

The datasets used to test the Quarb model and the associated betting strategy were twofold: the first (Dataset Two) sampled races for which a range of bookmakers offered fixed odds at 9 a.m., summarised in the trade press; the second (Dataset Three) sampled races for which Internet prices were available (acquired at 10.30 a.m. on race day).

Dataset Two contains odds arrays for 549 races, covering the period 1999–2003. Dataset Three has corresponding data for 700 races, covering 2001–2003. Races were drawn from Flat and National Hunt (jump) racing seasons during the respective periods. It was not possible to gather matched prices for the same races between Datasets Two and Three, as the 9 a.m. price matrices are obtained from *The Racing Post* Pricewise column, which covers only a small number of races (typically three or four per week); in order to collect data for a representative sample of races in Dataset Two we therefore had to sample from a period prior to that of Dataset Three. It was not possible to match the two datasets fully, as odds arrays on the Internet were not available before 2001.

Adjustments to nominal winning returns implied by the odds in the dataset had to be made for non-runners announced at 9 a.m. and 10.30 a.m., respectively. Odds paid out on winning horses in races where there are non-runners are governed by Weatherbys' Rule 4; a proportion of winnings is deducted to reflect the fact that the absence of one or more intended runners after a bet is struck effectively leaves bookmakers with likely losses due to an under-round book (where the sum of implied probabilities contained in the odds is less than 1). In practice, the application of this rule is not clear-cut, so a working rule was adopted for Datasets Two and Three whereby deductions from winnings were made by the multiplication of winning odds to the ratio:

$$\frac{\sum p_{nr}^s}{\sum p_{nr}^s + \sum p_{ij}^s}$$

where p_{nr}^s is the subjective probability of non-runners implied by the mean odds in the matrix prior to their withdrawal.

While this method was useful for adjusting actual returns for non-runners in specific races, it could not be used in relation to expected returns (outlined in section 4.5), as the latter had to be calculated from QIs, which could not be adjusted to reflect non-runners. This is because the structure of prices in a reformed market is typically significantly different from the original, reflecting subsequent race-specific information other than that relating to non-runners. For this reason we adjusted expected returns downwards by 3 per cent across the board in both datasets, this being an approximation of the impact of non-runners in aggregate, based on a comparison of nominal returns with adjusted returns for each dataset.

During the first two years of the sample period for Dataset Two, off-course deductions of 9 per cent of stakes were levied in the UK (comprising taxation of 6.75 per cent and other bookmaker levies). At the same time, however, bookmakers made competitive concessions to bettors on tax, in anticipation of the tax being abolished by the government. Our broad estimate of the overall impact of these influences in Dataset Two is 3–5 per cent of returns, but no downward adjustment is made to returns in Dataset Two, so as to facilitate comparison between the two datasets. Readers should therefore keep in mind the impact of tax on returns in Dataset Two. No other significant monetary transaction costs were apparent in relation to the two datasets.

4.5 Results

In table 4.1 we summarise the estimate of the functional relationship between objective and subjective probabilities referred to previously, from which our estimate of fl across the range of odds was derived. In table 4.2 we summarise the values of QI calculated in relation to Dataset Two, with corresponding returns to the chosen betting strategy outlined above (unit stake to win on sole top rated). Column (1) of table 4.2 shows the cumulative numbers of horses with top rated QIs up to specific values over 100. This amounts to a filter whereby initially only top-rated horses with an index of 100 are included, then increasing the filter ceiling incrementally by 1 per cent, until the highest-value QIs are reached. Adopting this approach enables us to identify any convergence of returns on their expected value as more races are drawn into the cumulative calculation, whilst enabling inference of the marginal impact of successively higher QI values on returns. Column (2) of table 4.2 indicates the cumulative win rate for each value of QI; column (3) shows the cumulative profit to a 1-point stake; column (4) gives the cumulative net profit at each filter level; and column (5) shows the corresponding return as a percentage of stakes. For reference, the return to all horses top rated between 90 and 100 is also included. Column (6) of table 4.2 shows the expected cumulative return, adjusted downwards by 3 per cent for non-runners, for each QI filter level weighted by runners (and hence stakes) in each cumulative QI category – these values are the returns we would predict to achieve over a long series of bets, if our assumption concerning the accuracy of the outlier relative to the mean is correct. In table 4.3 we summarise the corresponding information for Dataset Three. Finally, figures 4.1 and 4.2 show cumulative returns and expected cumulative returns against the QI filter level for Datasets Two and Three, respectively.

Table 4.2. *Quasi-arbitrage index (QI), profit, returns and expected returns, by filter level for Dataset Two*

(1) QI filter value Cumulative 100 to:	(2) Number of qualifiers	(3) Win rate (%)	(4) Net profit (points)	(5) Actual return (%)	(6) Expected return (%)
100	38	21.05	19.59	51.55	−3.00
101	59	23.73	39.22	66.48	−2.73
102	90	25.56	51.7	57.45	−2.23
103	118	27.12	73.03	61.89	−1.77
104	152	24.34	65.44	43.05	−1.22
105	184	21.20	40.24	21.87	−0.71
106	209	21.05	47.30	22.63	−0.30
107	229	19.65	38.30	16.72	0.05
108	244	19.67	36.81	15.09	0.33
109	264	18.56	24.81	9.4	0.73
110	280	18.21	20.31	7.25	1.07
111	296	17.57	19.31	6.52	1.42
112	312	18.27	26.44	8.47	1.79
113	322	18.01	25.44	7.9	2.03
114	327	18.04	29.44	9.00	2.16
115	332	17.77	24.44	7.36	2.30
116	334	17.96	31.44	9.41	2.36
117	342	17.84	28.44	8.32	2.62
118	350	17.71	30.98	8.85	2.89
119	355	17.46	25.98	7.32	3.07
120	358	17.32	22.98	6.42	3.18
121	360	17.22	20.98	5.83	3.26
122	365	16.99	15.98	4.38	3.46
123	369	16.80	11.98	3.25	3.63
124	371	16.71	9.98	2.69	3.72
129	373	16.62	7.98	2.14	3.84
130	375	16.53	5.98	1.59	3.95
131	376	16.49	4.98	1.32	4.02
133	377	16.45	3.98	1.06	4.08
136	378	16.40	2.98	0.79	4.15
90–100	143	23.78	44.67	31.24	−3 to −13
Non-runners	28				
N	549				

Table 4.3. *Quasi-arbitrage index (QI), profit, returns and expected returns, by filter level for Dataset Three*

(1) QI filter value Cumulative 100 to:	(2) Number of qualifiers	(3) Win rate (%)	(4) Net profit (points)	(5) Actual return (%)	(6) Expected return (%)
100	56	30.36	7.83	13.97	−3.00
101	96	28.13	4.94	5.15	−2.58
102	148	23.65	−10.15	−6.86	−2.03
103	176	23.86	−8.90	−5.06	−1.70
104	220	23.18	−14.90	−6.77	−1.16
105	251	23.11	−20.48	−8.16	−0.77
106	280	22.86	−20.58	−7.35	−0.38
107	299	23.75	−1.55	−0.52	−0.10
108	320	23.13	−2.55	−0.80	0.23
109	341	23.17	−3.72	−1.09	0.59
110	358	22.91	−4.97	−1.39	0.89
111	377	22.81	−5.68	−1.51	1.25
112	386	22.54	−10.35	−2.68	1.43
113	404	22.03	−18.85	−4.66	1.81
114	422	22.51	−6.94	−1.64	2.20
115	434	22.81	0.56	0.13	2.47
116	438	22.60	−3.44	−0.78	2.57
117	446	22.87	7.16	1.60	2.78
118	453	22.74	7.90	1.75	2.96
119	459	22.66	6.27	1.37	3.14
120	464	22.63	5.02	1.08	3.28
121	476	22.90	14.14	2.97	3.66
122	479	23.17	20.89	4.36	3.75
123	482	23.44	26.89	5.58	3.85
124	486	23.25	22.89	4.71	3.99
125	490	23.27	23.39	4.77	4.14
126	496	22.98	17.39	3.51	4.37
127	502	22.91	19.39	3.86	4.60
128	505	22.77	16.39	3.25	4.72
129	506	22.73	15.39	3.04	4.77
130	506	22.73	15.39	3.04	4.77
131	509	22.59	12.39	2.43	4.90
132	511	22.70	21.39	4.19	5.00
133	512	22.85	23.89	4.67	5.05
134	517	22.63	18.89	3.65	5.30
136	521	22.65	24.02	4.61	5.51
138	522	22.80	26.43	5.06	5.57

Table 4.3. *(cont.)*

(1) QI filter value Cumulative 100 to:	(2) Number of qualifiers	(3) Win rate (%)	(4) Net profit (points)	(5) Actual return (%)	(6) Expected return (%)
141	523	22.94	30.93	5.91	5.63
142	524	22.90	29.93	5.71	5.69
148	525	22.86	28.93	5.51	5.77
150	526	22.81	27.93	5.31	5.85
153	527	22.77	26.93	5.11	5.93
160	528	22.73	25.93	4.91	6.03
164	531	22.79	32.93	6.20	6.34
170	532	22.74	31.93	6.00	6.45
171	533	22.70	30.93	5.80	6.57
90–100	146	23.97	−15.77	−10.80	−3 to −13
Non-runners	21				
N	700				

4.6 Discussion

First, we consider Dataset Three, as the results conform with our expectation. As indicated in table 4.3 and figure 4.2, in respect of Dataset Three, actual returns at low QI filter values (100 and just over) are generally less than expected, but this can be explained by sampling error. As more races are drawn in as the filter value increases, actual returns converge reassuringly on expected returns. The overall pattern offers support for the concept of Quarbs in this market. Dataset Two presents a different picture, however. Actual returns at lower QI filter values considerably exceed their expected values; again, this could be due to sampling error. Convergence of actual and expected returns occurs up to a filter value of around 120, but actual returns beyond 120 continue to decline alarmingly; the record of top-rated horses with a QI value of over 120 in this sample was very poor. One explanation for this may be that the races chosen for the Pricewise matrix, from which the sample was exclusively drawn, have a high proportion of races with large fields of runners, often very competitive handicaps, where the average runner has a relatively low probability of winning. In such races, the QI of the most likely winners, according to the betting odds, tends to be inflated in the normalisation process outlined earlier, as the adjustment for the favourite-longshot bias reduces the index for the

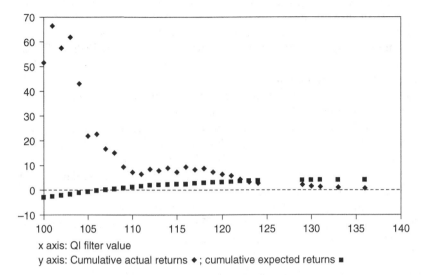

x axis: QI filter value
y axis: Cumulative actual returns ♦ ; cumulative expected returns ■

Figure 4.1 Cumulative actual and expected net returns per cent, by QI filter value, Dataset Two

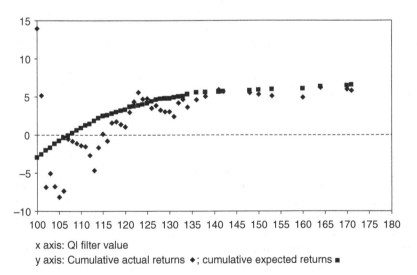

x axis: QI filter value
y axis: Cumulative actual returns ♦ ; cumulative expected returns ■

Figure 4.2 Cumulative actual and expected net returns per cent, by QI filter value, Dataset Three

majority of runners to very low levels. The marginal impact of this effect is probably influential at QI filter levels higher than 120, hence the rather systematic decline in returns. The same effect is not evident in Dataset Three, as the races for which fixed odds are available on the Internet at 10.30 a.m. tend to be more representative of the population of races, with a much wider variety of race types. The level of expected returns for Dataset Three, reinforced by their proximity to actual returns as QI increases, suggest the reasonable prospect of a profitable betting strategy based on Quarbs, with the proviso that there may be liquidity constraints on the degree to which stakes can be scaled upwards. The expected returns for Dataset Two do not encourage the same level of confidence that a similar betting strategy would pay in relation to 9 a.m. markets, especially when one factors in the impact of the abolition of deductions on bets arising from the radical overhaul of the system of UK betting taxation in October 2001. Indeed, the expected returns are not encouraging. Actual returns at low QI filter values over 100 are very high, but this may be due to sampling error. Our earlier observation of the inability of our estimate of the favourite-longshot bias to model the differential impact of the bias adequately in relation to field size provides a possible reason why we find higher returns for low QI values than for high values.

In respect of the dynamics of the market, we might expect to see Quarb values reducing between 9 a.m. and 10.30 a.m. The fact that actual returns converge on expected returns at approximately 3–3.5 per cent in Dataset Two, whereas they do so at approximately 5 per cent in Dataset Three, is contrary to this expectation. Changes in deductions and the distortions introduced by our normalisation procedure suggest, however, that we should not rely too much on this comparison. It is clear that further research into market dynamics will require a much more complete set of matched data as well as a somewhat modified Quarb model.

4.7 Conclusion

We find some evidence of weak form inefficiency in relation to our set of horse-race markets, using a simple Quarb model, enabling a profitable betting strategy based on an expected value rule. We find that the Quarb model is a good predictor of outcomes of races for which prices are available at 10.30 a.m. For races with prices available at 9 a.m., subject to sampling error, it appears that a betting strategy based on top rated QI filter values only marginally better than 100 would be more successful than one which uses high QI values (120 or over). This represents an anomaly in the model, which we explain by distortions caused by our normalisation procedure. Further exploration of Quarb opportunities in relation to these markets should include at least one other variable – i.e. the number of runners, in the initial estimation of the favourite-longshot bias.

Note

1 Vaughan Williams (2000, 2001) introduces this terminology.

References

Adams, M. (2002) *Secrets of Successful Betting*, Newbury: Raceform, pp. 147–50

Bird, R. and McCrae, M. (1987) 'Tests of the Efficiency of Racetrack Betting Using Bookmaker Odds', *Management Science*, 33(12), pp. 1552–62

Fama, E. F. (1970) 'Efficient Capital Markets: A Review of Theory and Empirical Work', *Journal of Finance*, 25(2), pp. 383–417

Hausch, D. B., Ziemba, W. T. and Rubinstein, M. (1981) 'Efficiency of the market for racetrack betting', *Management Science*, 27(12), pp. 1435–1452

Paton, D. and Vaughan Williams, L. (2005) 'Forecasting Outcomes in Spread Betting Markets: Can Bettors Use "Quarbs" to Beat the Book?', *Journal of Forecasting*, forthcoming

Shin, H. S. (1993) 'Measuring the Incidence of Insider Trading in a Market for State-Contingent Claims', *Economic Journal*, 103, pp. 1141–53

Tuckwell, R. (1983) 'The Thoroughbred Gambling Market: Efficiency, Equity and Related Issues', *Australian Economic Papers*, 22, pp. 106–8

Vaughan Williams, L. (1999) 'Information Efficiency in Betting Markets', *Bulletin of Economic Research*, 51(1), pp. 1–30

  (2000) 'Index Investment Markets and Information Efficiency', *Global Business and Economics Review – Anthology* 2000, pp. 24–9

  (2001) 'Can Bettors Win? A Perspective on the Economics of Betting', *World Economics*, 2(1), pp. 31–48

Vaughan Williams, L. and Paton, D. (1997) 'Why is there a Favourite-Longshot Bias in British Racetrack Betting Markets?', *Economic Journal*, 107(440), pp. 150–8

Weitzman, M. (1965) 'Utility Analysis and Group Behaviour: An Empirical Study', *Journal of Political Economy*, 73(1), pp. 18–26

5 The presence of favourites and biases in bookmakers' odds[1]

William Collier and John Peirson

5.1 Introduction

There is an extensive literature on the well-known longshot-favourite bias in the odds offered by bookmakers on horse-races, see Figgis (1951), Dowie (1976), Royal Commission on Gambling (1978), Tuckwell (1983), Crafts (1985), Henery (1985), Bird and McCrae (1987), Shin (1991, 1992, 1993), Jullien and Salanié (1994), Vaughan Williams and Paton (1997, 1998) and the authoritative survey by Vaughan Williams (1999). The motivation of this short chapter is to consider the empirical evidence and theory behind the proposition that the odds offered on a horse by bookmakers will depend on the other horses in the race. Past empirical evidence and theory appears not to have considered that the odds offered on a horse may depend on the other horses in the race.

Intuitively, one might expect that the most likely horse to affect the odds offered on other horses is the favourite. The odds on favourites vary from as little as 25 to 1 on to as much as 14 to 1 against. The bias in very short odds is minimal but for less strong favourites the bias is greater. It is suggested that strength of favourite may affect the degree of bias in the odds offered on other horses. On the basis of British flat horse-race statistics for 1993, it is shown that the degree of bias in odds offered on horses is positively related to the presence of strong favourites. Two possible explanations are proposed for this relation. First, for the bookmakers to make a reasonable profit on races with a strong favourite means that the bias on other horses must be substantial. However, in races with weak favourites, for bookmakers to make a reasonable return does not require them to offer dramatically unfair odds on the remaining horses. A second possible explanation is that in races without strong favourites, the horses are more similar and bookmakers offer more competitive odds than in races where the market is dominated by betting on a strong favourite. The underlying answer to the causes of the impact on bias on odds resulting from the presence of strong favourites is not answered completely in this chapter and remains open to further investigation.

5.2 Bias in British bookmakers' odds

In order to determine the impact of the presence of favourites on the odds offered on other horses, it is necessary to estimate the relation between bias and offered odds. This estimation is carried out on a large dataset of odds and outcomes of 3,388 British flat races run between March and November 1993.[2]

All possible odds categories were considered and, for each category, the observed probability, p_i, was calculated from the ratio of the number of horses winning and aggregate number of horses in the category. As the intervals between odds categories vary markedly,[3] the analysis in this chapter uses the price of a ticket that pays one pound on the horse winning. The relation between odds o_i, and the implied ticket price, q_i, is

$$q_i = \frac{1}{1 + o_i}$$

From the observed probabilities, it is possible to estimate relative biases, b_i, for each of the odds/price categories using the formula

$$b_i = \frac{p_i}{q_i} - 1$$

Figure 5.1 reports the data and estimated relationship between bias and price for the 34,789 horses which ran in British flat races between March and November 1993. Estimating a locally weighted regression of bias on price reveals a highly non-linear relationship and the standard longshot-favourite bias.[4]

5.3 The impact of offered odds of the presence of favourites

The major proposition under investigation in this study is the impact of favourites on the odds offered on other horses. The presence of a strong favourite in a horse race is likely to affect the betting on other horses. Strong favourites tend to attract a lot of betting and bookmakers tend to lose money on races in which a strong favourite wins. There is considerable anecdotal evidence to support this proposition; for example the *Royal Commission on Gambling* (1978: 471) reports that 'if one of the fancied horses wins, the bookmakers lose, but if one of the outsiders wins, they win'. The low bias and relatively large amounts bet on strong favourites may be explained by high elasticities of demand for betting on favourites.

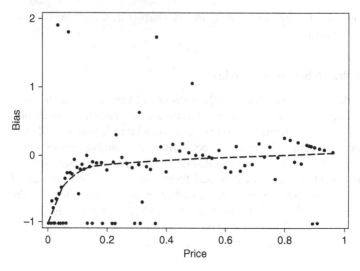

Figure 5.1 Estimated relationship between bias and price

High elasticities of demand for betting on a horse will result in fairer odds being offered by profit maximising bookmakers (see Peirson, 1988). Fairer odds and a high elasticity in turn lead to a relatively large amount being bet on favourites. The fairness in the odds and the relative amount bet are likely to increase with the strength of favourite. Additionally, the objective probability of the favourite winning increases with the strength of favourite and the level of bias decreases (see figure 5.1 for evidence on some of these propositions).

The previous analysis makes clear that favourites have three particular characteristics. They have the least bias in their prices, the highest probability of winning a race and the most amount bet on them. These characteristics all increase with the strength of favourite. It is thus of interest to examine how the strength of favourite affects the odds offered on other horses.

This analysis is carried out by dividing the data into races with strong favourites, moderate favourites and weak favourites.[5] The biases identified in figure 5.1 are caused by the observed probabilities of a horse winning in each price category. Thus, to investigate the relationship further one should consider the observed probabilities in the different race and price categories. Hence, for each class of race, we estimate the relationship between the probability of winning and price. Figure 5.2 gives the predicted probability and price relationship for horses in strong and weak favourite races using the locally weighted regression methods outlined in section 5.2.

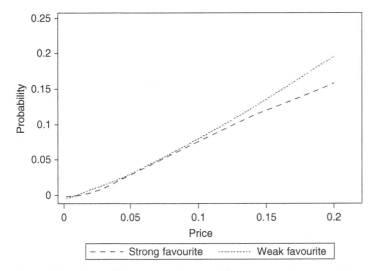

Figure 5.2 Estimated bias–price relationships for horses in races with either strong or weak favourites

It is clear that for horses in races with strong favourites, the predicted probabilities are relatively less than for similarly priced horses in races with weak favourites. Consequently, the bias for such horses is greater. Similar results hold for horses in races with moderate favourites when compared to those horses in races with either weak or strong favourites. It is important to demonstrate formally that the bias–price relationship differs significantly between these three race categories. To test this, we estimate a simple polynomial regression (cubic) between bias and price which includes intercept dummy variables capturing the type of favourite present in each race (i.e. strong, moderate or favourite). We find that this specification is rejected against a more general specification in which the slope as well as the intercept is allowed to differ between the different races. Furthermore, these interactive terms are both individually and jointly significant.[6] These results indicate that the bias–price differs substantially and statistically significantly between the different race categories.

5.4 Explanations of the impact of favourites on the biases in odds

The empirical analysis shows clearly that the presence of strong favourites is associated with greater biases in the prices of the other horses in a race.

Apart from the important exception of the presence of insiders,[7] little attention has been paid to possible causes in differences in biases between different races.

Three explanations are suggested to explain the impact of strong favourites on the biases in the prices of other horses. First, if a strong favourite runs in a race then the bias in the price will be low. For bookmakers to make a reasonable profit on such races requires the bias on the remaining horses to be high and relatively greater than in other races. This suggestion emphasises that bookmakers set a book of prices on a race and do not set prices horse by horse. For this to be a profit-maximising strategy. The demand for betting on non-favourites must be less elastic when there is a strong favourite. This allows a more biased profit maximising price to be set on these non-favourite horses.

The second and related suggestion is that in races with weak favourites, the horses are more similar and represent reasonably close substitutes. If horses in a race are similar and, in terms of betting, represent close substitutes, one would expect the profit-maximising price to be less biased than otherwise. Investigation of this suggestion requires measurement of the closeness of substitution between horses in a race.

The third suggestions relates to the existence of insider information. The most important development in the economics of setting of odds is the analysis of insider information and how it affects the bias in the bookmakers' odds; see Shin (1991, 1992, 1993) Vaughan Williams and Paton (1997) and Cain, Law and Peel (2001a, 2001b). The standard theory of insider information assumes that the probability of there being such information is the same across all races, see Shin (1991, 1992, 1993). To explain the above statistical results would require that the presence of insider information is more likely in races with a strong favourite. The average number of horses in races with a strong favourite is smaller than that observed in the other race categories.[8] The presence of a strong favourite and a smaller field of horses suggests that insider information may be less rather than more likely than that expected *a priori*. Though a possible explanation of the statistical result, the authors believe that a greater likelihood of insider information in races with a strong favourite is the least plausible of the offered explanations.

5.5 Conclusions

This chapter considers the impact of the odds offered on the favourite in a race on the bookmakers' odds on other horses. To the knowledge of the authors, empirical investigation of the relationship between odds and biases for horses in the same race has not been carried out before. It is shown that the presence of a strong favourite increases the bias in the prices offered on other horses in a race.

Three possible causes of this statistical observation are offered. First, in the presence of a strong favourite with nearly fair odds, bookmakers set more biased odds on the remaining odds to obtain a reasonable profit. Secondly, in races without a strong favourite, horses are more similar and the demand for betting on such horses is more elastic. Consequently, bookmakers have to set fairer odds than when demand is less elastic. The second and first causes are closely related. Finally, though perhaps least plausibly, bookmakers may believe that insider information is more likely to exist in races with a strong favourite.

Notes

1 We have benefited greatly from the assistance of Philip Blackburn. We are grateful for discussions with and comments from Leighton Vaughan Williams. Remaining errors and omissions in this chapter are the responsibility of the authors.
2 The data was collected from *Sporting Life 1993* and *Flat Results and Raceform 1993*, with the omission of races with deadheats.
3 For example, there is a gap of 100 units between 200/1 and 300/1, but a gap of only 0.1 between evens and 11/10.
4 See Goodall (1990) for a survey of smoothing techniques.
5 A 'strong favourite' is defined as having odds of less than or equal to evens, a 'moderate or equal to 3/1 and a 'weak favourite' has odds of greater than to 3/1.
6 A joint test of whether the coefficients on the interactive terms are equal to zero yields an F-statistic of $F(8,34777) = 2532.67$ ($p = 0.00$).
7 See Shin (1991, 1992, 1993), Vaughan Williams and Paton (1997) and Cain, Law and Peel (2001a, 2001b).
8 The average number of horses in races with strong, moderate or weak favourites is 8.86, 10.91 and 15.76, respectively.

References

Bird, R. and McCrae, M. (1987) 'Tests of the Efficiency of Racetrack Betting Using Bookmaker Odds', *Management Science*, 33(12), pp. 1552–62

Cain, M., Law, D. and Peel, D. (2001a) 'The Relationship between Two Indicators of Insider Trading in British Racetrack Betting', *Economica*, 68(169), pp. 97–104

(2001b) 'The Incidence of Insider Trading in Betting Markets and the Gabriel and Marsden Anomaly', *The Manchester School*, 69(2), pp. 197–207

Crafts, N. F. R. (1985) 'Some Evidence of Insider Knowledge in Horse Race Betting in Britain', *Economica*, 52, pp. 295–304

Goodall, C. (1990) 'A Survey of Smoothing Techniques', in J. Fox and J. S. Long (eds.), *Modern Methods of Data Analysis*, Newbury Park, CA, Sage, pp. 126–66

Jullien, B. and Salanié, B. (1994) 'Measuring the Incidence of Insider Trading: A Comment on Shin', *Economic Journal*, 104, pp. 1418–9

Peirson, J. (1988) 'The Economics of the Setting of Odds on Horse Races', Paper presented at the Fourth International Conference on the Foundations and Applications of Utility, *Risk and Decision Theory*, Budapest, June

Royal Commission (1978) *Royal Commission on Gambling* (Chairman Lord Rothschild), Cmnd. 7200-I & II, London: HMSO

Shin, H. S. (1991) 'Optimal Betting Odds against Insider Traders', *Economic Journal*, 101, pp. 1179–85

(1992) 'Prices of State Contingent Claims with Insider Traders, and the Favourite-Longshot Bias', *Economic Journal*, 102, pp. 426–35

(1993) 'Measuring the Incidence of Insider Trading in a Market for State-Contingent Claims', *Economic Journal*, 103, pp. 1141–53

Tuckwell, R. (1983) 'The Thoroughbred Gambling Market: Efficiency, Equity and Related Issues', *Australian Economic Papers*, 22, pp. 106–8

Vaughan Williams, L. (1999) 'Information Efficiency in Betting Markets: A Survey', *Bulletin of Economic Research*, 51(1), pp. 1–30

Vaughan Williams, L. and Paton, D. (1997). 'Why is There a Favourite-Longshot Bias in British Racetrack Betting Markets?', *Economic Journal*, 107, pp. 150–8

(1998). 'Why are Some Favourite-Longshot Biases Positive and Some Negative?', *Applied Economics*, 30, pp. 1505–10

6 Searching for semi-strong form inefficiency in the UK racetrack betting market

Ming-Chien Sung, Johnnie E. V. Johnson
and Alistair C. Bruce

While there is a large body of literature devoted to the study of various aspects of the efficiency of betting markets, and especially horse-race betting markets, there are contexts for and forms of analysis that remain significantly underrepresented. Hence, studies which seek to identify weak form inefficiency are relatively common compared with those which investigate the presence of semi-strong or strong form inefficiency. Equally, the dominant means of analysis has been to explore opportunities for pockets of abnormal returns associated with a single variable or a closely related set of variables, rather than a wider set of factors. This study seeks to redress these imbalances in the body of empirical work by focusing on semi-strong form efficiency of horse-race betting markets, using a multi-variable approach seen previously in only a limited number of studies.

Furthermore, while the overwhelmingly dominant setting for betting market analysis has been the US *parimutuel* market, this contribution focuses instead on the UK *bookmaker* market. The appeal of investigating the UK context is based on a number of institutional factors which discriminate it markedly from the US setting and which, *prima facie*, might give grounds for expecting differences in efficiency characteristics.

The following section offers a brief review of the literature relating to betting market efficiency and charts those characteristics of the UK horse-race betting market context which render it distinctive from other settings for empirical enquiry.

6.1 Literature and context

6.1.1 Semi-strong form betting market efficiency

Studies exploring semi-strong form efficiency in racetrack betting markets examine the degree to which publicly available information is efficiently

179

incorporated into odds. These studies fall into the following four broad categories, based on the type of publicly available information on which they focus:

(i) *Parallel market* studies (e.g. Gabriel and Marsden, 1990, 1991; Hausch and Ziemba, 1990; Leong and Lim, 1994; Bruce and Johnson, 2001; Cain, Law and Peel, 2001; Peirson and Blackburn, 2003).

(ii) *Professional prediction* studies (e.g. Figlewski, 1979; Snyder, 1978; Losey and Talbott, 1980; Bird and McCrae, 1987; Vaughan Williams, 2000; Smith, 2003).

(iii) Models based on a *single type of publicly available information*, such as *post-position* (e.g. Canfield, Fauman and Ziemba, 1987; Betton, 1994; Busche and Walls, 2000; Walls and Busche, 2003; Bruce, Johnson and Tang, 2004).

(iv) Models incorporating a *range of types of publicly available information* (e.g. Bolton and Chapman, 1986; White, Dattero and Flores, 1992; Benter, 1994; Chapman, 1994; Edelman, 2003; Gu, Huang and Benter, 2004).

The broad conclusion to emerge from the first set of studies is that differences exist in odds in parallel markets (e.g. odds offered in two different locations on the same race), but that technical difficulties and the costs involved in trying to exploit these differences may well prevent this information being used profitably. Studies exploring the value of professional predictions find that this information is discounted in final odds. Models incorporating a single type of publicly available information (e.g. post-position, betting volume) with odds have been shown to provide more information than those based on odds alone. However, these differences are often small and disappear in the longer run. Consequently, taken together, the first three sets of studies suggest that the horse-race betting market is largely semi-strong form efficient. In contrast, models for predicting the winning probability of a horse, based on a range of variables constructed from publicly available information, have been shown to produce profitable trading strategies. These contrasting results may occur because members of the betting public are able to successfully analyse and incorporate individual pieces of publicly available information (e.g. post-position) but have more difficulty in integrating all published information simultaneously.

The results of these multi-variable models have been in the public domain for several years and the efficient market hypothesis would suggest that profitable trading using these models should by now have been eroded. However, these models have largely been developed for races in the US and Hong Kong, in a parimutuel betting market, and it is our hypothesis that the betting context in the UK is so different that profitable trading based on a multi-variable model might still be possible. We now identify those distinctive features of the UK horse-race betting market context which may make this possible.

6.1.2 The betting context

The UK horse-race betting market has traditionally been regarded as unusual due to the co-existence of distinctly different market forms in terms of structure and process. Hence parallel bookmaker and parimutuel markets exist for all horse-racing events. The UK context is also relatively unusual in terms of the co-existence of on-course and off-course betting, while the nature of UK horse-racing, compared with that in the US, is notable for its great diversity in terms of track types, the structure of race meetings and even the style of racing itself. There are various ways in which one might hypothesise that the idiosyncrasies of the UK context could impact on semi-strong efficiency. On the one hand, these could include the competing away of pockets of abnormal return via cross-market arbitrage activity. On the other, there is the possibility of superior returns based on informational advantages enjoyed by on-course versus off-course bettors or by aficionados of a particular track and its eccentricities. The non-formulaic nature of odds-setting in bookmaker markets may also be a factor, where bookmakers may seek deliberately to manipulate odds in order to influence the perceptions (and actions) of bettors in relation to a particular horse's chances of success.

However, as indicated above, it is not the purpose of this chapter to frame narrow hypotheses around one or other potentially influential factor: rather, the aim is to conduct an exploratory, but extensive, analysis of a wide set of institutional and environmental variables in testing their collective ability to predict horses' probabilities of success.

Our hypothesis is that the unique context of the UK market will permit the achievement of positive returns using a similar multi-variable model to that adopted by Bolton and Chapman (1986) for races in the US and Benter (1994) and Chapman (1994) for races in Hong Kong; despite the fact that these models have been in the public domain for a number of years. We explain below the procedures adopted to test this hypothesis.

6.2 Methodology

6.2.1 Data and variables

As indicated above, racetracks in the UK, unlike the US and Hong Kong, are highly idiosyncratic in terms of configuration, ground conditions, size of market and relevant knowledge of market participants, etc. Consequently, the data employed in this study is limited to one racetrack, Goodwood, and involves 556 races (5,947 runners) run between May 1995 and August 2000. In order to mirror Bolton and Chapman's (1986) study, this sample includes only races involving horses of age 3 or more, thus reducing problems associated with incomplete form records and the instability of performances which can be associated with younger horses.

In order to test our hypothesis we have incorporated explanatory variables similar to those used by Bolton and Chapman (1986); these are based largely on the previous performances of both the horse and jockey. However, in the UK, because races are run on turf it is widely known that the ground (or going) conditions can have a significant effect on race results. In addition, races in the UK are generally run over a wider spectrum of distances than for the races in the US. Consequently, we include explanatory variables to account for some aspects of the going and distance. We also include some missing value indices in the model, because some of the explanatory variables which are derived from previous races run by a horse or a jockey may be missing. Consequently, if a particular variable is missing (e.g. a horse's speed rating in its previous race would be missing if the horse has not run before) it is given the value of zero and its missing value index takes the value 1. In so doing, we overcome the problem of having too many invalid values and it enables us to explore the statistical significance of missing values. The definitions of each variable used in our model are presented in table 6.1.

6.2.2 Method

Our aim is to develop a conditional logit model to predict the probability of a horse winning a given race based on both the fundamental variables indicated above and the public's perception of its likelihood of winning (determined from the bookmakers' final odds on the horse). We achieve this in three stages.

In the first stage we develop a conditional logit model to predict the probability of a horse i winning race j as follows:

$$p_{ij} = \frac{\exp(\beta V_{ij})}{\sum_{i=1}^{n_j} \exp(\beta V_{ij})}$$

where V_{ij} is the vector of fundamental variable values associated with horse i in race j (indicated in table 6.1), β is the vector of parameter values and n_j is the number of runners in race j. This model is estimated for 200 races run between May 1995 and May 1997, using maximum likelihood procedures.

Table 6.1. *Definitions of the independent variables employed in the model*

Independent variables	Definition of variables
avgsr4	The horse's speed rating in its last four races; value of zero when there is no past run
disavesr	The average speed rating of the past runs of each horse at this distance; value of zero when no previous run
disdummy	1 indicates that the horse has run at this distance before; 0 otherwise
draw	Post position in current race
eps	Total life-time earnings up to race date; i.e. (money prize earned by the horse when it finished first, second or third)/Number of races entered
go_avesr	The average speed rating of the all past runs of the horse on this going; value of zero when no previous run
godummy	1 indicates that the horse has run on the current race's going before; 0 otherwise
jnowin	The number of wins by the jockey from May 1995 to date of race
jst1miss	1 indicates the situation when variables calculated from the previous race run by each jockey are missing; 0 otherwise
jwinper	The winning percentage of the jockey from May 1995 to date of race
lst1miss	1 indicates the situation when variables calculated from the previous race run by each horse are missing; 0 otherwise
lst4miss	1 indicates the situation when variables calculated from the past four races run by each horse are missing; 0 otherwise
newdis_B	1 indicates a horse that ran three or four of its last four races at a distance of 80 per cent less than current distance, and 0 otherwise or missing values
pre_s_ra	Speed rating for the previous race in which the horse ran
weight	Weight carried by the horse in current race
win_run	The percentage of the races won by the horse since May 1995

Since our sample size (200) is relatively small we employ a process described by Chapman and Staelin (1982) to 'explode' the dataset. Essentially, this involves considering a given race as a set of independent horse races. Consequently, an explosion to depth two would include races to determine the overall winner of the race and races (excluding the ultimate winners) to determine which horse wins the race to be second. An explosion to depth three would also include the races (excluding the winner and the second) to determine which horse wins the race to be third, etc. There is a danger that once it becomes obvious to the jockey that the horse will not finish in the first three (where prize money is available) they will have little incentive to encourage it to run to its full potential. Consequently, the reliability of the rank order finishing data may decrease for such horses. Consequently, we restrict our search for the optimal 'depth of explosion' to a maximum of level three; that is, to those races for the first three finishers. In addition we observe the following value for models developed for depth of explosion one, two and three:

$$\widehat{R}^2 = 1 - \frac{L(\theta = \widehat{\theta})}{L(\theta = 0)}$$

where the numerator is the log-likelihood value of the model with the parameters estimated and the denominator is the log-likelihood value of a random choice model with no parameter estimated. When the estimated parameters completely explain the occurrence of the dependent variables, the numerator will approach zero; consequently, $\widehat{R}^2$ will approach unity. Therefore, the higher is the $\widehat{R}^2$, the better is the model. We investigate the $\widehat{R}^2$ for each depth of explosion; a reduction in $\widehat{R}^2$ would suggest that it has introduced unreliability to the rank order finish data. In addition, we also conduct a formal test suggested by Watson and Westin (1975), to explore whether the dataset based on the ultimate winner can be pooled with the dataset of races for second place (i.e. where the ultimate winner has been excluded), and so on.

Having determined the appropriate depth of explosion and the parameter values for the fundamental model at stage one we then seek to combine the probability estimates produced by this model with probability estimates derived from final odds. To achieve this we adopt the approach employed by Benter (1994). Consequently, at stage two we develop a second conditional logit model, where the probability of horse i winning race j is given as follows:

$$P_{ij} = \frac{\exp\left(\alpha O_{ij} + \delta p_{ij}^l\right)}{\sum_{i=1}^{n_j} \exp\left(\alpha O_{ij} + \delta p_{ij}^l\right)}$$

where O_{ij} is the log of the normalised probability of horse i winning race j derived directly from its final odds, p^t_{ij} is the log of the probability of the horse winning derived from the fundamental model developed at stage one and α and δ are parameters to be estimated (using maximum likelihood procedures) from a second set of 200 races (run between May 1997 and May 1999).

At stage three we develop a 'Kelly wagering strategy' (Kelly, 1956) based on the model developed at stage two, but applied to a holdout sample of 154 races run between May 1999 and August 2000. The Kelly strategy requires that in race j we bet a fraction $f_j(i)$ of our current wealth on horse i, and this is chosen by comparing the model probability with the odds of the horse, in such a way that the total wealth grows at an exponential rate, with a zero probability of ruin. If the betting strategy produces a positive return, this is taken as evidence that although the models of Bolton and Chapman (1986), Benter (1994) and Chapman (1994) have been in the public domain for a number of years, the unique context of the UK market results in this information not being fully discounted in final odds.

6.3 Results

6.3.1 Stage 1

The parameter values for the sixteen non-price-related (i.e. fundamental) variables in the conditional logit model discussed above, were estimated (for depths of explosion one, two and three) using the first subset of 200 races. The $\hat{R}^2$ values of these models increased slightly as the explosion depth increased from one to three (0.3905, 0.3944 and 0.4044, respectively) suggesting that the explosion process did not introduce random 'noise' resulting from an increase in the unreliability of the rank order finish data. We compute the log-likelihood (LL) values for models to predict the race winner (a) with all runners included ($E = 1$), (b) when the first past the post is excluded (i.e. the race to finish second) ($E = 2$) – ($E = 1$), (c) when the first two past the post are excluded (i.e. the race to finish third) ($E = 3$) – ($E = 2$)), (d) for races defined by (a) and (b) together (i.e. explosion depth two: ($E = 2$)) and (e) for races defined by (a), (b) and (c) together (i.e. explosion depth three: ($E = 3$)). These values are given in table 6.2. To test whether it is appropriate to explode the sample we employ the sequential pooling and hypothesis testing procedure suggested by Watson and Westin (1975), whereby a LL ratio test is used to compare the LL of the explosion depth two ($E = 2$) with that from ($E = 1$) and ($E = 2$) – ($E = 1$) combined; where the LL ratio is defined as -2 $\{LL(E = 2) - [LL(E = 1) + LL((E = 2) - (E = 1))]\}$. In a similar manner

Table 6.2. *Log-likelihood values for determining the optimal explosion depth*

Choice group	No. of races	Log-likelihood value	LL ratio	χ^2_{16} (0.05)
(E = 1)	200	− 414.5929		
(E = 2) − (E = 1)	199	− 394.5352		
(E = 3) − (E = 2)	198	− 380.8755		
(E = 2)	399	− 821.8538	25.4514	26.30
(E = 3)	597	− 1,209.3150	13.1714	26.30

we compare the *LL* of the explosion depth three (E = 3) with (E = 2) and (E = 3) − (E = 2) combined. The resulting values are distributed χ^2_n, where *n* is the number of parameters in the model (i.e. sixteen). The results of these tests are given in table 6.2 and it is clear that the test statistics for both explosion depths two and three are less than their critical values, suggesting that we cannot reject the view that these samples come from the same population. We conclude, therefore, that it is possible to pool the independent races (a), (b) and (c), defined above (i.e. to use explosion depth three).

Consequently, we report, in table 6.3, the parameter and associated *t* values for each of the sixteen non-price variables in the conditional logit model discussed above, for explosion depth three (i.e. 597 races) derived from the first subset of 200 races.

A *LL* ratio test, which compares the model indicated in table 6.3 with one where the parameter values are set to zero, indicates that, collectively, the sixteen fundamental variables offer considerable explanatory power (*LL* ratio = 1642.38, χ^2_{16} (0.05) = 26.30). It is not strictly appropriate to consider the influence of individual factors in terms simply of their individual statistical significance, and indeed the objective of this study is explicitly to consider the variable set as a whole. Nonetheless, the highly significant factors at least prompt some speculation as to what might be driving the overall significance of the variable set. Of the five individual variables which appeared as significant at the 5 per cent level, one was associated with the draw of the horse – that is, its starting position on the track – one with the lifetime earnings of the horse, two with the horse's speed rating and one with jockey-related variables. An obvious factor linking these is their status as relatively easily accessible public domain information which, were these the critical factors determining the predictive power of the model, might constitute a surprising basis for the generation of abnormal returns.

Table 6.3. *The 'first-stage' conditional logit model for explosion depth three*

Variable	Coefficient	Standard error	t-value	p-value
avgsr4	0.0075	0.0035	*2.1560	0.0311
disavesr	0.0008	0.0025	0.3282	0.7427
disdummy	0.1002	0.1632	0.6142	0.5391
draw2	0.0340	0.0126	*2.6925	0.0071
eps	0.2e-05	0.1e-05	*2.2504	0.0244
go_avesr	0.0010	0.0026	0.3880	0.6980
godummy	−0.1709	0.1737	−0.9836	0.3253
jnowin	0.0024	0.0009	*2.6241	0.0087
jst1miss	0.9022	0.4623	1.9518	0.0510
jwinper	1.4272	0.7719	1.8490	0.0645
lst1miss	−0.1232	0.2737	−0.4502	0.6526
lst4miss	−0.1484	0.1304	−1.1384	0.2549
newdis_b	−0.4234	0.3534	−1.1978	0.2310
pre_s_ra	0.0038	0.0019	*2.0416	0.0412
weight	0.0115	0.0066	1.7556	0.0792
win_run	0.3253	0.3587	0.9070	0.3644

Note: * = Significant at the 5 per cent level.

6.3.2 Stage 2

At the second stage we develop, using a second set of 200 races (May 1997–May 1999), a conditional logit model, which includes the natural logarithm of (a) the estimated probability from the first-stage model (p'_{ij}) and (b) the normalised probability implied by the final odds (o_{ij}). This model was estimated by exploding the 200-race dataset to depths of one, two and three. As in stage one, both the $\hat{R}^2$ values of these models (0.4219, 0.4242 and 0.4275, respectively, for depths one, two and three) and the Watson and Westin (1975) sequential pooling and hypothesis testing procedure confirmed that exploding to depth three was appropriate. The parameter values and test statistics for the explosion to depth three (594 races) are given in table 6.4.

The results suggest that the log of the probability value derived from final odds is most significant in explaining winning probability, but that the log of the probability derived from the fundamental variables is also significant (at the 6.86 per cent level). We compare the log-likelihood of the model combining both these variables with the log-likelihood of a model incorporating only the log of the probability value derived from the final odds, using a LL ratio test (LL of combined model $= -1156.64$,

Table 6.4. *The 'second-stage' conditional logit model for explosion depth three*

Variables	Coefficient	Standard error	t-value	p-value
O_{ij}	0.9620	0.0815	11.80	0.0000
p^l_{ij}	0.1677	0.0921	1.82	0.0686
Model statistics				
$L\,(\theta=0)$	$-2,020.31$			
$L\,(\theta=\hat{\theta})$	$-1,156.64$			
LL-ratio statistic	1,727.34			
(Critical value)				
$(\chi^2_2(.05))$	(5.99)			
$\hat{R}^2$	0.42750			

LL of odds-based model $= -1158.30$, LL ratio statistic $= 3.32$, χ^2_1 $(0.10) = 2.71$). This result is significant at the 10 per cent level, suggesting that while final odds clearly incorporate the bulk of information concerning winning probabilities, the addition of the fundamental variables to the model adds some predictive power over a model based on odds alone. In other words, the results from incorporating non-price data imply a semi-strong inefficiency, whereby prices fail to accommodate fully all outcome-relevant information.

6.3.3 Stage 3

The third stage of the process involves testing the robustness of the composite model by using it to generate predictions for a further dataset of 156 races (run between May 1999 and August 2000). The results of adopting a Kelly wagering strategy based on these probability predictions are shown in figure 6.1. The log of our cumulative wealth increases from zero (our initial wealth) to 0.31. This implies that our wealth increases by a factor of 1.36 as a result of betting on these 156 races. This compares very favourably with naïve strategies of placing £1 on every runner (wealth decreases by 25.60 per cent) or betting to obtain a return of £1 should a horse win, thereby lessening the impact of the favourite-longshot bias (wealth decreases by 16.51 per cent).

6.4 Interpretation and discussion

The results presented here are interesting, for two main reasons. First, and most central, is the ability of the non-price data to enhance the predictive

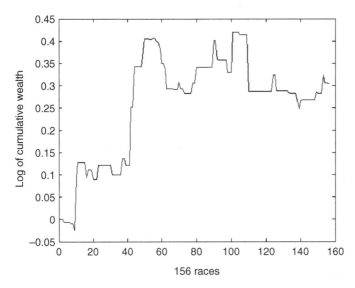

Figure 6.1 Cumulative wealth as a result of applying a full Kelly wagering strategy for holdout sample

value of a pure odds-based model. While the odds-only model is still significantly the most successful predictor, it seems clear that there is information somewhere within the fundamental variable set which is not fully factored into prices. The significance of this result is amplified when one considers that in the UK bookmaker market context, bettors are trading with active suppliers (bookmakers) who on average generate returns significantly in excess of US parimutuel operators. Yet it is in this comparatively unfavourable context that evidence for successful betting strategies emerges.

The second striking feature relates to the apparent robustness of the composite predictive model through time. Whilst the original fundamental model was developed using a set of horse-races from 1995–97, the model clearly continues to add value to predictions based on odds alone by stage three of the analysis, which employs data from 1999–2000. In addition, the model we develop is similar to the ones developed by Bolton and Chapman (1986), Benter (1994) and Chapman (1994) and yet the model appears to enable profitable trading at least five years after the details of these models have been published. What is interesting about this is how or why identified bases for semi-strong inefficiency appear to remain invulnerable to learning by agents in the betting market. This persistence of inefficiency may of course reflect the complexity of the relationship between the non-odds factors and race outcome – where, for example, complex interdependencies between variables might remain opaque to those populating the market. It is an accepted feature of decision-making in general, and horse-race betting in particular, that decisions will often be based on relatively simplistic partial use of information – involving, for example, the employment of heuristics in the face of complex and turbulent sets of diverse types of variable. Thus, for example, bettors' decisions may be driven by their belief that the jockey's current form, or the draw or the 'going', or some crude combination of these factors, constitutes a sensible heuristic device. There is clearly scope here for further work to identify the exact origin of the value added from the fundamental variables, though this is not likely to be straightforward and is manifestly outside the scope of this chapter.

It is interesting, nonetheless, to engage in some preliminary speculation as to why the UK bookmaker market seems to offer potential for the profitable exploitation of inefficiencies. Here, a starting point is to return to some of the broad environmental and institutional distinctions outlined earlier in this chapter. This might suggest that any tendency for cross-market arbitrage opportunities to erode profitable opportunities is less influential than the edge which certain subsets of the betting population might enjoy by virtue of, for example, their presence at the racecourse or their accumulated knowledge of racecourse idiosyncrasies. Yet, ultimately, arguments for such higher-performing subsets of the betting population based on racecourse attendance or specialist course knowledge or any other acquired expertise are difficult rationally to sustain when one considers that the suppliers who ultimately determine the market prices and with whom any such privileged bettors must engage are professional on-course bookmakers.

A rather different potential line of explanation might argue that the co-existence of parimutuel and bookmaker markets in the UK may lead to information overload on bettors, who (compared with, for example, their US counterparts) must not only weigh the relative value of each parallel market, but who, additionally, face a range of bookmakers with varying price menus. Consequently, their ability to, additionally, employ a complex model involving fundamental variables might be impaired. From the supply side point of view, of course, bookmakers in the UK, unlike parimutuel operators in the US or elsewhere, are aware that they are competing for betting revenue with other bookmakers and the parimutuel market. While, in general, bookmakers returns exceed parimutuel takes, this may be less marked, or even inverted, where the level of bookmaker competition is particularly high, as might be anticipated to be the case at a major venue such as Goodwood. The ability to trade profitably using composite models such as those developed here might therefore vary across different racetracks. To this end, there would seem to be some potential in extending the above type of analysis to other venues, with materially different degrees of inter-bookmaker competition.

Ultimately, the most appropriate conclusion to this analysis is that it generates some interesting evidence for the existence and durability of semi-strong inefficiency characteristics in UK bookmaker betting markets but that reliably isolating the origins of these inefficiencies requires further careful investigation.

References

Benter, W. (1994) 'Computer Based Horse Race Handicapping and Wagering Systems: A Report', in Donald B. Hausch, Victor S. Y. Lo and William T. Ziemba (eds.), *Efficiency of Racetrack Betting Markets*, New York: Academic Press, pp. 183–98

Betton, S. (1994) 'Post Position Bias: An Econometric Analysis of the 1987 Season at Exhibition Park', in Donald B. Hausch, Victor S. Y. Lo and William T. Ziemba (eds.), *Efficiency of Racetrack Betting Markets*, New York: Academic Press, pp. 511–26

Bird, R. and McCrae, M. (1987) 'Tests of the Efficiency of Racetrack Betting Using Bookmaker Odds', *Management Science*, 33, pp. 1552–62

Bolton, R. N. and Chapman, R. G. (1986) 'Searching for Positive Returns at the Track: A Multinomial Logit Model for Handicapping Horse Races', *Management Science*, 32, pp. 1040–60

Bruce, A. C. and Johnson, J. E. V. (2001) 'Efficiency Characteristics of a Market for State Contingent Claims', *Applied Economics*, 33, pp. 1751–4

Bruce, A. C., Johnson, J. E. V. and Tang, L. L. (2004) 'The Value of Trading Volume Information in a Market for State-Contingent Claims', Unpublished paper

Busche, K. and Walls, W. D. (2000) 'Decision Costs and Betting Market Efficiency', *Rationality and Society*, 12(4), pp. 477–92

Cain, M., Law, D. and Peel, D. A. (2001) 'The Incidence of Insider Trading in Betting Markets and the Gabriel and Marsden Anomaly', *The Manchester School*, 69, pp. 197–207

Canfield, B. R., Fauman, B. C. and Ziemba, W. T. (1987) 'Efficient Market Adjustment of Odds Prices to Reflect Track Biases', *Management Science*, 33, pp. 1428–39

Chapman, R. G. (1994) 'Still Searching for Positive Returns at the Track: Empirical Results from 2,000 Hong Kong Races', in Donald B. Hausch, Victor S. Y. Lo and William T. Ziemba (eds.), *Efficiency of Racetrack Betting Markets*, New York: Academic Press, pp. 173–81

Chapman, R. G. and Staelin, R. (1982) 'Exploiting Rank Ordered Choice Set Data Within the Stochastic Utility Model', *Journal of Marketing Research*, 19, pp. 288–301

Edelman, D. (2003) 'Adapting Support Vector Machine Methods for Horse-race Odds Prediction', Conference Paper for the 12th International Conference on Gambling and Risk Taking, Vancouver BC, June

Figlewski, S. (1979) 'Subjective Information and Market Efficiency in a Betting Market', *Journal of Political Economy*, 87(1), pp. 75–89

Gabriel, P. E. and Marsden, J. R. (1990). 'An Examination of Market Efficiency in British Racetrack Betting', *Journal of Political Economy*, 98(4), pp. 874–85

(1991) 'An Examination of Efficiency in British Racetrack Betting: Errata and Corrections', *Journal of Political Economy*, 99(3), pp. 657–9

Gu, M. G., Huang, C. and Benter, W. (2003) 'Multinomial Probit Mock for Competitive Horse Racing', *Working Paper of the Chinese University of Hong Kong*

Hausch, D. B. and Ziemba, W. T. (1990) 'Arbitrage Strategies for Cross-Track Betting on Major Horse Races', *Journal of Business*, 63, pp. 61–78

Kelly, J. L. (1956) 'A New Interpretation of Information Rate', *Bell System Technical Journal*, 35, pp. 917–26

Leong, S. M. and Lim, K. G. (1994), 'Cross-Track Betting: Is the Grass Greener on the Other Side?', in Donald B. Hausch, Victor S. Y. Lo and William T. Ziemba (eds.), *Efficiency of Racetrack Betting Markets*, New York: Academic Press, pp. 617–29

Losey, R. L. and Talbott, J. C. (1980) 'Back on the Track with the Efficient Markets Hypothesis', *Journal of Finance*, 35, pp. 1039–43

Peirson, J. and Blackburn, P. (2003) 'Betting at British Racecourses – A Comparison of the Efficiency of Betting with Bookmakers and at the Tote', in L. Vaughan Williams (ed.), *The Economics of Gambling*, London: Routledge Taylor & Francis, pp. 30–42

Smith, M. A. (2003) 'The Impact of Tipster Information on Bookmakers' Prices in UK Horse-Race Markets', in L. Vaughan Williams (ed.), *The Economics of Gambling*, London: Routledge Taylor & Francis, pp. 67–79

Snyder, W. W. (1978a) 'Horse Racing: Testing the Efficient Markets Model', *Journal of Finance*, 33, pp. 1109–18

Vaughan Williams, Leighton (2000) 'Can Forecasters Forecast Successfully? Evidence from UK Betting Markets', *Journal of Forecasting*, 19, pp. 505–13

Walls, W. D. and Busche, K. (2003) 'Breakage, Turnover and Betting Market Efficiency – New Evidence from Japanese Horse Tracks', in L. Vaughan Williams (ed.), *The Economics of Gambling*, London: Routledge Taylor & Francis, pp. 43–66

Watson, P. L. and Westin, R. B. (1975) 'Transferability of Disaggregated Mode Choice Models', *Regional Science and Urban Economics*, 5, pp. 227–49

White, E. M., Dattero, R. and Flores, B. (1992) 'Combining Vector Forecasts to Predict Thoroughbred Horse Race Outcomes', *International Journal of Forecasting*, 8, pp. 595–611

7 Models, markets, polls and pundits: a case study of information efficiency

Leighton Vaughan Williams

In this chapter, I will offer a brief perspective on alternative methodologies designed to gauge the state of the 2004 US Presidential election race at a given point in time and to forecast the outcome of the race. At the time of final data collection and completion (Tuesday, 5 October 2004) the election is four weeks away. The reader can make some judgement of the relative and absolute merits of the alternative methodologies with the advantage of the actual results to hand.

Section 7.1 considers econometric models and section 7.2 considers polling evidence. Section 7.3 considers the forecasts of a panel of 'experts'. Section 7.4 examines evidence from the various betting markets. Section 7.5 summarises the findings, and concludes.

7.1 Econometric studies

The application of economic indicators to forecast election outcomes can be traced to Kramer (1971) and Stigler (1973) for US congressional election, to Fair (1978) and Hibbs (1982) for US Presidential elections and to Lewis-Beck (1988) and Palmer and Whitten (1999) for elections in other industrialised countries.

A survey of economic models for predicting Australian elections (Wolfers and Leigh, 2002) indicates the importance of including unemployment and inflation as key factors in the forecasting mix, with Jackman and Marks (1994) noting an additional incumbency advantage. Jackman (1995) includes a 'honeymoon' effect for novice governments and Cameron and Crosby (2000) the impact of the world wars.

Recent econometric studies of US Presidential elections typically contain a 'share-of-the-vote' dependent variable for each of the major Presidential candidates, together with a number of predictors of that share.

Norpoth (2004) is a recent example of this sort of model. The parameters of his vote model are electoral support for the major-party candidates in the nominating phase – i.e. the 'primary' elections – long-term voter partisanship between the political parties – and the Presidential 'vote cycle'. These parameters are estimated using data from all Presidential elections since 1912 (see also Midlarsky, 1984; Norporth, 1996, 2001, 2002; Norpoth and Rusk, 2003). Norpoth's model estimates victory in the two-party share of the vote for George Bush in 2004 by 54.7 per cent to 45.3 per cent, figures first posted on 29 January 2004.

Abramowitz (2004) uses a 'time-for-change' model (see also Abramowitz, 1988, 1996, 2001) to predict the election outcome more than three months prior to polling day. This model is based on three variables – a 'time-for-change' dummy variable based on whether the President's party has controlled the White House for only one term or for more than one term, the change in real gross domestic product (GDP) during the first two quarters of the election year, and the incumbent President's net approval rating in the final Gallup Poll in June of the election year.

Estimating the time-for-change model with data from the Presidential elections ranging from 1948 to 2000 inclusive yields an estimate of 53.7 per cent for George Bush's share of the major-party vote in 2004 (with a standard error of plus or minus 2.0 percentage points).

Cuzan and Bundrick (2004a) – see also Cuzan, Heggen and Bundrick, 2003 – employ a 'fiscal model', which they add to Abramowitz's (2004) 'time-for-change' model to obtain results which they argue are superior to those obtained with Abramowitz's original model. To clarify, 'fiscal policy' is measured by a binary variable that takes two values– 'expansionary' and 'cutback'. Fiscal policy is defined as 'expansionary' if fiscal spending as a proportion of GDP has increased between Presidential elections at the same rate as or at a higher rate than in the previous term; it is defined as 'cutback' if, since the last election, there has been a deceleration in spending. Other things equal, they argue, an expansionary policy is associated with a reduced vote share for the incumbent and a cutback policy with an increased vote share.

Using their synthesis of the time-for-change and a fiscal model, they downgrade Abramowitz's (2004) estimate of the Bush two-party vote share from 53.7 per cent to 51.97 per cent (as of 3 April 2004), with a standard error of plus or minus 1.7 percentage points. Cuzan and Bundrick (2004b) update their estimates using revised GDP growth figures to estimate (as of 1 August 2004) a vote share figure for George Bush of 51.1 per cent, with a standard error of 1.9 percentage points.

Wlezien and Erikson (2004a) estimate an equation which uses Leading Economic Indicator (LEI) growth, Presidential approval ratings and, in one version, latest polling data on voting intention ('trial-heat' polling) to estimate vote share. Specifically, the LEI measure used is the weighted average of quarterly summaries of monthly growth, with each quarter weighted 0.90 as much as the following quarter. The measure of approval is, except for the last quarter of the election cycle (when the latest available month's figures are used), the average percentage of the public, according to 'Gallup', who approves of the President's performance during each particular quarter or the most recent quarter for which data is available. The 'trial-heat' polling is based on a selection of polls.

As of 28 June 2004, the model without the 'trial-heat' polling data predicts 52.8 per cent of the two-party vote for Bush, and with that polling data (judged by Wlezien and Erikson, 2004a as a more reliable forecast) a 52.2 per cent share of the vote. An updated forecast (August 27, 2004), provided by Wlezien and Erikson (2004b) yields an estimate of 52.9 per cent for Bush using the first model, and 51.7 per cent when adding in late-August trial-heat poll results.

Fair (2002a) – see also Fair (2002b) – uses data from all US Presidential elections between 1916 and 2000 to predict vote share on the basis of three economic variables (two measures of real *per capita* income growth and one of inflation) and four political variables (incumbency, terms in office, party and war). The war variable took on a dummy value of 1 for 1920, 1944 and 1948, but 0 otherwise.

At the beginning of November 2002, this model predicted a Bush two-party vote share of 55.57 per cent. By 29 April 2004, this had been revised upward to 58.74 per cent, and corrected to 57.48 per cent in an estimate provided at 31 July 2004 (Fair, 2004).

Hibbs (2004) – see also Hibbs (2000) – employs a 'bread and peace' model of US Presidential voting. The model is based on an economic variable and a war variable. The economic variable is a weighted average of quarterly growth rates of real disposable income *per capita*, calculated from the first full quarter of each Presidential term through to the election quarter. The war variable is derived from evidence of the electoral effect of the cumulative number of killed-in-action in the wars in Korea and Vietnam, which Hibbs shows to be linked negatively to the party in office when the war was initiated.

As of 26 July 2004, Hibbs estimates that the likely combinations of cumulative military fatalities in Iraq and weighted-average real income growth over the current Presidential term yield an expected two-party vote for George Bush of around 53 per cent.

Lewis-Beck and Tien (2004) – see also Lewis-Beck and Tien (2000, 2001) – offer a 'jobs model' which holds the two-party popular vote share to be a function of July presidential popularity, six-month GNP change (interacted with whether or not the President is running), incumbent party advantage

Table 7.1. *Estimates of two-party vote, 2004*

	Vote	
Model	Bush (%)	Kerry (%)
Norpoth (2004)	54.7	45.3
Abramowitz (2004)	53.7	46.3
Cuzan and Bundrick (2004b)	51.1	48.9
Wlezien and Erikson (2004b)	51.7	48.3
Fair (2004)	57.5	42.5
Hibbs (2004)	53	47.0
Lewis-Beck and Tien (2004)	49.9	50.1
Campbell (2004)	53.8	46.2

and job growth over the administration. All measures are taken mid-summer of the election year. Their regression model is estimated over the 1952–2000 period. As of 2 September 2004, their forecast for George Bush was that he would obtain 51.16 per cent of the two-party popular vote, with a standard error of 1.52 percentage points.

Campbell (2004) uses two variables in his forecasting model – the incumbent's share of the two-party vote in the first Gallup Poll published after US Labor Day and the growth rate for real GDP for the second quarter of the election year. Campbell (2001) explains the theoretical basis of the model. Campbell's model, as of 7 September 2004, predicted a share of the two-party vote for George Bush of 53.8 per cent.

A further perspective on the value of economic indicators in predicting election outcomes can be found in Jones (2002, 2004).

To summarise, the latest available estimates of the two-party vote share, using econometric modelling (Wlezien and Erikson 2004a), at the time of writing, are as in table 7.1.

7.2 The opinion polls

According to a study of the 2000 US Presidential election, conducted by the National Council on Public Polls (NCPP), the accuracy of the election projections based on the pre-election polls of 2000 was surpassed only by the polls of 1976 and 1960. Based on the final polls of ten polling organisations that used traditional methods for conducting their polls (live telephone interviews), the estimates had an average error of 1.1 percentage points for George Bush and Al Gore and an error of 1.3 per cent for Ralph Nader, who finished third in the popular vote.

Table 7.2. *Final poll estimates, 2000*

Polling organisation	Bush (%)	Gore (%)	Nader (%)	Undecided (%)	Other (%)
Zogby	46	48	5	0	1
CBS	44	45	4	5	2
Harris	47	47	5	0	1
Gallup/CNN/*USA Today*	48	46	4	0	2
Pew Research	49	47	4	0	0
IBD/CSM/TIPP	48	46	4	0	2
ICR/*Politics Now*	46	44	7	1	2
NBC/WSJ	47	44	3	4	2
ABC/*Washington Post*	48	45	3	3	1
Battleground	50	45	4	0	1
Actual result	**47.87**	**48.38**	**2.74**		**1.01**

Table 7.3. *Harris Interactive and Rasmussen estimates, 2000*

Polling organisation	Bush (%)	Gore (%)	Nader (%)	Undecided (%)	Other (%)
Harris Interactive	47	47	4	0	2
Rasmussen	49	40	4		
Actual result	**47.87**	**48.38**	**2.74**		**1.01**

The final estimates were as shown in table 7.2.

Harris also used an interactive online polling methodology (Harris Interactive), while Rasmussen used an automated recording interviewing system, with no live interviewer intervening. The results of these polling techniques were as shown in table 7.3.

There are three main issues which divide the methodological approaches of the major polling organisations.

- The first is whether to use live telephone interviews, automated digitally recorded telephone interviews, or on-line interactive interviews.
- The second is whether to weight the sample by the expressed party political allegiance or inclination of the respondents.
- The third is whether to weight the sample to include 'likely voters' or whether to use the entire sample of 'registered voters' – i.e. all voters who are registered and hence legally entitled to vote.

In the 2000 election, Rasmussen used an automated telephone interview system, skewed toward likely voters and unweighted by expressed party political preference. Since then, the methodology of the Rasmussen poll has changed in part to adjust for party weight and to reduce the tightness of the screening for likely voters (Scott Rasmussen, in e-mail correspondence with the author, 19 September 2004).

The CBS/*New York Times* survey for the 2004 race is unweighted by expressed party political preference, as are the Gallup and Pew Research surveys. The Zogby and NBC/*Wall Street Journal* polls, on the other hand, do adjust for self-described party identification. Zogby, for example, uses a party share of 39 per cent Democrats, 35 per cent Republicans and 26 per cent Independents to weight his poll (http://zogby.com/news/ReadNews.dbm?ID = 859). The basis for political weighting is the expressed political allegiance of the US electorate, derived from exit polls, comprised of self-identified Democrats, Republican and Independents.

Polling results are sometimes quoted with respect to the sample of all registered voters and sometimes of 'likely voters', measured differently depending on the methodology. For example, Gallup asks a series of questions that assigns voting probability to each respondent; it then uses their answers and an overall estimate of voter turnout to identify the likely electorate. A number of polling organisations quote findings for both 'likely' voters (as assessed) and 'registered' voters.

Convenient access to a selection of up-to-date polling surveys can be found at PollingReport (www.pollingreport.com), although this site does not list automated interview polls or Internet polls – see also: www.realclearpolitics.com.

As of Tuesday, 5 October 2004, polling figures from the following organisations stood as shown in table 7.4 (only polling taken after the first Presidential debate of 30 September, and concluding on or before 5 October is included).

7.3 The experts

Armstrong, Jones and Cuzan (2004) employ a forecasting methodology based on a survey of distinguished political scientists and other 'close observers' of the American electoral process. Their group of 'experts' use a procedure known as 'Delphi' to predict the two-party vote-share of the main candidates. In the Delphi procedure, each participant first makes an anonymous prediction of the most likely forecast of the vote, along with forecasts of a 'best case' and 'worst case' outcome for one of the candidates, offering reasons for each prediction. Next, panel members are shown the individual predictions made in the first round and the reasons given for them, as well as forecast averages and other descriptive statistics

Table 7.4. *Polling figures, 5 October 2004*

| | | | | Two-party share | |
Polling organisation	Bush (%)	Kerry (%)	Other responses (%)	Bush (%)	Kerry (%)
Zogby	46	43	11	51.7	48.3
CBS/*NY Times*	48	47	5	50.5	49.5
Gallup/CNN/*USA Today*	49	49	2	50.0	50.0
Pew Research	49	44	7	52.7	47.3
Newsweek	45	47	8	48.9	51.1
ABC/*Washington Post*	49	47	4	51.0	49.0
American Research Group	46	46	8	50.0	50.0
Democracy Corps (GQRR)	48	49	3	49.5	50.5
ICR	51	44	5	53.7	46.3
Fox/Opinion Dynamics	47	45	8	51.1	48.9
Rasmussen	47	47	6	50.0	50.0

for the group. Panellists are then asked to revise their estimates in light of this information.

On 2 August 2004, the median estimate (i.e. the group mid-point) was that John Kerry would obtain 50.5 per cent of the two-party vote. The panel was 95 per cent sure that Kerry's vote would be at least 48 per cent and not more than 54 per cent, again using the median scores. On 30 September 2004, the median estimate was that George Bush would obtain 51 per cent of the two-party vote. The panel was 95 per cent sure that Bush's vote would be at least 48 per cent and not more than 54 per cent. See Linstone and Turoff (2002) for further information on the Delphi methodology.

7.4 Betting markets

There are four basic types of betting market relevant to the US Presidential election – traditional fixed-odds (bookmaker) markets, real-money betting exchanges, play-money betting exchanges, and 'spread betting' markets.

In traditional markets, bookmakers offer odds on political events which are agreed (fixed) when the bet is struck. In a race such as the US Presidential election, where there are only two realistic outcomes, the fair odds would allow the bettor to break even by placing appropriate stakes on both candidates to win.

Say, for example, George Bush and John Kerry were both offered at 'Evens' (i.e. odds of 1 to 1). This means that a 1 unit stake on Bush would win 1 unit if Bush wins, with the stake returned. The stake on Bush is lost if Bush loses. A total stake of 2 units, therefore (1 on Bush and 1 on Kerry) yields a total return of 2 units if Bush wins and 2 if Kerry wins. These may be classified as 'fair' odds, in the sense that, with appropriate stakes, the bettor can guarantee a net profit/loss of zero, whoever wins. In general, odds are 'fair' if the sum of the implied probabilities in the odds equals 1.

In fact, bookmakers seek to make a profit and generally set odds which are less than fair – e.g. 0.5 to 1 about Bush, 1.5 to 1 about Kerry. A bettor must now stake 2 units on Bush to guarantee a net profit of 1, but that 1 unit staked on Kerry will earn a net profit of only 1.5 if Kerry wins. This is known as an 'over-round' book – i.e. the sum of the implied probabilities in the odds exceeds 1.

Although individual bookmakers seek to set an over-round book, bettors can choose among a range of bookmakers for the best price, so that it is often possible to find 'fair' odds (an over-round of 1), or even better, at best available odds. The concept of 'fair odds' does not imply that the odds reflect the objective probabilities, and indeed one of the prices may be very good value even if the combined odds are 'unfair' in the sense of an over-round book. Whatever the case, however, it is likely that bettor odds will be available by searching among a range of bookmakers than by consulting the price lists of just one firm.

There are a number of sites which list the odds available from a range of bookmakers, Oddschecker (www.oddschecker.com) being notable among these.

As of Tuesday, 5 October 2004, the over-round at best prices among the bookmakers selected by Oddschecker was 1.013, derived from a best price of 0.58 to 1 (implied probability = $1/1+0.58$) about Bush and a best price of 1.63 to 1 (implied probability = $1/1+1.63$) available about Kerry. The best prices available among mainstream bookmakers listed on the Oddschecker site were 0.53 (Bush) and 1.63 (Kerry), yielding an over-round (sum of implied probabilities) of: $1/(1+0.53)+1/(1+1.63) = 1.034$.

It is not clear, however, which of these prices is good value in terms of exceeding the unobserved objective probabilities of success, or whether one or both simply reflect or approximate to the actual objective probabilities, in which case the expected profit/loss to a bet is zero.

An analysis of the efficiency of bookmaker odds in predicting the outcome of the 2001 Australian Federal Election, in Wolfers and Leigh (2002), concluded that in fact the betting odds, as supplied by CentreBet, one of Australia's largest bookmakers, not only correctly forecast the outcome, but also provided very precise estimates of outcomes across a range of individual electorates.

'Betting exchanges' are a different type of betting medium, which operate without the need for a bookmaker. Instead, betting exchanges provide the technology to match up the best offers to back and lay an outcome on offer from clients of the exchange. This may or may not improve the predictive accuracy of the odds – in particular, Levitt (2004) argues that bookmakers are more skilled at predicting event outcomes than bettors.

Market leaders in the world of real-money exchanges are Betfair, Betdaq and Tradesports.

Tetlock (2004) surveys a range of data from Tradesports, finding evidence of a high degree of pricing efficiency in their financial contracts. Wolfers and Zitzewitz (2004) – see also Leigh, Wolfers and Zitzewitz (2003) – note, however, that trading responses in the Tradesports market about Iraq-related event outcomes suffered a slight lag relative to the responses in deeper financial markets. More generally, there is an obvious concern, particularly in relatively thin trading markets, that participants will be influenced by what they want to happen, rather than by a dispassionate assessment of the actual likelihoods. In particular, Forsythe, Rietz and Ross (1999) show evidence of biases in political trading based on party identification, while Strumpf (2004) demonstrates evidence of a similar bias by New York bettors towards the New York Yankees baseball team. An alternative hypothesis is that some traders may bet on the outcome they do not want to occur, as a means of hedging the potential disappointment. Wolfers and Zitzewitz (2004) make the important point, however, that market prices are driven by marginal traders, who are perhaps more likely to be motivated by profit than partisanship.

Another concern with betting markets is that they may be open to manipulation – for example, Wolfers and Leigh (2002) report candidates betting on themselves at long odds to create momentum, while Hansen, Schmidt and Strobel (2004) are sceptical of the use of what they term 'political stock markets' as substitutes for opinion polls based on evidence they find of political manipulation in identified political markets. Ultimately, the proof or otherwise lies in the results obtained, a point contained in Rhode and Strumpf's (2004) examination of wagering on US Presidential elections between 1868 and 1940. They conclude that betting markets over this period were fairly efficient despite the limited information of participants and despite attempts to manipulate the odds by political parties and newspapers.

The best offers available to anyone wishing to back either of the main candidates to win Election 2004, as of 5 October 2004, were as shown in table 7.5.

The Tradesports exchange works on a binary bet system – i.e. outcomes are classified on a 0 to 100 scale (100 = will happen, 0 = will not happen).

Table 7.5. *Odds on main candidates, 5 October 2004*

Organisation	Bush	Kerry	Over-round
Betfair	0.62	1.58	$1/1.62 + 1/2.58 = 1.005$
Betdaq	0.61	1.52	$1/1.61 + 1/2.52 = 1.018$

Bettors who 'buy' at the prevailing price win if the event happens and lose if it does not. Similarly, bettors who 'sell' at the prevailing price win if the event does not happen and lose if it does. In each case, profits/losses are in proportion to the difference between the expiry price (0 or 100) and the 'buy' or 'sell' price at the time of the bet, multiplied by the money at risk (calculated as a number of contracts). The prevailing market probability of a Bush win on Tradesports was 0.625, at the point of data collection, and 0.4 for Kerry. These translate to an over-round of: $0.625 + 0.4 = 1.025$. Converting these into odds gives the following:

Tradesports:

Effective Bush odds $= 1/0.625 - 1 = 1.6 - 1 = 0.6$ to 1

Effective Kerry odds $= 1/0.4 - 1 = 2.5 - 1 = 1.5$ to 1

Over-round $= 1/1.6 + 1/2.5 = 1.025$

'Play-money' exchanges – i.e. exchanges allowing bets without using real money – include Newsfutures (www.newsfutures.com), an exchange which specialises in news and current events issues, and the Foresight Exchange (www.ideosphere.com), which specialises in the outcomes of unresolved scientific and societal questions.

It is less clear that traders in these exchanges have the same incentive to use best available information, since real money is not at stake. However, a study of Foresight Exchange prices by Pennock, Lawrence, Giles and Nielsen (2001), based on information from 161 expired securities, finds that these prices did indeed correlate strongly with observed outcome frequencies. They found similar accuracy in another play-money market, the Hollywood Stock Exchange (www.hsx.com), in particular that prices of securities in Oscar, Emmy and Grammy awards correlated well with actual awards' outcome frequencies, and that prices of movie stocks accurately predicted real box office results. In a direct comparison of the forecasting efficiency of real-money and play-money markets, Servan-Schreiber, Wolfers, Pennock and Galebach (2004) examined the predictive power of prices from both types of market over the course of the

2003 National Football League (NFL) season, concluding that the real- and play-money markets yielded predictions that were of similar accuracy. Moreover, both sets of prices yielded more accurate predictions than all but a dozen of 3,000 people in an online contest.

The Newsfutures and Foresight exchanges work, like Tradesports, on a binary bet system – i.e. outcomes are classified on a 0 to 100 scale (100 = will happen, 0 = will not happen). The prevailing market probability of a Bush win on Newsfutures was 0.51, at the point of data collection, and 0.49 for Kerry. Converting these into odds gives the following:

Newsfutures:

Effective Bush odds = $1/0.51 - 1 = 1.96 - 1 = 0.96$ to 1

Effective Kerry odds = $1/0.49 - 1 = 2.04 - 1 = 1.04$ to 1

The prevailing market probability of a Bush win on the Foresight Exchange was 0.57, at the point of data collection, and 0.45 for Kerry. These translate to an over-round of: $0.57 + 0.45 = 1.02$. Converting these into odds gives the following:

Foresight exchange:

Effective Bush odds = $1/0.57 - 1 = 1.75 - 1 = 0.75$ to 1

Effective Kerry odds = $1/0.45 - 1 = 2.22 - 1 = 1.22$ to 1

The Iowa Electronic Markets (IEM), conducted by the University of Iowa College of Business, is one of the more long-standing markets (founded in 1988), and is operated for research and teaching purposes. Perhaps the best known of these markets is the Iowa Political Markets, which are designed so that prices should predict election outcomes (see also the Austrian Electronic Market and the University of British Columbia Election Stock Market). Members of the general public can trade in the Iowa political markets, but the maximum size of any individual trading account is $500. Bets can be placed on the winner of the popular vote in the Presidential election (the 'Winner-Takes-All' market), and the share of the two-party vote accruing to each candidate ('Vote-Share'). Berg, Forsythe, Nelson and Rietz (2001) – see also Berg and Rietz (2003) – survey the evidence for the efficiency of the Iowa markets as a predictor, concluding that 'its predictions were dramatically more accurate and stable than polls' (2003: 5). Berg, Forsythe and Rietz (1996) argue, however, that the forecasting efficiency of the market is linked to volume and the number of contracts – in particular, that larger more active markets (typically closer to the election) with fewer contracts (i.e. fewer candidates or parties) tend to be more accurate. More generally, empirical studies (Forsythe, Rietz and

Table 7.6. *Estimate of two-party vote-share Iowa markets*

Vote-share	Bush (%)	Kerry (%)
	51.4	48.6

Ross, 1999), laboratory investigations (Plott and Sunder, 1988) and policy proposals (Hanson, 1995) all argue that prices of real-money securities do indeed constitute accurate estimates of objective probabilities.

Chen and Ortner (1998) and Plott (2002) also find evidence that internal markets provided more efficient forecasts of specific aspects of company performance than did traditional planning tools.

The Iowa Electronic Markets work, like Tradesports, Newsfutures and the Foresight Exchange, on a binary bet system – i.e. outcomes are classified on a 0 to 100 scale (100 = will happen, 0 = will not happen). The prevailing market probability of a Bush popular vote win on the Iowa markets was 0.588, at the point of data collection, and 0.427 for Kerry. These translate to an over-round of: $0.588 + 0.427 = 1.015$. Converting these into odds gives the following:

Iowa political markets:

Effective Bush odds $= 1/0.588 - 1 = 1.7 - 1 = 0.7$ to 1

Effective Kerry odds $= 1/0.427 - 1 = 2.34 - 1 = 1.34$ to 1

Over-round $= 1/1.7 + 1/2.34 = 1.015$

The estimate of the two-party vote-share on the Iowa markets was as shown in table 7.6.

Spread betting originated in the UK in the mid-1970s, but developed rapidly in the late 1980s and 1990s. It is quite different to point spread betting, as operated in the US, which is essentially a fixed-odds 'handicap' betting system, in which bettors wager at fixed odds on one team to beat the other after points are artificially deducted from one of the teams. In spread betting, bettors are invited instead to buy or sell notional assets associated with an event (for example, corners in a soccer match), based on a 'spread' set by traders (bookmakers). If a bookmaker expects a match to contain, say, 11 corners, a typical spread may be set between 10.5 and 11.5. Bettors who expect the number of corners to exceed the top end of the spread (11.5) are invited to buy at this level. Similarly, bettors who expect the number of corners to fall short of the bottom end of the spread (10.5)

Table 7.7. *Offers by spread bookmakers, 5 October 2004*

Spread bookmaker	Electoral votes (Bush)	Electoral votes (Kerry)
IG Index	282–290	248–256
Sporting Index	280–288	250–258
IG Binary Bets	Bush 60–64	Kerry 36–40

are invited to sell at this level. The spread may move upwards or downwards before or during the course of the event until the value of the asset is known with certainty. At this point a bettor who bought (sold) the asset will win or lose the difference between the *ex post* value of the asset price at which the deal was made, multiplied by their original stake. The bettor may 'close' the trade at any time. Analysis of spread betting markets by Vaughan Williams (2000, 2001, 2004) and Paton and Vaughan Williams (2005), suggests that the mean of the mid-points of the spreads of all the companies offering a market (a 'Quarb' strategy') may, at least in some markets, provide the best indicator of the objective probability of occurrence of a defined outcome.

In terms of the US Presidential election, spread bookmakers typically set a spread about the number of electoral college votes that each candidate will win. Bettors may also be offered the opportunity to buy or sell on a scale of 0 to 100, with 100 being the payoff to a winning candidate, 0 the payoff to a losing candidate. A candidate on offer at, say, 2 to 1 against on the fixed-odds markets may, therefore, be on offer at, say, 31–35 on these markets (sometimes known as 'binary' markets.) In each case, the price reflects a probability of about 1 in 3 of the candidate winning the election.

As of 5 October 2004, offers by the spread bookmakers included those shown in table 7.7.

WSX, the US bookmaker, offers a binary-type bet of its own, which was offered at the time of data collection at:

Bush   60–64

Kerry   36–40

7.5 Summary and conclusion

The mean estimate of the two-party vote, using econometric models, on the latest figures available, was:

Bush share of the two-party vote: 53.2 per cent
Kerry share of the two-party vote: 46.8 per cent

The mean estimate of the two-party vote, using polling data, was:

Bush share of the two-party vote: 50.8 per cent
Kerry share of the two-party vote: 49.2 per cent

The mean updated estimate of the two-party vote, according to a panel of experts, using the Delphi forecasting technique, was:

Bush share of the two-party vote: 51.0 per cent
Kerry share of the two-party vote: 49.0 per cent

The estimate of the two-party vote, according to the Iowa electronic markets was:

Bush share of the two-party vote: 51.4 per cent
Kerry share of the two-party vote: 48.6 per cent

The estimate of the probability of a popular vote victory for each candidate, on the Iowa exchange, deflating the over-round to 1, was:

Bush probability of winning: 57.9 per cent
Kerry probability of winning: 42.1 per cent

The mean estimate of the probability of victory for each candidate, using the bookmaker odds, as listed on Oddschecker, adjusting for the margin in the odds (i.e. deflating the 'over-round', or sum of probabilities in the odds) to 1, was:

Bush probability of winning: 62.5 per cent
Kerry probability of winning: 37.5 per cent

The mean estimate of the probability of victory for each candidate, using the real-money traditional exchange Betfair odds, deflating the over-round to 1, was:

Bush probability of winning: 61.7 per cent
Kerry probability of winning: 38.3 per cent

The estimate of the probability of victory for each candidate, on the real-money binary exchange (Tradesports), deflating the over-round to 1, was:

Bush probability of winning: 61.0 per cent
Kerry probability of winning: 39.0 per cent

The mean estimate of the probability of victory for each candidate, using the play-money exchange odds, deflating the over-round to 1, was:

Bush probability of winning: 53.5 per cent
Kerry probability of winning: 46.5 per cent

The estimate of the probability of victory on the 'spread betting' (binary) markets, using the mid-point of the spread, was:

Bush probability of winning: 62 per cent
Kerry probability of winning: 38 per cent

The mean estimate of the number of electoral votes gained by each candidate (270 to win), using the mid-point of the spread, was:

Bush electoral votes: 285
Kerry electoral votes: 253

Armstrong (2001) – see also: http://morris.wharton.upenn.edu/forecast/Political/index.html – suggests combining some of these estimates according to a prescribed rule. For the purposes of this chapter, however, each of the estimates is left to stand independently.

In conclusion, we have a variety of snapshots and forecasts of the 2004 US Presidential election, sometimes very divergent in their assessments. In summary, the 'experts', the limited-stake trading exchange (Iowa 'vote-share' market) and the polling evidence all point to a similar outcome – i.e. George Bush with about 51 per cent of the two-party vote, and John Kerry with about 49 per cent. Although this is in line with one econometric forecasting model, the mean estimate of these models was significantly more favourable in respect of Bush (mean = 53.2 per cent Bush, 46.8 per cent Kerry).

As far as the probabilities of victory are concerned, the odds in all the real-money markets present a broadly similar picture – i.e. a 61–62 per cent chance for Bush, a 38–39 per cent chance for Kerry. The only exception is the Iowa market, played for limited stakes, which gives Bush a slightly smaller edge in terms of win probability (58 per cent compared to 42 per cent for Kerry). The play-money exchanges continue the trend, giving Bush a smaller edge still (a win probability of 53.5 per cent compared to 46.5 per cent for Kerry).

Should we rely exclusively on the econometric modelling, or an aspect of it, or the opinion polls, or an aspect of them, or the opinions of the 'experts' or one or more of the various types of betting markets, whether in assessing the objective probabilities of a given outcome at a given point in time or else as a forecast of a defined future point in time? Should we perhaps take an aggregate view which weights each of these methodologies in varying degrees? If so, what should an optimally weighted snapshot of the objective probabilities, or an 'optimally weighted forecast', look like, and is there a way of defining this through time? An examination of the final outcome of the 2004 US Presidential election should take us one further step along the path toward answering these critically important questions.

Appendix

On Tuesday, 2 November, at 12 noon GMT (7 am US Eastern time), the various methodologies offered the following results.

A.1 Econometric models

The mean estimate of the two-party vote, using econometric models, using the latest figures, was:

Bush share of the two-party vote: 53.2 per cent
Kerry share of the two-party vote: 46.8 per cent (table 7A.1)

Harris also used an interactive online survey, while Rasmussen used an automated recording interviewing system, with no live interviewer intervening (table 7A.3).

A.2 Opinion polls

The mean estimate of the two-party vote, using polling data, was:

Bush share of the two-party vote: 50.6 per cent
Kerry share of the two-party vote: 49.4 per cent (table 7A.2)

A.3 Panel of experts

In their final survey, completed in late October, the median estimate of the panel of experts was that George Bush would obtain 50.5 per cent of the two-party vote. The panel was 95 per cent sure that Bush's vote would be at least 48 per cent and not more than 53 per cent.

Table 7A.1. *Econometric models*

Model	Bush (%)	Kerry (%)
Norpoth (2004)	54.7	45.3
Abramowitz (2004)	53.7	46.3
Cuzan and Bundrick (2004b)	51.2	48.8 (updated, 29 October)
Wlezien and Erikson (2004a)	51.7	48.3
Fair (2004)	57.7	42.3 (updated, 29 October)
Hibbs (2004)	53.0	47.0
Lewis-Beck and Tien (2004)	49.9	50.1
Campbell (2004)	53.8	46.2

Table 7A.2. *Polling organisations*

Organisation	Bush (%)	Kerry (%)	Nader (%)
Zogby	48	47	1
CBS/*NY Times*	49	47	1
Harris	49	45	2
Gallup/CNN/*USA Today*	49	49	1
Pew Research	51	48	1
TIPP	51	48	1
NBC/*WSJ*	47	44	3
ABC/*Washington Post*	49	48	1
Battleground	50	46	1
Tarrance	51	48	1
Marist	49	50	1
Fox	46	48	1
Democracy Corps	49	50	1
ARG	48	48	1

Table 7A.3. *Harris and Rasmussen results*

Polling organisation	Bush (%)	Kerry (%)	Nader (%)
Harris online survey	47	49	2
Rasmussen	50	48	–
All polls average	48.9	47.7	1.3

A.4 Betting markets

The estimate of the two-party vote, according to the Iowa electronic markets was:

Bush 51.0 per cent; Kerry 49.5 per cent

The estimate of the probability of a popular vote victory for each candidate, on the Iowa exchange, deflating the over-round to 1, was:

Bush 52.0 per cent; Kerry 48.0 per cent

The mean estimate of the probability of victory for each candidate, using the bookmaker odds, as listed on Oddschecker, adjusting for the margin in the odds (i.e. deflating the 'over-round', or sum of probabilities in the odds) to 1, was:

Bush 56.2 per cent; Kerry 43.8 per cent

The mean estimate of the probability of victory for each candidate, using the real-money traditional exchange (Betfair) odds, deflating the over-round to 1, was:

Bush 56.0 per cent; Kerry 44.0 per cent

The estimate of the probability of victory for each candidate, on the real-money binary exchange (Tradesports), deflating the over-round to 1, was:

Bush 53.0 per cent; Kerry 47.0 per cent

The mean estimate of the probability of victory for each candidate, using the play-money exchange odds, was:

Bush 52.0 per cent; Kerry 48.0 per cent

The estimate of the probability of victory on the 'spread betting' (binary) markets, using the mid-point of the spread, was:

Bush 53 per cent; Kerry 47 per cent

The mean estimate of the number of electoral votes gained by each candidate (270 to win), using the mid-point of the spread, was:

Bush 272; Kerry 266

Actual share of the vote:
Bush 50.9 per cent; Kerry 48.1 per cent; Nader 0.3 per cent; others 0.6 per cent (does not add to 100 per cent because of rounding)
Source: Associated Press.
Actual electoral votes:
Bush 286; Kerry 252

References

Abramowitz, A. I. (1988) 'An Improved Model for Predicting Presidential Election Outcomes', *PS: Political Science and Politics*, 21, pp. 843–7
    (1996) 'Bill and Al's Excellent Adventure: Forecasting the 1996 Presidential Election', *American Political Quarterly*, 24, pp. 434–42
    (2001) 'The Time for Change Model and the 2000 Election', *American Politics Quarterly*, 29, pp. 279–82

(2004) 'When Good Forecasts Go Bad: The Time-for-Change Model and the 2004 Presidential Election', Unpublished paper, http://morris.wharton.upenn.edu/forecast/Political/PDFs/Abramowitz.pdf

Armstrong, J. S. (2001) 'Combining Forecasts', in J. S. Armstrong (ed.), *Principles of Forecasting: A Handbook for Researchers and Practitioners*, Boston: Kluwer Academic, pp. 417–39

Armstrong, J. S., Jones, R. J. and Cuzan, A. G. (2004) 'Experts Predict a Very Close Election; Slight Advantage to Kerry', August 2, unpublished, http://morris.wharton.upenn.edu/forecast/Political/Delphi_experts_prediction.html

Berg, J. and Rietz, T. (2003) 'Prediction Markets as Decision Support Systems', *Information Systems Frontiers*, 5(1), pp. 79–93

Berg, J., Forsythe, R. and Rietz, T. A. (1996) 'What Makes Markets Predict Well? Evidence from the Iowa Electronic Markets', in W. Albers, W. Guth, P. Hammerstein, B. Moldovanu and E. van Damme (eds.), *Understanding Strategic Interaction: Essays in Honor of Reinhard Selten*, New York: Springer, pp. 444–63

Berg, J., Forsythe, R., Nelson, F. and Rietz, T. (2001) 'Results from a Dozen Years of Election Futures Markets Research', in C. Plott and V. Smith (eds.), *Handbook of Experimental Economic Results*, New York: Elsevier

Cameron, L. and Crosby, M. (2000) 'It's the Economy Stupid: Macroeconomics and Federal Elections in Australia', *Economic Record*, 76(235), pp. 354–64

Campbell, J. (2001) 'An Evaluation of the Trial-Heat and Economy Forecast of the Presidential Vote in the 2000 Election', *American Politics Research*, 29, pp. 289–96

(2004) 'Election Forecast Calculator', unpublished paper, http://www.libarts.ucok.edu/yc/elect.php

Chen, K.-Y. and C. Plott (2002) 'Information Aggregation Mechanisms: Concept, Design and Field Implementation for a Sales Forecasting Problem', Social Science Working Paper, 1131, California Institute of Technology, March

Cuzan, A. G. and Bundrick, C. M. (2004a) 'Comparing the Time-for Change and Fiscal Models: A Synthesis?', Unpublished paper, http://morris.wharton.upenn.edu/forecast/Political/PDFs/CuzanandBundrick_Comparing_the_Time-for-Change.pdf

(2004b) 'Fiscal Effects on Presidential Elections: A Forecast for 2004', Paper prepared for presentation at the September meeting of the American Political Science Association, Chicago, 4 September, http://www.uwf.edu/govt/facultyforums/fiscaleffectsprselect2004.pdf

Cuzan, A. G., Heggen, R. J. and Bundrick, C. M. (2003) *Voters and Presidents: A Fiscal Model*, Philadelphia: Xlibris

Fair, R. (1978) 'The Effect of Economic Events on Votes for President', *Review of Economics and Statistics*, 60(2), pp. 159–73

(2002a) 'The Effect of Economic Events on Votes for President: 2000 Update, November 1, 2002', Unpublished paper, http://fairmodel.econ.yale.edu/rayfair/pdf/2002DHTM.HTM

(2002b) *Predicting Presidential Elections and Other Things*, Stanford: Stanford University Press

(2004) 'Presidential Vote Equation, July 31, 2004', http://fairmodel.econ.yale.edu/vote2004/vot0704.htm, http://fairmodel.econ.yale.edu/vote2004/computev.htm

Forsythe, R., Rietz, T. and Ross, T. (1999) 'Wishes, Expectations and Actions: Price Formation in Election Stock Markets', *Journal of Economic Behaviour and Organisation*, 39, pp. 83–110

Hansen, J., Schmidt, C. and Strobel, C. (2004) 'Manipulation in Political Stock Markets – Preconditions and Evidence', *Applied Economics Letters*, 11(7), pp. 459–63

Hanson, R. D. (1995) 'Could Gambling Save Science? Encouraging an Honest Consensus', *Social Epistemology*, 9(1), pp. 3–33

Hibbs, D. (1982) 'The Dynamics of Political Support for American Presidents among Occupational and Partisan Groups', *American Journal of Political Science*, 26(2), pp. 312–32

(2000) 'Bread and Peace Voting in US Presidential Elections', *Public Choice*, 104, pp. 149–80

(2004) 'Implications of the "Bread and Peace Model" of US Presidential Voting for the 2004 Election Outcome', Unpublished paper, http://www.handels.gu.se/~econdhib/election2004.htm

Jackman, S. (1995) 'Some More of All That: A Reply to Charnock', *Australian Journal of Political Science*, 30, pp. 347–55

Jackman, S. and Marks, G. (1994) 'Forecasting Australian Elections: 1993 and All That', *Australian Journal of Political Science*, 29(2), pp. 277–91

Jones, R. J., Jr. (2002) *Who Will Be in the White House? Predicting Presidential Elections*, New York: Longman

(2004) 'You Can Predict the 2004 Presidential Election (Maybe!)', Unpublished paper, http://morris.wharton.upenn.edu/forecast/Political/PDFs/JonesEssayIndicatorsModels%20_30Mar04_.pdf

Kramer, G. (1971) 'Short-term Fluctuations in U S Voting Behaviour, 1896–1964', *American Political Science Review*, 65(1), pp. 131–43

Leigh, A., Wolfers, J. and Zitzewitz, E. (2003) 'What do Financial Markets Think of the War in Iraq?', NBER Working Paper, 9587

Levitt, S. (2004) 'Why Are Gambling Markets Organised So Differently from Financial Markets?', *Economic Journal*, 114(495), pp. 223–46

Lewis-Beck, M. (1988) *Economics and Elections: The Major Western Democracies*, Ann Arbor: University of Michigan Press

Lewis-Beck, M. S. and Tien, C. (2000) 'The Future in Forecasting: Prospective Presidential Models', in J. E. Campbell and J. C. Garand (eds.), *Before the Vote: Forecasting American National Elections*, Thousand Oaks, CA: Sage Publications

(2001) 'Election 2000: How Wrong Was the Forecast?', *American Politics Research*, 29, pp. 302–6

(2004) 'Jobs and the Job of President: A Forecast for 2004', *PS: Political Science*, 37, pp. 753–8

Linstone, H. A. and Turoff, M. (eds.) (2002) 'The Delphi Method: Techniques and Applications', http://www.is.njit.edu/pubs/delphibook/index.html

Midlarsky, M. I. (1984) 'Political Stability of Two-Party and Multiparty Systems: Probabilistic Bases for the Comparison of Party Systems', *American Political Science Review*, 78, pp. 929–51

Norpoth, H. (1996) 'Of Time and Candidates. A Forecast for 1996', *American Political Quarterly*, 24(4), pp. 443–67

(2001) 'Primary Colors: A Mixed Blessing for Al Gore', *PS: Political Science & Politics*, 34, pp. 45–8

(2002) 'On a Short Leash: Term limits an Economic Voting', in H. Dorussen and M. Taylor (eds.), *The Context of Economic Voting*, London: Routledge, pp. 121–36

(2004) 'From Primary to General Election: A Forecast of the Presidential Vote', Paper prepared for presentation at the 100th Annual Meeting of the American Political Science Association, Chicago, 2–5 September, http://morris.wharton.upenn.edu/forecast/Political/PDFs/Norpoth.pdf

Norpoth, H. and Rusk, J. (2003) 'Wag the Dog: Congressional Elections and Political Change, 1828–2002', Paper for meeting of the American Political Science Association, Philadelphia, August

Ortner, G. (1998) 'Forecasting Markets – An Industrial Application', Technical University of Vienna, mimeo

Palmer, H. and Whitten, G. (1999) 'The Electoral Impact of Unexpected Inflation and Economic Growth', *British Journal of Political Science*, 29, pp. 623–39

Paton, D. and L. Vaughan Williams (2005) 'Forecasting Outcomes in Spread Betting Markets: Can Bettors Use "Quarbs" to Beat the Book?', *Journal of Forecasting*, 24(2), pp. 139–54

Pennock, D. M., Lawrence, S., Giles, C. L. and Nielsen, F. A. (2001) 'The Real Power of Artificial Markets', *Science*, 291, pp. 987–8

Plott, C. and Sunder, S. (1988) 'Rational Expectations and the Aggregation of Diverse Information in Laboratory Security Markets', *Econometrica*, 56, pp. 1085–1118

Rhode, P. W. and Strumpf, K. S. (2004) 'Historical Presidential Betting Markets', *Journal of Economic Perspectives*, 18(2), pp. 127–41

Servan-Schreiber, E., Wolfers, J., Pennock, D. and Galebach, B. (2004) 'Prediction Markets: Does Money Matter?' *Electronic Markets*, 14(3)

Stigler, G. (1973) 'General Economic Conditions and National Elections', *American Political Science Review*, 63, pp. 160–7

Strumpf, K. (2004) 'Manipulating the Iowa Political Stock Market', University of North Carolina, mimeo

Tetlock, P. C. (2004) 'How Efficient are Information Markets? Evidence from an Online Exchange', Harvard mimeo

Vaughan Williams, L. (2000) 'Index Investment Markets and Information Efficiency: Evidence from the UK', *Global Business and Economics Review – Anthology 2000*, pp. 24–9

(2001) 'Can Bettors Win? A Perspective on the Economics of Betting', *World Economics*, 2(1), pp. 31–48

(2004) 'Decision-Making in Betting Markets', *Significance*, 1(3), pp.109–12

Wlezien, C. and Erikson, R. S. (2004a) 'The Fundamentals, the Polls and the Presidential Vote', *PS: Political Science and Politics*, 37(4), pp. 747–51

(2004b), 'An Updated Forecast', Paper presented at the 100th Annual Meeting of the American Political Science Association, Chicago, 2–5 September, http://morris.wharton.upenn.edu/forecast/Political/APSA_Roudtable.html #Christopher_Wlezien_and_Robert_S._Erikson

Wolfers, J. and Leigh, A. (2002) 'Three Tools for Forecasting Federal Elections: Lessons from 2001', *Australian Journal of Political Science*, 37(2), pp. 223–40

Wolfers, J. and Zitzewitz, E. (2004) 'Prediction Markets', *Journal of Economic Perspectives*, 18(2), pp. 107–26

8 Longshot bias: insights from the betting market on men's professional tennis

David Forrest and Ian McHale

8.1 Motivation

The best known stylised fact to emerge from the area of research reflected in this volume is that, in horse and dog betting, financially superior returns (i.e. smaller losses) accrue to a strategy of wagering on short-odds rather than long-odds runners. This bias is sufficiently pronounced that expected returns may even be positive where one bets only on extreme favourites. The evidence for the existence of this bias in the odds dimension is impressively voluminous and has accumulated over more than five decades.[1]

The existence and persistence of such 'longshot bias' represents an anomaly when viewed within the tradition of treating wagering markets as examples of financial markets. According to the efficient markets hypothesis, prices (odds) should reflect all available information relevant to the outcome of a race. With all agents risk-neutral, expected returns, in equilibrium, would then be the same for all possible bets and so invariant with respect to odds. Further, it is more common in economics to assume risk aversion rather than risk-neutrality and in this case one would predict that bets at short odds should yield *lower* returns, on average, than bets at long odds. Certainly a premium to risk rather than its reverse is what is observed in most financial markets other than betting ones.

Early attempts to explain the 'longshot anomaly' within betting were typically based on attributing particular tastes to a representative bettor such that he would be willing to accept worse financial returns when betting on outsiders than when betting on favourites. For example, his utility function may be characterised by (locally) increasing marginal utility of wealth (Quandt, 1986). Or the typical bettor may gain fun from the betting process itself and this fun could be greater when betting on longshots because, when one does win, one can brag about the fact (Thaler and Ziemba, 1988). Or bettors, as is claimed by psychologists, may suffer from a more general tendency systematically to overestimate the

215

probability of unlikely events such as lightning strikes or wins by the worst horse in a field (Griffith, 1949).[2]

Representative bettor models such as these may well capture features of bettor behaviour that contribute to longshot bias (though it is hard empirically to test their importance relative to each other). However, they can offer only a partial explanation. Representative bettors may indeed be ill informed or bet for fun or because they are risk-loving. But why do other traders in the market, better informed, more orientated to financial goals and with a more conventional attitude to risk, not 'correct' the bias by taking advantage of the superior deal to be had by backing favourites and thereby, with the weight of their money, move the pattern of odds back towards efficiency? 'Noise' traders are present in many or most other financial markets but the activities of well-informed 'professional' traders appear often to limit their influence on the pattern of prices. A full explanation of the existence and persistence of longshot bias seems therefore to need to incorporate an understanding of the way in which different types of bettors in the market interact with each other. Accordingly the recent trend in the literature on longshot bias has been towards the construction of models which distinguish between categories of bettor such as 'informed' and 'uninformed' or 'professional' and 'amateur'. A conclusion common to all such modelling exercises is that high transactions costs are a potentially decisive obstacle to the achievement of efficiency in the pattern of odds. Typical of these models is that offered by Vaughan Williams and Paton (1998).[3]

The Vaughan Williams–Paton paper has the virtue of recognising that longshot bias has not been observed in every betting market studied. The authors themselves present evidence that bias is absent from the betting market on high-grade handicap racing in Britain and note that efficiency in the odds dimension appears also to characterise racetrack markets in Asia.[4] From the world of sports betting, there have even been reports of reverse or negative bias such that superior returns appear to accrue to long-odds bettors (compared with short-odds bettors) on American baseball and (ice) hockey.[5]

Vaughan Williams and Paton (1998) sought to construct a model that would account not only for the traditional (positive) bias observed in racetrack betting markets but also these cases of zero or negative bias. They distinguished between uninformed and informed bettors. Where uninformed bettors were present, they would fail to give full weight to the fact that one runner (in a two-horse race) was a stronger contender than the other and, as a group, would underbet the horse with the greater chance of winning. If *only* uninformed bettors were present, this would result in positive longshot bias in the odds.

Typically, though, there are some informed bettors active in the market. When the uninformed have placed their bets, the informed will recognise that the better horse is more attractively 'priced' than the other and will place wagers accordingly. This 'informed' money will move the odds in such a way as to moderate initial (positive) longshot bias. However, when the price on the favourite has shortened to the point where expected return is no longer acceptable, no more 'informed' money will be placed. With a high track take or bookmaker commission, this point may be reached with substantial residual bias still present in the odds. Given that track parimutuel operations in the US and bookmakers in the UK typically 'take' some 20 per cent of turnover, longshot bias can be expected to be the norm. The degree of positive bias will however vary and will be greater (i) the lower the proportion of betting turnover accounted for by informed bettors and (ii) the higher the transactions costs of betting.

Vaughan Williams and Paton also noted that, in a bookmaker market, bookmakers may adjust odds on outsiders as an insurance against bets by those with private information. An additional influence on the degree of bias is therefore how much of the information relevant to the outcome of the race is likely to be public knowledge. As information tends towards being fully available in the media, as the proportion of informed money increases and as transactions costs become more competitive, positive bias will tend to disappear. This proposition is consistent with the failure to detect bias in the betting markets on the highest-profile races in Britain and in the very high-volume racetrack markets of Asia.

Suppose now that only (risk-neutral) informed bettors were active in a particular betting market. This situation would tend to reduce the degree of positive bias in the odds towards zero if the event that was the subject of wagering was so high profile that all information was in the public domain. However, in such a market, Vaughan Williams and Paton proposed that it would be possible that bias would not only be eliminated but actually reversed. 'Negative' bias becomes possible if informed bettors are motivated not only by financial considerations but also by a desire for peer esteem. They suggest that the latter is earned by a high frequency of winning. If true, this would bias market participants to betting on favourites and the equilibrium pattern of odds could display negative bias. This is the Vaughan Williams–Paton explanation for published findings on the American professional team sports of baseball and hockey where casual bettors are relatively few, where betting commissions are much lower than in racing and where media interest is so frenzied that private information is liable quickly to become public.

The contribution of Vaughan Williams and Paton is the closest we have to a general theory of bias in betting markets. Longshot bias may be positive, zero or negative depending on:

(a) the relative importance of uninformed and informed betting
(b) the level of transactions costs
(c) (in bookmaker markets) the potential for some individual bettors to hold private information and
(d) whether and to what extent bettors gain utility from winning itself as well as from financial payoffs.

The construction of the Vaughan Williams–Paton model was informed by pre-existing studies of the nature and extent of longshot bias in various race betting markets and in the American team sports betting markets analysed by Woodland and Woodland, (1994, 2001, 2003). Its predictions are consistent with the positive, zero or negative biases identified in those markets. But it should be tested against data from other betting markets to establish how general a theory it can claim to be. We note that the Vaughan Williams–Paton model has broadly similar features to other models, referenced above, based on two categories of bettor and designed to give insights into the sources of longshot bias. Testing the ability of such models to predict bias in hitherto unconsidered betting markets would facilitate an evaluation of how fruitful recent developments in the literature on longshot bias have been.

The survey of the economics of wagering markets by Sauer (1998) illustrates the narrowness of focus of the empirical literature. Market efficiency has been tested repeatedly in horse and dog betting and to a limited extent for the markets on team sports. The study of betting on individual sports could generate new insights. Here we offer a chapter on the Internet betting market on singles matches in men's professional tennis.

8.2 The advantages of studying tennis betting

The tennis betting market is a specialised market without the influence of uninformed 'fun' bettors enjoying an outing at the racetrack. The level of transactions costs is extremely low and of an order of magnitude comparable to other types of financial market outside betting.[6] The complexity of the task of assessing the relative quality of the contestants is much less than in horse-racing and world rankings summarise a host of relevant information. Those who wish to become 'informed' can therefore do so relatively easily. The potential for insider information to be valuable is limited because players perform in public very frequently and so injuries are revealed quickly. Any inclination to hold back effort is likely to be particularly limited in the high-prize/high-prestige Grand Slam tournaments which we are able to analyse separately. The contrasts with the horse betting market are therefore such that, according to the propositions generated by the Vaughan Williams–Paton model, one would predict reduced, zero or even reverse bias in tennis betting.

An advantage to studying tennis compared with team sports is that in team sports, such as baseball and (ice) hockey, clubs have large numbers of fans with permanent, almost tribal, allegiance. They may wish to express their fidelity by backing their team in the betting market as well as in the stadium or arena. Avery and Chevalier (1999) illustrated the potential of 'sentiment' to distort the terms offered in the betting market by showing that those betting on 'glamorous' teams in the NFL suffered above-average losses. Strumpf (2003) obtained data from illegal sports books in the New York area and found that conspicuously ungenerous odds were offered for bets on local favourite teams. The negative longshot bias present in the odds on baseball and hockey betting therefore has an alternative explanation to that cited above (which stressed low transactions costs, a high proportion of informed bettors and a preference by bettors for high frequency of winning) – favourites in individual matches tend disproportionately often to be the more powerful clubs, the more powerful clubs have larger numbers of fans and bookmakers may exploit the loyalty of these fans by offering relatively unfair odds. Separating bias in the odds dimension from the influence of 'sentiment' will be difficult without multivariate analysis and there is potential for false conclusions to be drawn. The same danger is not present in tennis. As with horses, only rarely does a particular player attract fan(atical) allegiance. And if one looks at Internet betting, as we do, the influence of nationalistic sentiment will also be limited since the market is global.

To our knowledge, only one academic study investigates longshot bias in tennis. Cain, Law and Peel (2003) tabulated returns on betting, for broad odds ranges, for ninety-one matches at the 1996 Wimbledon tournament. No pattern emerged (except that rank outsiders appeared to be bad bets) but this is unsurprising given the small sample size.[7] In betting, the standard deviation of the return to an individual unit bet is very high since its value is always either minus one or a positive number. Finding statistically significant relationships between odds and return therefore requires a large dataset. We had the advantage of access to a substantial archive of odds on men's tennis.

8.3 Data and results

For tennis, an Italian website, www.infobetting.com, provides 'live' odds from a range of international bookmakers. Its archive lists 'best closing price' on players in each men's singles match (and the outcome of the match) held at tournaments on the men's professional tennis tour (the ATP Tour) since 2001. We employed data on the 5,892 matches recorded between January 2001 and April 2004. Thus we knew the outcome and return on 11,784 individual betting opportunities.

Table 8.1. *Returns to betting on favourites and underdogs, all years*

	2001	2002	2003–4	All years
Favourites	−0.002 (−0.10)	0.023 (1.36)	0.034 (2.41)	0.021 (2.31)
Underdogs	−0.122 (−3.81)	−0.111 (−3.29)	−0.148 (−4.95)	−0.129 (−7.02)
N	1,729	1,797	2,362	5,888

Note: *t*-statistics appear in parentheses.

A first indication of the nature and degree of longshot bias in this market was obtained from comparing the returns from two simple strategies – betting on the (bookmaker) favourite in each match and betting on the (bookmaker) underdog in each match. Table 8.1 shows the returns from following these strategies over the whole period and for each year separately. 2003 and 2004 are treated as a single year because the sample extended only to April 2004. Four matches are excluded because the odds listed were the same for the two players.

Over the whole period and for each subperiod, betting on underdogs yielded strong and statistically significant losses (11 per cent or worse). By contrast, betting on favourites allowed the bettor essentially to break-even in 2001 and to make a positive return in 2002 and in 2003–4 (statistically significant in the case of 2003–4). Over the whole period studied, the strategy of betting on favourites yielded a return of +2.1 per cent, and this was strongly statistically significant.

The evidence, then, is that this betting market is weak form inefficient. Knowledge of returns on bets in one year allowed participants to identify a strategy that yielded above-average returns in the following year. Moreover, the strategy tended actually to be profitable for the bettor. Market efficiency is thus rejected because there is a longshot bias similar to that found in horse betting markets.

Of course, there are degrees of favourite. In the early rounds of a tournament, many matches are competitively unbalanced because of the seeding system which is designed to prevent the top players meeting and knocking each other out. In such matches, favourites will tend to be very shortly priced. In later rounds, a 'favourite' might have odds only slightly different from those of the 'underdog'. In further analysis, we therefore investigated the returns to betting in different odds ranges.

On the website and in its archive, odds are quoted in the decimal format, standard in continental Europe. For example, quoted odds of 3.50 on the website would mean that, if a unit bet were placed and if it were successful, the bettor would subsequently be able to collect 3.50 units (2.50 profit, 1.00 return of original stake) from the bookmaker. In our statistical analysis, we express odds in another style, using *probability odds*. This is the reciprocal of the decimal odds, so that 3.50 in decimal format would be 0.286 in terms of probability odds. An interpretation of the probability odds figure is that it is the stake the bettor would be required to make to secure a claim of one unit against the bookmaker in the event that his wager was successful. Further, whether or not the expected return to any bet is positive will depend on whether or not the true probability of winning exceeds the probability odds.

Table 8.2 presents the returns to betting in different odds ranges, defined at intervals of 0.1 in the probability odds. Again, we report results for the whole period and for each of three subperiods. The evidence for positive longshot bias is very strong. Across 'all years', the return increases almost monotonically with probability odds. Betting on genuine longshots produces spectacularly negative returns. Indeed, every one of the sixty-four bets available in the probability odds range 0 to 0.1 lost. By contrast, good betting value was to be had from backing strong favourites. The highest return over the whole period was from backing players priced in the 0.8–0.9 range of probability odds. Here 803 bets were available and the return was +5.8 per cent (strongly statistically significant). For each of the three subperiods separately, the return was again positive (statistically significantly different from zero at the 10 per cent level in 2001 and at the 1 per cent level in 2002 and in 2003–4). Again we conclude that the market does not satisfy even weak form efficiency since it was possible to identify a profitable strategy in one period and pursue it to make a profit in the next.[8]

Different tennis tournaments take place on different types of surface: hard, grass, clay or indoors. The degree of predictability of individual matches may differ according to the type of surface and it is therefore of interest to check whether the strong longshot bias we have identified holds within subsets of matches defined by surface. Table 8.3 displays the results. For bets on indoor matches, there is no discernible pattern in the returns to bets in different odds categories; but this type of surface has the smallest sample size in our dataset. For grass, and especially hard court, tournaments, the pattern of superior returns at higher probability odds is very evident and strong positive returns are again associated with betting in the 0.8–0.9 range. On clay courts, a more attractive strategy would have been to bet on less strong favourites since the 0.6–0.7 range offered the highest number of bets and a return of +6.6 per cent but bets in the 0.8–0.9 range still generated a positive yield, albeit not statistically significant.

Another way of categorising tennis tournaments is by the levels of prestige and prize money on offer. Collectively, the Wimbledon and

Table 8.2. Returns to betting on odds ranges, all matches

Probability odds range	2001			2002			2003/04			All years		
	n	Yield	t-stat	n	Yield	t-stat	n	Yield	t-stat	n	Yield	t-stat
0.0–0.1	6	−1.000		15	−1.000		43	−1.000		64	−1.000	
0.1–0.2	118	−0.639	−4.78	149	−0.170	−0.87	328	−0.399	−3.67	595	−0.389	−4.75
0.2–0.3	373	−0.236	−2.90	390	−0.185	−2.30	571	−0.126	−1.82	1334	−0.174	−3.94
0.3–0.4	565	−0.038	−0.67	547	−0.042	−0.73	649	−0.081	−1.54	1761	−0.055	−1.72
0.4–0.5	580	−0.017	−0.37	603	−0.084	−1.84	707	−0.069	−1.64	1890	−0.058	−2.25
0.5–0.6	567	−0.037	−0.98	618	0.002	0.06	726	0.003	0.08	1911	−0.009	−0.45
0.6–0.7	645	−0.026	−0.88	629	0.023	0.79	691	0.077	2.83	1965	0.026	1.57
0.7–0.8	369	0.045	1.52	383	−0.005	−0.16	530	−0.003	−0.14	1282	0.010	0.61
0.8–0.9	198	0.048	1.66	215	0.073	2.93	390	0.055	2.85	803	0.058	4.29
0.9–1.0	45	0.083	26.60	45	−0.043	−0.85	89	0.023	0.87	179	0.022	1.15
N	3,466			3,594			4,724			11,784		

Table 8.3. *Returns to betting, by surface, all matches*

Probability odds range	Hard			Grass			Clay			Indoor		
	n	Yield	t-stat	n	Yield	t-stat	n	Yield	t-stat	n	Yield	t-stat
0.0–0.1	39	−1.000		9	−1.000		11	−1.000		5	−1.000	
0.1–0.2	285	−0.439	−3.93	105	−0.291	−1.27	163	−0.418	−2.88	42	−0.185	−0.53
0.2–0.3	503	−0.246	−3.52	196	−0.327	−3.09	468	−0.104	−1.35	167	0.024	0.18
0.3–0.4	636	−0.101	−1.92	233	−0.055	−0.62	637	−0.084	−1.59	255	0.131	1.49
0.4–0.5	675	−0.022	−0.51	242	−0.111	−1.56	690	−0.076	−1.80	283	−0.052	−0.78
0.5–0.6	695	−0.028	−0.80	250	0.034	0.60	693	−0.011	−0.32	273	0.001	0.01
0.6–0.7	691	0.033	1.20	272	−0.002	−0.05	708	0.066	2.45	294	−0.062	−1.39
0.7–0.8	487	0.046	1.81	183	0.060	1.47	446	−0.028	−0.98	166	−0.050	−1.04
0.8–0.9	357	0.069	3.49	130	0.111	4.14	245	0.029	1.08	71	0.011	0.22
0.9–1.0	96	0.036	1.60	34	−0.113	−1.60	43	0.086	27.41	6	0.097	18.98
N	4,464			1,654			4104			1,562		

American, Australian and French Open Championships are known as the 'Grand Slam' tournaments. At these events, upsets might be expected to be less likely to occur than usual because players have greater incentive to maximise effort and these will not be occasions to treat competitive matches as practice. Of course, in an efficient market, odds would be adjusted to take account of the different environment of a Grand Slam tournament. But table 8.4 reveals that, over our period, returns to betting on strong favourites (probability odds 0.8–0.9) were even greater when wagering was restricted to these high-profile events. Over 'all years' 329 bets would have returned +9.5 per cent; returns for the three subperiods were +6.4 per cent, +9.2 per cent and +11.6 per cent. We do not know how turnover varies across tournaments but it would not be unreasonable to speculate that more money is wagered in respect of the 'big' events. It thus appears that a 'thicker' market does not erode the striking positive longshot bias we have identified in the data.

8.4 Reflections

In his review of the history of the academic study of longshot bias, Sauer (1998) documented the supplanting of early representative bettor models by richer models that took account of heterogeneity among bettors in respect of the degree to which they were well informed. We focused above on the model presented by Vaughan Williams and Paton (1998) but all such models share an emphasis on the role of risk-neutral informed bettors in promoting efficiency and on the role of transactions costs as a barrier to efficiency. Such models predict that positive longshot bias will become less pronounced as the importance of uninformed bettors' money is reduced and as transactions costs fall.

We have identified a market where transactions costs are strikingly low compared with horse betting and where casual uninformed bettors such as are found at racetracks are likely to be relatively fewer in number. For these reasons, we might have anticipated that the odds in betting on tennis would exhibit less bias than has been repeatedly documented in the case of horse-racing. Yet we have found that there is strong positive longshot bias in the tennis betting market. And, as with bookmaker betting on horses, we have even been able to document positive returns to a strategy of backing very strong favourites. Indeed the return to this strategy is of a very similar order of magnitude to the 8.5 per cent reported for the same strategy applied to British horse betting by Dowie (1976).[9]

It cannot be doubted that models with heterogeneous bettors capture important features in betting markets. As Sauer (1998) points out, they can account, as earlier models could not, for the ability of some informed bettors

Table 8.4. *Returns to betting, by odds ranges, Grand Slams only*

Probability odds range	2001			2002			2003/04			All years		
	n	Yield	*t*-stat	*n*	Yield	*t*-stat	*n*	yield	*t*-stat	*n*	yield	*t*-stat
0.0–0.1	6	−1.000		13	−1.000		25	−1.000		44	−1.000	
0.1–0.2	74	−0.831	−7.00	94	−0.072	−0.27	139	−0.585	−3.99	307	−0.487	−4.41
0.2–0.3	131	−0.356	−2.74	113	−0.344	−2.49	173	−0.303	−2.65	417	−0.331	−4.54
0.3–0.4	135	−0.235	−2.14	121	0.194	1.52	144	−0.091	−0.81	400	−0.053	−0.79
0.4–0.5	114	−0.015	−0.14	136	−0.036	−0.37	130	−0.184	−1.93	380	−0.080	−1.41
0.5–0.6	130	−0.041	−0.52	137	−0.025	−0.32	135	0.048	0.61	402	−0.006	−0.13
0.6–0.7	132	0.091	1.50	140	−0.104	−1.60	141	0.164	2.91	413	0.050	1.40
0.7–0.8	113	0.111	2.27	98	0.051	0.92	161	0.023	0.50	372	0.057	1.99
0.8–0.9	88	0.064	1.56	97	0.092	2.74	144	0.116	4.80	329	0.095	5.22
0.9–1.0	39	0.082	23.53	39	−0.063	−1.10	50	0.038	1.27	128	0.021	0.95
N	962			988			1,242			3,192		

to earn positive returns. And in emphasising the role of transactions costs as an impediment to the achievement of efficiency, they incorporate a standard finding in the analysis of financial markets generally. But they may still have limitations and this is underlined by their failure here to predict correctly the short-odds/long-odds bias found in tennis betting. Seemingly old-fashioned representative bettor models may after all offer some insights that could be incorporated in newer theories.

Hurley and McDonough (1995), Terrell and Farmer (1996) and Vaughan Williams and Paton (1998) all assume risk-neutrality on the part of informed bettors. This assumption may be represented as being carried over from the study of conventional financial markets where the informed may fairly be termed professionals (obtaining positive returns at the expense of noise traders and transacting only when the expected return is positive). But the adoption of the efficient markets paradigm for the study of wagering activities may have distracted too much attention from the extent to which gambling is a *consumption* activity. In comparison to other financial markets, the highly informed in our experience include fewer 'professional' gamblers and more 'amateurs' for whom betting is nevertheless a passionate hobby for which they possess considerable knowledge and skill. Both those drawn to professional gambling as a career and those for whom it is a hobby on which they are willing to spend (i.e. lose money)[10] may be 'risk-lovers' in some sense. If the 'informed' group of bettors were characterised as risk-loving in the heterogeneous bettor models discussed above, positive longshot bias would not disappear if transactions costs and the number of uninformed bettors approached zero.

Horse and tennis betting share the characteristic that genuine longshot opportunities are common. This is not true of betting on handicap horseraces (where weights carried by horses are adjusted to equalise the chances of the runners). Nor is it true of results betting on team sports in America (where interventionist measures such as player drafts[11] or salary caps promote competitive balance) and Europe (where teams compete in hierarchical divisions). For a longshot opportunity in team sports betting, one has to wager on some aspect other than the winner (e.g. the exact score).

Positive longshot bias has been documented for most horse betting and for dog betting and, here, for tennis betting. It has also been reported in the betting market on exact scores in football (soccer) (Cain, Law and Peel, 2000). All these are activities where the range of odds is wide.

Positive longshot bias has been reported absent from betting markets on handicap horse-races,[12] American team sports[13] and English football results.[14] These are all activities where institutional arrangements narrow the range of odds because there are few outcomes that would shock.

We recommend further research in other betting markets to examine what we suspect to be a relationship between the width of odds and the presence or absence of positive longshot bias. A link would be consistent with bettors, even the well informed, being risk-lovers. In terms of the framework of the familiar expected utility of wealth model, narrowness in the odds implies that any normal-sized bet will be associated with alternative wealth outcomes (win or lose) that are very close to each other. Between these wealth levels, the utility of wealth will be so close to linear as to make no difference, so that presumed convexity in the utility function could have no influence in biasing odds. Where longshot opportunities exist however, there is scope for risk-loving bettors to exercise their willingness to tolerate more unfair odds on outsiders, so generating positive longshot bias. A separate possibility is that apparently risk-loving behaviour may be observed even amongst those who are risk-neutral because of discontinuities in the utility of wealth function. Thus a dollar return for a dollar bet may be less appealing at *any* wealth level than a bet with a $20 return, even if the latter is actuarially worse. A dollar is scarcely worth picking up but $20 would buy a Havana cigar!

If bettors are typically risk-loving (which could be defined not in the traditional economist's sense but alternatively in terms of a love of the excitement of the risk process itself), this alone cannot account for the negative longshot bias claimed to exist in some sports betting markets. Whereas Thaler and Ziemba (1998) attributed some of the preference for backing outsiders to the acquisition of 'bragging rights' if they won, Vaughan Williams and Paton accounted for the possibility of the bias being reversed by the desire of bettors to win frequently to gain peer esteem. These appear to be contradictory representations of bettor preferences but they may be reconciled if one accepts that width of odds will influence perceptions of what constitutes skilled betting. In a horse-race, little will be proved by successfully tipping a short-odds horse whereas a win on a longshot is likely to be noticed and admired. In team sports betting markets, all the odds will be similar so that little credit is earned by backing a (slight) outsider. Those concerned with winning peer group esteem will indeed be forced to focus on frequency of winning. This will increase betting on favourites and, *ceteris paribus*, induce negative bias in the odds.

Vaughan Williams and Paton entitled their 1998 paper 'Why are Some Favourite-Longshot Biases Positive and Some Negative?'. The question is important because the existence of exceptions to the general rule that betting short offers financially superior returns should discipline the search for a resolution of the longshot anomaly. They introduced a hypothesis about the preferences of informed betters (utility is gained from high frequency of winning, independent of financial returns). While this is consistent with observing negative bias in some markets, the species of model they were adapting still fails to predict the findings we have reported for tennis. Further consideration of bettor preferences appears to be required in order to adapt heterogeneous bettors models so as to make their predictions consistent with empirical evidence from betting markets beyond horse racing.

Notes

We are grateful to Graham Piggott, one of our students on the degree in Gambling Studies at the University of Salford, for suggesting to us that the tennis betting market would be a fruitful focus for research.

1 For surveys, see Vaughan Williams (1999) and Sauer (1998).
2 These are demand-side explanations of the longshot bias phenomenon. In American racetrack markets, all betting is parimutuel, with relative odds determined mechanistically by weight of bettors' money. In Britain, most betting is with bookmakers and there is therefore scope for supply-side influence as well. In particular, Shin (1991, 1992, 1993) demonstrated that an appropriate response by bookmakers to the threat posed by bettors with inside information would be to offer actuarially more unfair odds on outsiders. This would generate longshot bias. While this explanation has empirical support (Vaughan Williams and Paton, 1997); it lacks generality to the extent that it does not account for longshot bias being a feature of parimutuel as well as of bookmaking markets.
3 Other examples include Terrell and Farmer (1996) and Hurley and McDonough (1995).
4 Studies include Busche and Hall (1988), Busche (1994) and Busche and Walls (2000).
5 See Woodland and Woodland (1994, 2001, 2003).
6 Our dataset includes odds for each player in each of nearly 6,000 matches. Mean over-round is 1.76%. This is extremely low compared with horse and dog racing, partly because there are only two 'runners' in each event, partly because the Internet betting market is highly competitive and partly because our data source gave bettors access to 'best prices' across a range of bookmakers.
7 Similarly inconclusive results were reported for two other individual sports, snooker and boxing, with again very small sample sizes compared with what has been possible for racing.
8 In terms of decimal odds, the profitable strategy was to wager in the range 1.11–1.25. UK bookmakers follow a different convention in the quotation of odds; the relevant range following this convention would be 1/9–1/4.
9 In each case, the implication is that bookmakers lost money on strong favourites. Their willingness to do so is a puzzle to be resolved but it may be that, if no market were offered on strong favourites or they were offered at extremely short odds, this would undermine the market in bets on outsiders whose chances are even less than their long odds suggest.

10 As Crafts (1985) noted, profitable strategies may be identified but there may be frustratingly few occasions on which they may be implemented – too few occasions, perhaps, to satisfy those who gain consumption benefit from gambling.
11 The draft system allocates new players between clubs. The team with the weakest playing records in the previous season are given first pick from the pool of new talent.
12 Vaughan Williams and Paton (1998).
13 Woodland and Woodland (1994, 2001, 2003).
14 Forrest and Simmons (chapter 15 in this volume).

References

Avery, C. and Chevalier, J. (1999) 'Identifying Investor Sentiment from Price Paths: The Case of Football Betting', *Journal of Business*, 72, pp. 493–521

Busche, K. (1994) 'Efficient Market Results in an Asian setting', in D. Hausche, S. Y. Lo and W. T. Ziemba (eds.), *Efficiency in Racetrack Betting Markets*, London: Academic Press, pp. 615–16

Busche, K. and Hall, C. D. (1988) 'An Exception to the Risk Preference Anomaly', *Journal of Business*, 61, pp. 337–46

Busche, K. and Walls, W. D. (2000) 'Decision Costs and Betting Market Efficiency', *Rationality and Society*, 12(4), pp. 477–92

Cain, M., Law, D. and Peel, D. (2000) 'The Favourite-Longshot Bias and Market Efficiency in UK Football Betting', *Scottish Journal of Political Economy*, 47, pp. 25–36

    (2003) 'The Favourite-Longshot Bias, Bookmaker Margins and Insider Trading in a Variety of Betting Markets', *Bulletin of Economic Research*, 55, pp. 263–73

Crafts, N. (1985) 'Some Evidence of Insider Knowledge on Horse-Race Betting in Britain', *Economica*, 55, pp. 295–304

Dowie, J. (1976) 'On the Efficiency and Equity of Betting Markets', *Economica*, 43, pp. 139–50

Griffith, R. M. (1949) 'Odds Adjustment by American Horse Race Bettors', *American Journal of Psychology*, 62, pp. 290–4

Hurley, W. and McDonough, L. (1995) 'A Note on the Hayek Hypothesis and the Favourite Long Shot Bias in Parimutuel Betting', *American Economic Review*, 85, pp. 949–55

Quandt, R. (1986) 'Betting and Equilibrium', *Quarterly Journal of Economics*, 101, pp. 201–7

Sauer, R. (1998) 'The Economics of Wagering Markets', *Journal of Economic Literature*, 36, pp. 2021–64

Shin, H. (1991) 'Optimal Odds against Inside Traders', *Economic Journal*, 101, pp. 1179–85

    (1992) 'Prices of State Contingent Claims with Insider Traders, and Favourite-Longshot Bias', *Economic Journal*, 102, pp. 426–35

    (1993) 'Measuring the Incidence of Insider Trading in a Market for State-Contingent Claims', *Economic Journal*, 103, pp. 1141–53

Strumpf, K. (2003) 'Illegal Sports Bookmakers', University of North Carolina at Chapel Hill, mimeo

Terrell, D. and Farmer, A. (1996) 'Optimal Betting and Efficiency in Parimutuel Betting Markets', *Economic Journal*, 106, pp. 846–68

Thaler, R. and Ziemba, W. T. (1988) 'Anomalies – Parimutuel Betting Markets: Racetracks and Lotteries', *Journal of Economic Perspectives*, 2, pp. 161–174

Vaughan Williams, L. (1999) 'Information Efficiency in Betting Markets: A Survey', *Bulletin of Economic Research*, 51, pp. 1–30

Vaughan Williams, L. and Paton, D. (1997) 'Why is There a Favourite-Longshot Bias in British Racetrack Betting Markets?', *Economic Journal*, 107, pp. 150–8

(1998) 'Why are Some Favourite-Longshot Biases Positive and Some Negative?', *Applied Economics*, 30, pp. 1505–10

Woodland, L. and Woodland, B. (1994) 'Market Efficiency and the Favourite-Longshot Bias: The Baseball Betting Market', *Journal of Finance*, 49, pp. 269–79

(2001) 'Market Efficiency and Profitable Wagering in the National Hockey League: Can Bettors Score on Longshots?', *Southern Economic Journal*, 67, pp. 983–95

(2003) 'The Reverse Favourite-Longshot Bias and Market Efficiency in Major League Baseball: An Update', *Bulletin of Economic Research*, 55, pp. 113–23

9 Biases and insider trading in exotic bets on thoroughbreds

Les Coleman and Martin McGrath

This chapter examines exotic bets in Australian thoroughbred wagering to identify market anomalies and derive an estimate of the extent of insider trading. The analysis tests whether these markets are what Fama (1970) termed 'strongly efficient', which means monopoly information cannot be used profitably.

Although bookmakers operate in Australia, over 95 per cent of bets are placed with one of three parimutuel operators or totalisators ('Tote'). They accept bets up until the start of a race, then deduct a fixed proportion of the pool to cover taxes and operating costs, and divide the balance between winning bets.

All investors on the Tote receive the same odds. It is thus in the interests of skilled bettors and insiders to hide their bets so that they do not reveal their strategy to the less informed public and risk 'herd behaviour' and a fall in the odds. One way to achieve this is through 'exotic bets' whose odds (and hence volume invested) are not available to the betting public as is the case with win and place bets.[1] Exotics include: exactas, where bettors pick the first two horses in their finishing order; quinellas, in which bettors pick the first two horses in any order; and trifectas (called a tierce in Hong Kong), where bettors pick the first three horses in their finishing order. There is considerable anecdotal evidence that professional punters invest a substantial portion of their bets on exotics, including articles in the popular press (e.g. Kaplan, 2002) and personal communication with betting operators.

The remainder of this chapter proceeds in four parts. Section 9.1 discusses the meaning of 'insider bettor' and reviews previous studies. Section 9.2 introduces relevant features of wagering markets, and describes the setting and data for this study. Sections 9.3 and 9.4, respectively, report the analytical results and discuss the findings, including broader financial implications and suggestions for further research.

9.1 Insider trading in thoroughbred wagering markets

A stimulus for studies of insider trading is that it has proven difficult to explain movements of financial markets in terms of flows of publicly available information. For instance, Fair (2002) tracked the US S&P 500 futures contract between 1982 and 1999 to identify moves of greater than 0.75 per cent within any five minutes (about seven standard deviations above average). He found 1,159 examples, and then searched newswires at the time but found that 90 per cent had no identifiable cause.

With similar difficulty in using publicly available information to explain movements in other markets, there is a long history of research by finance scholars into insider or informed trading. The pioneering analysis by Fama (1970) encouraged studies of wagering markets that found evidence of insider trading and anomalies. More recent thinking is summarised by Cain, Law and Peel (2001); Vaughan Williams (1999) provides a comprehensive survey of efficiency in betting markets. Historical studies of insider betting have pursued a variety of analytical strategies, and interested readers should examine contributions by Dowie (1976), Crafts (1985), Shin (1993), Schnytzer and Shilony (1995), Vaughan Williams and Paton (1997) and Cain, Law and Peel (2001). Studies on Australian racetracks (Tuckwell, 1983; Bird and McCrae, 1987; Schnytzer and Shilony, 1995) show that insiders have been operating there for over twenty years. The general consensus is that insider trading comprises between 2 and 4 per cent of all bets (Shin, 1993 and Cain, Law and Peel, 2001, respectively).

Bettors who outperform the general public can be conveniently thought of as falling into two groups. One uses publicly available information, but processes it with superior skill. This could be achieved by technology, such as sophisticated analysis of comprehensive databases or intensive scrutiny of race videos. In other cases, it might be more intuitive. Such skilled bettors – 'professionals' to many people – do not invalidate strong market efficiency. The second group accesses information that is not generally available to generate superior financial returns and invalidates the wagering market's strong efficiency. Insider knowledge can come from owners, jockeys, trainers and industry figures who become aware that a horse is to run particularly well or badly. As it is not possible to separate skill from inside knowledge using market-level data, this chapter uses the generic term 'insider' to describe those bettors with superior skill and/or monopoly information.

The methodology of this chapter relies on a number of assumptions. The first is that the win market provides the best estimate of the probability that a horse will win the race. This estimate is typically biased by investors' behaviour, but the market's subjective probability can be corrected to provide an unbiased objective probability of winning.

A second assumption extends the hypothesis advanced by Harville (1973) that the second-finishing horse in any race would win in the absence of the winner, and the third-finishing horse would win in the absence of the first two. Thus finishing positions are independent events. Although this is logical and mathematically tractable, the limitations are obvious. Consider, for instance, a race where two stable mates finish first and second. Would the second finisher win if its stable mate had not been running? Thus when Harville (1973) reality checked his theoretical calculations against actual results, he found they understated the probabilities of horses running second and (less conclusively) third. This has been confirmed in our results. In other words, the second and third placegetters perform better than indicated by their win dividends. Thus the theoretical independence of runners needs to be relaxed to use their win dividends to predict the probability that any exotic bet will be successful.

The third assumption relates to the way that insiders distort wagering markets. Consider an unbiased, perfectly informed market: it will provide an accurate estimate of each runner's probability of winning; thus the returns from all runners will be the same and equal to the (negative) take of the Tote operator. Now assume that monopoly information becomes available to some bettors and they exploit it by betting on the winner. As the market tends to give a good indication of each runner's chances of winning, insider bets will tend to go towards shorter-priced horses. Thus the expected return from longer-priced horses will fall, as will the returns to outsider bettors. This pattern is termed the 'longshot bias' and its strength is used in this chapter to estimate the extent of insider knowledge.[2]

9.2 Description of the markets and data

9.2.1 The market

In Australia, there are two forms of legal wagering on thoroughbred races: bookmakers and the parimutuel system or totalisator ('Tote'). Bookmakers typically offer fixed odds and use an open-outcry system to compete with one another for bets; they usually pay a turnover tax. Their share of the betting market was 19 per cent in 1979, but is now below 3 per cent (The Tasmanian Gaming Commission, 2002). Bets with a bookmaker are at a marginal price, whereas dividends paid by the Tote are an average; in practice the distinction is minimal as most bets are placed close to the start of the race.

Table 9.1. *Nomenclature*

H	Number of horses starting in a race
X_h	Amount bet for a win on horse h
W	Pool for any race (ΣX_h)
α	Parimutuel operator's take
D_h	Win dividend on any horse
a_h	Win odds on any horse
p_h	Subjective probability of win based on bets that a horse will win (X_h/W)
π_h	Objective probability based on race results that a horse will win
γ	Adjustment to Harville formula
i	Proportion of pool that is bet by insiders
R_h	Expected return from win bet on horse h

Using the definitions and nomenclature which have usually been followed since first established by Griffith (1949) and Ali (1977) (table 9.1), let us determine returns from exotic bets.

Consider there are H horses in a race, and they are numbered in finishing order as 1 2 ... h ... H. Let X_h be the amount bet for a win on horse h, and the total win pool on the race is W, where:

$$W = \Sigma_{h=1}^{H} X_h$$

In parimutuel markets, the operator takes an amount, α, out of the pool to cover its costs and government taxes. This take ranges between about 15 and 25 per cent, and varies according to jurisdiction and type of bet; in Australia it is a maximum of 16 per cent. The win dividend paid on any horse is

$$D_h = \frac{(1-\alpha)W}{X_h}$$

In Australia, the Totes round all bets down to the nearest 10 cents: this means that published dividends will, on average, be 5 cents less than the dividend indicated by bettors' preferences. Thus the value of D_h used in this analysis is the published dividend plus 5 cents.

The win odds on any horse, a_h, equal $(D_h - 1){:}1$ and so

$$a_h = \frac{\{(1 - \alpha)W - X_h\}}{X_h}$$

The subjective probability that any horse will win, p_h, is established by bettor preferences and is equal to the proportion of the pool that is bet on any horse:

$$p_h = \frac{X_h}{W} = \frac{(1-\alpha)}{D_h} = \frac{(1-\alpha)}{(1+a_h)}$$

The objective probability that any horse will win, π_h, is the proportion of times a horse starting at any particular odds has historically won. Most wagering markets exhibit an important anomaly called the 'longshot bias' which arises because more money is wagered on longshot horses (i.e. high dividend) than can be justified by their objective probability of winning (Coleman, 2004). Thus p_h and π_h are not the same.

The expected return, R_h, is calculated as

$$R_h = \pi_h^* D_h - 1$$

$$= (1-\alpha)\frac{\pi_h}{p_h} - 1$$

Over 70 per cent of the variation in expected returns can be explained by an expression of the following form:

$$\text{Expected return}(\%), R_h = \beta_1 - \beta_2{}^* \text{in } (D_h)$$

where β_1 and β_2 are constants.

Turning now to exotic bets, Harville (1973) set out a formula which uses win probabilities of individual horses to calculate the theoretical return from exotic bets. Where π_1, π_2 and π_3 are, respectively, the objective probabilities that the first three placegetters will win:

$$\text{Quinella probability} = \pi_1.\frac{\pi_2}{(1-\pi_1)} + \pi_2.\frac{\pi_1}{(1-\pi_2)}$$

$$\text{Trifecta probability} = \pi_1.\frac{\pi_2}{(1-\pi_1)}.\frac{\pi_3}{(1-\pi_1-\pi_2)}$$

As noted above, these theoretical probabilities understate actual probabilities and so need to be adjusted. Clearly it is possible to make the adjustment using different assumptions and to vary it according to various race and runner parameters. We have elected to make the same adjustment to each placegetter's probabilities, y, the and calculate the adjustment so that the resulting objective win probabilities for trifecta bets match the Tote's negative take. Thus the formulae to calculate the theoretical returns from exotic bets become:

$$\text{Objective quinella probability} = \pi_1.\frac{\pi_2}{(1-\pi_1-y)} + \pi_2.\frac{\pi_1}{(1-\pi_2-y)}$$

$$\text{Objective trifecta probability} = \pi_1.\frac{\pi_2}{(1-\pi_1-y)}.\frac{\pi_3}{(1-\pi_1-\pi_2-2^*y)}$$

This adjustment has an important implication. Consider a bettor who can accurately assess the objective probability that horses will win. The win market provides a reasonable return to the bettor's estimates. However, the exotic markets have a higher probability (and hence lower dividend) than indicated by the bettor's estimates.[3]

How will the presence of insiders affect the market? In the absence of inside bettors, win dividends will provide an unbiased estimate of the probability that any horse will win. Thus π_h is equal to p_h.

Now consider that insiders (who possess information not available to other bettors) become involved. Let the amount they wager equal i proportion of the bets by 'outsiders', and assume that it is invested exclusively on the winner. If D_h^* is the dividend on the winner in a market where insiders operate:

$$D_h^* = \frac{\text{Net amount bet on the race}}{\text{Amount bet on winning horse h}}$$

$$= \frac{(1-\alpha) * (\text{Total bets of 'outsiders'}) * (1+i)}{(\pi_h + i)^* (\text{Total bets of 'outsiders'})}$$

$$= \frac{(1-\alpha) * (1+i)}{(\pi_h + i)}$$

From above :

$$D_h^* = \frac{(1-\alpha)}{p_h}$$

Therefore :

$$i = \frac{p_h - \pi_h}{1 - p_h}$$

Insiders will bet on exotic combinations while their assessment of the probability of the horses' success is higher than that of the market. They exploit monopoly information which is not available to outsider bettors, and the latter's expected return falls.

9.2.2 Data

This study uses data compiled by Martin McGrath for all thoroughbred race meetings held in Australia's principal capital cities (Adelaide, Brisbane, Melbourne, Perth and Sydney) during the period November 2002 to June 2004. About 60 per cent of the meetings were held on Saturdays, with about 20 per cent on Wednesdays. Both flat and jump races are included. To ensure the data reflect meaningful market activity, races with prize money of less than $20,000 were excluded. In addition, a small number of races with extreme outlier results (suggestive of incorrect data transmission) were removed from the analysis. This left a total of 4,700 races, with 50,700 runners. All dividend data relate to the parimutuel market operated by the listed public company Tabcorp Holdings Limited (hereafter, TAB).

9.3 Results

The first step in the data analysis was to examine the market for win bets. These results establish the objective probability that any horse will win, and this is used to calculate the theoretical dividends from exotic bets.

Figure 9.1 plots the win dividends of all runners and shows that they follow a lognormal distribution. The data are then used to derive the key parameters set out in table 9.2. The key features of table 9.2 are shown in figure 9.2.

These results show a strong longshot bias in the win market: counter-intuitively the return from betting rises with the probability that a horse will win. In this case, betting on favourites provides a better return (of negative 5–15 per cent) than betting on longshots (with a negative return below 20 per cent).

The results also show that the win market can accurately predict the probabilities that any horse will win. Some 99 per cent of the variance in win probabilities is explained by the following expression:

$$\text{Objective win probability} = 1.075^*(\text{Win dividend})^{-1.131}$$

That is $\pi_h = 1.075^* D_h^{-1.131}$

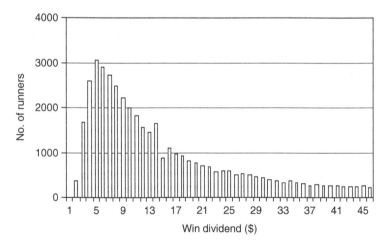

Figure 9.1 Win dividends of runners

Table 9.2. *Metropolitan races: win market data*

Range of starters' win dividends ($)	Races (no.)	Average win dividend of winners ($)	Objective win probability	Expected return (%)
<1.5	65	1.4	0.69	−2.9
1.6–2.6	494	2.2	0.38	−17.8
2.7–3.7	757	3.2	0.28	−9.4
3.8–4.9	770	4.4	0.20	−14.7
5.0–7.3	975	6.1	0.15	−11.4
7.4–12.1	845	9.5	0.09	−15.6
12.2–20.0	426	15.6	0.05	−22.3
20.1–33.0	222	25.8	0.03	−15.0
33.1–54.5	84	42.3	0.02	−31.4
54.6–89.9	33	69.7	0.01	−39.6
>90.0	10	145.3	0.00	−64.3
Total	4,680	27.9	0.09	−22.3

9.3.1 Analysis of trifecta bets

We start the analysis of exotic bets with trifectas. Their theoretical payout can be calculated using the objective winning probabilities calculated from win dividends. The process involves:

(i) Calculate an adjustment factor, y, which normalises the theoretical probability calculations to match observed returns from TAB

(ii) Calculate objective win probabilities for each of the three placegetters

(iii) Calculate the theoretical trifecta dividend using the objective win probabilities, Harville formula and historical TAB take

(iv) Compare the actual and objective dividends.

In each case, the calculations of probabilities and theoretical dividends took into account the TAB take including fractions of 15.2 per cent for win bets, 15.3 per cent for quinellas and 20.0 for trifectas.[4]

The value of y was 7.71 per cent. That is, the win market understates by 7.7 per cent the probability that any horse will run second.

The remaining results are shown in table 9.3.

The most important result from table 9.3 is shown in figure 9.3. Almost all the variance between the theoretical trifecta dividend and actual payments is explained by the following expression:

Expected return (%) = 42.5 − 12.4* ln (Average trifecta dividend)

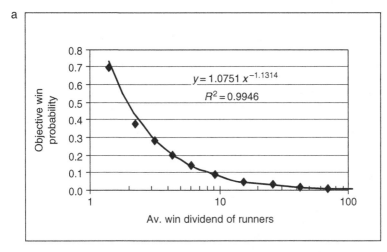

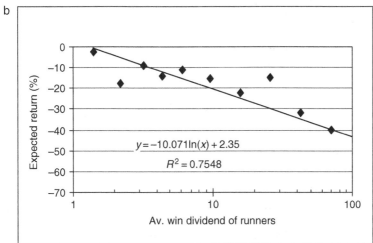

Figure 9.2 Win market wagering data: (a) Objective win probablity (b) Longshot bias in win bets

This shows a relatively strong longshot bias in the trifecta market with higher than expected payouts for trifectas which include short-priced horses.

9.3.2 Analysis of quinella bets

The next step is to replicate the analysis above using data for quinellas, and key data are shown in table 9.4.

Table 9.3. *Metropolitan races: trifecta data*

Maximum win dividend of placegetters ($)	Trifectas (no.)	Average trifecta dividend ($)	Objective win probability	Expected return (%)
<4.9	111	33.2	0.03832	(3.5)
5.0–7.3	526	80.2	0.02029	(10.9)
7.4–9.6	658	156.0	0.00999	(19.5)
9.7–12.4	716	276.3	0.00577	(25.3)
12.5–16.4	698	417.2	0.00364	(33.3)
16.5–24.5	805	810.0	0.00236	(35.9)
24.6–36.6	588	1507.4	0.00131	(45.5)
36.7–54.6	307	2248.8	0.00056	(59.2)
54.7–81.4	271	4420.6	0.00047	(61.3)
Total	4,680	867.0	0.00665	(20.2)

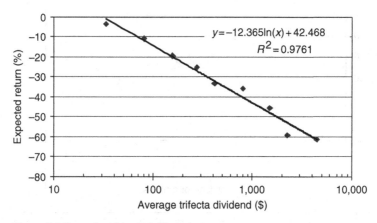

$$y = -12.365\ln(x) + 42.468$$
$$R^2 = 0.9761$$

Figure 9.3 Longshot bias in trifecta bets

Figure 9.4 plots the expected return from quinellas as a function of dividends. Just as with trifectas, the dividend for short-priced winners is substantially higher than would be expected from the adjusted Harville formula, and the size of the overpayment falls as the dividend rises.

In summary, there is a strong longshot bias in the quinella market (which matches the experience in Finland reported by Kanto, Rosenqvist and Suvas, 1992) so that a higher expected return comes from supporting short-priced horses in quinellas.

Table 9.4. *Metropolitan races: quinella data*

Maximum win dividend of placegetters ($)	Quinellas (no.)	Average quinella dividend ($)	Objective win probability	Expected return (%)
<4.9	573	$6.0	0.212	3.2
5.0–6.4	609	$10.5	0.113	−3.8
6.5–8.0	613	$15.4	0.078	−6.5
8.1–11.0	851	$22.6	0.051	−13.0
11.1–16.0	796	$38.3	0.028	−19.7
16.1–24.0	569	$64.6	0.017	−26.5
24.1–36.0	365	$96.5	0.013	−25.6
>36	304	$198.2	0.005	−45.8
Total	4,680	$42.9	0.069	−11.1

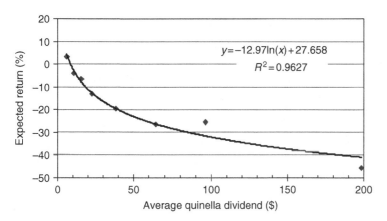

Figure 9.4 Longshot bias in quinella bets

9.3.3 Extent of insider trading

We now determine the extent of insider trading. The approach taken is to use the formula:

$$i = \frac{p_h - \pi_h}{1 - p_h}$$

where:

$i=$ insider bets as a proportion of bets by outsiders

$p_h=$ subjective probability of a win as calculated by win dividends

$\pi_h=$ objective probability of a win calculated from dividends in the win market and the adjusted Harville formulae

The results for the three wagering markets are shown in table 9.5. In the win market, 10 per cent of bets are by insiders; given this is an upper estimate, the conclusion matches advice from the Victorian TAB that 'professional punters comprise between three and six per cent of turnover' (personal communication, February 2003). The insiders' bets are heavily concentrated on shorter-priced horses.

The level of insider betting in the two exotic markets is considerably lower, and virtually all goes to exotic bets incorporating short-priced horses. Another feature of table 9.5 is that the extent of insider trading declines with complexity of the bets: in the win market where only first place is chosen, insiders make 10 per cent of bets; with quinellas which require two selections, they place about 2 per cent of bets; and their share of the complex trifecta market is tiny.

9.4 Discussion and implications

Anecdotal evidence suggests that insiders are more active in the trifecta market than the win market. On the other hand, the win market is by far the deeper of the two, with about three times the volume of bets. Intuitively one would expect that insiders would make more use of the deeper market where their bets will have less impact. In addition, dividends in the exotic markets are lower than expected from objective win probabilities, so that skill or knowledge is not as well rewarded. On balance, then, insiders should see exotic markets as less attractive than win markets. In fact this is borne out by the evidence in table 9.5 that shows that insiders are far more active in the win market than in the quinella and trifecta markets.

An important question then arises about insiders' strategy: why do they prefer to bet in the win market even though the instantaneous display of odds on screens publicly signals their bets to outsiders who might follow the momentum and depress the odds? The answer comes in a consistent feature of Australian parimutuel operators: in practice, last-minute changes in odds are not signalled to outsiders. Despite extensive computerisation of the Tote, a third of bets are not reflected in the odds until seconds before betting closes.[5] Thus it is quite common for outsider bettors to be physically unable to follow downward moves in odds that signal an insider plunge.

Table 9.5. *Insider trades as a proportion of bet value*

Win market		Quinella market		Trifecta market	
Range	Insiders (%)	Range	Insiders (%)	Range	Insiders (%)
≤1.5	26.5	≤4.9	4.6	≤4.9	0.68
1.6–2.6	0.4	5.0–6.4	1.5	5.0–7.3	0.21
2.7–3.7	3.3	6.5–8.0	0.8	7.4–9.6	0.01
3.8–4.9	0.7	8.1–11.0	0.1	9.7–12.4	−0.04
5.0–7.3	1.1	11.1–16.0	−0.2	12.5–16.4	−0.07
7.4–12.1	0.2	16.1–24.0	−0.3	16.5–24.5	−0.06
12.2–20.0	−0.3	24.1–36.0	−0.2	24.6–36.6	−0.06
20.1–33.0	0.1	>36	−0.3	36.7–54.6	−0.05
33.1–54.5	−0.3			54.7–81.4	−0.05
54.6–89.9	−0.3				
>90.0	−0.3				
Total (weighted by bet value)	9.9		2.2		0.3

The late flow of money is difficult to explain. Insider and/or professional bets are no more than 10 per cent of the bet volume; and bookmakers are only 3 per cent. Thus no more than 13 per cent of the bets can be explained by all professionals betting at the last minute and bookmakers laying off all their bets on the Tote. Moreover, leaving bets until the final seconds risks missing the race cut-off. One possibility is that a stream of bets is simply held up until the last minute. For instance, TABCORP's 2003 *Annual Report* says that self-service betting (such as touch tone telephones and internet) comprises 46 per cent of all bets. While it is beyond the scope of this chapter to consider further why computerised odds lag so far behind the flows of money, it is an important imperfection in the Tote market that should concern outsider bettors and perhaps industry regulators.[6]

Indirect confirmation that insiders are taking advantage of slow computer processing comes from the bookmaker markets. Although bookmaker odds are generally fixed and thus insiders should be largely unconcerned whether others follow their bets, plunges with bookmakers also occur late in the betting. This is consistent with the existence of a significant group of insiders who also bet on the Tote and wish to avoid signalling to outsiders.

The truism of gambling that 'You cannot beat the books!' is invariably confirmed by academic research into wagering markets that shows profitable strategies rarely exist. Although *ex post* mining of comprehensive market data sometimes points to profitable techniques, few can offset transaction costs, and many are not practical to execute in the face of the slow flow of dividend information.

The analysis above provides an example of a bias in the wagering market that theoretically might allow a profitable investment opportunity. In the case of trifectas, a profit after transaction costs can be made by betting on the 4.4 per cent of combinations that have a dividend of less than about $30 (the maximum dividend of placegetters is generally less than about $10; on average there are 4.4 such runners in each race).

Although betting on short-priced trifectas appears superficially attractive, there are a number of constraints preventing it. The most obvious is that trifecta dividends are not displayed until after the race is run, so that they must be inferred from win dividends. And because the majority of bets come close to the start of the race, odds on short-priced horses frequently change after betting is closed. Thus identifying the correct choices is often not practicable.

Looking beyond exotic bets, the conclusions of this study have broader implications than just those for bettors because wagering markets share many of the features of conventional financial markets.

The first broad implication is that simple investment strategies provide greatest returns to skill. At the racecourse, market structures mean that inside bettors can achieve better payouts in the win market than in exotics; and that is the way they seem to bet. A second implication is that insiders are active, controlling up to 10 per cent of investments; and most of their wagers are on high-probability (low-dividend) outcomes. A third implication is that outsiders are disadvantaged not only by a lack of knowledge, but also by structural features of the market such as late transmission of betting data.

These conclusions point to potentially rewarding areas for analysis in conventional financial markets. They should also encourage continuing analysis of insider trading in wagering markets, for instance by evaluating other types of dividends and results in markets outside Australia.

Notes

1 A 'place' bet in Australia pays if the chosen horse finishes first, second or third (but if there are seven runners or less, no third dividend is paid). This definition is used throughout.
2 There are other possible explanations for the longshot bias such as bettors' overestimation of the probability of occurrence of low-frequency events, or their assumption of an equal risk-weighted return from wagering and preference for the small chance of a large win. Moreover some of the bias may be caused by 'herd behaviour', rather than true insiders; and some insider bets may not go to the winner. Because there are several possible explanations for the longshot bias, ascribing the cause solely to insider trading, means that the estimate of insider trading derived here is probably high.
3 Although identifying the cause of this is beyond the capability of our data, one possibility is the practice of 'boxing' runners in exotic bets so that (say) three or four horses are chosen and boxed so that any two can constitute a quinella. This could set up relations between dividends on exotic bets that do not arise in win markets.
4 TAB take is displayed under 'Bet Rules' at www.tabracing.com.au. Fractions (called 'breakage' in the US) is additional and is the amount which comes from rounding dividends down to the nearest 10 cents.
5 A small sample of races in Australia showed that about 40 per cent of wagers are placed in the last minute of betting. Anecdotally the situation is similar in other wagering markets around the world.
6 The first author sent an e-mail to TABCORP seeking an explanation. They estimate that 30–60 per cent of bets are placed in the last 2–3 minutes of betting and believe this is a feature of bettors' behaviour and not within their control (personal communication: 15 September 2004).

References

Ali, M. M. (1977) 'Probability and Utility Estimates for Racetrack Bettors', *Journal of Political Economy*, 85, pp. 803–16

Bird, R. and McCrae, M. (1987) 'Tests of the Efficiency of Racetrack Betting Using Bookmaker Odds', *Management Science*, 33, pp. 1552–62

Cain, M., Law, D. and Peel, D. A. (2001) 'The Relationship Between Two Indicators of Insider Trading in British Racetrack Betting', *Economica*, 68, pp. 97–104

Coleman, L. (2004) 'New Light on the Longshot Bias', *Applied Economics*, 36, pp. 315–26

Crafts, N. F. R. (1985) 'Some Evidence of Insider Knowledge in Horse Race Betting in Britain', *Economica*, 52, pp. 295–304

Dowie, J. (1976) 'On the Efficiency and Equity of Betting Markets', *Economica*, 43, pp. 139–50

Fair, R. C. (2002) 'Events that Shook the Market', *Journal of Business*, 75, pp. 713–31

Fama, E. F. (1970) 'Efficient Capital Markets: A Review of Theory and Empirical Work', *Journal of Finance*, 25, pp. 383–417

Griffith, R. M. (1949) 'Odds Adjustment by American Horse Race Bettors', *American Journal of Psychology*, 62, pp. 290–4

Harville, D. A. (1973) 'Assigning Probabilities to Outcomes of Multi-entry Competitions', *Journal of the American Statistical Association*, 68, pp. 312–16

Kanto, A. J., Rosenqvist, G. and Suvas, A. (1992) 'On Utility Function Estimation of Racetrack Bettors', *Journal of Economic Psychology*, 13, pp. 491–8

Kaplan, M. (2002) 'The High Tech Trifecta', *Wired Magazine*, 10, pp. 10–13

Schnytzer, A. and Shilony, Y. (1995) 'Inside Information in a Betting Market', *Economic Journal*, 105, pp. 963–71

Shin, H. S. (1993) 'Measuring the Incidence of Insider Trading in a Market for State-Contingent Claims', *Economic Journal*, 103, pp. 1141–53

The Tasmanian Gaming Commission (2002) *Australian Gambling Statistics 1975–6 to 2001–2*, Hobart: Tasmanian Gaming Commission

Tuckwell, R. H. (1983) 'The Thoroughbred Gambling Market: Efficiency, Equity and Related Issues', *Australian Economic Papers*, pp. 6–118

Vaughan Williams, L. (1999) 'Information Efficiency in Betting Markets: A Survey', *Bulletin of Economic Research*, 51, pp. 1–30

Vaughan Williams, L. and Paton, D. (1997) 'Why is There a Favourite-Longshot Bias in British Racetrack Betting Markets?', *Economic Journal*, 107, pp. 150–8

10 On the improbability of informationally efficient parimutuel betting markets in the presence of heterogeneous beliefs

William Hurley and Lawrence McDonough

10.1 Introduction

A very useful laboratory for the study of the informational efficiency in markets is a parimutuel betting market. Participants assess the relative likelihoods that various horses will win and then bet on the basis of this analysis. From this betting we can deduce the market's aggregate assessment of the probability that a particular class of horse will win (the so-called *subjective probability*) and this can be compared to that class's *objective probability* of winning. The conventional view is that, if parimutuel betting markets were efficient, these probabilities ought to coincide. Unfortunately, a significant number of empirical studies have found they do not. Most often, favourites are underbet and long-shots overbet. However there have been studies which have reported a reverse bias (Busche and Hall, 1988; Woodland and Woodland, 1994). This mismatching of subjective and objective probabilities is termed the 'favourite-longshot bias'. The instance where favourites are underbet is termed the *usual* bias; where favourites are overbet, it is termed the *reverse* bias.

Not surprisingly there have been a number of explanations for the bias. The interested reader is referred to Thaler and Ziemba (1988) and Sauer (1998) for excellent summaries of the literature. One class of explanation appeals to bettor preferences. In particular, they posit that bettors are risk-lovers. This line of research would include the work of Weitzman (1965), Ali (1977), Quandt (1986), and Kanto, Rosenqvist and Suvas (1992). More recently Golec and Tamarkin (1998) have suggested that gamblers prefer return skewness rather than risk.

Another explanation appeals to asymmetric information among bettors. These models assume there is a class of bettor with superior information about the outcome of the contest and would include the work of

Shin (1992), Hurley and McDonough (1995a, 1996), Williams and Paton (1998) and Cain, Law and Peel (2003).

A third class of model turns on heterogeneous beliefs among bettors. Ali (1977) studies a two-horse-race where bettors have heterogeneous expectations and shows that the bias will obtain. Blough (1994) extends Ali's model to the case of an m-horse-race and finds that, under the condition of symmetric heterogeneous expectations, the bias will emerge.

The model we present here is based on heterogeneous bettor beliefs. It differs from those of Ali (1977) and Blough (1994) in that a large number of betters play sequentially. We do not model this sequential betting as a game. Rather, it has the flavour of an evolutionary game as set out in, say, Samuelson (1997). Effectively our sequence of bettors produces a stochastic process of parimutuel odds. We then examine the steady-state behaviour of this process. In this way, our model is different from those of Watanabe (1997) and Feeney and King (2001).

The steady-state behaviour has a number of interesting properties. In the two-horse-race, our steady-state results are identical to Ali's. However we show that the imposition of positive track take in the two-horse-race can result in the reverse bias if track take is sufficiently high. If there are at least three horses and 0 track take, the steady state can exhibit the usual and reverse biases depending on the distribution governing bettor beliefs. However our main result has to do with the likelihood that there is a bias. What drives our model is the probability distribution governing bettor beliefs. We assume that bettor beliefs are unbiased in the following sense. For a particular horse, a large number of betters form beliefs about the chance that horse will win. If we then take an average of these beliefs over a large number of bettors, the average is arbitrarily close to the horse's true probability of winning. With this assumption we show that it is highly unlikely that subjective probabilities will match the objective probabilities. Hence, we conclude that it is highly improbable that parimutuel betting markets characterised by heterogeneous beliefs will be efficient.

10.2 A two-horse-race

10.2.1 Preliminaries

Consider a horse-race where there are only two horses – a *Favourite* and a *Longshot*. The true probability that the Favourite wins is p_F; the probability that the Longshot wins is $p_L = 1 - p_F$.

There are N possible bettors where N is large. We model their behaviour as follows. We assume bettor n's beliefs about the probability the Favourite will win, p_n, is formed by a random drawing from a distribution with density function $g(\cdot)$ and a corresponding cumulative density function $G(\cdot)$. Hence our bettors have heterogeneous beliefs for a particular race, but we insist that, as a group, their collective estimate is unbiased. Mathematically we require that

$$E(p_n) = p_F \text{ for all } n \tag{10.1}$$

This assumption about individual behaviour gives rise to a Law of Large Numbers effect:

$$\frac{p_1 + p_2 + \ldots + p_N}{N} \xrightarrow{\text{pr}} p_F \tag{10.2}$$

So, even though individual beliefs are heterogeneous, these beliefs are unbiased in the sense that the average of bettor beliefs gets arbitrarily close to p_F as N gets large.

Bettors arrive one after the other, each to bet b units on the horse which provides the highest expected profit. Which horse is bet will depend on the subjective probability that a bettor places on the event that the Favourite wins the race and the current odds on the Favourite. At the time the first bettor places his or her bet, we assume that there has been some initial betting which leads to F_0 wagered on the Favourite and L_0 wagered on the Longshot. This assures that the profit function of the first bettor is well defined.

Suppose bettor n places an amount X_n on the Favourite. X_n either takes the value b or 0. If X_n takes the value 0, then the bettor is assumed to place b on the Longshot. Given these definitions, the total amount placed on Favourite after the nth bettor has placed his or her bet is

$$F_n = F_0 + \sum_{t=1}^{n} X_t \tag{10.3}$$

and on the Longshot,

$$L_n = L_0 + nb - \sum_{t=1}^{n} X_t \tag{10.4}$$

Note that $F_n + L_n = F_0 + L_0 + nb$.

The subjective probability on the Favourite after the nth bettor places a bet is defined

$$\theta_n = \frac{F_n}{F_n + L_n} \tag{10.5}$$

where F_n and L_n are the actual amounts bet on the Favourite and Longshot. Since there are only two horses in the race, the subjective probability on the Longshot is $1 - \theta_n$.

Now consider the $(n+1)$st bettor's decision. He or she perceives a bet b on the Favourite will give expected profit of

$$\pi_{n+1}^F = \frac{F_n + L_n}{F_n} b p_{n+1} - b = \left(\frac{p_{n+1}}{\theta_n} - 1\right) b \qquad (10.6)$$

and on the Longshot,

$$\pi_{n+1}^L = \frac{F_n + L_n}{L_n} b(1 - p_{n+1}) - b = \left(\frac{1 - p_{n+1}}{1 - \theta_n} - 1\right) b \qquad (10.7)$$

These payoff functions are consistent with the following assumptions about behaviour:

1. A bettor assumes that the current parimutuel payoffs are unbiased estimates of those that will prevail at the end of betting
2. A bettor assumes that the number of bettors is large enough that his or her bet will not affect the parimutuel payoffs and
3. A bettor allocates his or her wager, b, to maximise the expected value of profit as in (10.6) and (10.7).

Note from (10.6) that bettor $n+1$ will bet the Favourite if $p_{n+1} > \theta_n$ and this will happen with probability $1 - G(\theta_n)$.

10.2.2 Steady-state behaviour

The following results characterise the steady-state behaviour of the sub-jective probability on the Favourite.

> *Lemma 1:*
> The sequence of random variables, $\{\theta_1, \theta_2, \ldots, \theta_n, \ldots\}$, has a limit.

> *Proof:*
> See the appendix, p. 256.

> *Lemma 2:*
> Let θ^* solve $1 - \theta = G(\theta)$. Then $plim\,\theta_n = \theta^*$.

> *Proof:*
> See the appendix, p. 257.

Thus, the steady-state condition is

$$1 - G(\theta) - \theta = 0 \qquad (10.8)$$

and we are now in a position to give the relationship between the objective and subjective probabilities.

Proposition 1:
For a two-horse-race and a large number of bettors, the usual favourite-longshot bias obtains, or

$$p_F > 0.5 \Rightarrow \theta^* < p_F \tag{10.9}$$

Proof:
The steady-state condition in (10.8) can be rewritten

$$\theta + G(\theta) = 1 \tag{10.10}$$

Note that the left-hand side is an increasing continuous function for $\theta \in [0,1]$. Now suppose that $p_F > 0.5$ solves the steady-state condition. Substituting p_F into the left-hand side gives

$$p_F + G(p_F) = p_F + 0.5 \tag{10.11}$$

which is greater than 1 since p_F was assumed to be greater than 0.5. Thus it must be that $\theta^* < p_F$. And the proof is complete.

This proof is based on Ali's (1977) insight. Suppose the betting (subjective probabilities) reflected the true win probabilities, $(p_F, 1 - p_F)$, at some point in the betting sequence. Since $G(p_F) = 1 - G(p_F) = 0.5$, the next bettor would have an equal chance of betting either horse, but a steady state would require that the probability of betting on the Favourite would be equal to the win probability of the Favourite which is greater than $1/2$.

10.2.3 The effect of track take

Suppose the track extracts a percentage T of the win pool. Therefore a percentage $Q = 1 - T$ is returned to bettors. The expected payoff to a bet b on the Favourite is

$$\pi_{n+1}^F = \frac{(F_n + L_n)Q}{F_n} b p_{n+1} - b \tag{10.12}$$

and on the Longshot,

$$\pi_{n+1}^L = \frac{(F_n + L_n)Q}{L_n} b(1 - p_{n+1}) - b \tag{10.13}$$

Assuming a large number of bettors, the steady-state condition can be shown to be

$$\theta Q = \frac{1 - G(\theta)}{1 - G(\theta) + G(\theta + 1 - 1/Q)} \tag{10.14}$$

Note that, when there is no track take ($Q = 1$), this condition reduces to

$$1 - G(\theta) - \theta = 0 \tag{10.15}$$

the steady-state condition in the absence of track take.

Let θ_Q^* solve (10.14). Then as track take increases we can show that θ_Q^* increases. Since we know the usual favourite-longshot bias obtains when track take is 0 ($Q = 1$), it must be that the bias reverses itself as track take increases. Here is an example. Suppose bettors choose probabilities on the Favourite that are uniformly distributed on [0.4, 0.8] Note that the Favourite's objective probability of winning is 0.6. Under these assumptions, we can solve (10.14) for θ_Q^*:

$$\theta_Q^* = \frac{4}{7Q} = \frac{4}{7(1 - T)} \tag{10.16}$$

The following table presents values of θ_Q^* for various values of T:

T	θ_Q^*
0.00	0.571
0.05	0.602
0.10	0.635

(10.17)

Note that θ_Q^* increases as T increases. Hence track take can reverse the bias, but nonetheless there will be a bias, either the usual or reverse, for all but one value of T.

10.3 The steady-state condition for the m-horse-race

Now consider an m-horse-race. Proposition 2 characterises the steady state for such a race:

> *Proposition 2:*
> Let ϕ_n^i be the probability that bettor n bets horse i. Let θ_m^i be the subjective probability on horse i before bettor n places a bet. Then
>
> $$\lim_{n \to \infty} \Pr\left\{ \left| \varphi_n^i - \theta_n^i \right| < \varepsilon \right\} = 1 \text{ for } i = 1, 2, \ldots, m \tag{10.18}$$
>
> *Proof:*
> See the appendix, p. 259.

The proposition states that, as the number of bettors becomes large, the probability that a bettor chooses horse i converges to the subjective probability on horse i. Let

$$plim \; \varphi_n^i = \varphi^i \tag{10.19}$$

Then to get the steady-state subjective probabilities, we need to solve the following system:

$$\theta^i = \varphi_i \text{ for } i = 1, 2, \ldots, m-1 \tag{10.20}$$

$$\sum_i \theta_i = 1 \tag{10.21}$$

10.4 A three-horse-race

Now consider a three-horse-race where there is a Middle horse as well as a Favourite and Longshot. Let the objective probabilities of winning be p_F, p_M and p_L, where $p_F > p_M > p_L$ Throughout this section we assume that track take is 0.

One of the difficulties in modelling heterogeneous bettor expectations is selecting the subjective probabilities in such a way that they lie on the unit simplex. For instance suppose we draw a set of subjective probabilities, $\{p_F, p_M, p_L\}$, from normal distributions centred on each horse's objective probability of winning. Then there is no guarantee that these will sum to 1. The *expectation* of the sum is 1, but a specific *realisation* will be different than 1. Since we will ultimately show that the direction of the bias depends critically on the variance of the distributions we employ, it is important that we be careful about how the variance structure of beliefs is modelled.[1] Hence the problem: how do we draw a set of subjective probabilities which lie on the unit simplex, which are centred at the objective probabilities, and which have a specified variance structure?

Our normalisation is this:

$$\rho_i^N = \rho_i - \lambda_i \left(\sum_i \rho_i - 1 \right) \quad \text{for } i = F, M, L \tag{10.22}$$

where $\sum_i \lambda_i = 1$, and $\lambda_i > 0$ for all i. Note that $\sum_i \rho_i^N = 1$ and that $E(\rho_i^N) = p_i$. In addition, if the ρ_i are selected from normal distributions, then ρ_i^N will also have a normal distribution. The details of this method are provided by Hurley and McDonough (1995b).

Now consider a representative bettor. Without loss in generality, suppose he draws $\{\rho_F, \rho_M, \rho_L\}$, from independent normal distributions having respective means p_F, p_M, p_L and variances σ_F^2, σ_M^2, σ_L^2. This drawing is then normalised using (10.22) to produce $\{\rho_F^N, \rho_M^N, \rho_L^N\}$ where λ_i is chosen to be p_i. Moreover we also suppose that the variances of these distributions are small enough that ρ_i^N turns out to be in the interval $[0,1]$ for $i = F$, M and L. We can show that the joint distribution of $(\rho_F^N, \rho_M^N, \rho_L^N)$ is multivariate normal with means

$$E\left(\rho_i^N\right) = p_i, \quad \text{for } i = F, M, L \tag{10.23}$$

and a covariance matrix with ij element

$$\text{cov}\left(\rho_i^N, \rho_j^N\right) = -\lambda_i\sigma_i^2 - \lambda_j\sigma_j^2 + \lambda_i\lambda_j\sum_{k=1}^{3}\sigma_k^2 \tag{10.24}$$

Our representative bettor will wager the Favourite if the expected profit of a bet on the Favourite exceeds the expected profit of a bet on the Middle horse *and* the expected profit of a bet on the Longshot, which corresponds to the probability

$$\varphi_F = Pr\left\{\rho_F^N \geq \left(\frac{\theta_F}{\theta_M}\right)\rho_M^N \text{ and } \rho_F^N \geq \left(\frac{\theta_F}{\theta_L}\right)\rho_L^N\right\} \tag{10.25}$$

Under the distributional assumptions made, and noting that $\theta_F + \theta_M + \theta_L = 1$, we have

$$\varphi_F = \int_{-\infty}^{\infty}\int_{\theta_F}^{\infty}\int_{1-\rho_F^N(1-\theta_F)/\theta_M}^{\rho_F^N\theta_M/\theta_F} f_N\left(\rho_F^N, \rho_M^N, \rho_L^N\right)d\rho_M^N \, d\rho_F^N \, d\rho_L^N \tag{10.26}$$

where $f_N\left(\rho_F^N, \rho_M^N, \rho_L^N\right)$ is the multivariate normal distribution specified above. The probability of betting on the middle horse is

$$\varphi_M = \int_{-\infty}^{\infty}\int_{\theta_M}^{\infty}\int_{1-\rho_M^N(1-\theta_M)/\theta_F}^{\rho_M^N\theta_F/\theta_M} f_N\left(\rho_F^N, \rho_M^N, \rho_L^N\right)d\rho_F^N \, d\rho_M^N \, d\rho_L^N \tag{10.27}$$

Based on Proposition 2, the steady-state conditions for the three-horse-race are

$$\theta_F = \varphi_F$$

$$\theta_M = \varphi_M$$

$$\theta_F + \theta_M + \theta_L = 1 \tag{10.28}$$

To see that the direction of the bias is affected by choice of second moment, consider the following instance:

$$p_F = 0.45 \qquad p_M = 0.35 \qquad p_L = 0.20$$

$$\sigma_F = 0.25p_F \quad \sigma_M = 0.25p_M \qquad \sigma_L = 0.25p_L \tag{10.29}$$

Note that all standard deviations are set at 25% of their respective means. Under these assumptions system (10.28) yields

$$\theta_F^* = 0.4402$$

$$\theta_M^* = 0.3490$$

$$\theta_L^* = 0.2109 \tag{10.30}$$

and the usual bias obtains. Now suppose we raise the standard deviation on the Favourite to $\sigma_F = 0.3p_F$. In this case the steady-state probabilities are

$$\theta_F^* = 0.4557$$

$$\theta_M^* = 0.3431$$

$$\theta_L^* = 0.2011 \tag{10.31}$$

Note, now, that the Favourite is overbet. Hence, based on this example, we can conclude two things: there will be a bias; and the direction of the bias will depend critically on the variance structure of beliefs.

Of some interest are the standard deviations which result in the objective probabilities being equal to the subjective probabilities. If bettor beliefs are formed according to

$$p_F = 0.45 \qquad p_M = 0.35 \qquad p_L = 0.20$$

$$\sigma_F = 0.133631 \quad \sigma_M = 0.099192 \qquad \sigma_L = 0.042029 \tag{10.32}$$

we have that

$$\theta_F^* = p_F = 0.45$$

$$\theta_M^* = p_M = 0.35$$

$$\theta_L^* = p_L = 0.20 \tag{10.33}$$

We can show that the only other points which give this result form a lower dimensional subspace. Hence there will be a bias with probability 1.

10.5 Comparison with market-maker betting markets

It is well known that market microstructure can have a significant effect on the efficiency of trade. Betting markets are no exception. They are generally organised in two ways. One is the parimutuel mechanism; the other is where market-makers (bookies) stand ready to take bets at fixed odds. The two are fundamentally different. For a market-maker microstructure, we have shown (see Hurley and McDonough, 2004) that, in the presence of heterogeneous beliefs, there will be no bias as long as these bookie betting markets are perfectly competitive. In this sense, market-maker betting markets have the potential to be efficient regardless of the distribution of bettor beliefs and in this sense they are superior to parimutuel markets.

10.6 Conclusions

The main contribution of the chapter is this. We have considered a model of sequential parimutuel betting where bettors have heterogeneous beliefs. Yet these heterogeneous beliefs are correct in the sense that if they were averaged they would correspond to the objective probabilities that various horses will win. In our view these assumptions are not inconsistent with what actually happens at the track. Under these assumptions, we show that it would be quite improbable for the subjective and objective probabilities to coincide in parimutuel betting markets. Hence our conclusion that parimutuel betting markets are not likely to be efficient.

The explanation turns on the variance structure characterising bettor beliefs. *Ceteris paribus*, as the variance of beliefs on a particular horse is raised, it is more likely that a particular horse will be bet, and hence the horse's subjective probability of winning will increase. To get the special case where objective and subjective probabilities coincide, we would have to get a particular set of variances, one of an infinite number of possibilities. Hence, we would be extremely lucky to observe efficiency in such a market.

Appendix

> *Proof of Lemma 1:*
> To prove that the sequence has a limit, we employ the Cauchy criterion and show that
> $$\lim_{n\to\infty} \Pr\{|\theta_{n+m} - \theta_n| \geq \varepsilon\} = 0 \tag{10A.1}$$

For any non-negative random variable, Y, it is always true that

$$\Pr\{Y \geq \alpha\} \leq \frac{E(Y)}{\alpha} \tag{10A.2}$$

Letting $\Delta_{nm} = \Pr\{|\theta_{n+m} - \theta_n| \geq \varepsilon\}$, we have that

$$\Delta_{nm} \leq \frac{E|\theta_{n+m} - \theta_n|}{\varepsilon}$$

$$= \frac{1}{\varepsilon} E \left| \frac{F_0 + \sum_{t=1}^{n} X_t + \sum_{t=1}^{m} X_{n+t}}{F_0 + L_0 + (n+m)b} - \frac{F_0 + \sum_{t=1}^{n} X_t}{F_0 + L_0 + nb} \right|$$

$$= \frac{1}{\varepsilon} E \left| \frac{-mb\left(F_0 + \sum_{t=1}^{n} X_t\right)}{(F_0 + L_0 + (n+m)b)(F_0 + L_0 + nb)} - \frac{\sum_{t=1}^{m} X_{n+t}}{F_0 + L_0 + (n+m)b} \right|$$

$$\leq \frac{1}{\varepsilon} E \left| \frac{-mb\left(F_0 + \sum_{t=1}^{n} X_t\right)}{(F_0 + L_0 + (n+m)b)(F_0 + L_0 + nb)} \right|$$

$$+ \frac{1}{\varepsilon} E \left| \frac{\sum_{t=1}^{m} X_{n+t}}{F_0 + L_0 + (n+m)b} \right|$$

$$= \frac{1}{\varepsilon} E \left\{ \frac{mb\left(F_0 + \sum_{t=1}^{n} X_t\right)}{(F_0 + L_0 + (n+m)b)(F_0 + L_0 + nb)} \right\}$$

$$+ \frac{1}{\varepsilon} E \left\{ \frac{\sum_{t=1}^{m} X_{n+t}}{F_0 + L_0 + (n+m)b} \right\}$$

$$\leq \frac{1}{\varepsilon} \frac{mb(F_0 + nb)}{(F_0 + L_0 + (n+m)b)(F_0 + L_0 + nb)}$$

$$+ \frac{1}{\varepsilon} \frac{mb}{F_0 + L_0 + (n+m)b} \tag{10A.3}$$

since $\sum_{t=1}^{k} X_t \leq k$. For any kb. For any m, both terms on the right-hand side of the inequality in (10A.3) go to 0 as $n \to \infty$. Therefore we have that

$$\lim_{n \to \infty} \Pr\{|\theta_{n+m} - \theta_n| \geq \varepsilon\} < 0 \tag{10A.4}$$

which implies that

$$\lim_{n \to \infty} \Pr\{|\theta_{n+m} - \theta_n| \geq \varepsilon\} = 0 \tag{10A.5}$$

since probabilities are non-negative. And the proof is complete.

Proof of Lemma 2:
Before proceeding with the general line of proof, we demonstrate that

$$\lim_{n \to \infty} E \left[\frac{F_0 + \sum_{t=1}^{n} X_t}{F_0 + L_0 + nb} \right] = \lim_{n \to \infty} E \left[\frac{\sum_{t=1}^{n} X_t}{nb} \right] \tag{10A.6}$$

To see this, note that

$$\lim_{n\to\infty} E\left[\frac{F_0 + \sum_{t=1}^n X_t}{F_0 + L_0 + nb}\right] = \lim_{n\to\infty} E\left[\frac{F_0}{F_0 + L_0 + nb}\right] + \lim_{n\to\infty} E\left[\frac{\sum_{t=1}^n X_t}{F_0 + L_0 + nb}\right]$$

$$= \lim_{n\to\infty} E\left[\frac{\sum_{t=1}^n X_t}{F_0 + L_0 + nb}\right]$$

$$= E\left[\lim_{n\to\infty} \frac{\sum_{t=1}^n X_t/n}{F_0/n + L_0/n + b}\right]$$

$$= E\left[\lim_{n\to\infty} \left(\frac{\sum_{t=1}^n X_t}{nb}\right)\right]$$

$$= \lim_{n\to\infty} E\left[\left(\frac{\sum_{t=1}^n X_t}{nb}\right)\right] \qquad (10A.7)$$

The main line of proof is by contradiction. Suppose $plim\ \theta_n = \theta'$, and that $\theta \neq \theta'$. Then

$$\lim_{n\to\infty} E(\theta_n) - \theta' = 0$$

$$\Rightarrow \lim_{n\to\infty} E\left[\frac{F_0 + \sum_{t=1}^n X_t}{F_0 + L_0 + nb}\right] - \theta' = 0$$

$$\Rightarrow \lim_{n\to\infty} E\left[\frac{\sum_{t=1}^n X_t}{nb}\right] - \theta' = 0$$

$$\Rightarrow \lim_{n\to\infty} \frac{1}{nb}[E(X_1) + E(X_2) + \ldots + E(X_n)] - \theta' = 0$$

$$\Rightarrow \lim_{n\to\infty} \frac{1}{nb}[b(1 - G(\theta_0)) +$$

$$b(1 - G(\theta_1)) + \ldots + b(1 - G(\theta_{n-1}))] - \theta' = 0$$

$$\Rightarrow \lim_{n\to\infty} \frac{1}{nb}[nb - b\{G(\theta_0) + G(\theta_1) + G(\theta_{n-1})\}] - \theta' = 0$$

$$\Rightarrow 1 - \lim_{n\to\infty} \frac{1}{n}\sum_{t=0}^{n-1} G(\theta_t) - \theta' = 0$$

$$\Rightarrow 1 - G\left(\lim_{n\to\infty} \frac{1}{n}\sum_{t=0}^{n-1} \theta_t\right) - \theta' = 0$$

$$\Rightarrow 1 - G\left(\theta'\right) - \theta' = 0 \qquad (10A.8)$$

which is impossible since θ^* solves $1 - G(\theta) - \theta = 0$. Therefore, by contradiction, $plim\ \theta_n = \theta^*$ And the proof is complete.

Proof of Proposition 2:

By proposition 1 we have that

$$\lim_{n\to\infty} \Pr\left\{ \left| \theta_{n+1}^i - \theta_n^i \right| < \varepsilon \right\} = 1$$

$$\Rightarrow \lim_{n\to\infty} \Pr\left\{ \left| (E(\theta_{n+1}^i) - \theta_n^i) + (\theta_{n+1}^i - E(\theta_{n+1}^i)) \right| < \varepsilon \right\} = 1$$

$$\Rightarrow \lim_{n\to\infty} \Pr\left\{ \left| E(\theta_{n+1}^i) - \theta_n^i \right| < \varepsilon \right\} = 1 \qquad (10A.9)$$

since

$$\Pr\left\{ \left| (E(\theta_{n+1}^i) - \theta_n^i) + (\theta_{n+1}^i - E(\theta_{n+1}^i)) \right| < \varepsilon \right\}$$

$$\leq \Pr\left\{ \left| E(\theta_{n+1}^i) - \theta_n^i \right| < \varepsilon \right\} \qquad (10A.10)$$

Letting s_n^i be the amount placed on horse i before bettor n places a bet, we have that

$$E(\theta_{n+1}^i) = \left[\frac{s_n^i + 1}{\sum_j s_n^j + 1} \right] \varphi_n^i + \left[\frac{s_n^i}{\sum_j s_n^j + 1} \right] (1 - \varphi_n^i)$$

$$(10A.11)$$

and, hence, the difference

$$E(\theta_{n+1}^i) - \theta_n^i = \left[\frac{s_n^i + 1}{\sum_j s_n^j + 1} \right] \varphi_n^i + \left[\frac{s_n^i}{\sum_j s_n^j + 1} \right] (1 - \varphi_n^i) - \frac{s_n^i}{\sum_j s_n^j}$$

$$= \frac{s_n^i + \varphi_n^i}{\sum_j s_n^j + 1} - \frac{s_n^i}{\sum_j s_n^j}$$

$$= \frac{1}{\sum_j s_n^j + 1} \left[\varphi_n^i - \frac{s_n^i}{\sum_j s_n^j} \right]$$

$$= \frac{1}{\sum_j s_n^j + 1} \left[\varphi_n^i - \theta_n^i \right] \qquad (10A.12)$$

Substituting this into (10A.9) gives

$$\lim_{n\to\infty} \Pr\left\{ \left| \frac{1}{\sum_j s_n^j + 1} \left[\varphi_n^i - \theta_n^i \right] \right| < \varepsilon \right\} = 1$$

$$\Rightarrow \lim_{n\to\infty} \Pr\left\{ \left| \varphi_n^i - \theta_n^i \right| < \bar{\varepsilon} \right\} = 1 \qquad (10A.13)$$

where $\bar{\varepsilon} = \varepsilon \left(\sum_j s_n^j + 1 \right)$. And the proof is complete.

Notes

1 To see this consider the normalisation

$$\rho_i^N = \frac{\rho_i}{\sum_i \rho_i} \quad \text{for } i = F, M, L$$

Note that $\Sigma_i \, \rho_i^N = 1$. However, in general, $E(\rho_i^N) \neq p_i$. Thus this normalisation may introduce the very bias we are trying to measure. Another is to draw ρ_F and ρ_M and then let

$$\rho_L = 1 - \rho_F - \rho_M$$

The difficulty with this approach is that an unusually high variance is placed on the Longshot.

References

Ali, Mukhtar M. (1977) 'Probability and Utility Estimates for Racetrack Bettors', *Journal of Political Economy*, 85, pp. 803–15

Blough, Stephen R. (1994) 'Differences of Opinion at the Racetrack', in Donald B. Hausch, Victor S. Y. Lo and William T. Ziemba (eds.), *Efficiency of Racetrack Betting Markets*, New York: Academic Press, pp. 323–41

Busche, Kelly and Hall, Christopher D. (1988) 'An Exception to the Risk Preference Anomaly', *Journal of Business*, 61, pp. 337–46

Cain, Michael, Law, David and Peel, David (2003) 'The Favourite-Longshot Bias, Bookmaker Margins and Insider Trading in a Variety of Betting Markets', *Bulletin of Economic Research*, 55, pp. 263–73

Golec, Joseph and Tamarkin, Maurry (1998) 'Bettors Love Skewness, Not Risk, at the Horse Track', *Journal of Political Economy*, 106, pp. 205–25

Feeney, Rob and King, Stephen P. (2001) 'Sequential Parimutuel Games', *Economic Letters*, 72, pp. 165–73

Hurley, William J. and McDonough, Lawrence C. (1995a) 'A Note on the Hayek Hypothesis and the Favourite-Longshot Bias in Parimutuel Betting', *American Economic Review*, 85, pp. 949–55

  (1995b) 'A Note on Simulating Unbiased Heterogeneous Expectations', *Computers and Mathematics with Applications*, 30, pp. 29–32

  (1996) 'The Favourite-Longshot Bias in Parimutuel Betting: A Clarification of the Explanation that Bettors Like to Bet Longshots', *Economics Letters*, 52, pp. 275–8

  (2004) 'Bookmaker Competition, Heterogeneous Expectations', Department of Economics Working Paper, 2004–1, Kingston, Ontario: Royal military College of Canada

Kanto, Antti, Rosenqvist, Gunnar and Suvas, Arto (1992) 'On Utility Function Estimation of Racetrack Bettors', *Journal of Economics and Psychology*, 13, pp. 491–8

Quandt, R. E. (1986), 'Betting and Equilibrium', *Quarterly Journal of Economics*, 101, pp. 201–7

Samuelson, Larry (1997) *Evolutionary Games and Equilibrium Selection*, Cambridge, MA: MIT Press

Sauer, Raymond D. (1998) 'The Economics of Wagering Markets', *Journal of Economic Literature*, 36, pp. 2021–64

Shin, Hyun Song (1992) 'Prices of State Contingent Claims with Insider Traders, and the Favourite-Longshot Bias', *Economic Journal*, 102, pp. 426–35

Thaler, Richard H. and Ziemba, William T. (1988) 'Parimutuel Betting Markets: Racetracks and Lotteries', *Journal of Economic Perspectives*, 2, pp. 161–74

Watanabe, Takahiro (1997) 'A Parimutuel System With Two Horses and a Continuum of Bettors', *Journal of Mathematical Economics*, 28, pp. 85–100

Weitzman, Martin (1965) 'Utility Analysis and Group Behaviour: An Empirical Study,' *Journal of Political Economy*, 73, pp. 18–26

Williams, L. V. and Paton, David (1998) 'Why Are Some Favourite-Longshot Biases Positive and Others Negative?', *Applied Economics*, 30, pp. 1505–10

Woodland, Linda M. and Woodland, Bill M. (1994) 'Market Efficiency and the Favourite Longshot Bias: The Baseball Betting Market', *Journal of Finance*, 49, pp. 269–80

11 Modelling gambling demand in a laboratory casino: discovering the importance of individual-specific effects

W. David Walls and Patrick J. Harvey

11.1 Introduction

Gambling has become an important source of government revenue all around the globe at the local, regional and national levels. Governments seek to maintain, and where possible to increase, the inflow of gambling revenues. Gambling businesses operate with a profit maximisation objective and find increasing government taxation a serious threat to profitability. One way to approach the problem between firms and tax authorities is to first analyse how to increase the size of the aggregate pie to be divided between the two. The key variable of analysis is the aggregate house take-out percentage, since this is the essential element of the price of gambling from the perspective of potential consumers. Our analysis focuses on the question of how to set this take-out percentage so that the aggregate revenue collected from gamblers is maximised.[1] However, the analysis presented in this chapter is useful for other policy purposes because it quantifies the demand curve.

Reduced consumption, in addition to the amount of revenue raised, is also of interest to certain government entities, particularly those concerned with social issues such as problem gambling, crime and other social ills that are sometimes seen to be negative externalities of legal gambling markets. For these other purposes, it is also worthwhile to have an estimate of the responsiveness of gambling demand to increases in the house take-out rate. Without knowledge of demand, it is not possible to adjust the house take-out percentage to obtain any desired outcome, whether it is to maximise tax revenue or to reduce gambling activity by a particular amount.

Market researchers often conduct surveys or organise focus groups as a way of gathering information on how consumers will respond to a new product or to a new policy. The counterpart to this type of market research in the academic environment is to conduct laboratory studies. Laboratory investigations have rigorous, controlled conditions, and the results should be readily repeatable by other interested academicians. Certain disciplines lend themselves more readily to application of the accepted scientific method – such as those investigating physical laws which can be readily demonstrated – while other disciplines are seemingly precluded from systematic scientific examination due to their less tangible nature.

Unfortunately for the gaming industry, many of the most interesting features revolve around those less tangible qualities such as motivation, risk preferences and potential loss absorption capacity of individual gamblers. These attributes are not readily generalisable, nor is there a definitive test or method for discovering the intensity of these attributes. Therefore, rigorous scientific investigation is not normally seen as an available means to test gaming behaviour or responses to changes in the gaming environment. But there is a technique in the social sciences which has largely been underutilised for academic pursuit without specific applications to gambling.

An economic experiment can be used to generate laboratory market data – data that could not be generated or collected using market transactions in a non-laboratory setting.[2] It is important to emphasise that the econometric technique used to analyse the data relies on revealed preference and not on stated preference, so the analysis proceeds in the same manner as it would for data generated in any non-experimental economic market.

In this chapter, we conduct an economic experiment to quantify the demand for alternative wagers in response to changes in the effective rate of gambling taxation, also known as the 'house advantage'. The data generated in the economic experiment permit the estimation of binary choice models that are based on the revealed choices of the subjects and not on their stated choices. The experimental design and a description of the data generated in the trials is contained in section 11.2. Statistical models used to quantify gaming demand are set out in section 11.3. Empirical results are presented in section 11.4 and their implications for casino management are discussed and illustrated numerically in section 11.5. Concluding remarks are made in section 11.6.

11.2 The experimental gambling market

The methodology of experimental economics is based on the pioneering work of Nobel Economics Laureate Vernon Smith.[3] Although experimental economics studies cannot in themselves generate universally valid solutions or claims, the effects observed in such studies are credible evidence of the existence of incentive effects on the behavioural response of the individuals participating. The controlled laboratory setting also offers the advantage of reducing the confounding effects of outside influences, and by enabling the researcher to implement an orthogonalised experiment design it helps to isolate the comparative statics.

An economic experiment was used to generate the data analysed in this chapter. It is important to emphasise that the econometric technique used to analyse the data relies on revealed preference and not on stated preference, so the analysis proceeds in the same manner as it would for data generated in a non-experimental economic market. The actual experimental market was conducted at the Casino Lab at University of Nevada, Las Vegas, lending the element of realism to the controlled environment.

All participants were undergraduate students familiar with gaming and they represented a diverse cross-section of majors at the university. To elicit effort, participants were compensated in real money with their rate of pay tied to their choices as set out below. Each subject was trained in the mechanics of the experiment and satisfactorily completed a quiz on this prior to undertaking the experiment. The experiment instructions and the quiz are displayed in box 11.1. At the conclusion of the experiment, each subject was required to complete a post-experimental questionnaire prior to being paid his or her 'winnings'. On the exit survey, 100 per cent of the participants were satisfied with their rate of pay.

Each participant was responsible for tracking his or her own winnings. The player simply marked in the appropriate column what he or she chose to do for that round of the experiment, and then recorded the associated realised payoff. The expected value of the payoff naturally decreases as the number of green spaces – the effective tax rate – increases. At some point (identifying this point is one of the goals of the experiment) subjects will choose to participate in the coin flip rather than the roulette wheel spin. Participants are free at any time to choose between the two options, and may switch back and forth at will. The order of tax rate increases/decreases was randomised in the experiments.

The experiment implementation consists of repeated trials of ten different levels of taxation as set out in table 11.1. In total, the experiment consisted of one hundred rounds in which participants were faced with the various tax rates and provided with the opportunity to gamble or not. The experiment has two parts. First, the opportunity to gamble, with a roulette wheel serving as the element of chance. This option employed the variable tax assessment on gambling by requiring the participants to bet on either red or black, with the traditional 2 to 1 payoff. The green slots on the roulette wheel represent the gaming tax. Tax rates vary from zero to about 24 per cent by adding additional green spaces by covering over existing red or black spaces.

BOX 11.1 INSTRUCTIONS RECEIVED BY EXPERIMENT PARTICIPANTS

Experiment instructions

This experiment is designed to investigate gaming behaviour.

Every participant will play 100 rounds. You will have the chance to make a decent amount of money, and you certainly will be paid something tangible for your efforts. You will be paid in cash at the end of the experiment, so make your decisions based on the prospects of receiving money for the choices you make.

You have basically two alternatives. The first is to play roulette. Unlike roulette in the casinos, you may only bet on 'red' or 'black'. For each spin, you are allocated 20 cents. Your bet always must be for the entire 20 cents allocated to that particular round; in other words, you cannot split your bet half red and half black. The payoff is if the ball stops in the color you bet on, you receive 40 cents. If it does not land on the color you select, you receive nothing. Example: you bet on 'red' and the ball lands in a 'red' space. You are paid 40 cents for that round, and the next round is played. Example: you bet on 'red' and the ball stops on 'black'. You receive nothing for that round, and the next round is played. If the ball lands on 'green', no one wins. Notice that the number of 'green' slots on the wheel are varied; there may be many, few, or none at all. These changes will be announced, so there is no surprise.

The second alternative is to not play roulette, and to observe a coin flip instead. A coin is flipped, and if the coin lands on tails, you receive 25 cents. If it lands on heads, you receive 15 cents. You cannot 'choose' heads or tails, the payoffs are already set.

You may choose either the coin flip or the roulette spin for each round without any restriction. You can alternate from one to the other whenever you wish, with no limit or restriction.

Each player keeps track of their own winnings on the score sheet provided. An example of the score sheet is included with these instructions. The results of each round are marked on the sheet, and at the end of the experiment you will fill out a questionnaire regarding the experiment, and then be paid your earnings in cash. We are marking the sheet instead of paying after each round to save time and speed up the experiment.

If you have any questions, ask the instructor.

Quiz

If I bet on roulette and I win, how much do I win?
If I choose the coin toss, and a head is flipped, how much do I win?
How much do I win if 'green' is the roulette spin?
True or false: I will be paid in cash at the end of the experiment.
If I choose the coin toss, and a tail is flipped, how much do I win?

Table 11.1. *Experimental design and outcomes: effective tax rates and gaming choices*

Green spaces	Effective tax rate	No. of trials	Gaming percentage	Standard deviation
0	0.00	10	89.13	31.19
1	2.63	10	80.00	40.09
2	5.26	10	83.48	37.22
3	7.89	10	61.30	48.81
4	10.53	10	56.96	49.62
5	13.16	10	59.57	49.18
6	15.79	10	51.30	50.09
7	18.42	10	50.43	50.11
8	21.05	10	40.87	49.27
9	23.68	10	39.57	49.01
		Total 100	Average 61.26	

The second option for the participant is to not gamble at all. If this option is chosen, the participant receives a payoff based on the flip of a coin. Since no decision as to heads or tails is made by the participant, this represents a lottery determined by nature and not a gamble. The payment will be either 15 cents if a 'head' is tossed, or 25 cents if a 'tail' is tossed. The expected value is 20 cents, which is the payment per round for both gamblers and non-gamblers. There is no tax associated with this activity, and it also lacks the element of personal utility in the gambling action.

As shown in table 11.1, the proportion of subjects choosing to actively gamble varies from about 89 per cent to about 40 per cent, corresponding to effective gaming tax rates of 0 per cent and 24 per cent. The expected value of not gambling and accepting the coin flip is always 20 cents, and the expected value of gambling varies from 20 cents when there are no green spaces to about 12 cents when there are nine green spaces. It is clear from the tabulated choices in table 11.1 that the subjects are not risk-neutral money-maximisers, for if they were they would never choose to gamble when the expected return is less than 20 cents. We do not view this as evidence of market inefficiency, risk preference, or bad experiment design. Instead, this is simply a description of the behaviour of subjects in our study and it is not inconsistent with the behaviour of actual gamblers.

11.3 Statistical models of gaming demand

The experiment outlined in section 11.2 is designed to investigate gaming behaviour and see how the rate of gambling taxation affects gambler participation. In this section, we demonstrate how the data generated in the economic experiment can be quantitatively modelled. In particular, we propose a probabilistic model of the gambler participation as a function of the tax rate. The parameters of the models can be estimated by standard maximum likelihood techniques and the revenue-maximising tax rate can be computed directly. In this way we demonstrate concretely the use of laboratory economics as a practical tool for the gambling industry and for quantitative policy analysis.

We employ a statistical model to analyse the representative consumer's choice of whether or not to play roulette.[4] Consumers make a marginal benefit–marginal cost calculation based on the utilities received from choosing to gamble or not to gamble. Since we can not observe their marginal utilities, they are modelled statistically by the unobserved variable $y^* = \mu_i + \beta' x_i + \varepsilon_i$ where ε is the stochastic disturbance. What we do observe is the decision y of whether a subject chooses to gamble: $y = 1$ (gamble) if $y^* > 0$ and $y = 0$ if $y^* \leq 0$. The probability that a consumer chooses to gamble is $\Pr(y^* > 0) = F(\mu_i + \beta' x_i)$ where $F(\cdot)$ is a cumulative distribution function. The most common cumulative distribution functions used in practice for ε are the Gaussian and the logistic, yielding the familiar probit and logit models of binary choice. In the model set out above, we have permitted each individual consumer i to differ in the coefficient. We have done this to allow for individual-specific effects, permitting gamblers to differ in their propensity to gamble. Not allowing for individual-specific effects by restricting $\mu_i = \mu$ results in a pooled model that we can test against. In the estimation below, we treat the individual-specific effects as random variables so that we can make marginal inferences on the population based on our sample of experimental subjects. Treating the individual-specific effects as fixed would permit us to make statistical inferences that are *conditional* on the fixed effects in our sample of subjects. Making such conditional inferences is not useful for policy purposes, because we want any policy inferences to apply to the entire population and not to be restricted to the subjects who participated in the experimental trials. In the statistical analysis we estimate random-effects models and compare them with simple pooled models.

11.4 Estimation results

We estimate the simple pooled and random-effects probit and logit choice models directly by the method of maximum likelihood. Because the magnitude of the parameter estimates is difficult to interpret directly, we also compute and report the marginal probabilities – the change in the probability that a consumer chooses to actively gamble for a unit change in the house take-out percentage.

Table 11.2 presents the simple pooled and random-effects probit estimates of the demand for gambling. In the probit model we reject the simple pooled probit model in favour of the random-effects model: the likelihood ratio test

Table 11.2. *Probit estimates of the demand for gaming*

Variable	Simple pooled probit		Random-effects probit	
	Coefficient estimates[a]	Marginal probability[b]	Coefficient estimates[a]	Marginal probability[b]
Constant	1.0111 (0.0551)		1.4635 (0.0865)	
House take-out percentage	−0.2187 (0.0096)	−0.0222 (0.0014)	−0.0886 (0.0049)	−0.0324 (0.0019)
σ_μ			0.8382 (0.0452)	
ρ^c			0.4127 (0.0261)	
Log-likelihood	−1407.7314		−964.1825	
Observations	2300		2300	

Notes:

[a] Estimated standard errors are reported in parentheses.

[b] The marginal probabilities represent the change in the probability of choosing to play roulette for a one percentage point change in house take, evaluated at mean values.

[c] For convenience we report ρ, the proportion of total variance contributed by the individual-specific panels. When $\rho = 0$, the pooled estimator and the random-effects estimator yield identical results.

of the null hypothesis that the proportion of total variance contributed by the individual-specific panel component is zero (i.e. $\rho = \sigma^2_\mu / (1 + \sigma^2_\mu) = 0$) results in a chi-square statistic with one degree of freedom of 887.10, as compared to the 1 per cent critical value of 6.63. This means that individual-specific effects are important and that we are likely to make mistakes of inference if we use the pooled model to make statistical inferences. The random-effects probit estimates show that the house take-out percentage is statistically significant at the 1 per cent level, and the marginal probability is estimated to be about –0.0324, meaning that a one percentage point increase in the effective tax rate on gaming will reduce the numerical probability of choosing to gamble by that amount. If we were to ignore the random effects and use the pooled probit estimates, the corresponding marginal probability corresponding to the house take-out percentage is –0.0222. The numerical difference may seem small, but there is a 46 per cent difference in this key behavioural parameter which is the primary instrument of policy. In section 11.5 we will illustrate the practical implications of using the fixed-effects parameter estimate instead of the pooled estimate.

The random-effects models estimated in this chapter make use of Gauss–Hermite quadrature to compute the log likelihood and its derivatives. The quadrature approximation in random-effects models can be inaccurate due to large group sizes and/or large correlations within groups. This can occur because the quadrature procedure approximates the product of normal density functions with a high-order polynomial, and this assumption is no longer approximately valid with large groups or correlations within groups. As a check on the quadrature approximation, we have re-estimated the model using two different numbers of quadrature points using the coefficient estimates of the original model for starting values in the numerical optimisation. We then compare the log-likelihood and coefficient estimates of the original model to the two re-estimated models. If the quadrature approximation is invalid, then the estimates will be sensitive to the number of quadrature points.

Table 11.3 shows the results of the quadrature check for the random-effects probit estimation. The original model was estimated with twelve quadrature points, and the model was re-estimated with eight and sixteen quadrature points. The relative difference between the log-likelihood value for the original model and the re-estimated models is 0.006 and –0.001. For the key parameter, the coefficient on the house take-out percentage, the relative difference between the original point estimate and the re-estimated values is –0.0175 and –0.0243. A common rule of thumb is that a relative difference greater than 0.01 warrants further investigation. For this reason, we proceed by estimating the same random-effects model of gambling demand using a logit model as an alternative to the probit model.

Table 11.3. *Quadrature check for random-effects probit estimation*

	Comparison quadrature 8 points	Comparison quadrature 16 points
Log-likelihood	−969.99198	−963.09986
Difference	−5.809436	1.0826825
Relative difference	0.00602524	−0.0011229
House take-out	−0.08706166	−0.08646148
Difference	0.00155256	0.00215274
Relative difference	−0.01752044	−0.02429341

Table 11.4. *Logit estimates of the demand for gaming*

Variable	Simple pooled probit		Random-effects probit	
	Coefficient estimates[a]	Marginal probability [b]	Coefficient estimates[a]	Marginal probability[b]
Constant	1.6436		2.4941	
	(0.0939)		(0.1394)	
House take-out	−0.0953	−0.0223	−0.1584	−0.0360
percentage	(0.0063)	(0.0015)	(0.0092)	(0.0021)
σ_μ			1.6753	
			(0.0877)	
ρ^c			0.4604	
			(0.0079)	
Log-likelihood	−1408.6471		−956.4571	
Observations	2300		2300	

Notes:

[a] Estimated standard errors are reported in parentheses.

[b] The marginal probabilities represent the change in the probability of choosing to play roulette for a one percentage point change in house take, evaluated at mean values.

[c] For convenience we report ρ, the proportion of total variance contributed by the individual-specific panels. When $\rho = 0$, the pooled estimator and the random-effects estimator yield identical results.

The estimates of the simple pooled and random-effects logit coefficients, their marginal probabilities, and the associated estimated standard errors are reported in table 11.4. The coefficient estimates are of the anticipated sign and all significantly different from zero at the 1 per cent marginal

Table 11.5. *Quadrature check for random-effects logit estimation*

	Comparison quadrature 8 points	Comparison quadrature 16 points
Log-likelihood	−961.43353	−954.30416
Difference	−4.9764563	2.1529223
Relative difference	0.00520301	−0.00225093
House take-out	−0.15843585	−0.15973979
Difference	−0.00004206	−0.001346
Relative difference	0.00026553	0.00849781

significance level. In the logit specification for the choice model, we also reject the simple pooled specification in favour of the random-effects specification: the likelihood-ratio test of the null hypothesis that $\rho = 0$ results in a chi-square statistic with one degree of freedom of 904.38, as compared to the 1 per cent critical value of 6.63. The marginal probabilities indicate that a one percentage point increase in the house take-out is associated with a −0.0360 decrease in the probability that a consumer chooses to actively gamble. The simple pooled logit specification yields a marginal probability on the house take-out percentage of −0.0223, almost identical to the values estimated from the simple pooled probit model. This value differs significantly from the estimate obtained from the random-effects model as was the case in the probit specification. Also of interest is that the random-effects logit point estimate of the marginal probability of the house take-out percentage differs from the corresponding estimate from the probit model (0.0324), but that the difference is not statistically significant.

The random-effects logit model also makes use of the Gauss–Hermite quadrature, so we again check to determine the fragility or robustness of our numerical results in relation to the number of quadrature points used in the polynomial approximation. Table 11.5 displays the quadrature check results comparing the log-likelihood and coefficient estimates from the original model with twelve quadrature points and the model re-estimated with eight and sixteen quadrature points. The log-likelihood of the original model and the re-estimated model differs by less than one half of one per cent. The coefficient on the house take-out per cent differs by less than one per cent. Since the relative difference of the log-likelihood and the house take-out coefficient are both less than 10^{-2} it appears that the Gauss–Hermite quadrature is a reasonable approximation.

11.5 Implications for decision making

The optimal house take is that level that maximises the magnitude of the house take with respect to the house take-out percentage. From the probability model of gaming demand, we can represent an individual's probability of gaming as a function of the house take-out percentage t: $F(t)$. The dollar value of the house take is then $R(t) = t \times F(t)$. Maximising $R(t)$ with respect to t is a straightforward calculus problem, with the optimal take-out rate being the rate where $dR(t)/dt = 0$. The optimal take can be computed numerically given demand parameter estimates reported above. We now provide an example of how the analytics are combined with the statistical estimates.

Given an effective tax rate t, defined so that in expectation the gross return on each dollar bet is $1 - t$ dollars, each individual makes the binary choice to gamble or not to gamble. Let us define the binary variable g that assumes a value of unity if the individual chooses to gamble, and zero otherwise. The exogenous variable that affects the gambling choice is the tax rate $t \in [0, 1]$. The probability that an individual chooses to gamble is

$$\Pr(g = 1) = F(t) \tag{11.1}$$

where $F(t)$ represents any cumulative distribution function. While any cumulative distribution function could be used in theory, the logistic cumulative distribution function and the Normal distribution function are most often used in applied work, and they correspond to the probit and logit (or logistic regression) models. The logit model is more convenient for the purpose of exposition, though none of our substantive empirical results depends on which model is used.

The logit model, which can be derived from Luce's (1959) random utility model of individual choice, has the following closed-form solution for the choice probability

$$\Pr(g = 1) = 1/(1 + \exp(-\beta_1 - \beta_2 t)) \tag{11.2}$$

where β_1 and β_2 are parameters to be estimated from the experimental data on t and the choices of the subjects. Given estimates of these parameters, we can proceed to determine the revenue-maximizing tax rate t^*. Define the tax revenue function to be

$$R(t) = t \times F(t) = t/(1 + \exp(-\beta_1 - \beta_2 t)) \tag{11.3}$$

Then solve the maximisation problem for revenue with respect to t by solving the first-order condition

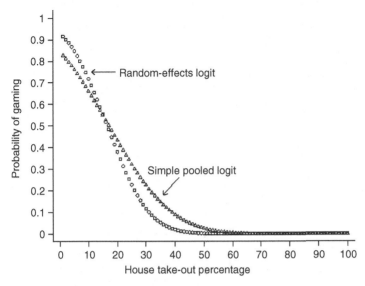

Figure 11.1: Probability of gaming from simple pooled and random-effects logit models

$$\mathrm{d}R(t)/\mathrm{d}t = (1 + (1 + \beta_2 t)\exp(-\beta_1 - \beta_2 t))/$$
$$(1 + \exp(-\beta_1 - \beta_2 t))^2 \qquad (11.4)$$

We can numerically solve this equation for the optimal tax rate after inserting our estimates of β_1 and β_2.

Figure 11.1 shows the probability than an individual chooses to actively gamble in response to the house take-out percentage corresponding to the logit estimates displayed in table 11.4. The proportion of subjects choosing to gamble decreases as the take-out percentage increases, and the curves differ substantially depending on whether or not the estimation accounted for the individual-specific effects. To maximise the aggregate monetary value of the house take, the probability of gambling must be balanced against the take-out percentage.

Figure 11.2 plots the expected revenue generated through the house take as a function of the house take-out percentage. When individual-specific effects are controlled for in the estimation, the optimal take-out rate is estimated to be about 15 per cent. This differs substantially from take-out rate of 19 per cent that would be calculated from the model that ignores individual-specific effects. These results suggest that controlling for individual-specific effects is extremely important in econometric models

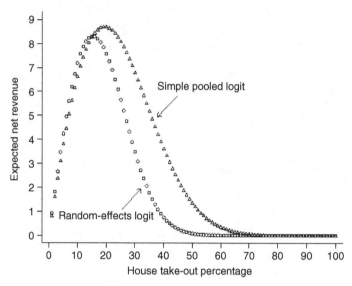

Figure 11.2: Expected net revenue from simple pooled and random-effects logit models

of the demand for gambling. Failing to control for individual-specific effects results in an overestimate of the optimal take-out percentage from the perspective of maximising the aggregate revenue to be divided between the gambling concession operator and the government taxation authority.

11.6 Conclusions

In this chapter we have shown that laboratory economics is a useful tool of analysis in the study of gambling markets. To illustrate the methodology of experimental economics applied to gambling, we conducted an economic experiment in which demand for various wagers could be quantified using data generated in a laboratory casino. The methodology of experimental economics, together with the wealth of econometric methods developed to analyse market data, can be used to find pragmatic and scientifically rigorous answers to practical real-world questions. In our application, the data on individuals' choices can reveal the response of gaming demand to various effective rates of gaming taxation, and the estimates of the statistical models of gaming choice were used to estimate the revenue-maximising rate of gaming taxation.

Our empirical results show that individual-specific effects are important in modelling the demand for gambling. Omitting individual-specific effects in estimating the demand relation leads to an underestimate of the price elasticity of demand for gambling and this has substantive implications. Accounting for individual-specific effects, the revenue-maximising rate of gambling taxation is estimated to be about 15 per cent; not accounting for the individual-specific effects, one would estimate the revenue-maximising tax rate to be about 19 per cent. Individual-specific variation appears to be an important component of gambling demand that should be modelled explicitly in future work.

Notes

1 We do not in this chapter address the bargaining problem between the government and the gambling operator. Joint maximisation of the taxation authority and the gambling operator dictates that the aggregate revenue would be maximised first and then later divided.
2 Commercial transactions are proprietary, and this is one reason why doing empirical work in microeconomics can sometimes be nearly impossible. For example, the empirical study of 'black markets' is difficult due to the dearth of market data, but these illegal markets can be studied in a laboratory setting (Harvey and Walls, 2003).
3 See Smith (1982) for a clear and concise introduction to the use of controlled laboratory experiments to test the implications of microeconomic theory. Also see Luce (1959), Smith (1962, 1965, 1976, 1989), Plott (1982, 1989), Kagel and Roth (1995), Binmore (1999) and Loewenstein (1999) for an introduction to this fascinating literature.
4 See Greene (1997) for a readable introduction to discrete choice models, and Ben-Akiva and Lerman (1985) and Train (1986) for a more detailed treatment.

References

Ben-Akiva, M. and Lerman, S. R. (1985) *Discrete Choice Analysis: Theory and Application to Travel Demand*, Cambridge, MA: MIT Press
Binmore, K. (1999) 'Why Experiment in Economics?', *Economic Journal*, 109(453), pp. F16–24
Greene, W. H. (1997) *Econometric Analysis*, 3rd edn., New York: Prentice-Hall
Harvey, P. J. and Walls, W. D. (2003) 'The Revealed Demand for Pirate Goods: Probit Analysis of Experimental Data', *International Journal of Management*, 20(2), pp. 194–201
Kagel, J. H. and Roth, A. E. (eds.) (1995) *The Handbook of Experimental Economics*, Princeton: Princeton University Press
Loewenstein, G. (1999) 'Experimental Economics from the Vantage-Point of Behavioural Economics', *Economic Journal*, 109(453), pp. FM23–F34
Luce, R. D. (1959) *Individual Choice Behaviour: A Mathematical Analysis*, New York: Wiley

Plott, C. R. (1982) 'Industrial Organisation Theory and Experimental Economics', *Journal of Economic Literature*, 20(4), pp. 1485–1527

(1989) 'An Updated Review of Industrial Organisation: Applications of Experimental Methods', in R. Schmalensee and R. Willig (eds.), *Handbook of Industrial Organisation, Handbooks in Economics*, 2, Amsterdam: North-Holland, pp. 1101–76

Smith, V. L. (1962) 'An Experimental Study of Competitive Market Behaviour', *Journal of Political Economy*, 70, pp. 111–37

(1965) 'Experimental Auction Markets and the Walrasian Hypothesis', *Journal of Political Economy*, 75, pp. 387–93

(1976) 'Experimental Economics: Induced Value Theory', *American Economic Review*, 6(2), pp. 274–9

(1982) 'Microeconomic Systems as an Experimental Science', *American Economic Review*, 72(5), pp. 923–55

(1989) 'Theory, Experiment and Economics', *Journal of Economic Perspectives*, 3(1), pp. 151–69

Train, K. (1986) *Qualitative Choice Analysis: Theory, Econometrics, and an Application to Automobile Demand*, Cambridge, MA: MIT Press

12 Market efficiency of the 50–30–20–10 horse-racing spread betting market

Paul M. Twomey

12.1 Introduction

In this chapter we seek evidence to suggest that market signals in fixed-odds betting markets can be used to identify profitable spread betting opportunities. It is the belief that *inside information* is still largely exclusive to the fixed-odds markets that drives this work; potential spread bettors observe the changes in the fixed-odds prices offered by the fixed-odds bookmakers, use these changes to calculate the expected spread points for each horse and then take advantage of discrepancies between their estimates of the points and the spread being offered by the spread betting firm to place promising bets. For this endeavour to be successful, there are two main requirements of the markets in question. The first is that the evolution of the fixed-odds prices must be such that the probability estimates based upon the odds tend to improve. There are several previous studies that suggest that this is the case – see, for example, Crafts (1985) for British racing, Asch, Malkiel and Quandt (1982) for US racing and Schnytzer and Shilony (1995) for Australian racing. The second requirement is that the spread betting firms are slow to react, or do not react at all, to the fixed-odds price changes.

For each spread betting market the spread firm offers a spread (a, b) such that $a < b$. Once the market is complete the final value of the market, c, will be known. The return to a *sell* bettor for a stake of x units per point, $x > 0$, is $x(a-c)$ while the return to a *buy* bettor is $x(c - b)$ for a similar stake of x units per point. If this return is negative then the bettor must pay this amount to the spread firm; no money changes hands until after the result is known. Spread betting is more volatile than fixed-odds betting as the bettor is not sure of the magnitude of his losses for an unsuccessful bet until after the market has been completed.

As an example, consider the market for total runs in an innings of cricket for some team. In this instance the firm may offer a spread of (280, 300).

277

Bettors who think that the team will not achieve the sell price of 280 runs should place a *sell* bet, whilst bettors who think the team will get more than 300 runs should place a *buy* bet; those who think the score will be between these two figures should not place a bet on this market. Now suppose that we have two bettors, one has sold at 280 for £1 per point, while the other has bought at 300 for £1 per point. If the team does poorly and score only 200 runs, the *sell* bettor will make a profit of £80 but the *buy* bettor will lose £100. On the other hand if the team does well and score 350 runs then the *buy* bettor will make a profit of £50 but the *sell* bettor will have lost £70. If the team score a number of runs within the range of the spread, say 287, both *buy* and *sell* bettors will lose; in this instance, the *sell* bettor will lose £7 and the buy bettor *will* lose £13. Note that in all three cases the aggregate result for the spread betting firm from these two bettors is a profit of £20. If the spread firm can set the market so that they attract equal bets on both sides of the spread then a profit is guaranteed regardless of the outcome of the market.

The market that we will be considering in this chapter is the 50–30–20–10 horse-racing market. Here, the first four horses to finish the race are awarded these numbers of points, respectively, with all other horses receiving no points. In section 12.2, we will introduce a simple method for converting fixed-odds prices into spread betting points. In section 12.3, we will use a large number of actual race results to analyse how accurate the method is at predicting spread betting points. In section 12.4, we apply the method to a number of races for which the changing odds and spread betting prices were considered simultaneously. Potential betting strategies with particular reference to the risks will also be considered in this section. Section 12.5 will draw some conclusions.

12.2 The Harville method

Fixed-odds prices generally give only an indication of a horse's chance of winning a race, but for the application being considered here we need also to estimate the probability of each horse finishing in each of the first four positions, respectively. The simplest method that attempts to do this, which we use here, is that of Harville (1973). There are several other methods that have also been considered – see, for example, Henery (1981), Stern (1990), Bacon-Shone, Lo and Busche (1992), Lo and Bacon-Shone (1992).

Before making use of the Harville method, the fixed-odds prices of the horses must be converted into win probabilities. The standard method to achieve this in a race with n runners, letting p_i denote the probability of horse i winning, is to let

$$p_i = \frac{1/(1 + O_i)}{\sum\limits_{j=1}^{n} 1/(1 + O_j)}$$

where O_i is the odds of horse i. The numerator of this expression denotes the 'fair' probability associated with this horse, 'fair' in the sense that if the horse had this chance of winning then the expected return to a bet would be the stake itself. The denominator of the expression should, for each bookmaker, add up to more than one. The amount by which this quantity exceeds one is often referred to as the over-round on the bookmaker's market and is a measure of the bookmaker's expected profit margin. By dividing the fair probability by the denominator, this process essentially scales the fair probabilities down in the same ratio for each horse.

It is a well-known phenomenon that when the probabilities are arrived at in this manner, they are seen to exhibit the *favourite-longshot bias*. This bias is essentially that, in the long run, favoured horses tend to win more often than is suggested by these probabilities, while longshots win less often than is expected.

The Harville method is applied to the probabilities p_i to arrive at the probability associated with any possible ordering permutation of any number of the horses. The probability of horse a winning the race and horse b finishing second, p_{ab}, is given by

$$p_{ab} = p_a \frac{p_b}{1 - p_a}$$

This formula tells us that the race for second place, given that horse a wins the race, is akin to a race with one fewer runner with all of the remaining probabilities scaled up to account for the missing probability of the winner.

For our application, the probability that horses a, b, c and d finish in positions first to fourth, respectively, p_{abcd}, is given by

$$p_{abcd} = p_a \frac{p_b}{(1 - p_a)} \frac{p_c}{(1 - p_a - p_b)} \frac{p_d}{(1 - p_a - p_b - p_c)}$$

Again, the race for each subsequent finishing position is akin to a race with all the horses that have already finished being removed and the probabilities of the remaining horses being scaled up to account for this.

With all possible ordering permutations calculated in this way, the probability of horse i finishing in position j, $p_i(j)$, is arrived at by summing over all permutations in which this is observed. Harville did this for a set of 335 races from Ohio and Kentucky. He observed that a bias in the opposite direction to that of the favourite-longshot bias is apparent for second and third place, and that this bias tends to cancel out the favourite-longshot bias so that when the probabilities are combined to arrive at the overall probability of the horse finishing in the first two or three positions the estimates are reasonable.

For our application, having calculated p_i (j) for each horse i, our estimate of its expected spread betting points will be given by S_i where

$$S_i = 50p_i(1) + 30p_i(2) + 20p_i(3) + 10p_i(4)$$

12.3 Testing the model

The dataset used to compare expected and actual spread betting points is the set of 3,861 UK flat races that took place during the months of January to September 2001, inclusive. To simplify matters, those few races in which there was a dead heat for any of the first four positions, or the race had fewer than four runners, were removed. This reduced the dataset to 3,729 races.

The horses were ordered by increasing number of expected spread points and then starting with the horses with lowest points they were placed into groups of 2,000 plus ties. The aim here was to group horses with similar expected points so that the observed and actual number of spread points for the horses could be compared. The results of this grouping are shown in table 12.1. The final column is perhaps the most pertinent, giving the average difference between the observed and the expected spread points per horse for each of the groups. Ideally, if there were no systematic bias we would expect the positive and negative quantities in this column to be randomly scattered. It appears that this is not the case as the negative signs are generally clumped together for the groups of horses with the greater number of spread betting points, with just a few exceptions. As this column deals with the observed spread points deducted from the expected spread points, the bias is such that it tends to underestimate the spread points for favoured horses but overestimate the points for longshots. In using this method to predict spread betting points to try to identify favourable bets it may be important to be aware of this bias.

One way of overcoming these problems can be seen in figure 12.1. For none of the groups is the bias ever in excess of 1 spread point from that which is observed. This suggests that perhaps a betting strategy incorporating some kind of filtering process may be sensible. For example, we might choose to place bets only where the expected spread points is more than a point outside of the spread offered, so a horse with spread of (12,15) would be bet upon only when its expected spread points were less than 11 or more than 16. The problem with a filter such as this is that it will limit our betting opportunities and so this must be balanced against the

Table 12.1. *Comparing observed and actual spread points for the 2001 dataset*

Range of expected spread points	Horses in group	Average expected spread points per horse	Average observed spread points per horse	Average expected minus observed spread points per horse
0–1.764	2005	1.28	0.71	0.57
1.765–2.375	2001	2.08	1.49	0.59
2.376–2.805	2001	2.59	1.80	0.79
2.806–3.270	2000	3.04	2.39	0.65
3.271–3.767	2004	3.52	3.21	0.30
3.768–4.237	2000	4.00	4.07	−0.06
4.238–4.764	2000	4.50	4.25	0.25
4.765–5.298	2003	5.03	4.33	0.69
5.299–5.829	2000	5.56	5.34	0.23
5.830–6.403	2007	6.11	6.22	−0.11
6.404–7.061	2001	6.72	6.97	−0.25
7.062–7.752	2000	7.40	7.20	0.20
7.753–8.571	2002	8.15	8.08	0.07
8.572–9.528	2001	9.04	9.72	−0.68
9.529–10.671	2002	10.08	10.72	−0.64
10.672–11.931	2000	11.30	11.89	−0.59
11.932–13.439	2000	12.67	13.51	−0.84
13.440–15.392	2007	14.39	15.22	−0.83
15.393–17.977	2000	16.65	17.04	−0.39
17.978–21.469	2000	19.61	19.48	0.14
21.470–27.143	2000	24.00	23.94	−0.06
27.144–50	1686	32.31	32.59	−0.27

increased confidence that the filter provides. These ideas will be explored in section 12.4.

12.4 Betting systems

In this section our dataset consists of eighty races, forty from July 2002 and forty from July 2003. The fixed-odds prices and the spreads were collected manually from various websites associated with spread and fixed-odds companies at two different times, 15 minutes and 2 minutes prior to the scheduled start time of each race respectively. This second time of 2 minutes prior to the race was deemed the latest cut-off allowing sufficient time to run the computer program to calculate the expected spread points and place any spread bets before the race commenced.

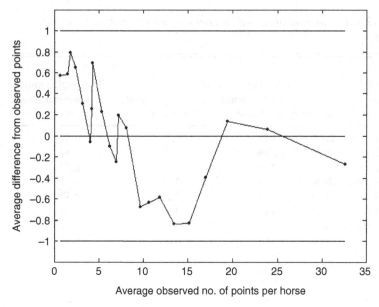

Figure 12.1 Observing the bias in using the Harville method to predict spread betting Points

Table 12.2 reports the results of betting strategies for these races. The profit/loss figures are for a unit stake placed on each horse that the betting strategy indicated a bet upon. It can clearly be seen that as the filter increases the number of bets decreases. The dataset consists of 940 horses and so the strategies with filter 0.0 lead to betting on around 35% of the horses in the dataset. This figure seems far too high, simply because it seems so unlikely that the spread firm could offer spread prices that give so many good betting opportunities. This observation is supported by the actual results of these betting strategies, with the strategies at both times producing heavy losses. The filter of 1 spread point leads to around 100 bets at each time, around 10% of horses, and this seems a reasonable number. As the filters increase to 1.5 points the bets become fairly infrequent with only around one bet every other race being placed and when we reach 2 points the bets are about one in every three to four races.

Table 12.2 splits the bets into *sell* bets and *buy* bets and it appears that the *sell* bets tend to be more favourable than the *buy* bets, with eight of the ten strategies being profitable. For the total of *buy* and *sell* bets combined it can be seen that both the strategies with largest filters, 1.5 and 2.0, are profitable based upon the data from both time periods;

Table 12.2. *Results of filtering strategies for eighty races*

	15 minutes prior to race					2 minutes prior to race				
Filter	0.0	0.5	1.0	1.5	2.0	0.0	0.5	1.0	1.5	2.0
Number of *buy* bets	188	96	52	24	12	161	101	51	21	12
Number of *sell* bets	169	100	51	28	20	151	91	44	23	11
Total number of bets	357	196	103	52	32	312	192	95	44	23
Buy bets profit/loss	−245	−191	−31.5	−43	−22.5	−125	24	−27	−3	27.5
Sell bets profit/loss	70.5	141	108	82	31	−13	40	−114	12	36
Total profit/loss	−174.5	−50	76.5	39	8.5	−138	64	−141	9	63.5

unfortunately, as our dataset here consists of only eighty races, the number of bets comprising these results for these larger filters is small and as such strong conclusions cannot be drawn. However, these results suggest that further analysis based upon larger datasets may lead to evidence that the spread betting market may not be efficient.

12.5 Conclusions

Unfortunately, without access to large amounts of spread betting data it is not possible to draw firm conclusions with regard to the market efficiency of the spread betting markets. I approached several of the spread betting firms requesting the historical data that, combined with the fixed-odds prices, could have been used to test the efficiency of the market, but none were prepared to release this information. However, the Harville method as used in this chapter does appear to be a reasonable method for predicting spread betting points based solely on the fixed-odds prices. In Twomey (2005), I look at other methods for predicting the spread points. Although some of these do appear to outperform the Harville method it is not clear to what extent they are better and, again, without access to more spread data it is impossible to draw strong conclusions. This thesis also contains more sophisticated betting strategies such as the Kelly strategy (Kelly, 1956), which maximises the long-term growth of capital by betting a fixed proportion of your wealth at each stage.

Having collected the data for eighty races and observed the changing price patterns of the horses I believe there is some evidence to suggest that it may be possible to identify favourable spread bets in a manner similar to that described in this chapter. Note that these ideas are presented only as observations noted when obtaining the data and seeing the price movements in each of the markets; again, there is no overwhelming evidence to substantiate these ideas.

Consider as an example the horse Skram, which ran in the 3.35 race at Uttoxeter on 16 July 2003. This horse's odds moved from 6 to 1 to 10 to 1 in the time between the two readings of the odds; this movement equated to the expected spread points moving from 13.7 points to 10.0 points yet the spread remained fixed at (13,16) at all times. If the spread firms were responding to changes in the fixed-odds markets then it would have been expected that this horse's spread prices should decrease. The reason that the spread firms may choose not to do this is simply that they have near equal exposure on both sides of the bet and so it is not really in their interests to move the spread.

Another reason that spread firms may choose not to move their prices, even if they were aware of the market signals from the fixed-odds markets, is that if they move their spread too far this gives some bettors the opportunity to close out their bet for a profit before the race has even taken place.

A second example horse gives an even greater indication that the spread firms consider their own exposure first and foremost. Here we consider the horse General Hawk, which ran in the 3.15 race at Carlisle on 19 July 2002. This horse drifted out to 5 to 1 from 7 to 2, meaning that its expected spread points decreased from 17.0 to 13.2 yet its spread offered by the firm actually increased from (13,16) to (14,17). It seems even less likely that if the spread firms were taking into account fixed-odds market signals they would choose to move the price in this way. The most likely explanation is that the firm were exposed on the *buy* side of the spread and so chose to move their spread up to account for this. This is completely rational behaviour on their part. It is also good news for bettors who attempt to make money using signals in the fixed-odds markets as outlined in this chapter, as it suggests that if the inefficiencies do exist they are likely to continue to do so.

A final point that should be made with this particular betting application is that unlike most other attempts to make a profit from market inefficiencies, this application has the advantage that the bettor placing a spread bet is guaranteed the price at which the bet is struck. In many other studies, such as Hausch, Ziemba and Rubinstein (1981), for example, one problem that arises is that the market in which the bets are being placed are parimutuel markets and so no matter how late bets are placed there is no guarantee of this price persisting; bets that look favourable when placed may not remain so.

Notes

I would like to thank the *Racing Post* website for supplying me with the starting prices for the large set of horse races in 2001 and my PhD supervisor John Haigh for his helpful comments with regard to this work.

References

Asch, P., Malkiel, B. G. and Quandt, R. E. (1982) 'Racetrack Betting and Informed Behaviour', *Journal of Financial Economics*, 10, pp. 187–94

Bacon-Shone, J., Lo, Y. and Busche, K. (1992) *Logistic Analyses for Complicated Bets*, Research Report, 16, Department of Statistics, University of Hong Kong

Crafts, N. F. R. (1985) 'Some Evidence of Insider Knowledge in Horse Racing Betting in Britain', *Economica*, 52, pp. 295–304

Harville, D. A. (1973) 'Assigning Probabilities to the Outcome of Multi-Entry Competitions', *Journal of the American Statistical Association*, 68, pp. 312–16

Hausch, D. B., Ziemba, W. T. and Rubinstein M. (1981) 'Efficiency of the Market for Racetrack Betting', *Management Science*, 27, pp. 1435–53

Henery, R. J. (1981) 'Permutation Probabilities as Models for Horse Races', *Journal of the Royal Statistical Society, Series B*, 43, pp. 86–91

Kelly, J. L., Jr. (1956) 'A New Interpretation of Information Rate', *Bell Systems Technical Journal*, 35, pp. 917–26

Lo,V. S. Y. and Bacon-Shone, J. (1992) 'An Approximation to Ordering Probabilities of Multi-Entry Competitions', Research Report, 16, Department of Statistics, University of Hong Kong

Schnytzer, A. and Shilony, Y. (1995) 'Inside Information in a Betting Market', *Economic Journal*, 105, pp. 963–71

Stern, H. (1990) 'Models for Distributions on Permutations', *Journal of the American Statistical Association*, 85, pp. 558–64

Twomey, P. M. (2005) PhD thesis, University of Sussex, in progress

13 Insider trading and bias in a market for state-contingent claims

Adi Schnytzer and Yuval Shilony

13.1 Introduction

This chapter aims to shed light on the functioning of a market for state-contingent claims with inside traders. Many markets are beset by clandestine and illegal insider activity, which much effort has been made to control. The Melbourne horse betting bookmakers' market considered in this chapter is unusual in that insider trading is legal there. In many markets for state-contingent claims, including most betting markets, a favourite-longshot bias is observed throughout, but decreases over time. In the context of a horse betting market, a favourite-longshot bias implies that favourites are underpriced relative to longshots. The explanations given in the literature for this common phenomenon, which is seemingly incongruent with market efficiency, are briefly summarised below for the case of bookmaking markets. Although the typical market for horse bets lasts 30 minutes at most, it goes through several phases with more than one set of prices, as explained below. The analysis presented in this chapter suggests new explanations for this phenomenon.

In contrast to (legal) US horse betting markets,[1] which are only parimutuel, betting on-course in Australia takes place with both a parimutuel and bookmakers. In parimutuel betting, the bettors on horses do not know the return odds until all betting is completed and the total revenue, minus tax and costs, is divided among the winners, proportionally to the bets made. Bookmakers, on the other hand, offer bets at fixed odds, which are more amenable to profitable exploitation by shrewd insiders. The initial set of prices posted before betting begins is called the set of opening prices (OP). In the course of betting, prices change and the last set of prices before the race starts is called the set of starting prices (SP).

Shin (1991, 1992, 1993) developed a theoretical model based on explaining the bias as a consequence of insider trading in the British horse betting market. His model differs from the one proposed in this chapter in

287

exclusively focusing on SP. In his model, insiders only bet at SP and always win, implying that they bet off-course, where SP betting is available. SP on-course betting is not available in the UK since, by definition, it is determined by the equilibrium at the close of betting.

Henery (1985) offers a different model to explain the favourite-longshot bias in SP in the British horse betting market. According to him, it is a consequence of the bettors' underestimation – by a constant amount – of the probabilities of all the horses losing a race. He does not offer an explicit model for bookies' behaviour, but simply assumes they charge competitive prices that take into account the bettors' error. There are no inside traders in Henery's model.

Schnytzer and Shilony (1995) provided an indirect demonstration of insider trading in the Melbourne parimutuel horse betting market. Comparing the betting behaviour of on- and off-course gamblers, the former were shown to perform significantly better than the latter. According to them, this is due to the (visible) plunge phenomenon, whereby insiders bet heavily with bookmakers on a particular horse. Inside information is thus openly provided during the course of betting.

In this chapter, we model both OP and SP. OP is modelled as the equilibrium of an expected profit-maximising cartel. We show that, in the presence of inside traders, bookmakers include a favourite-longshot bias in OP. Furthermore, even in the absence of insiders, OP is always biased if bookmakers make mistakes in setting prices, which is unavoidable. This novel explanation of bias is not related to whether there is inside money in the market. However, the insiders' behaviour allows the empirical determination of pricing mistakes. At the outset of betting, insiders look for opening prices which have been set too low, which they then arbitrage at the bookmakers' expense via plunges. The bias becomes apparent provided the direction of the mistake is known. However, since the only way that mistakes can be observed is via plunge behaviour, the implications of our OP model can be empirically tested only in the presence of insider trading. Note that hindsight knowledge of the race result would not reveal mistakes since all horses had a positive probability of winning (and one of them indeed won).

In section 13.2, we present a brief description of the operation of the Melbourne market. In section 13.3, we model the determination of OP by bookmakers acting as a cartel showing, in section 13.4, that inside money is necessary to induce a planned bias, via optimising the monopoly. In section 13.5, we show that the empirically observed bias reflects the inevitable pricing mistakes made by the bookie for lack of better information.

In section 13.6, a novel explanation for the persistence of the bias in SPs, in spite of its decrease over time, is provided. Betting induces competition among bookmakers, therefore decreasing the extent of the favourite-long-shot bias. If prices were continuous and the market operated until the establishment of a competitive equilibrium, there would be no bias. Discrete pricing, in conjunction with markets of relatively short duration, seems to prevent complete removal of the bias and also ensures a small profit margin for bookmakers even at SP. Various empirically verifiable hypotheses concerning OP and SP are derived, which are tested in section 13.7. Section 13.8 draws a brief conclusion.

13.2 The Melbourne bookmaking market

In Australian horse betting markets, bookmakers are permitted to operate only on the race courses. Betting off-course is available via a parimutuel, which also operates on-course. There are four racing venues in Melbourne[2] and the OP and SP as well as results for all races during the 1993–4 season provide the data for this chapter. For prices deviating from a monotonic downward trend between OP and SP, prices during the betting are also available. Bookmakers operate in betting rings, with as many as fifty members. All odds are made clearly visible to bettors at all times. Between 15 and 30 minutes before a race, bookmakers set their odds for accepting bets on the horses in the race. Prices are simply odds expressed as probability equivalents. As betting proceeds, bookmakers are free to adjust odds as they see fit. Virtually all transactions are in cash, and betting is concluded just before the race. Immediately after the race, all debts are settled. A winning bettor is paid the amount of the bet times one plus the odds on display at the time it was made. This gives bookmakers a competitive advantage over the parimutuel, since the latter's winning payoff becomes known to bettors only after the race. It should be noted that only some sixty different odds are offered, and, therefore, prices are not continuous. The odds are shown on a printed board made available to all bookies and thus individual bookies cannot easily offer a price that does not appear on the board.[3] Tables 13.1 and 13.2 show the different opening and starting odds respectively, which were offered during the 1993–4 season, together with the number of horses and number of winners in each odds category.

Bookmakers in the main betting ring – the 'rails' – in Melbourne entrust the initial setting of opening odds to one member in their group, who has a reputation for knowing about the horses' form, and the others more or less follow. Betting commences and inside traders often bet via several agents who are instructed to bet, at predetermined odds, simultaneously with a number of bookmakers. This ensures that relatively large sums are placed on particular horses at odds deemed desirable by the insider. (Course

Table 13.1. *Opening odds (OP)*

Opening odds (OP)	Horses	Winners	Opening odds (OP)	Horses	Winners
0.25	1	1	6.5	35	3
0.5	9	5	7	570	55
0.571428	4	4	8	717	64
0.666666	13	6	9	42	2
0.727272	4	4	10	790	44
0.8	19	9	12	710	30
0.9	9	3	14	413	10
1	37	17	15	157	8
1.111111	12	5	16	501	15
1.25	42	19	20	578	18
1.375	14	9	25	600	9
1.5	62	23	30	5	0
1.625	7	4	33	525	9
1.75	101	31	40	73	1
2	116	37	50	386	1
2.25	152	40	66	153	0
2.5	198	55	80	3	0
2.75	56	6	100	189	0
3	285	56	125	8	0
3.25	42	3	140	1	0
3.5	316	49	150	5	0
4	370	36	200	21	0
4.5	329	54	250	5	0
5	507	49	330	1	0
5.5	119	12	500	1	0
6	514	42			

regulations place an upper limit on the size of the bookmakers' contingent debts.) This highly visible heavy betting act is called a 'plunge'. Inside information is passed on to outsiders in this way. This differs from the situation in other financial markets, where noise traders obscure insider trading. It should be noted that insiders should utilize any special information they have during the betting, since it loses all value when the race starts. Furthermore, as noted above, since insider trading is both legal – only jockeys are forbidden to bet – and takes place at fixed prices, insiders have no incentive to hide their trading behaviour from outsiders. However, such information may no longer be valuable since the odds available about a particular horse would be lower after a plunge.

Table 13.2. *Starting odds (SP)*

Starting odds (SP)	Horses	Winners	Starting odds (SP)	Horses	Winners
0.363636	1	1	7.5	13	3
0.571428	5	3	8	452	34
0.615384	5	3	9	275	19
0.666666	7	3	10	600	55
0.727272	5	3	11	96	4
0.8	14	8	12	552	44
0.9	14	6	14	448	19
1	21	11	15	249	6
1.111111	17	10	16	537	19
1.25	20	8	20	692	25
1.375	18	10	25	595	13
1.5	44	16	30	41	2
1.625	23	12	33	530	10
1.75	56	21	40	301	3
1.875	18	10	50	369	7
2	105	36	60	11	0
2.25	102	33	66	277	2
2.5	100	22	80	54	0
2.75	97	24	100	244	0
3	150	43	125	127	0
3.25	105	19	140	62	0
3.5	208	39	150	9	0
3.75	31	9	160	23	0
4	248	30	200	73	0
4.5	213	32	250	22	0
5	309	39	330	13	0
5.5	208	35	400	10	0
6	371	40	500	15	0
6.5	132	13	660	4	0
7	480	44	999	6	0

In modelling bookmakers' behaviour, it seems reasonable to consider setting OP as monopolistic. Thus, in section 13.3, the bookmakers as a group are referred to as 'the monopoly bookie', when OP is discussed. Furthermore, inside trade is defined as a bet(s) on a horse which increases its price. This assumption seems reasonable, given that the competition among bookmakers, which takes place after OP has been set, tends to drive prices down. Thus, for the 1993–4 Melbourne racing season, the mean sum of OP per race was 1.40, while the mean sum of SP was only 1.20. In addition, the sum of OP exceeded the sum of SP in every race.

13.3 The model

There are n horses in a race. A monopoly bookmaker sells contingent claims on each horse. The contingent claim on horse i costs q_i and pays 1 if horse i wins, and zero otherwise. A price q_i implies odds $\frac{1-q_i}{q_i}$.

There are two populations of bettors on a race with n horses: outsiders and insiders. Outsiders demand, Y, which depends on the price level – i.e. the 'round', $\sum_{i=1}^{n} q_i$. Y is the amount bet and $Y'\left(\sum_{i=1}^{n} q_i\right) < 0$. If demand were totally inelastic, the prices charged by a monopolist would be unbounded. The insiders have a maximal budget, Z, that may be wagered, partly or totally. A budget Z is assumed rather than allowing the insiders to borrow and freely optimise their bets since, on average, the bookies lose to insiders, who have better information. Both bookies and insiders make their profits at the expense of outsiders. If Z is too large for given demand by outsiders, it would rock the market by putting bookies out of business, to the insiders' own detriment. Assume this budget is divided among n insiders – one associated with each horse in the race – in the manner described below.

13.3.1 Information

Suppose that the horses' true winning probabilities are given by $p_1, \ldots p_n$, where $\sum_{i=1}^{n} p_i = 1$. Assume that nobody, not even an insider, knows in advance which horse is going to win the race, in contrast to Shin (1991, 1992, 1993), who assumed that insiders know which horse will win the race. Assume that an insider knows only the true winning probability of one horse i, p_i, but does not know how $1 - p_i$ is distributed among the other horses. A risk-neutral insider would wager on horse i if $p_i > q_i$. It stands to reason that the more confident insiders are, the more eager and successful they are in raising betting funds. Thus, assume that p_i is the fraction of all inside money, Z, wagered by insider i on horse i, if $p_i > q_i$. Therefore, a maximum bet of $p_i Z$ dollars would be placed on horse i. We do not make any assumptions concerning the likelihood of inside traders *vis-à-vis* either favourites or longshots.

The vector $(p_1, \ldots, p_n)$ may be viewed as a realisation of the current situation of the horses' and jockeys' condition, which is known only to insiders. Non-insiders are more in the dark, which can be represented as an n-variable distribution function over the possible realisations of the winning probabilities $(p_1, \ldots, p_n)$. Denote by $g(p_1, \ldots, p_n)$ the density function defined over the n-dimensional simplex, $\sum_{i=1}^{n} p_i = 1$, $p_i \geq 0$ and by $g_i(p_i)$ the marginal density of horse i. We assume that while the monopoly bookmaker knows the density g in its entirety, the outsiders, who spend less on information gathering and processing and resort to popular sources, such as racing periodicals, know only the means of the marginal distribution. That is, for each horse i, they know $e_i = E p_i = \int_0^1 p_i g_i(p_i) \mathrm{d}p_i$. The outsiders support the horses in proportion to their expected winning probabilities, $e_1, \ldots, e_n$. These expectations may be thought of as the winning probabilities, as implied by 'public information'. Hence, outsiders wager $e_i Y$, dollars on horse i. In summary, there are three levels of information regarding horse i's winning chances: insiders know the true winning probability, p_i, bookies know the density g and outsiders know only the means of the marginal distributions, $e_1, \ldots, e_n$.

Trading proceeds in a number of stages, the first and the last of which we consider here. At stage 1, a proportion of the outsiders, α, $0 < \alpha < 1$ bet in the market at the OP set by the bookie. Also, all insiders may bet should the opportunity arise. At the other stages, the rest of the outsiders bet at new updated prices set by the bookie after having observed the insider trading pattern. As noted in section 13.2, insiders are said to have bet on a horse when the money they place on it in a single bet leads to an increase in the horse's price.[4] Insiders, if they feel it is worthwhile, can bet on horses at the reduced prices at the second stage. Price updating effectively continues until SP are fixed, and equilibrium prices are reached at the end of betting. Since – in contrast to the British market – there is no legal SP betting in the Australian market, these prices may be assumed to embody all the available useful information regarding the race's outcome.

13.3.2 Stage 1: monopoly

The monopolist bookie sets the optimal prices, $q_1, \ldots, q_n$, before the betting starts, knowing both the distribution of winning probabilities and the behaviour of both types of bettors. Regarding insiders, he knows their total budget Z and that some of them would like to support horse i with $p_i Z$ dollars, if p_i, which is unknown to him but known to the respective insider, turns out to be larger than q_i, or with zero dollars otherwise. As regards outsiders, he knows the fraction α who bet at OP, their demand

$Y\left(\sum_{i=1}^{n} q_i\right)$ and e_i, the proportion supporting horse i. The cost to the bookie is constant, c per dollar of revenue and includes 2 per cent turnover tax and operating costs.

Given these assumptions, the bookie's expected profit in stage 1, R_1, is:[5]

$$R_1(q_1,\ldots,q_n) = \alpha Y\left(\sum_{i=1}^{n} q_i\right)\left[1 - \sum_{i=1}^{n}\frac{e_i^2}{q_i} - c\right]$$

$$+ Z\sum_{i=1}^{n}\int_{q_i}^{1} p_i(1 - \frac{p_i}{q_i} - c)g_i(p_i)\mathrm{d}p_i \qquad (13.1)$$

where αY is the betting revenue from outsiders. $\$\alpha e_i Y$ is bet on horse i by outsiders and if it wins, the expected probability of this event is e_i, for each $\$1$ bet on it, $\$1/q_i$ is paid out. If horse i's true winning probability is p_i then only if $p_i > q_i$ are inside bets laid on i. The expected profit from insiders is the expectation over $q_i \leq p_i \leq 1$ of the amount bet, $p_i Z$, times the (negative) term in brackets $(1 - \frac{p_i}{q_i} - c)$.

Note from (13.1) that, for every horse i for which contingent claims are sold at a profit, the price must satisfy $q_i > e_i$. To illustrate this, consider the ith component of (13.1):

$$e_i\alpha Y\left(1 - \frac{e_i}{q_i} - c\right) + Z\int_{q_i}^{1} p_i(1 - \frac{p_i}{q_i} - c)g_i(p_i)\mathrm{d}p_i \qquad (13.2)$$

Since the second term is always negative, in order to make money on horse i, the first term should be strictly positive, which implies $q_i > e_i/(1 - c)$.

Assuming the monopolist bookie is indifferent to risk, he would maximize R_1. Differentiating with respect to q_k:

$$\frac{\partial R_1}{\partial q_k} = \alpha Y'\left(\sum_{i=1}^{n} q_i\right)\left[1 - \sum_{i=1}^{n}\frac{e_i^2}{q_i} - c\right] + \alpha Y\left(\sum_{i=1}^{n} q_i\right)\frac{e_k^2}{q_k^2}$$

$$+ \frac{Z}{q_k^2}\int_{q_k}^{1} p_k^2 g_k(p_k)\mathrm{d}p_k + cZq_k g_k(p_k) = 0 \qquad (13.3)$$

The n equations such as (13.3) for $k = 1,\ldots,n$, cannot be solved explicitly for $q_1,\ldots,q_n$ without the knowledge of Y, Z and $g_1,\ldots,g_n$.

As the insiders add a negative term to the bookie's profit, they pose a threat that calls for measures of caution. Raising prices turns out to be an adroit defence.

Claim 1:

For sufficiently small $|Y''|$, the sum of the optimal prices rises with the inside budget at $Z = 0$ that is $\sum_{i=1}^{n} \frac{\partial q_i^*}{\partial Z}\Big|_{Z=0} > 0$.

Proof: See the appendix, p. 306.

Note from the proof that although $\sum_{i=1}^{n} \frac{\partial q_i^*}{\partial Z} > 0$, this does not guarantee that $\frac{\partial q_i^*}{\partial Z} > 0$ for all i. The numerator of (13A.2) has both positive and negative terms. However since $\frac{d}{dy} \frac{1}{y^2} \int_y^1 x^2 g(x) dx < 0$, for all positive functions $g(x)$, $\frac{\partial q_i^*}{\partial Z}$ would tend to be greater for longshots – i.e. horses i with q_i, which are smaller than for favourites. According to this claim, the sum of OP should increase with the extent of insider trading. We are unable to test this hypothesis empirically since we have data only on the extent of price changes over the entire betting period as a consequence of a plunge, *inter alia*. While these data are sufficient to indicate insider trading, they do not permit accurate estimation of its extent.

13.4 The optimally planned favourite-longshot bias in OP

We now proceed to show that inside money underlies the deliberate bias optimally planned by the bookie. This explains the observed bias in OP. Define $B_{kj} = \frac{e_k}{q_k} - \frac{e_j}{q_j}$ as the bias between two horses k and j, the former of which is better – i.e. $e_k > e_j$. Note that the true winning probabilities are not observable, and their best estimates are the winning frequencies of groups of horses. In the following, we make use of the observed tendency of better horses to be more dependable, or less risky, which is assumed in claim 2 (p. 296). Denote by $G_k(s) = \int_0^s g_k(x) dx$ the cumulative marginal distribution function of horse k. Assuming that horse k is less risky means that its support is more concentrated around its mean than for j. In other words, $G_j(x + e_k - e_j)$ is a mean preserving spread of $G_k(x)$. Such relation between distributions is called 'second-degree stochastic dominance', which in turn has three interpretations, amounting to three equivalent definitions of the statement 'horse k is less risky than horse j':

1. Horse j is equal to horse k plus 'noise'
2. Horse j's distribution has more weight in its tails than that of horse k
3. All risk-averse individuals prefer horse k to horse j, *ceteris paribus*.

See Rothschild and Stiglitz (1970) for a proof of this. A slightly stronger version, which we shall assume for simplicity, occurs if $G_k(x)$ crosses $G_j(x + e_k - e_j)$ only once and from below.

Claim 2:
1. Without inside money there is no *intended* favourite-longshot bias on the bookie's part; that is, for all pairs of horses k and j, $B_{kj}|_{Z=0} = 0$.
2. For $Z > 0$, intended bias is part of the monopolist's optimal policy. That is, for small enough c, if $e_k > e_j$ and in addition k is less risky than j in the sense that $G_k(x)$ crosses $G_j(x + e_k - e_j)$ only once at e_k and from below, then $\frac{dB_{kj}}{dZ}\Big|_{Z=0} > 0$.

Proof: See the appendix, p. 307.

13.5 Pricing mistakes and the observed bias

Until this point, we have studied a 'theoretical' planned bias; that is, a bias in terms of the unobservable e_j and e_k, which holds in theory. A bias may, of course, exist in practice whatever the value of Z if $\frac{q_k}{q_j} \neq \frac{p_k}{p_j}$. However, the probabilities $(p_1, \ldots, p_n)$ are also unobservable. Thus, when we refer to observed bias, we mean $\frac{q_k}{q_j} \neq \frac{f_k}{f_j}$, where f_i is the observed winning frequency of horses with price q_i. These frequencies can be calculated from table 13.1 and are the best estimates of the respective groups' probabilities of winning. Note that p_i is the winning probability of a given horse in a given race and e_i is its average probability. However, empirically, there are many races and groups of horses, so that the difference between p_i and e_i is blurred and both may be represented by f_i.

To explain the observed bias, we advance a new argument. The hindsight knowledge of the OP-pricing mistakes induces a bias in the data under plausible conditions. That is, if we can somehow separate the data into two sets – (1) horses priced too high and (2) horses priced too low – then a bias would be expected in the data. The bias is a reflection of the pricing mistakes and it is possible to observe it through the knowledge of how to separate the two sets. It is not the product of inside money and may exist without insider trading. However it is the inside money that permits, via observed plunges, the above separation in the data. Note that the race results do not reveal mistakes since all the horses had a positive probability of winning. If we take a horse from set 1 and another from set 2, it is trivial to show that bias is inevitable. For two horses from set 1, assumptions concerning the distribution functions are required. We prove the above for any such separation even if $Z = 0$, but use the language of plunges as the cause of the separation, since our data relates to this and can, in principle, be tested empirically.

Since we are compelled to deal with winning frequencies, the theoretical counterpart of the available data cannot be winning probabilities but, rather, expectations of probabilities, applying general or conditional distributions on a case-by-case basis.

We now investigate the conditions under which the model predicts a favourite-longshot bias in the available OP data. Let us take two horses j and k, where k is better, which simply means it has a higher expected winning probability $e_k > e_j$, which implies from (13.2) that $q_k > q_j$.

Such a pair of classes of horses, (j, k), can be either both underpriced (plunged), one underpriced and one overpriced, or both overpriced. We consider these three possibilities in turn.

13.5.1 Horse j and k are both overpriced

If a horse j is known to be overpriced, then $p_j < q_j$ implying that its *a priori* density, g_i, should be updated by incorporating the new information. Denote by

$$g_j\left(x\,\middle|\,x<q_j\right) = \frac{g_j(x)}{\int_0^{q_j} g_j(x)\mathrm{d}x}, \quad 0 \le x \le q_j$$

its conditional density, and its conditional expectation by

$$e_j(p_j<q_j) = \int_0^{q_j} xg_j\left(x\,\middle|\,x<q_j\right)\mathrm{d}x$$

A favourite-longshot bias in this pair would be expected if

$$\frac{q_k}{q_j} < \frac{e_k(p_k<q_k)}{e_j(p_j<q_j)}$$

Claim 3:

Let j and k be two horses priced too high with $e_j < e_k$ and OP $q_j < q_k$. Then

$$\frac{q_k}{q_j} < \frac{e_k(p_k \le q_k)}{e_j(p_j \le q_j)} \quad \text{if } G_k(x)$$

$$- G_j(x - e_k + e_j)\begin{cases} \le 0 \text{ for } x \le e_k \\ \ge 0 \text{ for } x > e_k \end{cases}$$

and even if $Z = 0$

Note:

As the proof makes clear, instead of the more intuitive crossing-once-from-below condition, a much weaker condition suffices:

$$\frac{\int_0^q G(x)\mathrm{d}x}{G(q)} \leq \frac{\int_0^q F(x)\mathrm{d}x}{F(q)} \text{ for } q<e$$

Proof of Claim 3: See the appendix, p. 309.

13.5.2 Horse j is overpriced and horse k is underpriced

Claim 4:

If horse k is underpriced, while horse j is overpriced; that is, $p_k > q_k, p_j < q_j$, then regardless of both their riskiness, a favourite-longshot bias is expected:

$$\frac{q_k}{q_j} \leq \frac{e_k(p_k > q_k)}{e_j(p_j \leq q_j)} = \frac{\int_{q_k}^{1} xg_k(x)\,\mathrm{d}x \Big/ \int_{q_k}^{1} g_k(x)\,\mathrm{d}x}{\int_{0}^{q_j} xg_j(x)\,\mathrm{d}x \Big/ \int_{0}^{q_j} g_j(x)\,\mathrm{d}x}$$

Proof:

Since

$$q_k \int_{q_k}^{1} g_k(x)\,\mathrm{d}x \leq \int_{q_k}^{1} xg_k(x)\,\mathrm{d}x \text{ and } q_j \int_{0}^{q_j} g_j(x)\,\mathrm{d}x \geq \int_{0}^{q_j} xg_j(x)\,\mathrm{d}x$$

for any density functions g_k, g_j, the result follows directly. ∎

13.5.3 Horse j and k are both underpriced

In the case of two underpriced horses, bias cannot be proved. One can easily show examples of bias in any direction. Since two plunged horses would be involved in a race, this category only a includes a minuscule proportion of the data, so it could not possibly affect the observed bias profile. Interestingly, bias is not observed in this case; see below. On average 12 per cent of horses are plunged, so even under independence between plunges, the chance of two plunges in a race is 1.5 per cent, and in reality even less because of plausible negative dependence. The other two possibilities hold for 21 per cent and 77.5 per cent of all possible pairs, (j, k).

13.6 Stage 2: competition and starting prices

By observing insider trading pattern, the bookie can learn a great deal about a race. For a horse i, which is plunged, the bookie may obtain a reasonable estimate of the amount bet on the horse, $p_i Z$. Thus, if Z is either known or estimated on the basis of experience, the bookie may deduce the horse's true winning probability. For a non-plunged horse j, he can find out that $p_j < q_j$ and then update the probability estimate using Bayes' Law.

The bursts of new information provided by plunges break the monopolistic behaviour of the bookmakers' cartel. The OP provide a useful focus for bookies as long as they are in the dark regarding horses' true winning probabilities. They have to defend themselves against plunges, which occur sporadically and affect some bookies more than others, by changing prices in a manner independent of other bookies. The focal point is gone and competition sets in. The prices of plunged horses go up while the others go down, thereby possibly giving rise to further plunges. We have no complete data on this intermediate stage of the betting. Consequently, we consider the determination of SP in our model, which are the prices the market reached during the course of unfolding competition when time has run out and the race started. During this period, inside information is used and revealed, probabilities are updated and consequently prices are changed under the pressure of competition.

The incentive to raise the price on a plunged horse is immediate and strong. A bookie hit by a plunge comes to the painful realisation that he has sold the horse cheaply. He must defend himself by continuing to increase the price as long as the trend continues. Regarding the non-plunged horses, the bookies are still in the dark. They realise, from the fact that these horses were not plunged, that their winning probabilities are inflated and they are therefore overpriced, but do not know by how much. Large price decreases may attract a new plunge. A prudent bookie would lower prices gradually, watching the other bookies closely to avoid being caught with prices that are too low. This process is time-consuming and may not have a chance to run its full course before the race begins. To understand this better, it is useful to analyse fully the somewhat unrealistic benchmark case in which SP are the final market prices after all inside information has been revealed and competition has run its full course. Since plunges and their consequences are clear to outsiders, they also learn and update their winning probabilities and reach the same conclusions as the bookmakers. We assume that all true winning probabilities, $p_1, \ldots p_n$, are known to all the players, and that the SP, $t_1, \ldots, t_n$, are perfectly competitive under the constraint of non-negative profits to bookies.

Consider the implications of zero-profit condition. Suppose that after all the plunges have taken place, a proportion, β, of outsiders still has to bet, where $\beta \leq 1 - \beta$. Noting that outsiders now back horses in proportion p_i, instead of e_i, due to the better information, the expected total profit for all the bookies at this last stage of market functioning is given by:

$$R_2 = \beta Y \sum_{i=1}^{n} \left\{ p_i \left[1 - \frac{p_i}{t_i} - c \right] \right\} \tag{13.4}$$

If competition could drive profits down to zero, the limit for each horse i would be expected such that $1 - \frac{p_i}{t_i} - c = 0$ or $t_i = \frac{p_i}{1-c}$. No bias is implied by such complete competition since according to the above $t_k/t_j = p_k/p_j$.

Competitors, however, are not free to choose any price they wish. In Melbourne bookmaking, there are only around sixty prices (odds) to choose from and only sixty were offered during the 1993–4 season. The discretisation of prices is not as innocent as it may seem. It gives rise to profits for bookmakers even under the strongest competition. Indeed, it may be considered a collusive device to keep the bookmaking oligopoly away from zero profit at SP. While competition is more vigorous in the second stage than in the first, when only about forty prices are employed, it still manifests some trade restraint. A by-product of discretisation, which concerns us here, is the favourite-longshot bias.

Suppose the feasible prices, listed in table 13.1, are $V_1, V_2, \ldots V_{60}$. If it so happens that for the ith horse, $V_j < \frac{p_i}{1-c} < V_{j+1}$ to avoid losing money on horse i, bookmakers should set $t_i = V_{j+1}$, which implies a mark-up of ε_i of the magnitude:

$$\varepsilon_i = t_i - \frac{p_i}{1-c} = \min_{j} \left(V_j | V_j \geq \frac{p_i}{1-c} \right) - \frac{p_i}{1-c} \tag{13.5}$$

Note that although $\frac{p_i}{1-c}$ for a particular horse i in a particular race is assumed to be known to the betting public in stage 2, it is not known to us, the students of the market. So a measured bias necessarily refers to the statistical treatment of large groups of horses with the same price. Taking all the horses in all races in our sample with the price $t = V_{j+1}$, the probability of winning p satisfies $V_j < \frac{p}{1-c} \leq V_{j+1}$ or $(1-c)V_j < p \leq (1-c)V_{j+1}$, and p for a particular horse can fall at any point in this interval. Consequently, taking two horses k and i with SP $t_k > t_i$, then:

$$\frac{t_k}{t_i} = \frac{\min\limits_{j} \left(V_j | V_j \geq \frac{p_k}{1-c} \right)}{\min\limits_{j} \left(V_j | V_j \geq \frac{p_i}{1-c} \right)} = \frac{\frac{p_k}{1-c} + \varepsilon_k}{\frac{p_i}{1-c} + \varepsilon_i} \tag{13.6}$$

This ratio may be smaller, equal to or larger than $\frac{p_k}{p_i}$ so the bias could go either way depending on particular realisations of p_k, p_i and therefore $\varepsilon_k, \varepsilon_i$ could have any value in the respective intervals between two feasible prices. However, if one considers two large groups of horses with the prices t_k and t_i, reasonably assuming that all members of a group have the same price distribution, (13.6) is replaced, denoting conditional (on the respective price) means by bars, by

$$\frac{t_k}{t_i} = \frac{\frac{\bar{p}_k}{1-c} + \bar{\varepsilon}_k}{\frac{\bar{p}_i}{1-c} + \bar{\varepsilon}_i} \tag{13.7}$$

This ratio is smaller than $\frac{\bar{p}_k}{\bar{p}_i}$, which implies the favourite-longshot bias, if and only if $\frac{t_k}{t_i} > \frac{\bar{\varepsilon}_k}{\bar{\varepsilon}_i}$ or $\frac{\bar{\varepsilon}_k}{t_k} < \frac{\bar{\varepsilon}_i}{t_i}$. Let us now study the relationship between the ratios of mean mark-ups of prices. For simplicity, write the interval of a given group of horses $(1-c) \, V_j < p \leq (1-c) \, V_{j+1}$ as $a < p \leq b$ and their density as g, then the mean mark-up of the group is

$$\bar{\varepsilon} = b - \frac{1}{1-c} \left(\frac{\int_a^b xg(x)\mathrm{d}x}{\int_a^b g(x)\mathrm{d}x} \right) \tag{13.8}$$

If the mark-ups are the same for two different groups of horses it creates a bias because the mark-ups differ percentage-wise. Example: consider two groups of horses, one with odds 20/1 (i.e. price 0.047619) and the other with 1.970695/1 (0.336622). If these are true winning probabilities, then the market odds would be 16/1 (0.058824) and 15/8 (0.347826), respectively, with the same mark-ups at 0.011204. There is a favourite-longshot bias because $0.347826/0.336622 < 0.058824/0.047619$. By differentiating (13.8) with respect to a and b, the next claim tackles the problem of whether the expected mark-ups are indeed equal or close enough.

Claim 5:

1. $\dfrac{\partial \frac{\bar{\varepsilon}}{b}}{\partial a} < 0$

2. If in $[a, b]$, g is non-increasing, satisfies

$$\int g(x)\mathrm{d}x \leq [g(a) + g(b)](b - a)/2 \, (\text{e.g., convex})$$

and, in addition, is not too steep,

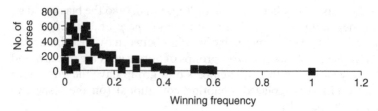

Figure 13.1 Sample distribution of horses by winning frequency

$$\text{i.e.} \quad \frac{g(a)}{g(b)} < \frac{3a^2 + b^2}{a^2 + b^2}$$

then

$$\frac{\partial \frac{\bar{\varepsilon}}{b}}{\partial b} > 0$$

3. If in $[a, b]$, g is non-increasing and satisfies

$$\int g(x)\mathrm{d}x \le [g(a) + g(b)](b - a)/2$$

then

$$\frac{\partial \frac{\bar{\varepsilon}}{b}}{\partial a} + \frac{\partial \frac{\bar{\varepsilon}}{b}}{\partial b} < 0$$

Proof: See the appendix, p. 310.

Consider the implications of claim 5. First, note that the price of a group is $t = b/(1-c)$. Points 1 and 2 imply that increasing the interval $[a, b]$ increases the mark-up-to-price ratio. Comparing two groups, $t_k > t_i$, if the better horses have a narrower interval, then $\frac{\bar{\varepsilon}_k}{t_k} < \frac{\bar{\varepsilon}_i}{t_i}$, implying a bias. According to point 3, moving the same interval to the right decreases the ratio, again implying a bias if the two groups have similar intervals. Deducing a bias from claim 5 is possible only if: (1) g satisfies its conditions; and (2) the SP structure selected by the industry manifests increasing, constant, or not sharply decreasing intervals in the horses' quality. As to the shape of g, the empirical distribution of horses by price in our sample, given in figure 13.1, may provide some insights. It is reasonable to assume that the distribution of horses with price t_i is not far from the distribution in figure 13.1, conditional on the interval between $(1-c)t_i$ and $(1-c)$ times the next

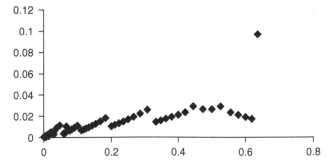

Figure 13.2 Width of interval as function of price

lower price. The *g* suggested by figure 13.1 is decreasing and convex for most horse groups. As for the structure of SP, as one moves to higher prices, the intervals between adjacent prices tends to increase and then to decline, see figure 13.2. Note that bookies are interested in profit, and not bias *per se*. A larger interval implies a higher mark-up, so it makes monopolistic sense to charge a higher price at intervals where there is greater or less elastic demand, by making them wider. Thus, with only partial support from claim 5, the bias in SP turns out to be an empirical question. As the regression below shows, there is indeed a bias. The main explanation is the failure of the market to reach the competitive equilibrium in the short trade duration. The prices of plunged horses are corrected immediately and they tend to be favourites. The prices of other horses follow more sluggish behaviour and may end up too high, which constitutes the bias. In addition, claim 5 may explain some of the bias although conflicting forces may be at work.

13.7 Empirical tests

The data used in this chapter are drawn from all the races in Melbourne during the 1993–4 racing season: a total of 848 races with 9,827 horses. Data are the official market OP and SP for each horse, irrespective of whether it won the race and the distance losers finished behind the winner (the 'margin'). With prices deviating from a downward trend between OP and SP, the prices during the betting are also available. The winning probabilities used below are estimated as follows: a horse was deemed plunged if its price rose above the OP during betting; this occurred in 1,129 out of the 9,827 running horses. The sample was divided into plunged and non-plunged horses. Both sets were grouped by SP and the winning frequencies calculated. For regressions involving SP data, the winning frequencies were taken as estimates of winning probabilities.

It should be noted that the number of different OP offered by bookies differed from the number of SP. Thus, winning frequencies based on SP could not be regressed directly on OP, as required by claims 3 and 4. In this case, each horse was assigned a winning frequency according to the SP, which are based on the most accurate information, which was then normalised, so that the estimated probabilities in each race summed to 1. These estimates were then regressed on OP, as described below. For all regressions, estimated winning probabilities are denoted by $\tilde{p}$.

13.7.1 Opening price tests

Claim 1:
According to this claim, the OP round-up rises because of inside money. As noted on p. 295, we are unable to test this claim.

Claim 2:
According to this claim, all horses should display a favourite-longshot bias in OP in races with inside money – i.e. plunges. To test this claim, we regress winning probabilities on OP in all races in which there were plunges. This claim requires a negative intercept. The following result was obtained:

$$\tilde{p} = \underset{(-27.768)}{-0.0196} + \underset{(188.145)}{0.8759 OP} \qquad\qquad \overline{R^2} = 0.8136, n = 8111$$

Claim 3:
According to this claim, non-plunged horses should display a favourite-longshot bias. This requires that the intercept in the regression of winning probabilities on OP should be negative, giving the following result:

$$\tilde{p} = \underset{(-32.503)}{-0.0198} + \underset{(201.908)}{0.8217 OP} + \underset{(15.381)}{0.1625 OPDUM} + \underset{(10.984)}{0.0227 PLUNGE}$$
$$\overline{R^2} = 0.8552, n = 9827,$$

where *PLUNGE* is a dummy variable, which equals 1 for plunged horses and zero otherwise, $OPDUM = OPPLUNGE$ and *t*-values are shown in parentheses.

Claim 4:
According to this claim, the ratio of winning probability to OP is higher for plunged than for non-plunged horses. The mean ratios and their standard deviations for horses separated into plunged (1,129) and

non-plunged (8,698) groups were 0.99 and 0.53, and 0.55 and 0.27, respectively. Based on a simple t-test the null hypothesis (i.e. the claim does not hold at all conventional levels of significance) is rejected. Among 2,193 ($= 4,351$) possible pairings, the claim holds in 1,828 (85.31 per cent) of cases.

Bias among plunged horses

The regression equation presented under the test of claim 3 implies a positive intercept $(-0.0198 + 0.0227 = 0.0029)$ for plunged horses, showing that a reverse bias cannot be rejected in this case. However, the intercept was not significant if the regression was run only on plunged horses, suggesting the absence of bias.

An important assumption underlying claim 2 is that the more favoured a horse, the greater its reliability. This is examined below using the distance a horse finished behind the winner in the race – the so-called 'margin' – as a measure of reliability. The standard deviations of the margins are calculated for horses grouped according to SP. To avoid generating a truncated endogenous variable, we proceed as follows.[6] Let A be the maximal SD of the data. Define a variable $y = \ln [SD/(A\text{-}SD)]$, which varies from minus infinity to infinity. More favoured horses may be said to be more reliable than longshots if OP received a negative coefficient. The following result was obtained:

$$y = -0.71975 - 2.9715OP \qquad \overline{R^2} = 0.6242, n = 58$$
$$\;\;\;\;\;\;\;(-15.4)\;\;\;\;\;\;(-9.782)$$

In this regression, the coefficient of OP is negative and significant above 1 per cent, thereby refuting the hypothesis that more favoured horses are not more reliable than longshots.

13.7.2 Starting price tests

Equation (13.7) was tested for bias. The regressions obtained were as follows:

$$\tilde{p} = -0.0183 + 1.024SP - 0.0694SPDUM + 0.0046PLUNGE$$
$$\;\;\;\;\;\;(-3.044)\;\;\;\;(20.909)\;\;\;\;\;\;\;\;(-0.655)\;\;\;\;\;\;\;\;\;\;\;\;(0.204)$$
$$\overline{R^2} = 0.8494, n = 108$$

where $SPDUM = SPPLUNGE$ and the regression was weighted by the number of horses in each price category. Both the negative constant and the coefficient of SP greater than 1 imply bias.

Note that the sample mean mark-up over all races and horses, measured as $SP - \tilde{p}$, is 0.0044. A positive mark-up suggests that the final equilibrium is not completely competitive.

13.8 Conclusions

In this chapter, we presented and tested empirically a theoretical model of a market for state-contingent claims with inside traders: the Melbourne horse betting bookmakers' market. Based on the above analysis of the informational structure of this market, the following conclusions may be drawn:

1. In the absence of inside information, when betting opens, sellers price contingent claims without bias.
2. The characteristic favourite-longshot bias in the market is the result of the bookmakers' attempt to defend themselves against adverse selection due to the presence of insiders.
3. The hindsight knowledge of OP-pricing mistakes induces a bias in the data if it is possible to separate between horses priced too high and too low. This bias is not the result of inside money and may exist without insider trading. However, it is the inside money, via observed plunges, which allows the above separation. Clearly, a bias is inevitable between one horse from the first set and another from the second.
4. As betting proceeds, the extent of the bias is attenuated by competition among bookmakers.

However, even if prices were continuous, complete eradication of the bias might not be possible in the 30 minutes of trade before the race starts, which is not long enough for all the relevant information to be revealed. In addition, use of discrete pricing prevents the market from reaching a fully competitive equilibrium, and, in turn, the complete removal of bias.

Appendix

Proof of claim 1:
Differentiating (13.3) with respect to Z:

$$\frac{\mathrm{d}}{\mathrm{d}Z}\frac{\partial R_1}{\partial q_k} = \alpha Y'' \left(1 - \sum_{i=1}^{n}\frac{e_i^2}{q_i} - c\right) \sum_{i=1}^{n}\frac{\partial q_i}{\partial Z} + \alpha Y' \sum_{i=1}^{n}\frac{e_i^2}{q_i^2}\frac{\partial q_i}{\partial Z}$$

$$+ \alpha Y' \frac{e_k^2}{q_k^2}\sum_{i=1}^{n}\frac{\partial q_i}{\partial Z} - 2\alpha Y\frac{e_k^2}{q_k^3}\frac{\partial q_k}{\partial Z}$$

$$+ \frac{1}{q_k^2}\int_{q_k}^{1} x^2 g_k(x)\mathrm{d}x - \frac{2Z}{q_k^3}\int_{q_k}^{1} x^2 g_k(x)\mathrm{d}x\frac{\partial q_k}{\partial Z} + cq_k g_k(q_k)$$

$$- (1-c)Z g_k(q_k)\frac{\partial q_k}{\partial Z} + cZ g_k'(q_k)\frac{\partial q_k}{\partial Z} = 0 \qquad (13\text{A}.1)$$

from which one gets

$$\frac{\partial q_k}{\partial Z} =$$

$$\frac{\frac{1}{q_k^2}\int_{q_k}^{1} x^2 g_k(x)\mathrm{d}x + cg_k(q_k) + \left[\alpha Y''\left(1 - \sum_{i=1}^{n}\frac{e_i^2}{q_i} - c\right) + \alpha Y'\frac{e_k^2}{q_k^2}\right]\sum_{i=1}^{n}\frac{\partial q_i}{\partial Z} + \alpha Y'\sum_{i=1}^{n}\frac{e_i^2}{q_i^2}\frac{\partial q_i}{\partial Z}}{2\alpha Y\frac{e_k^2}{q_k^3} + Z\left((1-c)g_k(q_k) + \frac{2}{q_k^3}\int_{q_k}^{1} x^2 g_k(x)\mathrm{d}x - cq_k g'_k(q_k)\right)}$$

(13A.2)

The denominator of (13A.2) is positive, except for the last term where $\mathrm{d}g/\mathrm{d}q$ could take any sign but is multiplied by small c, as well as the first two terms of the numerator. Note now:

1. Both $\sum_{i=1}^{n}\frac{\partial q_i}{\partial Z} < 0, \sum_{i=1}^{n}\frac{e_i^2}{q_i^2}\frac{\partial q_i}{\partial Z} < 0$ cannot hold since then $\frac{\partial q_k}{\partial Z} > 0$ for all k, if Y'' is negative or small enough, contradicting the assumption.

2. Since for $Z = 0$, $\frac{e_i}{q_i} = \frac{e_k}{q_k}$ for all i and k, $\sum_{i=1}^{n}\frac{e_i^2}{q_i^2}\frac{\partial q_i}{\partial Z} = \frac{e_k^2}{q_k^2}\sum_{i=1}^{n}\frac{\partial q_i}{\partial Z}$ and both expressions in 1 must have the same sign, which according to 1, is non-negative. ■

Proof of Claim 2:
1. Note from (13.3), where the first element is common to all horses k, that if $Z = 0$, for any two horses k, j:

$$\frac{e_k^2}{q_k^2} = \frac{e_j^2}{q_j^2} \text{ so } \frac{e_k}{q_k} = \frac{e_j}{q_j}$$

Therefore, in this case, bias would not be expected.
2. The bias may be written as

$$B_{kj} = \left[\left(\frac{e_k}{q_k}\right)^2 - \left(\frac{e_j}{q_j}\right)^2\right]\frac{q_k q_j}{e_k q_j + e_j q_k}$$

Equating $\frac{\partial R_1}{\partial q_k} = \frac{\partial R_1}{\partial q_j}$ in (13.3) gives:

$$B_{kj} = \frac{Z}{\alpha Y}\frac{q_k q_j}{e_k q_j + e_j q_k}\left[\frac{1}{q_j^2}\int_{q_j}^{1} x^2 g_j(x)\mathrm{d}x - \frac{1}{q_k^2}\int_{q_k}^{1} x^2 g_k(x)\mathrm{d}x + c\left(q_j g_j(q_j) - q_k g_k(q_k)\right)\right]$$

(13A.3)

$$\frac{dB_{kj}}{dZ}\bigg|_{Z=0} = \frac{1}{\alpha Y} \frac{q_k q_j}{e_k q_j + e_j q_k} \left[\frac{1}{q_j^2} \int\limits_{q_j}^{1} x^2 g_j(x) dx - \frac{1}{q_k^2} \int\limits_{q_k}^{1} x^2 g_k(x) dx \right.$$

$$\left. + c \big(q_j g_j(q_j) - q_k g_k(q_k) \big) \right]$$

$$(13A.4)$$

To prove that (13A.4) is positive for a small enough c, requires showing the following:

$$\frac{1}{q_j^2} \int\limits_{q_j}^{1} x^2 g_j(x) dx - \frac{1}{q_k^2} \int\limits_{q_k}^{1} x^2 g_k(x) dx > 0$$

Suppose that G_k and G_j are identically shaped, then:

$$g_k(x) = g_j(x - a) \quad \forall x, \text{where } a = e_k - e_j > 0$$

It follows that:

$$\frac{1}{q_j^2} \int\limits_{q_j}^{1} x^2 g_j(x) dx > \frac{1}{(q_j + a)^2} \int\limits_{q_j}^{1} (x + a)^2 g_j(x) dx$$

$$= \frac{1}{(q_j + a)^2} \int\limits_{q_j}^{1} (x + a)^2 g_k(x + a) dx$$

$$= \frac{1}{(q_j + a)^2} \int\limits_{q_j + a}^{1} x^2 g_k(x) dx > \frac{1}{q_k^2} \int\limits_{q_k}^{1} x^2 g_k(x) dx$$

$$(13A.5)$$

The first inequality in (13A.5) follows from $\left(\frac{x}{q_j}\right)^2 > \left(\frac{x+a}{q_j+a}\right)^2 > 1$. The second one follows from:

1. The absence of bias at $Z = 0$ so $q_k = q_j \frac{e_k}{e_j} = q_j \frac{e_j + a}{e_j} = q_j + \frac{q_j a}{e_j} > q_j + a$; and

2. $\frac{d}{dy} \frac{1}{y^2} \int_y^1 x^2 g(x) dx$ for all positive values of the function $g(x)$. However, if $G_k(x)$ crosses $G_j(x + e_k - e_j)$ only once and from below, the inequality in (13A.5) is even stronger, as proved by the following lemma:

Lemma:
If F and G have the same support $[0,1]$ and mean e, and G crosses F once and from below at e, then for all $e \leq q \leq 1$ $\int\limits_{q}^{1} x^2 dF > \int\limits_{q}^{1} x^2 dG$.

Proof: Integrating by parts:

$$\int_q^1 x^2 dG = x^2 G(x)\Big|_q^1 - 2\int_q^1 G(x)dx = 1 - qG(q) - 2\int_q^1 G(x)xdx < 1 - qF(q)$$

$$- 2\int_q^1 F(x)xdx$$

$$= \int_q^1 x^2 dF. \tag{13A.6}$$

The inequality follows from the crossing at e. For $x > e$, $F(x) < G(x)$, and $xF(x) < xG(x)$. Therefore, the same inequality holds between the respective integrals. ∎

Proof of claim 3:
Suppose that G_k and G_j are identically shaped, therefore:

$$g_k(x) = g_j(x - a) \quad \forall x, \text{where } a = e_k - e_j > 0$$

Then it follows that: $g_j\left(x\big|x < q_j\right) = g_k\left(x + a\big|x + a \le q_j + a\right)$ for any x. Thus:

$$e_j(p_j \le q_j) = \int_0^{q_j} xg_j(x|x \le q_j)dx = \int_a^{q_j+a} (x - a)g_k(x|x \le q_j + a)dx$$

$$= \int_a^{q_j+a} xg_k(x|x \le q_j + a)dx - a$$

$$= e_k(p_k \le q_j + a) - a < e_k(p_k \le q_k) - a$$

The latter inequality, $e_k(p_k \le q_j + a) < e_k(p_k \le q_k)$, would follow if $q_j + a < q_k$. This follows from (13.2), which for $Z = 0$, gives $q_k = q_j \frac{e_k}{e_j}$, which, in turn, implies:

$$q_k - q_j = q_j\left(\frac{e_k - e_j}{e_j}\right) = \frac{q_j}{e_j}a > a$$

Therefore:

$$\frac{e_j(p_j \le q_j)}{q_j} < \frac{e_k(p_k \le q_k) - a}{q_k - a} < \frac{e_k(p_k \le q_k)}{q_k}$$

since $e_k(p_k \leq q_k) < e_k < q_k$.

If $G_k(x) \neq G_j(x - e_k + e_j)$ but, instead, G_k crosses $G_j(x - e_k + e_j)$ as stipulated, then the conditional expectation $e_k(p_k \leq q_k)$ rises, making the inequality $\frac{q_k}{q_j} < \frac{e_k(p_k \leq q_k)}{e_j(p_j \leq q_j)}$ even stronger. That is, we show that, for any two distributions, G and F, of equal mean e, if G crosses F from below at e, then for any $q > e$:

$$\frac{\int_0^q x \, dF}{\int_0^q dF} \leq \frac{\int_0^q x \, dG}{\int_0^q dG}$$

Applying integration by parts to the numerators yield:

$$\frac{xF(x)\Big|_0^q - \int_0^q F(x)dx}{F(q)} \leq \frac{xG(x)\Big|_0^q - \int_0^q G(x)dx}{G(q)}$$

or

$$q - \frac{\int_0^q F(x)dx}{F(q)} \leq q - \frac{\int_0^q G(x)dx}{G(q)}$$

Now, $F(q) \leq G(q)$ as a result of this crossing, and $q > e$. Also, $\int_0^s G(x)dx \leq \int_0^s F(x)dx$ for any $0 < s \leq 1$ as a result of the crossing and the equality, $\int_0^1 F(x)dx = \int_0^1 G(x)dx = 1 - e$ which follows from integration by parts of $\int_0^1 x \, dF$ and $\int_0^1 x \, dG$. This completes the proof. ■

Proof of claim 5:

All integrals are over the interval $[a,b]$. Note that for a non-increasing g,

$$a < \bar{e} = \frac{\int xg(x)dx}{\int g(x)dx} \leq \frac{a+b}{2} \tag{13A.7}$$

Also, for g values below the straight line connecting $[a, g(a)]$ and $[b, g(b)]$,

$$\int g(x)dx \leq [g(a) + g(b)](b - a)/2 : \tag{13A.8}$$

1. $\frac{\partial \bar{e}}{\partial a} = -\frac{-ag(a)b \int g(x)dx - g(a)b \int xg(x)dx}{\left(b \int g(x)dx\right)^2} = \frac{g(a)}{b \int g(x)dx}\left(a - \frac{\int xg(x)dx}{\int g(x)dx}\right) < 0$ from (13A.7).

2. $\dfrac{\partial \bar{\varepsilon}}{\partial b} = -\dfrac{-b^2 g(b) \int g(x)\mathrm{d}x - \left[\int g(x)\mathrm{d}x + g(b)b\right] \int x g(x)\mathrm{d}x}{\left(b \int g(x)\mathrm{d}x\right)^2} = (1/b)\left[\dfrac{g(b)}{\int g(x)\mathrm{d}x}(b - \bar{\varepsilon})\right.$

$\left. -\bar{\varepsilon}/b\right]$, which is positive if the expressions in brackets are positive – i.e.

$$\bar{\varepsilon} < \frac{b^2 g(b)}{\int g(x)\mathrm{d}x + bg(b)}$$

This follows from:

$$\bar{\varepsilon} < \frac{a+b}{2} < \frac{b^2 g(b)}{(b-a)[g(a)+g(b)]/2 + bg(b)} < \frac{b^2 g(b)}{\int g(x)\mathrm{d}x + bg(b)}$$

The first inequality comes from (13A.7), the second follows from the condition $\dfrac{g(a)}{g(b)} < \dfrac{3a^2+b^2}{a^2+b^2}$ in the claim and the third from (13A.8).

3. $\dfrac{\partial \bar{\varepsilon}}{\partial a} + \dfrac{\partial \bar{\varepsilon}}{\partial b} = \dfrac{1}{b \int g(x)\mathrm{d}x}\left(g(a) + g(b) - \bar{\varepsilon}\left[g(a) + g(b) + \dfrac{\int g(x)\mathrm{d}x}{b}\right]\right)$ is negative if

$$\bar{\varepsilon} < \frac{g(a)+g(b)}{g(a)+g(b)+[\int g(x)\mathrm{d}x]/b}$$

which can be shown by

$$\bar{\varepsilon} < \frac{a+b}{2} < \frac{g(a)+g(b)}{g(a)+g(b)+(b-a)[g(a)+g(b)]/2}$$
$$< \frac{g(a)+g(b)}{g(a)+g(b)+[\int g(x)\mathrm{d}x]/b}$$

The first inequality comes from (13A.7), the second is demonstrated below and the third is from (13A.8). The second is equivalent to

$$[g(a)+g(b)]\left(2 - a - b - (b^2 - a^2)/2b\right) > 0$$

The term in round brackets is minimised at $a = b$, and equals $2 - 2b > 0$ for $0 < a \leq b < 1 < a \leq b < 1$. ∎

Notes

1 See, for example, Ali (1977), Asch and Quandt (1987), Thaler and Ziemba (1988) and Hurley and McDonough (1995).
2 The tracks are Caulfield, Flemington, Moonee Valley and Sandown.
3 In the UK, bookies use chalk and blackboard to offer odds. Thus, in theory they could always change prices.
4 This is equivalent to the assumption that many bets are placed simultaneously on a particular horse with different bookmakers – i.e. when the horse is plunged.

5 For ease of exposition, we assume that prices are continuous for the remainder of this section.
6 We thank an anonymous referee for making us aware of this potential problem.

References

Ali, M. (1977) 'Probability and Utility Estimates for Racetrack Betting', *Journal of Political Economy*, 85, pp. 803–15

Asch, P. and Quandt, R. E. (1987) 'Efficiency and Profitability in Exotic Bets', *Economica*, 54, pp. 289–98

Henery, R. J. (1985) 'On the Average Probability of Losing Bets on Horses with Given Starting Price Odds', *Journal of the Royal Statistical Society, A*, 148, part 4, pp. 342–9

Hurley, W. and McDonough, L. (1995) 'A Note on the Hayek Hypothesis and the Favorite-Longshot Bias in Parimutuel Betting', *American Economic Review*, 85, pp. 949–55

Rothschild, M. and Stiglitz, J. E. (1970) 'Increasing Risk I: A Definition', *Journal of Economic Theory*, 2, pp. 225–43

Schnytzer, A. and Shilony, Y. (1995) 'Inside Information in a Betting Market', *Economic Journal*, 105, pp. 963–71

Shin, H. S. (1991) 'Optimal Betting Odds against Insider Traders', *The Economic Journal*, 101, pp. 1179–85

(1992) 'Prices of State Contingent Claims with Insider Traders, and the Favorite-Longshot Bias', *Economic Journal*, 102, pp. 426–35

(1993) 'Measuring the Incidence of Insider Trading in a Market for State-Contingent Claims', *Economic Journal*, 103, pp. 1141–53

Thaler, R. H. and Ziemba, W. T. (1988) 'Parimutuel Betting Markets: Racetracks and Lotteries', *Journal of Economic Perspectives*, 2, pp. 161–74

14 Rationality and efficiency in lotto games

Victor A. Matheson and Kent R. Grote

14.1 Introduction to the 'lotto' game

'Lotto' is among the most popular games offered by state lottery associations accounting for roughly one-quarter of total revenues for state-run US lotteries in the late 1990s and early 2000s. As of August 2004, forty states had state-run lotteries, and every state with a lottery offered some version of a lotto game either through their own game or through a multi-state association such as the twenty-seven-state Multi-State Lottery Association (Powerball) or the eleven-state Big Game/Mega-Millions association.

Lotto games generally consist of an individual picking a set of five or six numbers from a group of approximately 35–55 choices. Winning numbers are then randomly selected at a weekly or bi-weekly drawing. A player whose ticket matches all of the winning numbers wins the jackpot prize, which is funded by allocating a percentage of ticket sales to the jackpot prize pool. Players matching some but not all of the winning numbers win smaller consolation prizes. If more than one ticket matches all the numbers, the money in the fund is divided evenly among the number of winning tickets while if no ticket matches the winning numbers, the money in the fund is carried over into the next drawing and is added on to the allocated funds from ticket sales in the next period. Because the jackpot prize fund is allowed to roll-over in this manner, the jackpot prize can become quite large if no one hits the jackpot in a large number of successive periods. Indeed, lotto derives its popularity from the large jackpot prizes that can be won, and advertised jackpots have been known to exceed $250 million.

Since the price of a lotto ticket and the odds of winning remain fixed regardless of the size of the jackpot, the expected return from the purchase of a lottery ticket continuously changes along with the size of the jackpot. This varying return from a repeated game with fixed odds makes lotto almost unique among games of chance. Craps, slots, roulette, bingo, keno, instant win lottery tickets and lotto games without a roll-over component all have fixed odds but also constant expected returns. Horse-racing provides varying rates of return but is not a repeated game with fixed odds. Perhaps the only other similar gamble is blackjack when played by an expert card-counter where the game exhibits fixed payoffs but varying odds of winning depending upon which cards have already been played. The non-constant nature of the expected return of lotto has made the game the subject of extensive academic research and provides for interesting opportunities to explore the efficiency of betting markets and the rationality of gamblers.

Some may question whether one can ever consider rational any gambling activity with a negative expected return. While this is a valid concern, gambling clearly offers non-pecuniary benefits to players in the form of thrills or excitement. In the words of one Big Game ticket buyer during the record $363 million, May 2000 drawing: 'One dollar is a small price to pay to be able to dream about winning $300 million.'

Accepting the idea of gambling itself as rational behaviour, one may address more detailed concepts of rationality and market efficiency. At least three notions of rationality can be explored using lotto games. First, rationality requires that individual bettors choose the gamble with the highest expected return per dollar played. Second, as expected return rises, more bettors should enter into the market and existing bettors should gamble more. Finally, lotto games should never provide a positive expected return. Sections 14.2–14.4 explore each of these ideas in turn.

14.2 Lotto returns and number selection

It is generally conceded that state lotteries have among the worst average expected payoffs among games of chance. While sports betting returns 91 per cent, slot machines return 89 per cent, bingo returns 74 per cent and blackjack returns 97 per cent, state lotteries return only 40 per cent–60 per cent gross revenues to players in the form of prizes on average. Several theories explain the popularity of lottery tickets in the face of such low expected returns.

First, lottery tickets are an extremely convenient form of gambling. While horse-racing and dog-racing are offered at roughly 150 and 45 tracks around the US, respectively, and casino gambling is legal in about 1,200 American casinos (roughly two-thirds of which are in just five states: Nevada, Montana, California, Washington and Oklahoma), lottery tickets are sold at over 150,000 retailers across the country. Furthermore, unlike casinos and racetracks, which are specialized gambling institutions, most lottery tickets are sold in gas stations and convenience stores and can be purchased along with other items.

Second, most lotteries widely advertise that the proceeds from the game go to public works such as education or state parks. Therefore, gamblers can rationalise their purchases as a charitable contribution in a way that other gambling cannot. Similarly, bingo, which is often offered by churches or other non-profit organisations, also offers a relatively low return.

Finally, Forrest, Simmons and Chesters (2002) have suggested that lotto players are attracted by the high jackpots and not the expected return, and lotto is popular due to the 'skewness' of the bet rather than its expected return. Cook and Clotfelter (1993) have posed the possibility that players are concerned with the frequency that the jackpot is won rather than the overall odds of a single ticket winning, and therefore as long as the media continues to print frequent stories about big winners, lotto will remain popular despite its low return.

Once the decision to play lotto over other gambles is made, players can increase their expected returns by playing 'rare' numbers. Most lotto games either allow a computer to randomly select numbers or allow players to choose their own numbers. When players select their own numbers, certain combinations such as multiples of 7, birthdays, or vertical or diagonal columns on the play slip, are more commonly played than others. Since the jackpot prize is shared if there are multiple winners, and since some lotto games also pay the lower tier prizes in a parimutuel fashion, playing rarer combinations allows the ticket buyer to earn an expected return above the average payout.

For example, an examination of the first 801 drawings in the Texas Lotto shows that the average payout for choosing 5 out of 6 numbers correctly was $1,656 and $105 for choosing 4 of 6 correctly. However, in the 6 drawings where the smallest number drawn was 29 or higher, the average payouts were $2,040 and $141, respectively, while in the 13 drawings where the highest number drawn was 28 or lower, the average payouts were $922 and $67 on average. Playing rare numbers, in this case numbers that did not correspond with dates, resulted in roughly a 25 per cent increase in return above the average and over a 100 per cent increase over the 'common' numbers.

The ability to earn above-normal returns is limited by the amount to which the distribution of numbers played deviates from a uniform distribution. Since roughly 70 per cent of all lotto tickets sold use computer-generated numbers, which can be reasonably assumed to follow a uniform distribution, any supernormal expected returns are limited to the deviation from uniformity by the 30 per cent of tickets that are sold to players who select their own numbers. Furthermore, as lotto jackpots grow, the percentage of players selecting their own numbers falls, further reducing any ability of players to select advantageous numbers during periods of high jackpots. Still, this phenomenon is a clear violation of rationality and has been widely examined by Thaler and Ziemba (1988), Clotfelter and Cook (1989) and MacLean, Ziemba and Blazenko (1992).

14.2.1 Lotto fever and lotto apathy

The second notion of rationality proposes that ticket buyers should respond to changes in the expected return of the ticket. Specifically, as the expected return from the purchase of a lottery ticket increases, ticket sales must also increase. A higher expected return lowers the net expected price of a lottery ticket, and as price falls, demand for tickets should increase. If ticket sales do not strictly increase with the expected return of a ticket, then lottery players' actions in the aggregate are not rational. We term this phenomenon 'lotto apathy'.

A corollary condition required for player rationality is that as lottery ticket sales increase, the increase in ticket sales must be justified by an increase in expected return. Since if two or more tickets match all of the winning numbers the jackpot is split among the winners, a higher jackpot may actually reduce the expected return of the lotto if ticket buying reaches such a frenzied pace that the higher return due to the increased jackpot is more than offset by the prospect of having to share this jackpot among competing players. Lottery players' actions in the aggregate are irrational if the expected return falls as ticket sales increase. We term this second condition 'lotto fever'.

Lotto apathy is most easily examined within jackpot cycles. As mentioned previously, if the jackpot is not won in a particular sales period, the money in the jackpot fund rolls-over into the next period and is added to the money allocated to the jackpot fund from ticket sales in the next period. Because the jackpot prize fund rolls-over in this manner, the advertised jackpot always increases from drawing to drawing until there is a winner. The cycle is completed once the jackpot is won.

Examining ticket sales within cycles is useful because it allows one to ignore the impact on ticket sales of other variables, such as demographic change, population growth, the business cycle and the availability of alternative forms of gambling. While these factors clearly influence ticket sales, their rate of change is small enough to cause little impact on ticket sales within a particular cycle. Therefore, while in the long run, ticket sales for a lotto drawing with a specific expected return may rise or fall depending on the aforementioned variables, within a single drawing cycle ticket sales are likely to be influenced largely by the expected return.

Over the short run, if lottery players are rational, total ticket sales should increase as the expected return of the drawing rises. Assuming a fixed number of ticket buyers, as the jackpot increases in size, the expected return from the purchase of a lottery ticket also increases. Since the jackpot is strictly increasing with each draw in the cycle, ticket sales should also be strictly increasing within each cycle. Of course, rationality will not be satisfied if the ticket-buying response to a higher jackpot is so great that the expected value falls, but this condition will be tested later in this section.

Examining ticket sales within cycles also means that this rationality condition is valid even if one includes non-monetary benefits in a player's utility function. Since the jackpot is strictly increasing within every draw of the cycle, the non-pecuniary benefits must also be strictly increasing within every draw of the cycle, assuming that the thrill of gambling increases with the size of the potential jackpot. Since both monetary and non-monetary returns increase with the size of the jackpot, ticket sales must also be strictly increasing with the size of the jackpot within any given cycle.

14.2.2 Drawings within the cycle

One particular factor complicates testing for strictly increasing ticket sales. The majority of lotto games hold drawings twice a week. Because the sales period of these drawings is of an uneven length (three days versus four days) and because players' ticket-buying habits are affected by the day of the week (with ticket sales typically being higher on weekends), ticket sales may not rise uniformly throughout a drawing cycle and may instead follow a stepwise increase in sales. Gulley and Scott (1993, 1995) and Forrest, Simmons and Chesters (2002) all note the complexities introduced by bi-weekly drawings. For games with a bi-weekly drawing, every other draw within a cycle should exhibit strictly increasing ticket sales so that sales should strictly increase between one draw and the draw in the following week corresponding to the same portion of the week. In the handful of lotteries that have tri-weekly drawings, ticket sales should be strictly increasing between every third drawing in a cycle.

To test lottery player rationality, ticket sales in thirty-four state and multi-state lotteries were observed to determine if they were indeed strictly increasing for each drawing within a cycle (or with every second or third drawing for bi- and tri-weekly drawings). Table 14.1 shows each lottery, the dates of drawings, the number of drawings examined, the number of violations that occurred for each lottery and notable explanations for those violations. Note that table 14.1 separates lottery games into two groups: independent lotto games, which are the large multi-state lotteries (Powerball and Big Game/Mega-Millions) and the lottery games run by the states that are not a part of either of the two large multi-state games,

Table 14.1. *Instances of lotto apathy*[a]

Lottery	Drawings	Violations	Holidays	Roll-over	Other	Unexp.
Multi-'The Big Game'/'Mega-Millions'	745	22	10	12	0	0
Multi-'Powerball'	1,274	43	6	33	2	2
California 'Super Lotto'	1,796	35	4	31	0	0
Colorado 'Lotto'	1,149	8	1	3	0	4
CT 'Lotto'	1,023	27	2	22	2	1
Florida 'Lotto'	778	5	0	5	0	0
New Jersey 'Pick 6 Lotto'	405	7	4	3	0	0
New York 'Lotto'	373	1	1	0	0	0
Ohio 'Super Lotto'	1,076	1	0	1	0	0
Pennsylvania 'Super 6'	299	22	8	7	0	7
'Lotto Texas'	1,152	1	0	0	0	1
Virginia 'Lotto'	649	1	0	1	0	0
Washington 'Lotto'	249	0	0	0	0	0
Subtotal (independent games)	10,968	173	36	118	4	15
Multi-'Tri-State Megabucks'	210	12	4	4	1	3
Multi-'Tri-State Win Cash'	177	42	7	9	2	24
Multi-'Tri-West/Wild Card Lotto'	977	260	49	16	5	190
Multi-'Hot Lotto'	234	61	11	4	0	46
Arizona 'Lotto'	49	4	0	0	0	4
CT 'Classic/Wild-Card Lotto' #3	695	98	33	8	0	57
Delaware 'All-Cash Lotto'	85	6	1	1	2	2
Georgia 'Lotto'	255	20	3	7	0	10
Illinois 'Lotto'	528	21	10	4	1	6
Indiana 'Hoosier Lotto' #1	840	134	41	26	0	67

Kansas 'Cash'	425	21	3	16	2	0
Kentucky 'Lotto'	668	138	28	20	0	90
Louisiana 'Lotto'	112	28	8	7	0	13
Maryland 'Megabucks'	158	47	11	8	0	28
MA 'Mass Millions'	691	209	41	1	0	167
MA 'Megabucks'	691	199	44	45	0	110
Michigan 'Lotto'	213	35	6	16	0	13
Minnesota 'Gopher 5'	1,060	23	4	19	0	0
Missouri 'Lotto'	457	104	25	20	0	59
Oregon 'Megabucks'	634	62	13	8	0	41
South Dakota 'Dakota Cash'	828	156	33	4	0	119
Wisconsin 'Megabucks'	1,251	236	65	3	1	167
Colorado 'Lotto'	299	39	7	10	0	22
New Jersey 'Pick 6 Lotto'	530	82	23	31	0	28
Ohio 'Super Lotto'	324	17	2	7	0	8
'Lotto Texas'	72	10	2	0	0	8
Virginia 'Lotto'	278	5	1	3	0	1
Subtotal (secondary games)	12,741	2,069	475	297	14	1,283

[a] The maximum expected return (Max. ER) is expressed per dollar wagered.

and 'secondary' lotto games run by states that are also members of either the Powerball or Mega-Millions. Five states (Colorado, New Jersey, Ohio, Texas and Virginia) are included in both tables, indicating time periods both before and after they joined one of the multi-state games. The reason for this division of lottery games will be made evident in the discussion of the results.

The results indicate that ticket sales largely reflect rational decision making on the part of consumers. Only 173 of the 10,968 drawings (1.6 per cent) examined for the independent games showed violations. Of these 173 drawings where rationality was rejected, 36 occurred during a holiday period, usually around Christmas/New Year's Day holiday but also including drawings over Thanksgiving, Labor Day, the Fourth of July, and Memorial Day.[1] It is completely reasonable to conclude that even rational consumers will alter their ticket-buying habits during these periods. Another four rejections of rationality can be explained by other reasons such as weather events (blizzards or hurricanes), the events of 11 September 2001 or some sort of significant change in the structure of the lotto game. The results for the secondary games are not as robust in demonstrating the rationality of lotto players: 2,069 of the 12,741 drawings (16.2 per cent) showed violations. As before, many of these can be explained by holidays (475 drawings) or other reasons (14 drawings).

While it can be concluded that ticket sales largely reflect rationality on the part of ticket buyers, there are two trends that reflect true irrationality on the part of ticket buyers. First, lottery ticket sales tend to be high in the sales period immediately following a large jackpot being won. The publicity following the award of a large jackpot prize apparently influences later consumers to make lottery ticket purchases despite the fact that the jackpot prize, and hence the expected value of the ticket, falls back to lower levels following the payoff of a large jackpot. By a full week following a large jackpot award, the excitement over the previous jackpot has subsided, and lottery ticket sales may therefore fall. We observed that 118 of the 173 violations for the independent games and 297 of the 2,069 violations for the secondary games occurred either in the third or fourth drawing of a bi-weekly cycle or the second drawing of a weekly cycle. In other words, following a large jackpot, the drawings in the first following week of roll-overs tend to be lower than in the week directly following the large jackpot.

The second widespread violation of player rationality comes in the form of strong substitution and complementary effects between lotto games in states that host both a state lottery and one of the two large multi-state games. For example, nearly every lotto game in states that were also members of the Powerball game experienced declines in their own state lotto game sales in the week following the record $295 million Powerball jackpot in August 1998. Similarly, over one quarter of the violations in the Wisconsin game that are not explained by other reasons occurred in the week after a large drawing was won in the Powerball game. This pattern is repeated in other games offering both a state lottery and a multi-state game. Apparently lotto games are complementary goods: as sales of Powerball tickets increase, sales of state lotto tickets in states selling Powerball tickets also increase. While this may at first seem irrational, the phenomenon can be explained from the viewpoint of opportunity costs. While lottery players are already purchasing tickets for the huge Powerball jackpot, it is very convenient to also purchase tickets for the other lotto game. The explanation could also be that players mistakenly purchase tickets for the wrong game. A final explanation for the frequency of violations in states offering both types of lotto games is that in states where players must keep track of two separate jackpot amounts for two different games it is reasonable to believe that increases in the jackpot of the smaller game may go unnoticed or may receive scant advertising. Therefore, one should expect that lottery players would have a more muted reaction to increases in state lotto jackpots in states where Powerball or the Big Game tickets are also offered.

The data supports this line of reasoning as the frequency of unexplained violations in states where two or more lotto games are played is 10.07 per cent with twenty-five of the twenty-seven games examined showing at least one violation while those states offering only a single game have a frequency of unexplained violations of a mere 0.14 per cent with only five of the thirteen games displaying any unexplained violations. The full extent of lotto game substitutability is beyond the scope of this chapter, but is certainly a topic that suggests further research.

Overall, over 90 per cent of the drawings displayed rationality on the part of ticket buyers. Of the unexplained violations of rationality, many occurred in lottery games where total ticket sales were low and where advertised jackpots, therefore, grew at slow rates. For example, in a game such as the Tri-State (Maine, Vermont and New Hampshire) 'Win Cash' lottery, average ticket sales are so low that the advertised jackpot typically rises by less than $50,000 per drawing, which represents a median drawing-by-drawing increase in the size of the jackpot of less than 8 per cent. Ticket buyers are simply not responsive enough to expected return for these tiny increases in the jackpot to be reflected in consistent drawing-by-drawing increases in ticket sales. Simple random fluctuations in ticket sales are frequently enough to overwhelm the effects of the regular increases in the jackpots.

14.3 Lotto fever

14.3.1 Occurrence

As stated earlier, lotto fever is defined as an increase in ticket sales despite a fall in the expected return for a lottery from one drawing to the next. This occurs as a result of overpurchasing of tickets as jackpots climb to peak levels, resulting in a greater likelihood of having to share the jackpot should it be won and, like lotto apathy, discussed previously, should be considered a violation of player rationality.

The occurrence of lotto fever in state-run lotto games is discussed in detail in Matheson and Grote (2004), in which occurrences of lotto fever are determined by comparing the rate at which the jackpot grows to the rate at which ticket sales grow between drawings. A more direct way to discover instances of lotto fever is simply to calculate the *ex post* expected return for each drawing of a lottery. Using (14.1) (p. 323), a mere twelve instances of lotto fever, which are shown in table 14.2, were found among the roughly 23,000 drawings in this dataset.

Three items in particular should be noted about these results. First the instances of lotto fever have occurred during advertised jackpots that were at or near the then-record levels for the individual games. Second, all of the examples of lotto fever occur in large states or in large multi-state games, where there is a large enough population to generate the required increase in

Table 14.2. *Instances of lotto fever*

Date	Game	Jackpot	ER^a per $1 wagered	Previous ER per $1 wagered
04/06/88	California 'Super Lotto'	$ 51.2 million	$0.599	$0.618
29/10/88	California 'Super Lotto'	$ 60.8 million	$0.606	$0.615
21/02/90	California 'Super Lotto'	$ 68.6 million	$0.584	$0.611
07/04/90	Florida 'Lotto'	$ 58.3 million	$0.507	$0.575
15/09/90	Florida 'Lotto'	$106.5 million	$0.503	$0.562
17/04/91	California 'Super Lotto'	$118.8 million	$0.650	$0.737
26/10/91	Florida 'Lotto'	$ 89.8 million	$0.571	$0.590
15/02/92	Virginia 'Lotto'	$ 25.0 million	$0.682	$0.698
08/04/98	California 'Super Lotto'	$102.0 million	$0.577	$0.586
29/07/98	Multi-state 'Powerball'	$295.7 million	$0.726	$0.727
07/03/01	Lotto Texas	$ 85.0 million	$0.699	$0.722
11/07/01	Ohio 'Super Lotto Plus'	$ 54.0 million	$0.946	$0.955

^{a} ER: Expected return.

ticket sales that must happen in order for lotto fever to occur. Third, the inclusion of non-pecuniary benefits to gambling may serve to explain away even the rare cases of 'lotto fever.' For example, while the monetary return of the 29 July 1998 Powerball drawing fell slightly from $0.727 per dollar played in the previous drawing to $0.726 per dollar played, it is easily conceivable that the excitement of a $296 million drawing versus a 'mere' $180 million drawing generates well in excess of $0.001 in non-monetary benefits per ticket. Therefore, even lotto fever may not necessarily indicate irrationality on the part of bettors. Overall, lotto fever is an extremely rare occurrence, especially in comparison to the lotto apathy discussed previously.

14.3.2 Fair bets in the lottery

A third test for lottery efficiency, one proposed by Gulley and Scott (1995), is that lottery games should rarely, if ever, provide their participants with a fair bet – that is, a bet with a positive expected value. Testing whether lotto games present a fair bet requires an estimate of the expected return from the purchase of a lottery ticket. Several researchers have presented estimates of this expected return starting with Clotfelter and Cook (1989) and including DeBoer (1990), Gulley and Scott (1993, 1995), Krautmann and Ciecka (1993), Shapira and Venezia (1992), and Matheson (2001).

Following Matheson (2001), which presents the most detailed function, expected return, ER_t, from the purchase of a single lottery ticket with randomly selected numbers is shown in (14.1).

$$ER_t = \left[\sum^i w_i V_{it} + \frac{(AV_{jt}/dvr_t)}{B_t} \left(1 - e^{-B_t w_j}\right) \right]$$

$$(1 - \theta) + \left[\sum^i w_i + w_j \right] \theta\tau \tag{14.1}$$

where w_i is the probability of winning lower-tier prize i, V_{it} is the cash value of lower-tier prize i at time t, w_j is the probability of winning the jackpot prize, AV_{jt} is the advertised jackpot prize at time t, dvr_t is a divisor used to convert the advertised annuitised jackpot into a net present value, B_t is the number of other ticket buyers for the drawing in period t, θ is the tax rate and τ is the price of a ticket. As mentioned previously, by playing rarer combinations a ticket buyer can earn an expected return above this average expected payout, so the expected value in (14.1) should be seen as lower bound for the game.

To test for fair bets in the lottery, data on jackpot size, ticket sales and game format were collected from thirty-four state and multi-state lotto games representing over 22,000 individual drawings. For each drawing, the w_is and w_j can be calculated in a straightforward manner based on the game matrix of the specific lotto, and dvr_t can be closely estimated using prevailing interest rates and the annuity length of the jackpot prize. The value of the lower-tier prizes is also available by examining the specific game rules, and the expected jackpot is widely advertised by lottery associations prior to each drawing. A marginal tax rate of $\theta = 30$ per cent was assumed.

A true representation of the *ex ante* expected value of purchasing a lottery ticket requires that the player be able to make an accurate estimation of the number of other ticket buyers. In order to facilitate the examination of a large number of lotto games, this chapter will instead examine the *ex post* expected return from the purchase of a lotto ticket based on actual ticket sales rather than buyer-forecasted ticket sales. While it is certainly true that the *ex post* and *ex ante* ticket sales (and hence *ex post* and *ex ante* returns) may differ from one another if players inaccurately estimate ticket sales, previous research has found that players can quite closely estimate ticket sales and do not generally make systematic forecasting errors (Gulley and Scott, 1995; Matheson and Grote, 2003). Given these results, it can be said that the *ex ante* and *ex post* estimates approximately match one another on any individual drawing and that on average over many drawings will exactly match. For simply ascertaining the relative frequency of fair bets in the lottery, the *ex post* method gives a good approximation with a significant reduction in computational difficulty.

The results presented in table 14.3 both confirm and counter the prevailing literature. Overall, it is shown that fair bets are indeed rare occurrences with slightly over 1 per cent of drawings providing a player with a fair bet. On the other hand, the instances of fair bets may be significantly more common than previously believed. Half of the games studied showed at least one instance of a fair bet, and numerous games provided players with even odds on a relatively frequent basis. Several of the states exhibited even odds in 4 per cent or more of the drawings, and in the extraordinary case of the Mass Millions game over 10 per cent of all drawings examined provided a fair bet thanks to a remarkable twenty-month stretch where the jackpot rolled-over 178 straight times.

It is also worthwhile to note that among the lotteries providing fair bets, several have maximum net expected payoffs well in excess of the price of the ticket with Kansas, Massachusetts and Missouri having a maximum expected gain of 40 per cent or more and Oregon having a maximum expected return of over $2.20 on the purchase of a single one dollar ticket. Another fact that can be observed in table 14.3 is the lotteries with positive maximum expected payoffs tend to be in smaller states. The eye-popping jackpots advertised in the Powerball and Big Game Lotteries, as well as

Table 14.3. *Fair bets for single and Trump Ticket purchases*[b]

Lottery	Highest jackpot ($ Million)	Single ticket				Trump Ticket		
		Draws	Max. ER[a] ($)	# > $1	% > $1	Max. ER ($)	# > $1	% > $1
Multi-state 'Powerball'	315	1,276	0.739	0	0.00	1.097	19	1.49
Multi-state 'Big Game'	363	749	0.861	0	0.00	1.161	16	2.14
Tri-State 'Megabucks'	8.2	214	0.719	0	0.00	1.114	3	1.40
Tri-State 'Win Cash'	2.3	179	0.973	0	0.00	1.443	33	18.44
Multi-state 'Wild Card'	2.1	979	1.067	2	0.20	1.583	131	13.38
Multi-State 'Hot Lotto'	6.2	236	0.402	0	0.00	0.778	0	0.00
Arizona 'Lotto'	10.1	51	0.921	0	0.00	1.434	14	27.45
California 'Super Lotto'	193	1,798	0.829	0	0.00	1.202	31	1.72
Colorado 'Lotto'	27	1,451	1.293	4	0.28	1.775	165	11.37
Connecticut 'Lotto'	26	719	1.251	10	1.39	1.767	202	28.09
Delaware 'All Cash'	1.1	88	0.888	0	0.00	1.438	30	34.09
Florida 'Lotto'	107	783	0.945	0	0.00	1.321	23	2.94
Georgia 'Lotto'	30.4	258	1.027	1	0.39	1.368	28	10.85
Illinois	33	241	1.253	6	2.49	1.745	43	17.84
Indiana	42	851	1.292	9	1.06	1.812	127	14.92
Kansas 'Cash'	2.0	428	1.565	21	4.91	2.055	93	21.73
Kentucky 'Lotto'	20	670	1.444	29	4.33	2.014	227	33.88
Louisiana	2.1	114	0.660	0	0.00	0.982	0	0.00
Maryland	18.5	160	1.144	5	3.13	1.545	45	28.13
Mass. 'Megabucks'	14.3	693	1.340	29	4.18	1.764	159	22.94
Mass. 'Millions'	50.7	693	1.971	82	11.83	2.465	310	44.73

Table 14.3. (*cont.*)

Lottery	Highest jackpot ($ Million)	Single ticket				Trump Ticket		
		Draws	Max. ER[a] ($)	# > $1	% > $1	Max. ER ($)	# > $1	% > $1
Michigan 'Lotto'	40	497	1.159	10	2.01	1.488	60	12.07
Minnesota 'Gopher 5'	1.40	1,062	0.918	0	0.00	1.338	76	7.16
Missouri 'Lotto'	11.6	459	1.546	22	4.79	1.911	102	22.22
New Jersey	48.5	937	1.198	13	1.39	1.602	119	12.70
New York	45	375	0.691	0	0.00	1.043	3	0.80
Ohio 'Super Lotto'	75	1,402	1.154	5	0.36	1.443	76	5.42
Oregon 'Lotto'	18	636	2.204	32	5.03	2.498	96	15.09
Pennsylvania 'Pick 6'	73	303	0.843	0	0.00	1.173	27	8.91
South Dakota 'Cash'	0.34	834	0.884	0	0.00	1.330	47	5.64
Texas 'Lotto'	145	1,223	1.033	1	0.08	1.529	94	7.69
Virginia 'Lotto'	28	929	1.168	6	0.65	1.670	127	13.67
Washington	24	251	1.042	2	0.80	1.305	19	7.57
Wisconsin	20.3	1,253	1.016	1	0.08	1.540	181	14.45
Total		22,792		290	1.27		2,726	11.96

[a] The maximum expected return (Max. ER) is expressed per dollar wagered.
[b] The number of drawings in tables 14.1 and 14.3 may differ due to data quality that might allow only one question or the other to be answered. A complete description of the data is available from the authors upon request.

those in the bigger states such as California, Florida, Texas and New York attract large numbers of buyers diminishing the expected value of the ticket. As hypothesised by Forrest, Simmons and Chesters (2002), players perhaps react to big jackpots rather than big expected returns.

14.4 The 'Trump Ticket'

It has been suggested that there may be conditions during which it may be profitable to corner a lottery game by purchasing every possible combination of numbers for a given drawing. Krautman and Ciecka (1993) and Matheson (2001) dub this strategy the 'Trump Ticket.' Calculating the expected payoffs requires some additional calculations. Assuming that other lottery players' decisions on whether to buy tickets remain constant regardless of whether another player buys the Trump Ticket, the purchase of a Trump Ticket does not affect the probability of any single ticket winning the jackpot, nor does it change the expected number of winning tickets among the other buyers in the particular drawing. The purchase does, however, increase the size of the jackpot that the jackpot winner(s) receives. Since the purchase of the Trump Ticket necessitates a large purchase of tickets, if a specific portion of ticket sales is allocated to the jackpot prize pool, as in most games, the purchase of the Trump Ticket will cause a significant increase in the size of the jackpot. Mathematically,

$$AV_{jt}^{TT} = AV_{jt} + \tau \; \alpha_j \; dvr_r / \; w_j \tag{14.2}$$

where AV_{jt}^{TT} is the advertised jackpot after the purchase of the Trump Ticket and α_j is the percentage of gross sales allocated to the jackpot pool. Since all number combinations are chosen under a Trump Ticket strategy, it is also not necessary to assume that other players' number selections are uniformly distributed.

The issue of taxation must again be considered. As with the purchase of a single ticket, any winnings are fully taxable at the rate θ, but the Trump Ticket purchaser may deduct the cost of the tickets purchased to the extent of any winnings. If the purchaser's winnings exceed the cost of the Trump Ticket then the winnings less the cost of the Trump Ticket are taxable. If the purchaser's winnings are less than the cost of the Trump Ticket, then the full cost of the Trump Ticket is not deductible, but the purchaser will not have to pay taxes on any of the winnings, either.

The final three columns of table 14.3 show the maximum expected return per dollar played for a Trump Ticket purchase, as well as the number and percentage of Trump Ticket drawings providing a fair bet. In comparing the single ticket and Trump Ticket columns, the first obvious conclusion is that Trump Ticket purchases are more often associated with positive expected returns than are single ticket purchases. As noted by Matheson (2001), the purchase of a Trump Ticket always has a higher expected return per dollar played than the purchase of a single ticket because of the higher jackpot and because the purchaser of the Trump Ticket has a much higher chance of being able to deduct the price of the tickets from applicable taxes than the purchaser of a single ticket. Therefore, a significantly greater number of the lotteries studied provide opportunities for positive expected returns for the Trump Ticket purchaser than for the single ticket purchaser. With only one exception, each lottery examined shows at least one instance of the Trump Ticket providing greater than even odds.

The other startling aspect of table 14.3 is simply the extraordinarily high number of times that the Trump Ticket presents a fair bet. Overall, 11 per cent of the drawings examined provided an even odds bet for the purchase of the Trump Ticket with over one-quarter of the games presenting a fair bet during at least 20 per cent of draws. The size of the potential winnings is also surprising, with many games offering an after-tax expected rate of return of over 50 per cent at their highest point.

The presence of frequent drawings where the purchase of a single ticket provides a positive expected return is a violation of market efficiency because these occurrences beg the question of why more people are not wagering on the lotto. The existence of drawings where the Trump Ticket offers a fair bet does not suggest a violation of market efficiency in quite the same way. The fact that investment consortiums do not routinely attempt to corner lotto jackpots is likely due to the transaction costs and sheer physical difficulty associated with the purchase of every number combination rather than a failure of efficiency.

14.5 Conclusions

This chapter has explored several notions of rationality and efficiency in lotto games. The results of an examination of over 23,000 American state lotto drawings suggests that lotto players generally exhibit rationality and that lotto markets are efficient, but significant exceptions to this rule exist. The primary exceptions are the higher returns that can be earned by playing rare numbers, the exceptionally high number of ticket buyers immediately following a large jackpot, lotto apathy, particularly for secondary lotto games, and the common occurrence of fair bets in the lottery for the purchase of the Trump Ticket. Other exceptions to rationality, including the possibility of a fair bet for the purchase of a single ticket and lotto fever, also occur but are relatively rare.

Note

1 One state, Massachusetts, also consistently exhibited a change in consumer purchases (lower than expected) over the Columbus Day weekend.

References

Clotfelter, C. and Cook, P. (1989) *Selling Hope*, Cambridge, MA: Harvard University Press

Cook, P. and Clotfelter, C. (1993) 'The Peculiar Scale Economies of Lotto', *American Economic Review*, 83(3), pp. 634–43

DeBoer, L. (1990) 'Lotto Sales Stagnation: Product Maturity or Small Jackpots?', *Growth and Change*, Winter, pp. 73–7

Forrest, D., Simmons, R. and Chesters, N. (2002) 'Buying a Dream: Alternative Models of Demand for Lotto', *Economic Inquiry*, 40(3), pp. 485–96

Gulley, D. and Scott, F. (1993) 'The Demand for Wagering on State-Operated Lotto Games', *National Tax Journal*, 1, pp. 13–22

(1995) 'Testing for Efficiency in Lotto Markets', *Economic Inquiry*, April, pp. 175–88

Krautman, A. and Ciecka, J. (1993) 'When are State Lotteries a Good Bet?', *Eastern Economic Journal*, Spring, pp. 157–64

MacLean, L., Ziemba, W. and Blazenko, G. (1992) 'Growth Versus Security in Dynamic Investment Analysis', *Management Science*, 38, pp. 1562–85

Matheson, V. 'When are State Lotteries a Good Bet? (Revisited)', *Eastern Economic Journal*, Winter, pp. 55–70

Matheson, V. and Grote, K. (2003) 'Jacking up the Jackpot: Are Lotto Consumers Fooled by Annuity Payments?', *Public Finance Review*, 31(5), pp. 550–67

(2004) 'Lotto Fever! Do Lottery Players Act Rationally Around Large Jackpots?', *Economics Letters*, 84(2), pp. 233–37

Shapira, Z. and Venezia, I. (1992) 'Size and Frequency of Prizes as Determinants of the Demand for Lotteries', *Organisational Behaviour and Human Decision Processes*, July, pp. 307–18

Thaler, R. and Ziemba, W. (1988) 'Anomalies: Paramutuel Betting Markets: Racetracks and Lotteries', *Journal of Economic Perspectives*, Spring pp. 161–74

15 Efficiency of the odds on English professional football matches

David Forrest and Robert Simmons

15.1 Motivation

This chapter considers two dimensions of efficiency that we suspect may be related. In the context of results betting on English professional football (soccer), we test for the presence of longshot bias and for the influence of 'sentiment' on the odds offered by bookmakers.

Positive longshot bias (such that superior returns accrue to bets on short-odds outcomes) is a well-documented feature of many horse-race betting markets. However, Woodland and Woodland (1994, 2001, 2003) present evidence of reverse or negative bias in the odds for two American team sports, (ice) hockey and baseball. It is potentially interesting to investigate whether their finding that it is financially more rewarding to bet on underdogs generalises to team sports in other countries. If it does, analysing differences in the betting markets between horse-racing and team sports is likely to be instructive since any convincing theory on the source of longshot bias needs to be able to account for cases of both positive and negative bias (Vaughan Williams and Paton, 1998).

One of the more obvious points of difference between horse-racing and team sports is that enthusiasts for the latter tend to pledge their allegiance to a particular club and have a long-term interest in and commitment to the success of 'their' team. This phenomenon of 'the fan' may then have a real impact in the betting market. Clubs attract thousands or even millions of supporters and profit from their loyalty by selling them high-priced souvenirs such as replica shirts. Similarly, according to American evidence, bookmakers exploit fans' desire to express allegiance by selling them high-priced bets that their team will win. Thus Avery and Chevalier (1999) show that worse than average returns are associated with placing bets (with Las Vegas sports books) on 'glamorous' teams in the National Football League (NFL). And Strumpf (2003), in a study of illegal bookmaking in the New York area, finds that particularly unfair odds are offered for wagers on the success of the local favourite baseball team.[1]

It is conceivable that measurement of longshot bias in sports betting markets could be open to misinterpretation if the role of 'sentiment' is ignored. It is tempting to attribute the difference between results for horse-race betting and for the team sports betting markets studied by Woodland and Woodland to factors highlighted in the literature on horse betting – for example, the presence of informed bettors or the potential for relevant information to remain private (Vaughan Williams and Paton, 1998). But the distinctive influence of 'sentiment' in sports betting markets could in fact be the root cause of any apparent reverse bias. This possibility we set out to test.

Clubs with the largest numbers of fans tend, as a consequence of market size, to be the wealthiest and can therefore recruit the best players. Across a large number of matches, such clubs will disproportionately often be the favourites to win. If bookmakers exploit the greater willingness to pay (i.e. to accept worse odds) of supporters who enjoy the act of betting on their team, odds-on favourites will typically then be shortened to less than team strength justifies and favourites will become 'bad bets'. If transactions costs are positive, betting by neutrals may be insufficient to correct any negative longshot bias that results. In statistical analysis, longshot and 'sentiment' biases may then be conflated. Here we employ multivariate analysis to test for longshot bias in the soccer betting market with a measure of team support introduced as a control variable. By measuring any longshot bias net of the influence of levels of support for different clubs, a more meaningful comparison with horse betting markets may then be made.

Although our primary goal is to illuminate the debate on longshot bias in wagering markets, our findings will be of interest also to sports economists. Empirical analyses of attendance demand for baseball and English football have addressed the important issue of the role of outcome uncertainty in stimulating spectator interest by employing betting odds to proxy the degree to which a match is expected to be closely contested. Such studies (Knowles, Sherony and Haupert, 1992, and Rascher, 1999, for American baseball, Peel and Thomas, 1988, 1992, for English football) rely on an assumption that sports betting markets are efficient. In the case of baseball, their reliability is called into question by the findings of Woodland and Woodland (1994, 2003). For football, Forrest and Simmons (2002) demonstrate that findings with respect to whether outcome uncertainty matters for attendance are very sensitive to whether uncertainty is proxied by odds or by odds adjusted for apparent biases. However their argument is illustrated with respect to only part of a single season.

This chapter looks again at the efficiency of odds on results of English football matches. The analysis employs four seasons of data covering the

5,838 Premier and Football League games played between August 1997 and May 2001 for which odds were available from an electronic archive, Mabel's Tables. The odds used are those of Super Soccer, a specialist odds-setting firm which supplies entry forms with odds to virtually all the small, independent bookmakers of the UK.[2] As is usual for UK football betting, the quoted odds remained available during a betting period, typically three or four days long, up to the start of the match (i.e. in contrast to Las Vegas sports books, terms of bets were not altered in response to new information or weight of money).

Previous attempts to investigate longshot bias in football betting have yielded mixed results. Cain, Law and Peel (2000) reported, on the basis of data from a single season, 1991–2, that superior returns were associated with a strategy of backing strong favourites – i.e. the market displayed positive longshot bias such as is found in most horse-race betting. By contrast, Dixon and Pope (2004), working with two seasons' data from the mid-1990s, found the same negative or reverse bias observed by Woodland and Woodland for American sports betting. In neither case was account taken of the strong correlation between possession of home advantage and shortness of odds: any apparent longshot bias may in reality reflect a home–away bias that bookmakers impose on the odds (either because they think bettors give an incorrect weighting to home advantage or because a significant market is fans betting on the game they attend). In neither case is there control for the role of 'sentiment'. Forrest and Simmons (2002) allowed for sentiment but, like Cain, Law and Peel (2000), employed what is likely to have been an inadequate dataset in that it related to only a single season. This is a serious deficiency because the literature on American sports betting includes many examples of biases noted from study of short data periods that were found no longer to exist in subsequent investigation (Sauer, 1998). The present chapter tests for longshot bias in each of a run of four seasons by estimating the relationship between odds and the probability of winning, for home win, draw and away win betting. Testing for 'sentiment' bias is implemented by including a control variable, *DIFFATTEND*. This is the mean home attendance of the home club in the previous season *minus* the mean home attendance of the away club in the previous season.[3] The measure reflects different levels of fan support that may be taken into account when bookmakers set odds for a fixture.

15.2 The model

We estimate a linear probability model as follows:

$$\text{Pr (home win)} = a_0 + a_1 BOOKPROB(H) + a_2 DIFFATTEND$$

$$(15.1)$$

$$\text{Pr (draw)} = b_0 + b_1 BOOKPROB(D) + b_2 DIFFATTEND$$
(15.2)

$$\text{Pr (awaywin)} = c_0 + c_1 BOOKPROB(A) + c_2 DIFFATTEND$$
(15.3)

The *BOOKPROB* terms indicate the probabilities of a home win (*H*), draw (*D*) and away win (*A*) that are implicit in the published odds. The values of *BOOKPROB* were obtained by taking the probability odds for a particular outcome in a particular match and dividing by the sum of the three probability odds offered on the three possible outcomes of the match. For each match, the sum of the *BOOKPROB* terms is therefore always equal to one. Efficiency in the odds requires that the constant terms equal zero, that the coefficients on the *BOOKPROB* terms equal one and that the coefficients on the *DIFFATTEND* terms equal zero.

Dobson and Goddard (2001) employed a similar framework (though without the inclusion of a variable to account for the influence of 'sentiment') for testing for efficiency in the odds (in a single season, 1998–9). However, they estimated the three equations independently whereas the three are not independent: the three events of home win, draw and away win are mutually exclusive and the sum of the dependent variables for each observation therefore always equals one. There will thus be a gain in efficiency from estimating the three equations as a system, using Zellner's method of seemingly unrelated regressions (Zellner, 1963).

In recognition that, for any observation,

$$BOOKPROB(D) = 1 - BOOKPROB(H) - BOOKPROB(A),$$

(15.2) is rewritten as

$$\begin{aligned}
\text{Pr (draw)} &= b_0 + b_1\{1 - BOOKPROB(H) - BOOKPROB(A)\} \\
&\quad + b_2 DIFFATTEND \\
&= b'_0 + b'_1\{BOOKPROB(H) + BOOKPROB(A)\} \\
&\quad + b_2 DIFFATTEND
\end{aligned}$$
(15.4)

where $b'_0 = b_0 + b_1$ and $b'_1 = -b_1$.

Estimation by seemingly unrelated regressions is then of (15.1), (15.4) and (15.3) with the null hypothesis of market efficiency tested by

$$a_0 = 0, \ a1 = 1, \ a2 = 0$$
$$b'_0 = 1, b'_1 = -1, \ b_2 = 0$$
$$c_0 = 0, \ c_1 = 1, \ c_2 = 0$$

15.3 Results

Results from our regression analysis are displayed in table 15.1. The estimated coefficient on the variable *DIFFATTEND* is statistically significant in the home win equation in two of the four seasons for which data were examined. In the case of away bets, *DIFFATTEND* is significant three times out of four. There is therefore evidence that bookmakers indeed took account of levels of team support and that 'sentiment' played a role in this market.

The signs on the coefficient estimates indicate that bets on teams with greater fan support were *more* likely to win than their odds suggested. This implies that bookmakers adjusted price to be *more* favourable for those betting on more popular teams. This is the opposite result to those reported

Table 15.1. *Estimation coefficents*

	1997–8	1998–9	1999–2000	2000–1	Null hypothesis
a_0	0.191**	0.139*	0.058	0.011	0
	(0.062)	(0.056)	(0.050)	(0.054)	
a_1	0.676**	0.680**	0.788*	0.895	1
	(0.134)	(0.122)	(0.096)	(0.103)	
a_2	0.56E-06**	5.97E-06**	0.00235	0.000129	0
	(1.83E-06)	(1.57E06)	(0.00161)	(0.00186)	
b'_0	0.759**	0.781**	0.924	1.010	1
	(0.099)	(0.090)	(0.080)	(0.088)	
b'_1	−0.675**	−0.680**	−0.788*	−0.895	−1
	(0.134)	(0.123)	(0.097)	(0.106)	
b_2	−2.49E-06	−1.66E06	0.000651	−0.000859	0
	(1.46E-06)	(1.26E06)	(0.00127)	(0.00155)	
c_0	0.049	0.080*	0.019	−0.022	0
	(0.039)	(0.036)	(0.032)	(0.035)	
c_1	0.676**	0.680**	0.788*	0.895	1
	(0.134)	(0.122)	(0.096)	0.103)	
c_2	−3.15E-06*	−4.31E06**	−0.00300*	0.000730	0
	(1.58E-06)	(1.42E06)	(0.00143)	(0.00165)	
Matches	1,373	1,491	1,585	1,389	

Notes:
Standard errors are shown in parentheses.
** and * indicate that the parameter estimate is significantly different (at the 1 per cent and 5 per cent levels, respectively) from the value proposed by the null hypothesis.

by Avery and Chevalier (1999) and Strumpf (2003) for two American sports betting markets.

We suspect that the contrast between our own and previous results is related to market structure. Avery and Chevalier used data from Las Vegas where, with one exception, all the casino sports books quote odds/spreads supplied to them by a single specialist agency. Price competition is therefore not a feature of this market and such arrangements facilitate monopoly pricing. Similarly, Strumpf's context was that of illegal betting in New York. There, individual bookmakers serve particular neighbourhoods and clients have long-term relationships with their bookmaker (trust between the parties is highly desirable when enforcement of contracts via the courts is not an option and a bettor may need to build up a track record of paying his bills before a bookmaker will accept his telephone bets). This institutional setting again permits exercise of monopoly power by bookmakers.

The situation in the betting industry in Britain is very different. Four national chains of bookmakers account for over half the market but, on typical high streets, bettors can choose between two or three of them and local or regional independent operators as well. Further, telephone and Internet betting on football is legal and easily accessible. Competition is therefore strong and the demand for a particular wager at any one bookmaker is likely to be elastic. In these circumstances it is easy to envision that competition for the largest markets (bets on more popular teams) might drive the prices down for followers of those teams.

Even controlling for levels of team support, inefficiency in the odds dimension emerges as a second key finding from our analysis. For each of the first three seasons included in our empirical analysis, the 95% confidence interval for the coefficient measuring the relationship between true probability and bookmaker probability lies entirely below one. This suggests the presence of negative or reverse longshot bias such that long-odds bets offer superior value to short-odds bets. Combining this effect with the estimated constant terms allows us further to comment that, as proposed by Dobson and Goddard (2001), long-odds away bets were particularly attractive from the bettor perspective.[4]

As with the influence of 'sentiment', we are unable to identify inefficiency in the odds dimension in the final year of our data period. For 2000–1, we cannot reject that the set of odds offered on English professional football was efficient. It is a matter for future research whether this change from previous years was a one-off phenomenon or whether it reflected the emergence of new pressures to propel the market more strongly towards efficiency. 2000–1 was the first full season after all the principal UK bookmakers had established off-shore branches where bettors using the telephone or the Internet could avoid betting tax. This put UK bookmakers in a much stronger position, *vis-à-vis* betting firms based in Europe or the Americas, to attract football bets from international clients (of whom many high rollers were based in Asia where English football is a popular subject for betting). If the new money in the market were neutral to risk and between teams, it could have had the effect of correcting biases linked purely to local bettor preferences.[5]

15.4 Conclusions

We set out to examine in the context of the British football betting market whether odds were subject to any bias arising from the influence of 'sentiment' and whether, controlling for the influence of 'sentiment', odds were characterised by longshot bias. We found that in three of four years studied, bookmakers appeared systematically to offer more generous odds to bettors on whichever team in a match had the bigger fan base. The significance of this finding is that it demonstrates empirically that the influence of 'sentiment' can work to the advantage as well as against followers of 'big' teams. The previous literature on 'sentiment' documents only examples of the second possibility. In principle, it should be no surprise that the effect can work either way because the optimal strategy for bookmakers will vary with the odds elasticity of demand by fan bettors and with the importance of fan bettors in the potential aggregate market for wagers on a particular contest.

We also identified bias in the odds dimension for three of four years studied. Specifically we found evidence of negative longshot bias in the odds. This is consistent with the findings of Woodland and Woodland (1994, 2001, 2003) with respect to betting markets on two American team sports and reinforces the notion that it may be generally true that longshot biases in horse-race and team sports betting markets have opposite sign. If further studies of team sports betting were to raise this tentative observation to the status of stylised fact, this would provide a discipline to the long and (as Coleman 2004, comments) fascinatingly inconclusive attempt to resolve the celebrated 'longshot anomaly'.

Notes

1 For English soccer, Kuypers (2000) proposed that UK bookmakers would similarly bias odds for teams with large numbers of fans. However, he offered no empirical test.

2 Odds were also available for each of four large national bookmaker chains. These odds were highly correlated with each other and with those of Super Soccer. Our findings were barely affected by which set of odds we used in the analysis reported below.

3 Mean attendances were calculated from figures in successive editions of *The Rothmans Football Yearbook*.

4 The structure of the model imposes the same slope coefficient on bookmaker probability across the home win, draw and away win equations but differences between the values of the intercepts permit evaluation of home–away bias at given odds.

5 The migration of business off-shore led to the reform of betting taxation in October 2001. A turnover tax was replaced by a tax on take-out at a rate such that the tax burden on betting was reduced sharply. Most UK bookmakers then repatriated their off-shore branches but the UK industry, with a favourable tax regime now combining with its strong reputation for probity, retained its new competitive position in the international market.

References

Avery, C. and Chevalier, J. (1999) 'Identifying Investor Sentiment from Price Paths: The Case of Football Betting', *Journal of Business*, 72, pp. 493–521

Cain, M., Law, D. and Peel, D. (2000) 'The Favourite-Longshot Bias and Market Efficiency in UK Football Betting', *Scottish Journal of Political Economy*, 47 pp. 25–36

Coleman, L. (2004) 'New Light on the Longshot Bias', *Applied Economics*, 36 pp. 315–26

Dixon, M. and Pope, P. (2004) 'The Value of Statistical Forecasts in the UK Association Football Betting Market', *International Journal of Forecasting*, 20, pp. 697–711

Dobson, S. and Goddard, J. (2001) *The Economics of Football*, Cambridge: Cambridge University Press

Forrest, D. and Simmons, R. (2002) 'Outcome Uncertainty and Attendance Demand: The Case of English Soccer', *Journal of the Royal Statistical Society (Series D), The Statistician*, 51, pp. 229–41

Knowles, G., Sherony, K. and Haupert, M. (1992) 'The Demand for Major League Baseball: A Test of the Uncertainty of Outcome Hypothesis', *American Economist*, 36, pp. 72–80

Kuypers, T. (2000) 'Informational Efficiency: An Empirical Study of a Fixed Odds Betting Market', *Applied Economics*, 32, pp. 1353–63

Peel, D. A. and Thomas, D. A. (1988) 'Outcome Uncertainty and the Demand for Football', *Scottish Journal of Political Economy*, 35, pp. 242–9

(1992) 'The Demand for Football: Some Evidence on Outcome Uncertainty', *Empirical Economics*, 17, pp. 323–31

Rascher, D. (1999) 'A Test of the Optimal Positive Production Network Externality in Major League Baseball', in J. Fizel, E. Gustafson and L. Hadley (eds.), *Sports Economics: Current Research*, Westport, CT: Praeger, pp. 27–45

Sauer, R. (1998) 'The Economics of Wagering Markets', *Journal of Economic Literature*, 36, pp. 2021–64

Strumpf, K. (2003) 'Illegal Sports Bookmakers', University of North Carolina at Chapel Hill, mimeo

Vaughan Williams, L. and Paton, D. (1998) 'Why are Some Favourite-Longshot Biases Positive and Some Negative?', *Applied Economics*, 30, pp. 1505–10

Woodland, L. and Woodland, B. (1994) 'Market Efficiency and the Favourite-Longshot Bias: The Baseball Betting Market', *Journal of Finance*, 49, pp. 269–79

(2001) 'Market Efficiency and Profitable Wagering in the National Hockey League: Can Bettors Score on Longshots?', *Southern Economic Journal*, 67, pp. 983–95

(2003) 'The Reverse Favourite-Longshot Bias and Market Efficiency in Major League Baseball: An Update', *Bulletin of Economic Research*, 55, pp. 113–23

Zellner, A. (1963) 'Estimates for Seemingly Unrelated Regression Equation: Some Exact Finite Sample Results', *Journal of the American Statistical Association*, 58, pp. 987–92

16 Modelling distance preference in flat racing via average velocity

David Edelman

16.1 Background

While there is a growing academic literature in horse-race betting and other wagering markets (see Vaughan Williams, 2003 and, earlier, Hausch, Lo, and Ziemba, 1994), the overwhelming emphasis in serious academic work (as distinct from commercially orientated 'get rich quick' offerings) has focused on the study of overall characteristics of markets, such as in favourite-longshot bias issues, rather than in the study of underlying factors which may be used to model racing outcomes themselves. In particular, there appears to have been only one serious published attempt to mathematically model what is arguably one of the most important factors affecting horses' chances of winning, the manner in which different horses are individually affected by changes in distance, which was by Benter, Miel and Turnbough (1996). In their paper, distance preference, or degree of advantage or disadvantage which should be given a particular horse relative to others when handicapping at a particular distance, is first introduced in relation to models for human running, such as the Hill–Keller model (Keller, 1973; see Benter *et al.* 1996) and in acknowledgement of work in the physiology of energy expenditure such as Noble (1986), ultimately reducing in principle to a distance preference index for a particular horse, modelled by a quadratic function of distance. Benter *et al.*'s index was not identified with any particular observable characteristic, such as runtime or average velocity, but rather by a certain notion in relation to competitiveness, where the conjecture from previous work was that each horse has an optimum distance, away from which its competitiveness decreases monotonically. Benter, Miel and Turnbough (1996) then go on to present statistical methods for estimating such functions for various horses, with an emphasis on estimation stability as enhanced by fictitious data, or 'tack' points.

By contrast, in the present study, the average velocity over a race will be studied in detail as an observable variable, and while heuristic motivation

339

from previous work on physiology will not be invoked, the rigorous statistical testing which had not been presented in Benter will be held paramount here.

It will be argued that for use either as a latent variable or as an end in itself, a log-linear (i.e. not quadratic) model for average velocity as a function of distance is sufficient, and may (arguably) be used as a proxy for distance preference. Statistical methods alternative to those presented in Benter, Miel and Turnbough (1996) will be discussed to enhance accuracy and to ensure stability.

16.2 Methodology and modelling

For modelling average velocity over a race as a function of distance travelled, the overall relationship appears to be approximately linear in the logarithm of distance (Edelman, 2002) (see figure 16.1, velocity in km/hr), subject to certain track idiosyncracies.

Superimposed on this log-linear relationship are a number of other effects, the most significant of which should be accounted for in any serious modelling attempt.

To begin with, it is reasonable to imagine a significant herd or 'within-race-culture' effect (which those familiar with racing might attribute chiefly to a combination of 'pace', 'class', 'weight', and 'competitiveness' effects), which can mean that horses within the same race tend to run either more slowly, on average, or more quickly than might be usual for them. This effect we shall call the 'Race' effect, which shall be modelled by an indicator variable for each race. Clearly, this masks, or 'confounds' the component of the effect of distance which is common to all horses, as well as any consistent track idiosyncracies, as all horses in a given race run approximately the same distance (subject to how close to the rail they run).

Another variable which must be included as a predictor is carried weight, which can be expected to have a negative marginal effect on velocity, other factors being held constant.

Next, we shall include an 'ability at 1400 m' variable for each horse (1400 m chosen as a median race distance, and often seen as significant borderline between sprint and distance races), followed by a 'distance gradient' variable, a linear function of logarithm of distance for each horse.

Crucial to the study will be an additional variable, 'distance convexity', in this case, a coefficient for each horse for the square of logarithm of distance (in relation to 1400 m), which can allow for potential nonlinear or 'curved' relationships in distance preference as measured by average velocity.

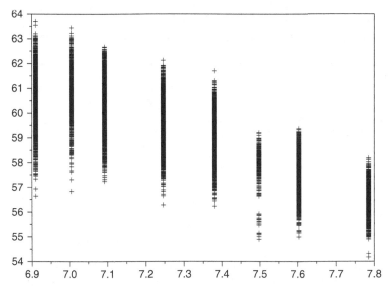

Fig. 16.1 Average velocity versus logdistance

In symbols, then, letting R denote a given race and H a particular horse in that race, the linear model may be written

$$\nu_{R,H} = a_w Wt_{R,H} + \nu_R + \nu 1400_H + d\nu_H \log(Dist_R/1400)$$
$$+ d\nu 2_H \log(Dist_R/1400)^2 + \text{error}$$

where the coefficients to be estimated are a_w, and the $\nu 1400_H$, $d\nu_H$ and $d\nu 2_H$ for every horse, as well as the nuisance parameters ν_R for each race (which in fact may be avoided by centring all variables by race).

While it is of interest to verify the extent and character of the contributions of the terms in the above model, the chief question which will be addressed here is whether the linear distance preference model is sufficient ($d\nu 2 \equiv 0$ above), or whether a non-linear term, as measured by $d\nu 2$ (after Benter, Miel and Turnbough 1996) appears to be necessary in a statistical sense.

16.3 Results

As a case study, we select a dataset of 1,381 races (representing 16,462 runs) over distances ranging from 1,000 m to 2,400 m, held at Randwick racecourse in Sydney, Australia between 1995 and 1998, where the 'going', or track condition, was officially rated as 'Good'. At the expense of

Table 16.1. *Linear distance preference model*

Variable	Coeff.	Partial R^2(%)	$\mathcal{F}$	df	Z-equiv.
Weight	− 0.0167	7	409.3	1	20.2
Race	−	95	75.0	1380	1943.8
Horse$_{1400}$	−	90	6.86	6797	341.6
Horse$_{dist.gr.}$	−	41	1.33	2839	12.43

considering the general case, it was considered desirable to control as many aspects as possible to help gain insight.

We begin by fitting the linear model discussed in section 16.2, with the non-linear term omitted

$$v_{R,H} = a_w W t_{R,H} + v_R + v1400_H + dv_H \, log(Dist_R/1400) + error$$

first verifying that each term is necessary, and then discussing the contribution and character of each. We will follow by adding the non-linear (quadratic) term, and testing for a significant improvement in error variance.

The resulting R^2 of the linear distance preference model is 94.9 per cent, with a regression F of 9.13 with numerator degrees of freedom 5,444 and denominator degrees of freedom 11,017, which is highly significant.[1] The estimated residual standard deviation is approximately 0.362(km/h), down from 1.45(km/h) overall.

The results are presented in table 16.1.

The $\mathcal{F}$ and partial R^2 statistics are the result of comparing the full model with and without a given factor. While all factors appear to have extremely high significance, in terms of explaining variation, it appears that overall horse ability and race (culture) together explain a very large portion of the variation here. Weight has a very small but nevertheless very clear explanatory effect, where 6kg would appear to decrease velocity by 0.1km/h, on average.

It should be noted that the estimation of only 2,839 'distance preference' parameters out of the 6,798 horses is due to the fact that most runners in the sample apparently ran only at one distance, and hence it was possible to fit a distance gradient coefficient only for the 2,839 minority.

It remains to test whether the inclusion of a quadratic term in distance preference adds significantly to the model, acknowledging that only 1,159 horses had had runs in the sample at more than two distinct distances.

The improvement in sum of squares for including the quadratic term (where possible) is seen to be 21 per cent, but the improvement in sum of squares comes at the expense of 1,159 parameters, or degrees of freedom (adjusted for degrees of freedom, the R^2 is just 4 per cent). Therefore, the F-test must be performed to determine whether this is statistically significant. The F is computed to be 0.994, which is very close to what might be expected by mere chance, indicating that the linear nature of distance preference cannot, on the basis of this sample, be rejected in favour of the quadratic.

16.4 Discussion

It would appear that, in distinction from the approach of Benter, Miel and Turnbough (1996) it may in fact be unnecessary to go beyond linear modelling to capture distance preference.

Paradoxically, however, this does not rule out the possibility of 'distance specialists' at intermediate distances such as is often noted (perhaps somewhat anecdotally?) at 1400m. This is illustrated by figure 16.2. Suppose for pedagogical purposes that with regard to distance preference, horses are divided into three types: (A) Sprinters, who perform well at short distances, but whose (linear) deterioration in velocity with (log) distance is much larger than average (indicated by the North-West to South-Eastward sloping line in the figure), (C) Stayers, who perform well at long distances, but do not travel much faster over shorter distances (South-West to North-East), and (B) Average horses (as represented by the horizontal line in figure 16.2), whose deterioration in velocity with distance is about average.

As can be seen, the 'Average' – type of horse is, in a relative sense, advantaged by intermediate distance, tempting a modeller to potentially model overall distance preference as a parabola opening downwards, whereas perhaps a pure linear model might suffice. The graph in figure 16.2 might also explain why 'distance specialist' horses are not generally regarded as 'class' horses, as the most extreme horse–distance combinations tend to appear at either of the two extremes.

It should be stressed that the intention here has been to suggest an approach to distance preference modelling, rather than how to optimise the estimation of the requisite parameters, the latter being beyond the scope of the present discussion. However, it is important to understand that the raw least-squares estimates used to test significance above will be much too erratic to be used in practice without modification. In Benter, Miel and Turnbough (1996), the use of 'tack points' is suggested as an ad hoc approach to stabilising the individual estimates. Much more widely accepted by linear models practitioners would be the ridge regression ('empirical Bayes') approach of regressing each individual estimate, either for distance preference or overall ability, towards the respective group

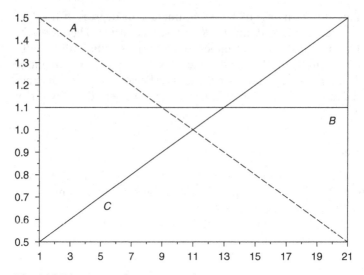

Fig. 16.2 Distance preference example

average. Such a modification can be shown by cross-validation to produce far superior estimates of distance preference than raw least-squares.

It also deserves mentioning that the a generalisation of the study presented here, including the effects of pace (the manner in which a race is run – see Brohamer (2000) – might be expected to yield even greater insight. Also, the quantification of the effect of recency (a measure of how recently a horse has been racing) as a function of distance can be expected to have significant importance.

In any case, it is hoped that the study here may provide insight, and perhaps help somewhat clarify the modelling of distance preference in flat racing.

Note

1 For large degrees of freedom, the F-distribution is very well approximated by the Normal with mean 1 and variance $\frac{2}{\nu_1}$ where ν_1 is the numerator degrees of freedom (as with the Student T, the denominator degrees of freedom of the $\mathcal{F}$ ceases to matter for large sample sizes). Here the standard deviation of the $\mathcal{F}$-ratio under the hypothesis that all parameters have been estimated spuriously (i.e. that there is no *real* underlying effect) is thus $\sqrt{\frac{2}{5444}} = 0.0192$. The Z-equivalent in terms of standard deviations is therefore $(9.13-1)/0.00192=424.1$ suggesting a p-value (for those interested in such details) smaller than the inverse of the number of particles in the universe.

References

Benter, W. F., Miel, G. J. and Turnbough, P. D. (1996) *Modelling Distance Preference in Thoroughbred Racehorses*, Proceedings of the Third Mathematics and Computers in Sport Conference (3MCS), Bond University

Brohamer, T. (2000) *Modern Pace Handicapping*, New York: DRF Press

Edelman, D. (2002) *The Compleat Horseplayer*, Sydney: De Mare Consultants Press

  (2003) 'A Competitive Horse-Racing Handicapping Algorithmn Based on Analysis of Covariance ', in Leighton Vaughan Williams (ed.) *The Economics of Gambling*, London: Routledge Taylor & Francis

Keller, J. B. (1973) 'A Theory of Competitive Running', *Physics Today*, 26, pp. 42–7

Noble, B. J. (1986) *Physiology of Exercise and Sport*, St Louis: Times Mirror/ Mosby College Publishing

Hausch, D. B., Lo, V. S. Y. and Ziemba, W. T. (eds.), (1994) *The Efficiency of Racetrack Betting Markets*, London: Academic Press

Vaughan Williams, L. (ed.), (2003) *The Economics of Gambling*, London: Routledge Taylor & Francis

17 Testing for market efficiency in gambling markets: some observations and new statistical tests based on a bootstrap method

I. A. Paya, D. A. Peel, D. Law and J. Peirson

17.1 Introduction

There have been numerous empirical analyses of the efficient markets hypothesis when applied to gambling markets (see, e.g., Sauer, 1998, and Vaughan Williams, 1999, for recent comprehensive surveys). The literature suggests that the null of market efficiency – at least where risk-neutrality is assumed – can be consistently rejected in three major areas of research application. However many of the rejections of the restrictions, required by the efficiency hypothesis, that are reported in the literature are based on classical least-squares regression procedures even though the regression residuals exhibit sometimes very pronounced deviations from normality and heteroscedasticity. As a consequence the inferences based on classical methods are suspect as the true size of the relevant test statistics is not the one hypothesised. Our purpose in this chapter is to reconsider some of the violations of efficiency, employing recently suggested bootstrap estimation procedures which allow for heteroscedasticity and any non-normality in OLS regression residuals. The procedures we employ might be found useful by other researchers in the area. At least they allow for more robust statistical inference than has hitherto often been the case. The chapter is organised as follows. In section 17.2 we first set out the wild bootstrap and then apply the wild bootstrap on a variety of datasets (sections 17.3 – 17.5). Section 17.6 draws some conclusions.

17.2 The bootstrap methods, statistical inference

Recent advances in computing offer an alternative approach to hypothesis testing when the error term in a regression is heteroscedastic and potentially non-normal.[1] Under such conditions the wild bootstrap has been shown to be an appropriate method for determining appropriate critical values for t- and F-tests (see, e.g. Wu, 1986; Mammen, 1993; Davidson and Flachaire, 2001). The intuition behind the approach is to identify the distributions of relevant test statistics when the null hypothesis holds and the distribution of regression residuals is based on the relevant sample distribution. We illustrate the bootstrap procedure with reference to the equation

$$T_i = \alpha + \beta SP_i + u_i \tag{17.1}$$

where T_i are the Tote winning odds net of stake in the ith race, SP_i are the bookmaker odds net of stake in the ith race, α, β are constants and u_i is the error term in the ith race. Equation (17.1) is that estimated by Gabriel and Marsden (1990, 1991) (also by Cain, Law and Peel, 2001) to compare the returns to winning bets in Tote market with those offered by bookmakers at starting prices. The procedure is as follows:

We estimate (17.1) by ordinary least squares. The residuals from this regression we denote by $\hat{u}_i$. We create a new series of residuals based on the OLS residuals as:

$$u_{bi} = \hat{u}_i \omega_{bi} \tag{17.2a}$$

or

$$u_{bi}^1 = \hat{u}_i \varepsilon_{bi} \tag{17.2b}$$

Where ω_{bi}, ε_{bi} are drawn from the two-point distributions:

$$\omega_{bi} = \begin{cases} -(5^{0.5} - 1)/2 \text{ with probability } p = \frac{(1+5^{0.5})}{2(5^{0.5})} \\ (5^{0.5} + 1)/2 \text{ with probability } (1 \quad p) \end{cases} \tag{17.3}$$

or

$$\varepsilon_{bi} = \begin{cases} 1 \text{ with probability } p = 0.5 \\ -1 \text{ with probability } p = 0.5 \end{cases} \tag{17.4}$$

The errors ω_{bi} and ε_{bi} are mutually independent drawings from a distribution independent of the original data and their distribution has the following properties:

$$E\omega_{bi} = 0, E\omega_{bi}^2 = 1, E\omega_{bi}^3 = 1, E\omega_{bi}^4 = 2 \tag{17.5}$$

or

$$E\varepsilon_{bi} = 0, E\varepsilon_{bi}^2 = 1, E\varepsilon_{bi}^3 = 0, E\varepsilon_{bi}^4 = 1 \tag{17.6}$$

Because the errors ω_{bi}, ε_{bi}s are independent any structure of heteroscesdasticity in the estimated residuals, $\hat{u}_i$, is preserved in the created residuals, u_{bi}, u_{bi}^1.[2] In addition, any excess skewness or kurtosis in the residual distribution will be allowed for to some extent. The generated errors, u_{bi}, from the two-point distribution (17.3) will replicate any skewness in the distribution of the original regression residuals whilst overstating kurtosis. The generated errors, u_{bi}^1, from the two-point distribution (17.4) will replicate any excess kurtosis in the estimated residuals but understate any skewness.

We create 10,000 sets of bootstrap residuals. Subsequently for each bootstrap iteration a series of *fake or artificial* Tote returns is constructed, imposing the null hypothesis: $\alpha = 0$, $\beta = 1$ in (17.1), so that

$$T_{bi} = SP_i + u_{bi}$$

or

$$T_{bi} = SP_i + u_{bi}^1 \tag{17.7}$$

$$i = 1, 2, \ldots 10000$$

As indicated by (17.7), the generated sequence of artificial Tote returns has a true intercept of zero and true slope of unity. We have imposed the null hypothesis of market efficiency (assuming risk-neutrality) on the artificially generated data. However, when we regress the artificial Tote returns on SP_i for a given bootstrap sample, the estimated values of the slope and slope parameters will, in general, differ from zero and one, respectively. The end result of this procedure is an empirical distribution for $\hat{\alpha}, \hat{\beta}$ and their associated standard errors that is based solely on re-sampling the residuals of the original regression. The idea in 10,000 replications is to determine the appropriate critical values of the pivotal test statistics such as the t and F statistic at the 5 per cent level of significance. These critical values can then be employed to determine whether the test statistics using the estimates obtained in the OLS estimation of (17.1) reject the null. We now apply the wild bootstrap methods to a number of different data sets.

17.3 Tote returns in British horse racing

Gabriel and Marsden (1990) and (1991), in a very original contribution, noted that British race-horse punters can bet in two ways, either with the 'Tote' or with bookmakers.[3] They compared the returns to winning bets in Tote market with those offered by bookmakers at starting prices employing data from the 1978 racing season. Gabriel and Marsden

(1990: 879, 883) suggested that 'tote payouts were consistently higher than identical bets made at [bookmakers'] starting price odds'. Since, they suggested, both betting systems involve similar risk and the payoffs were widely reported their analysis suggests that the market fails to satisfy semi-strong efficiency. Sauer (1998), in his survey, states that the econometric evidence presented by Gabriel and Marsden (1990) is an important anomaly and calls for explanation.

In fact, as noted by Cain, Law and Peel (2001), and Peirson and Blackburn (2003), the difference between the reported average winning pay-outs of the Tote and bookmakers of some 84 and 90 per cent, respectively, implies that for some odds at least, bookmakers must offer more favourable odds than the Tote. The important issue, as a basis for analysis, is whether the differences between returns exhibit a systematic pattern. Bruce and Johnson (2000) for the 1996 season, Cain, Law and Peel (2001, 2002) and Ioannides and Peel (2003) using data from 1978, and essentially that of Gabriel and Marsden (1990) and Peirson and Blackburn (2003) using data for the racing season 1993 reported a systematic pattern. On average, more favoured horses pay out with bookmakers than the Tote with the reverse pattern for longer shots. This finding was obtained by examining the mean of bookmaker and Tote odds in various SP ranges in the majority of analyses and by OLS regression in some.

We examine returns to winning bets in the Tote market with those offered by bookmakers at starting prices for the 1993 season employing the dataset previously employed by Peirson and Blackburn (2003).[4]

We estimate by least squares the linear models:

$$T_i = \alpha + \beta SP_i + u_i \tag{17.8}$$

and

$$T_i = \alpha^1 + \beta^1 OP_i + u_i^1 \tag{17.9}$$

where variables are defined as above, OP_i is the opening odds, α^1, β^1 are constants and u_i^1 is the error term. Because the starting prices and opening prices are essentially known they can be regarded as forecasts of the unknown Tote returns. The imposition of the hypothesis of market efficiency, under risk-neutrality, requires the joint restriction, α, $\alpha^1 = 0$, β, $\beta^1 = 1$.

In table 17.1 we report the results of the estimates. The residuals are heteroscedastic ($p = 0$) as shown by the White-test and non-normal ($p = 0$). Consequently, we estimate the equations using the White heteroscedastic consistent covariance matrix, and then we bootstrap the White corrected standard errors to test the single and joint restrictions of $\alpha^1 = 0$, β, $\beta^1 = 1$. In addition, we also present the p-values of the test using

Table 17.1. *Efficiency test*

Regression $T=\alpha+\beta SP$	α	Test $\alpha=0$	β	Test $\beta=1$	Wald $\alpha=0, \beta=1$	R^2	JB^a	Test White^b
	-1.172		1.538			0.72	0.00	0.000
White		(0.007)		(0.000)	(0.000)			
Bootstrap ω_{bi}		[0.032]		[0.000]	[0.000]			
Bootstrap ε_{bi}		{0.031}		{0.000}	{0.000}			
Regression $T=\alpha+\beta OP$	-1.228		1.754			0.63	0.00	0.000
White^c		(0.005)		(0.000)	(0.000)			
Bootstrap $\omega_{bi}{}^c$		[0.029]		[0.000]	[0.000]			
Bootstrap $\varepsilon_{bi}{}^c$		{0.022}		{0.000}	{0.000}			

Notes:

[a] JB denotes the p-value of the Jarque–Bera test for normality of residuals.
[b] Test White denotes the p-value of the White heteroscedasticity test of regression residuals.
[c] The figures in the rows labelled as White, Bootstrap ω_{bi}, and Bootstrap ε_{bi} represent the p-values of the corresponding tests using the White standard errors, the bootstrapped White standard errors with two-point distribution ω_{bi} and the bootstrapped White standard errors with two-point distribution ε_{bi}, respectively.

the two wild bootstrap procedures detailed above. The empirical results obtained from the wild bootstrap for different samples produce a consistent result.

The joint null hypothesis of α, $\alpha^1 = 0$, β, $\beta^1 = 1$ is rejected in favour of the alternative α, $\alpha^1 < 0$, β, $\beta^1 > 1$. Employing the wild bootstrap, the computed critical values of the pivotal test statistics in this case do not differ markedly from their 'classical' counterparts[5] with the exception of the significance when the constant term is tested individually. In this case, the wild bootstrap methodology would not reject the null of no significance at the 1 per cent level.

The appropriate conclusion from this analysis is that bookmaker odds are on average higher than Tote odds for low odds (high probability) and lower for long odds (low probability) winners.

Cain, Law and Peel (2003a) provide one theoretical justification for this result. Gabriel and Marsden's (1990) hypothesis that 'both betting systems involve similar risk and the payoffs' is questionable. Tote odds are in fact uncertain and bookmaker odds essentially certain. Consequently, equality of average returns, when the joint restriction holds, would be expected to occur only if agents are risk-neutral.[6] Cain, Law and Peel (2003b) show that in a model in which the representative agent model has, for instance, a Markowitz utility function so that they are risk-loving over low odds (favourites) and risk-averse over longshots, the outcome $\alpha < 0$, $\beta > 1$ would be expected to occur.

Though implicit in Cain, Law and Peel (2003a) it is worth stressing that the empirical relationship between Tote and bookmaker returns rules out certain functional forms of the utility or value function – at least if an explanation of the empirical result based on a representative agent has any validity.

As bookmaker odds are known and the Tote odds uncertain the expected utility from a unit stake bet has to be equal across the two betting mediums in equilibrium. Consequently as in Cain, Law and Peel (2003b)

$$g^+(p)U(w + SP) + g^-(1 - p)U(w - 1) = g^+(p)E(w + T)$$
$$+ g^-(1 - p)U(w - 1)$$

or

$$U(w + SP) = E(W + T) \tag{17.10}$$

with variables defined as above and U = utility or value function, p = Win probability, W = Wealth.

$g^+(p) = p$, $g^-(1 - p) = 1 - p$ in cases where objective and subjective win probabilities are equal. Otherwise they are weighting functions where subjective win probabilities are assumed to be greater (lower) than objective win probabilities over low (high) win probabilities (see Kahneman and Tversky, 1979; Tversky and Kahneman, 1992).

Now if agents are everywhere risk-averse over gains – from a reference point, as in Kahneman and Tversky's (1979) non-expected utility theory, then from Jensen's inequality

$$EU(T) < U(ET) \tag{17.11}$$

so that from (17.10)

$$ET > SP \tag{17.12}$$

Similarly if agents are assumed risk-loving over long shots, as in the cubic specification of utility of Golec and Tamarkin, then in this domain of the utility function

$$ET < SP \tag{17.13}$$

Consequently the empirical nature of the relationship between Tote and SP returns, reported above, offers from the perspective of a representative agent model support for the Markowitz specification of utility (as set out by Cain, Law and Peel, 2003b) but is inconsistent with non-expected utility theory, as set out by Kahneman and Tversky (1979), or a cubic specification of utility, as set out by Golec and Tamarkin (1998).

In future work it will be interesting to analyse further properties of Tote and bookmaker returns data, employing the methods outlined above, to see if other components of the data-generation process are consistent with a Markowitz utility function: in particular, Tote and bookmaker place returns, or win and place returns, and Tote data that incorporates information on losing bets.[7]

17.4 Empirical evidence on the favourite-longshot bias and some observations on its theoretical underpinnings

Until relatively recently it appeared that *ex post* returns from gambling markets exhibited a favourite-longshot bias; where bets on longshots (low-probability bets), have low mean returns relative to bets on favourites, or high-probability bets.

This has been documented by numerous authors for racetrack data for both the UK (bookmaker returns) and the US parimutuel system (see, e.g., Dowie, 1976; Ali, 1977; Golec and Tamarkin, 1998; and Cain, Law and Peel, 2003a). However, for some tracks in the Far East the favourite-longshot bias has not been replicated. For example Busche and Hall (1988) report a reverse bias for Hong Kong and Walls and Busche's (2003) results for Japanese race tracks appear consistent with risk-neutrality. Woodland and Woodland (2003) report a reverse bias in the market for Major League baseball. These conflicting results appear to represent a challenge and we consider further the empirical results, which endeavour to explain the results in terms of representative agent's risk preferences.[8]

The framework employed by Ali (1977) is routinely followed. It is assumed that bettors have identical utility functions, $u(.)$; that they bet their full wealth, w; and that win odds are in units of w dollars. A losing bet on horse h returns zero to the bettor and a winning bet returns X_h, where X_h equals one plus the win odds, O_h. Under the assumptions of expected utility a bettor's expected utility from the gamble is

$$EU = p_h U(X_h) + (1 - p_h) U(0) \tag{17.14}$$

If $U(0) = 0$ and $U(X_H) = 1$, where H represents the highest-odds horse, and if bettors are indifferent between bets on any horse h in a race, then

$$EU = p_h U(X_h) = p_H U(X_H) = p_H \tag{17.15}$$

As a consequence the utility function is defined as

$$\frac{p_H}{p_h} = U(X_h) \tag{17.16}$$

Ali (1977) fits the power function,

$$U(X_h) = A(X_h)^{\alpha} \tag{17.17}$$

He finds an estimate of α greater than one which is consistent with risk-loving behaviour over the range of outcomes.

More recent work by Golec and Tamarkin (1998), in an influential paper, and Walls and Busche (2003) have endeavoured to allow for a more complex form of utility function. They approximate the unknown utility function by a third-order Taylor series expansion and estimate:

$$\frac{P_H}{p_h} = a + bX_h + cX_H^2 + dX_H^3 \tag{17.18}$$

They suppose that risk neutrality is implied when estimates of $c, d = 0$, and risk aversion when $b > 0$, $c < 0$ and $d > 0$. One motivation for this exercise is provided by Golec and Tomarkin (1998), who suggest that the favourite-longshot bias is consistent with bettors being risk-averse but who prefer skewness.

In fact, though appealing, this argument, at least for the case of simple gambles they consider, is erroneous as pointed out by Cain, Law and Peel (2002). The expected utility from a simple gamble can be written as a function of any two, but only two, moments. The conceptual experiment of considering the expected return–skewness trade-off while holding variance fixed is invalid in this context. As a matter of fact the expected return–skewness frontier is positively and not negatively sloped over longshot bets for a risk-averse agent. Rather than craving skewness a risk-averse gambler would demand a higher expected return to compensate for the increased skewness in the simple gamble context. We can show this simply by writing

$$EU = pU(w + O) + (1 - p)U(w - 1) \tag{17.19}$$

and noting that

$$O = \frac{\mu}{p} - 1 \tag{17.20}$$

$$\mu_3 = \mu^3 \frac{(1 - 2p)(1 - p)}{p^2}) \tag{17.21}$$

where μ is the expected rate of return, and μ_3 is skewness of return. By substituting from (17.20) and (17.21) into (17.19) we can write

$$EU = U(\mu, \mu_3, w) \tag{17.22}$$

Consider the utility function

$$U = 1 - e^{-\beta w}$$
$$\beta > 0 \tag{17.23}$$

and suppose the agent bets all of their wealth of one unit. The agent is globally risk-averse. The expected return–skewness frontier is shown in figure 17.1, for this exponential function. Over longshot bets the frontier is positively sloped and not negatively as conjectured by Golec and Tamarkin (1998). The Taylor expansion of (17.23) is given by

$$U = 1 - e^{-\beta(1+O)} + \beta e^{-\beta(1+\bar{O})}(O - \bar{O}) - 0.5\beta^2 e^{-\beta(1+\bar{O})}(O - \bar{O})^2$$
$$+ 6^{-1}\beta^3 e^{-r(1+\bar{O})}(O - \bar{O})^3 \tag{17.24}$$

This agent has a preference for skewness in the sense that the third derivative of the utility function is positive. However, the agent will not bet at actuarially unfair odds. In order to bet at actuarially unfair odds the agent has to be risk-loving in some domain of the utility function, or behave as if risk-loving. For instance, an agent who is risk-averse over gains, such as in the non-expected utility theory of Kahneman and Tversky (1979), and Tversky and Kahneman (1992), can appear risk-loving over longshot bets, so that the expected return objective probability frontier is positively sloped, due to the effect of the probability weighting function (see Cain, Law and Peel 2004). Different specifications of the utility function and probability weighting function will, naturally, have (different) implications for the shape of the expected return–probability frontier over its full range. However, what is clear is that from the perspective of a model of the representative agent a variety of different specifications of utility functions and weighting functions are consistent with the expected returns and probabilities observed in US horse-racing. To illustrate in figures 17.2(a) we plot the expected return–probability frontier implied by a Markowitz utility function (Markowitz, 1952). In figures 17.2(b) and 17.2(c) we plot power functions with different specifications of the probability weighting function. The weighting functions have parameters that are reflective of those found in the literature – in case 17.2(b) Kahneman and Tversky (1992), in case 17.2(c) Wu and Gonzalez (1996). Figure 17.2(c) illustrates how an agent with a globally

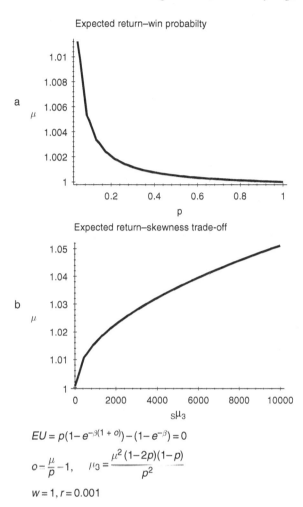

$$EU = p\left(1 - e^{-\beta(1+o)}\right) - \left(1 - e^{-\beta}\right) = 0$$

$$o = \frac{\mu}{p} - 1, \quad \mu_3 = \frac{\mu^2(1-2p)(1-p)}{p^2}$$

$$w = 1, r = 0.001$$

Figure 17.1 Expected return–win probability and expected return–skewness trade-off (a) Expected return–win probabilty (b) Expected return–skewness trade-off

risk-averse power utility function could appear risk-loving over the observed range of expected returns and probabilities in horse-racing.

Approximating the underlying utility function by a cubic form seems likely, *a priori*, to give misleading answers. The approximations in different ranges of the utility function will typically be radically different, implying instability in the estimates of the relationship over different ranges and very imprecise estimates of the underlying function. This is precisely what we observe in the analysis of Golec and Tamarkin (1998: 215, table 4). The

Markowitz utility function

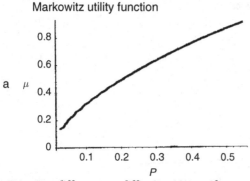

$$EU = p(1 - e^{-r\alpha so} - r\alpha soe^{-r\alpha so}) - (1-p)k(1 - e^{-\alpha s} - \alpha se^{-\alpha s}) = 0$$
$r = 2,\ k = 2.1,\ \alpha = 0.01,\ s = 1$

Power utility function with weighting function

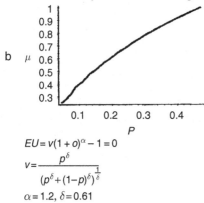

$$EU = v(1 + o)^{\alpha} - 1 = 0$$

$$v = \frac{p^{\delta}}{(p^{\delta} + (1-p)^{\delta})^{\frac{1}{\delta}}}$$

$\alpha = 1.2,\ \delta = 0.61$

Power utility function with weighting function

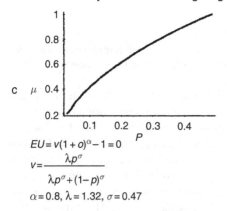

$$EU = v(1 + o)^{\alpha} - 1 = 0$$

$$v = \frac{\lambda p^{\sigma}}{\lambda p^{\sigma} + (1-p)^{\sigma}}$$

$\alpha = 0.8,\ \lambda = 1.32,\ \sigma = 0.47$

Figure 17.2 Expected return–objective win probability frontiers (a) Markowitz utility function (b) Power utility function with weighting function (c) Power utility function with weighting function

estimates for favourites and longshots exhibit marked differences[9] while those for the standard power utility model are much more stable. Given the observational equivalence of many competing models of utility over the relevant range of probabilities and expected returns (or odds) observed in horse-racing markets and the difficulties in estimating directly the parameters of the utility function we follow a simpler approach to 'determining the stylised facts'. This is to estimate the relationship between expected returns and observed win probabilities directly.[10] We run the following regressions:

$$\log(\mu) = a_0 + b_0 \log p + u_0 \tag{17.25}$$

$$\log(\mu) = a_1 + b_1 \log p + c_1 p + u_1 \tag{17.26}$$

a_0, a_1, b_0, b_1 and c_1 are constants and u_0 and u_1 are error terms.

An estimate of $b_0 = 0$ in (17.25) implies risk-neutrality. An estimate of $b_0 > 0$ implies risk-seeking behaviour. Equation (17.25) is in fact the precise relationship implied in the analysis of Ali (1977) with a power utility function. Estimates of $b_1 = 0$ and $c_1 = 0$ imply risk-neutrality, while an estimate of $c_1 \neq 0$ in (17.26) implies rejection of the Ali (1977) model and a more complex explanation of the data.

To illustrate, we use the dataset employed by Walls and Busche (2003). Their dataset reports the outcome of more than 13,000 races run at eighteen Japanese horse tracks in 1999 and 2000. They employ the method of Golec and Tamarkin (1998) and their estimates of the cubic utility function exhibit dramatic differences between high-turnover (JRA) and small-turnover (NAR tracks).

In table 17.2, 17.3 and 17.4, we report OLS estimates of (17.25) and (17.26) and standard errors and critical values for the various hypothesis employing the wild bootstrap. We report results for all races and JRA and NAR tracks separately when the data is restricted to be conditional on a heavy favourite. The results are interesting. In the case of JRA and NAR races the Ali (1977) model is rejected in both cases while it cannot be rejected for all races. Moreover, for the JRA races risk-neutrality is also rejected.[11]

Reconciling these results with those from US horse tracks is clearly an interesting challenge for future work.

17.5 Testing efficiency in football fixed-odds betting markets

Pope and Peel (1989) first considered the efficiency of the fixed odds posted by fixed-odds betting firms. The odds for these bets on the results of English football matches are fixed by the bookmakers a few days before the match and are not adjusted before the outcome. Pope and Peel

Table 17.2. *Risk-neutrality test, JRA Japanese races conditional on heavy favourite*

Regression $\log(\mu) = a_0 + b_0\log(p)$	a_0	b_0			R^2	JB^a	Test White[b]
	0.211	0.268			0.44	0.93	0.045
White[c]	(0.044)	(0.000)					
Bootstrap $\omega_{bi}{}^c$	[0.042]	[0.000]					
Bootstrap $\varepsilon_{bi}{}^c$	{0.057}	{0.000}					
	a_1	b_1	c_1	F-test $a_0 = 0,$ $b_0 = 0$	R^2	JB	Test White[b]
Regression $\log(\mu) = a_0 + b_0\log(p) + c_1 p$	1.109	0.483	−1.769		0.58	0.12	0.056
White[c]	(0.000)	(0.000)	(0.000)	(0.000)			
Bootstrap $\omega_{bi}{}^c$	[0.001]	[0.000]	[0.002]	[0.000]			
Bootstrap $\varepsilon_{bi}{}^c$	{0.001}	{0.000}	{0.005}	{0.000}			

Notes:

[a] JB denotes the p-value of the Jarque–Bera test for normality of residuals.
[b] Test White denotes the p-value of the White heteroscedasticity of regression residuals.
[c] The figures in the rows labelled as White, Bootstrap ω_{bi} and Bootstrap ε_{bi} represent the p-values of the significance tests of the coefficients using the OLS standard errors, the bootstrapped standard errors with two-point distribution ω_{bi} and the bootstrapped standard errors with two-point distribution ε_{bi}, respectively.

assumed a proportional margin over the home, draw and away outcome and adjusted the odds to obtain the implied probabilities.

They tested the weak form efficiency hypothesis by estimating the linear probability model

$$y_{i0} = a_{i0} + b_{i0}p_{i0} + u_{i0} \tag{17.27}$$

$i = 1, 2, 3$
for each outcome, where

> y_{10} is a 1, 0 variable taking the value 1 if the home team wins and zero otherwise
> y_{20} is a 1, 0 variable taking the value 1 if the away team wins and zero otherwise

Table 17.3. *Risk-neutrality test, NAR Japanese races conditional on heavy favourite*

Regression $\log(\mu) = a_0 + b_0\log(p)$	a_0	b_0			R^2	JB^a	Test White^b
	−0.241	0.006			0.00	0.52	0.013
White^c	(0.000)	(0.738)					
Bootstrap $\omega_{bi}{}^c$	[0.000]	[0.789]					
Bootstrap $\varepsilon_{bi}{}^c$	{0.000}	{0.794}					
	a_1	b_1	c_1	F-Test $a_0 = 0,$ $b_0 = 0$	R^2	JB	Test White
Regression $\log(\mu) =$ $a_0 + b_0\log(p) + c_1 p$	−0.606	−0.103	0.529		0.22	0.95	0.021
White^c	(0.000)	(0.002)	(0.002)	(0.006)			
Bootstrap $\omega_{bi}{}^c$	[0.000]	[0.001]	[0.002]	[0.003]			
Bootstrap $\varepsilon_{bi}{}^c$	{0.000}	{0.002}	{0.005}	{0.012}			

Notes:

$^{a\,b}$ as table A.2.
^{c} as table A.1.

y_{30} is a 1, 0 variable taking the value 1 if the match is drawn and zero otherwise

p_{10}, p_{20}, p_{30} are the probabilities of a home win, away win and draw respectively

a_{i0}, b_{i0} are constants, efficiency requires that $a_{i0} = 0$, $b_{i0} = 1$.

Since OLS estimation of the linear probability model produces a heteroscedastic error structure, Pope and Peel (1989) used weighted least squares (WLS) to estimate (17.27). Subsequent work has employed a systems estimator such as ordered probit to examine efficiency. However, the functional form fitted in such a method has the unfortunate property that it forces the observed probabilities to be biased estimates of the outcomes, particularly for low and high probabilities, even when they are efficient.

We would suggest that employing the linear probability model is an appropriate method for examining the efficiency of observed probabilities.[12] Here we note that under the null of efficiency the residuals from the

Table 17.4. *Risk-neutrality test, all Japanese races conditional on heavy favourite*

Regression $\log(\mu) = a_0 + b_0\log(p)$	a_0	b_0			R^2	JB[a]	Test White[b]
	−0.209	0.023			0.04	0.90	0.188
OLS[c]	(0.000)	(0.128)					
Bootstrap $\omega_{bi}{}^c$	[0.000]	[0.158]					
Bootstrap $\varepsilon_{bi}{}^c$	{0.000}	{0.135}					
	a_1	b_1	c_1	F-test $a_0 = 0,$ $b_0 = 0$	R^2	JB	Test White
Regression $\log(\mu)$ $= a_0 + b_0\log(p) + c_1p$	−0.254	0.010	0.070		0.02	0.94	0.424
OLS[c]	(0.045)	(0.184)	(0.271)	(0.405)			
Bootstrap $\omega_{bi}{}^c$	[0.079]	[0.350]	[0.292]	[0.495]			
Bootstrap $\varepsilon_{bi}{}^c$	{0.074}	{0.400}	{0.320}	{0.551}			

Notes:

[a][b] as table A.2.
[c] as table A.1.

linear probability model do not just exhibit variances that depend on the probabilities observed in a particular match but also skewness and kurtosis that depend on the probabilities observed. In particular, the moments of the residuals are given by

$$variance = \sigma_{u_{i0}}^2 = p_{i0}(1 - p_{i0})$$
$$skewness = p_{i0}(1 - p_{i0})(1 - 2p_{i0})$$
$$kurtosis = p_{i0}(1 - p_{i0})(1 - 3p_{i0} + 3p_{i0}^2)$$

The wild bootstrap appears a suitable method for determining the appropriate critical values of the WLS estimator in (17.27) and we report an example in table 17.5, employing data for 8,939 matches over the seasons 1997–2001. Efficiency can be rejected in either home win and away win matches. However, in the case of home win matches the individual coefficient of $b_0 = 1$ can be rejected at 5 per cent level when the robust wild bootstrap standard errors are calculated. In the case of matches that ended up in a draw, efficiency can be strongly rejected.

Table 17.5. *Efficiency test, English football match*

	α	Test $\alpha_0 = 0$	β	Test $\beta_0 = 1$	Wald $\alpha_0 = 0$, $\beta_0 = 1$	R^2	JB[a]	Test White[b]
				Home win regression $y_0 = \alpha_0 + {}_0P$				
	−0.035		1.081			0.06	0.00	0.000
WLS[c]		(0.056)		(0.051)	(0.143)			
Bootstrap ω_{bi}[c]		[0.061]		[0.046]	[0.133]			
Bootstrap ε_{bi}[c]		{0.066}		{0.045}	{0.135}			
				Away win regression $y_0 = \alpha_0 + \beta_{0p}$				
	−0.005		0.996			0.03	0.00	0.000
WLS[c]		(0.639)		(0.933)	(0.358)			
Bootstrap ω_{bi}[c]		[0.644]		[0.935]	[0.361]			
Bootstrap ε_{bi}[c]		{0.642}		{0.940}	{0.160}			
				Draw regression $y_0 = \alpha_0 + \beta_{0p}$				
	−0.171		1.674			0.00	0.00	0.000
WLS[c]		(0.005)		(0.004)	(0.008)			
Bootstrap ω_{bi}[c]		[0.006]		[0.001]	[0.000]			
Bootstrap ε_{bi}[c]		{0.003}		{0.002}	{0.001}			

Notes:

[a] JB denotes the *p*-value of the Jarque–Bera test for normality of the residuals.

[b] Test White denotes the *p*-value of the White heteroscedasticity test of regression residuals.

[c] The figures in the rows labelled as WLS, Bootstrap ω_{bi} and Bootstrap ε_{bi} represent the *p*-values of the corresponding tests using the weighted least squares standard errors, the bootstrapped WLS standard errors with two-point distribution ω_{bi} and the bootstrapped WLS standard errors with two-point distribution ε_{bi}, respectively.

17.6 Conclusions

A priori, heteroscedasticity and non-normality might be anticipated features of residuals obtained from regression analysis in datasets obtained from gambling markets. An appropriate method for determining critical values in such circumstances is to employ the wild bootstrap. We illustrated the method on three datasets. Though the method did not make a dramatic difference to inferences obtained under more standard methods in these cases it was, of course, not known that this was the case *ex ante*. The procedures might be found useful by other researchers in the area. At least they allow for more robust statistical inference than hitherto might have been the case.

Notes

1 Note that few of the prior studies in this area report tests for non-normality of residuals or employ standard errors modified for heteroscedasticity in their analysis. We also note that the White (1980) heteroscedasticity consistent-adjusted standard errors can be biased in small samples (see e.g. MacKinnon and White, 1985).
2 Analysis by Goncalves and Kilian (2002) is suggestive, in a slightly different context, that the wild bootstrap will perform as well as the conventional bootstrap, which is based on re-sampling of residuals with replacement, even when the errors are homoscedastic. The converse is not true.
3 The Tote is essentially the UK equivalent of the American race-tracks parimutuel betting system. Consequently if a horse wins the return from a bet with the Tote is based on the amount of money bet on the winning horse relative to the total bet in the winning pool minus track take-out. A bettor in the UK also has the option of placing bets with a bookmaker. Bets with the bookmaker can be placed either at fixed odds, offered at the time of the bet, or at what is termed, 'starting price' (SP) odds. In the SP bet the odds are determined as the average of a set of the largest (or 'ring') bookmakers at the racecourse just before the race starts. SP odds represent the odds at which a sizeable bet could have been made on the course just before the off.
4 Data was collected from *Sporting Life 1993 Flat Results* and *Raceform 1993 Flat Annual*. A total of 3,388 races from March to November were included. Races with dead heats for first place were excluded.
5 Ioannides and Peel (2003) find more difference using the wild bootstrap based on the two-point distribution (17.3) for the 1978 dataset.
6 Of course, the assumption that the representative bettor is risk-neutral could not explain, at least for UK and US markets, the stylised fact that there is a favourite-longshot bias.
7 Bruce and Johnson's (2000) paper analyses such a dataset using averages of returns in different SP ranges. This is an important contribution to determining

the stylised facts, and further analysis confirming their results more formally is warranted.

8 Some of the other explanations are based on transaction costs (Vaughan Williams and Paton, 1998a, 1998b), market size (Busche and Walls, 2001, Walls and Busche, 2003) and information disparities (Hurley and McDonough, 1996; Terrell and Farmer, 1996).

9 It is not clear in fact what it means to have a cubic specification of utility over both favourites and longshots.

10 As suggested by, e.g., Cain and Peel (1999).

11 These results differ in some cases, depending on the standard errors used to do the inference. In table 17.5, the intercept term of (17.25) cannot be rejected to be zero at the 5 per cent level when using the bootstrap $_{bi}$.

12 In subsequent work, we intend to employ an appropriate system estimator for the linear probability model.

References

Ali, M. M. (1977) 'Probability and Utility Estimates for Racetrack Bettors', *Journal of Political Economy*, 85, pp. 803–15

Bruce, A. C. and Johnson, J. E. V. (2000) 'Investigating the Roots of the Favourite-Longshot Bias: An Analysis of Decision Making by Supply- and Demand-Side Agents in Parallel Betting Markets', *Journal of Behavioural Decision Making*, 13, pp. 413–30

Busche, K. and Hall, C. D. (1988) 'An Exception to the Risk Preference Anomaly', *Journal of Business*, 61, pp. 337–46

Busche, K. and Walls, W. D. (2001) 'Breakage and Betting Market Efficiency: Evidence from the Horse Track', *Applied Economics Letters*, 8, pp. 601–4

Cain, M. and Peel, D. (1999) 'The Utility of Gambling and the Favourite-Longshot Bias', University of Bangor, mimeo

Cain, M., Law, D. and Peel, D. (2001) 'The Incidence of Insider Trading in Betting Markets and the Gabriel and Marsden Anomaly', *The Manchetser School*, 69, pp. 197–207

    (2002) 'Skewness as an Explanation of Gambling by Locally Risk Averse Agents', *Applied Economics Letters*, 9, pp. 1025–8

    (2003a) 'The Favourite-Longshot Bias and the Gabriel and Marsden Anomaly: An Explanation Based on Utility Theory', in L. Vaughan Williams (ed.), *The Economics of Gambling*, London: Routledge, pp. 2–13

    (2003b) 'The Favourite-Longshot Bias, Bookmaker Margins and Insider Trading in a Variety of Betting Markets', *Economic Bulletin*, 55, pp. 263–73

    (2004) 'Why Do agents Gamble on Odds on Favourites?', mimeo

Davidson, R. and Flachaire, E. (2001) 'The Wild Bootstrap, Tamed at Last', Department of Economics, Queen's University, Kingston, Ontario, mimeo

Dowie, D. (1976) 'On the Efficiency and Equity of Betting Markets', *Economica*, 43, pp. 139–50

Gabriel, P. E. and Marsden, J. R. (1990) 'An Examination of Market Efficiency in British Racetrack Betting', *Journal of Political Economy*, 96, pp. 874–85

(1991) 'An Examination of Market Efficiency in British Racetrack Betting: Errata and Corrections', *Journal of Political Economy*, 99, pp. 657–9

Golec, J. and Tamarkin, M. (1998) 'Bettors Love Skewness, Not Risk, at the Horse Track', *Journal of Political Economy*, 106, pp. 205–25.

Goncalves, S. and Kilian, L. (2002) 'Bootstrapping Autoregressions with Conditional Hetereroskedasticity of Unknown Form', University of Michigan, mimeo

Hurley, W. and McDonough, L. (1996) 'The Favourite-Longshot Bias in Parimutuel Betting: A Clarification of the Explanation That Bettors Like to Bet Longshots', *Economics Letters*, 52, pp. 275–8

Ioannides, C. and Peel, D. A. (2003) 'Testing for Market Efficiency in Gambling Markets: When Errors are Non-Normal; An Application of The Wild Bootstrap', University of Cardiff, mimeo; forthcoming in *Economics Letters*

Kahneman, D. and Tversky, A. (1979) 'Prospect Theory: An Analysis of Decision under Risk', *Econometrica*, 2, pp. 263–91

MacKinnon, J. G. and White, H. (1985) 'Some Heteroskedasticity Consistent covariance Matrix Estimators with Improved Finite Sample Properties', *Journal of Econometrics*, 29, pp. 305–25

Mammen, E. (1993) 'Testing Parametric versus Nonparametric Regression', *Annals of Statistics*, 21, pp. 1926–47

Markowitz, H. (1952) 'The Utility of Wealth', *Journal of Political Economy*, 56, pp. 151–4

Peirson, J. and Blackburn, P. (2003) 'Betting at British Racecourses; A Comparison of the Efficiency of Betting with Bookmakers and at the Tote', in L. Vaughan Williams (ed.), *The Economics of Gambling*. London and New York: Routledge. pp. 30–42

Pope P. F. and Peel D. A. (1989) 'Information, Prices and Efficiency in a Fixed-Odds Betting Market', *Economica*, 56, pp. 323–41

Sauer, R. D. (1998) 'The Economics of Wagering Markets', *Journal of Economic Literature*, 36, pp. 2021–64

Tversky, A. and Kahneman, D. (1992) 'Advances in Prospect Theory: Cumulative Representation of Uncertainty', *Journal of Risk and Uncertainty*, 5(4), pp. 297–323

Terrell, D. and Farmer, A. (1996) 'Optimal Betting and Efficiency in Parimutuel Betting Markets with Information Costs', *Economic Journal*, 106, pp. 846–68

Vaughan Williams, L. (1999) 'Information Efficiency in Betting Markets: A Survey', *Bulletin of Economic Research*, 51, pp. 307–37

Vaughan Williams, L. and Paton, D. (1998a) 'Why are some Favorite-Longshot Biases Positive and Some Negative?', *Applied Economics*, 30, pp. 1505–10

(1998b) 'Do Betting Costs Explain Betting Biases?', *Applied Economics Letters*, 5, pp. 333–35

Walls, D. W. and Busche, K. (2003) 'Breakage, Turnover, and Betting Market Efficiency: New Evidence from Japanese Horse Tracks', in L. Vaughan Williams (ed.), *The Economics of Gambling*, London and New York: Routledge

Woodland L. M. and Woodland B. M. (2003) 'The Reverse Favourite-Longshot Bias and Market Efficiency in Major League Baseball: An Update', *Economic Bulletin*, 55(2), pp. 113–23

White, H. (1980) 'A Heteroskedasticity-Consistent Covariance Matrix Estimator and a Direct Test for Heteroskedasticity', *Econometrica*, 48, pp. 817–38

Wu, C. F. J. (1986) 'Jackknife, Bootstrap and Other Resampling Methods in Regression Analysis (with Discussion)', *Annals of Statistics*, 14, pp. 1261–95

Wu, G. and Gonzalez, R. (1996) 'Curvature of the Probability Weighting Function', *Management Science*, 42, pp. 1676–88

18 Information (in)efficiency in prediction markets

Erik Snowberg, Justin Wolfers and Eric Zitzewitz

18.1 Introduction

This chapter examines a new class of markets at the intersection of traditional betting and traditional financial markets. We call these 'prediction markets'. Like both financial and betting markets, prediction markets focus on uncertain outcomes and involve trading in risks. Prices from these markets establish forecasts about the probabilities, mean and median outcomes, and correlations among future events. These prices have been used to accurately predict vote shares in elections, the box office success of Hollywood movies and the probability that Saddam Hussein would be deposed by a certain date. Other names for these markets include 'virtual stock markets', 'event futures', and 'information markets'.

Financial economists have long known about the information-aggregating properties of markets. Indeed, the efficient markets hypothesis, a centrepiece of financial theory, can be stated simply as, 'market prices incorporate all available information'. While financial instruments can be very complex, prediction markets tend to be analytically simple. Their current simplicity, however, belies their powerful potential future as a way to hedge against geopolitical and other forms of risk as envisioned by Athanasoulis, Shiller and van Wincoop (1999) and Shiller (2003).

Currently, most prediction markets are quite small, with turnover ranging from a few thousand dollars on the early political markets run by the University of Iowa, to several million bet in the 2004 election cycle on TradeSports, to hundreds of millions bet on the announcement of economic indicators in Goldman Sachs and Deutsche Bank's 'Economic Derivatives' market. The most famous prediction market is the Iowa Electronic Market (IEM), which was started in 1988 to predict the vote share of the two major party presidential candidates. Since then, they have amassed a record of more accurate prediction than polls, all while limiting trading positions to a cap of $500.

The small size and relative newness of these markets can exacerbate the types of deviations from the efficiency seen in traditional financial markets. A key focus of this chapter is understanding the conditions under which market prices are most likely to provide accurate predictions. Some of our diagnoses are well understood, and simply require increased liquidity to rectify them, while others are more speculative, and should form the basis of further research. Better understanding of the sources and types of failures in prediction markets can only enhance their eventual usefulness.

This chapter also emphasises more complex contracts that are in active use today. These contingent contracts, or 'decision markets', hold the promise not just of predicting uncertain events, but also of providing useful forecasts under alternative scenarios, which may inform decision making.

We begin by briefly describing some simple types of contracts that are currently traded. We then examine the advantages and potential pitfalls of these markets. Finally, we survey the performance of existing markets, discuss contingent contracts, and conclude.

18.2 Design of prediction markets

Prediction market contracts are simply gambles on uncertain future events. Depending on the construction of the gamble, the price yields the market's expectation of different parameters. The simplest contract is one that pays a dollar if a certain event happens. The price of that contract at any given time is simply the market's belief about the percentage chance that the event will happen.[1]

Another common gamble is 'spread betting' where participants take an even money bet on a particular outcome. This sort of betting is often practised in American football and basketball: one bets that a favoured team will win by a point spread of at least y points. In a political context, this might be a bet that pays off if a candidate earns over y percent of the vote. In both cases, the market, or market-maker, must adjust y such that supply equals demand, which requires that half of the bets fall on either side. Thus, the spread reveals the market's expectation of the median of $F(y)$.[2]

A final type of contract, which has proved less popular in sports betting is an 'index' bet. This contract pays off at the value of a particular parameter. For instance, sports bettors can buy a contract that pays off according to the number of runs a cricket team scores. This contract would thus reveal the market's expectation of the mean number of runs. This type of contract is most commonly used to predict a political candidate's share of the vote – much as a poll might.

By using variants and/or bundles of these three types of contracts, it is possible to construct contracts that will reveal the market's expectation of higher-order moments and more complicated parameters of the distribution of outcomes. One such variant, the contingent contract, pays off only if two or more events happen simultaneously. We discuss this type in greater detail later.

18.3 Applications and evidence

Prediction markets, in their most basic form, have been around since at least the beginning of the 1900s.[3] However, until recently, there were very few active markets. The proliferation of the Internet and its use for sports betting has enabled an explosion of prediction contracts. Indeed, most of the examples in this chapter are taken from contracts that have been set up in the last few years. There are still many questions that need to be rigorously examined as the data becomes available, but already we can draw a few generalisations.

First, market prices tend to respond rapidly to new information. The following anecdote provides an interesting example. On 15 October 2003 the Cubs faced the Marlins in game six of the National League Championship Series. The Cubs were favoured to win at the beginning of the game and soon built a comfortable 3–0 lead. In the top of the 8th a contract that paid $100 if the Cubs won was trading for over $95. Then Steve Bartman, a fan, reached over and spoiled Moises Alou's catch of a foul ball. The Marlins proceeded to score 8 runs in the remainder of the inning. By the end of the 8th, the contract on the Cubs winning was trading at around $5. Figure 18.1 shows the rapid incorporation of information into the contract price as the game progressed.

Not only is information rapidly incorporated into prices, but additional information also contributes to the accuracy of the forecasts made by prediction markets. Figure 18.2 shows the accuracy of the predictions of the IEM vote share market as a function of the time before election day. It is clear that as election day approaches and more information is revealed and incorporated into market prices, the accuracy of the prices as predictors increases.

Second, very few arbitrage opportunities exist. They appear briefly and represent small profit opportunities. Figure 18.3 shows the bid and ask prices on a contract that paid $100 if Arnold Schwarzenegger was elected California's Governor in 2003, sampling data on bid and ask prices from two online exchanges every four hours. Both prices show substantial variation, but they move in lockstep. Arbitrage opportunities are virtually absent.

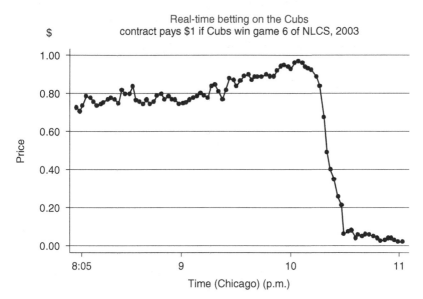

Figure 18.1 Rapid incorporation of information
Source: www.tradesports.com.

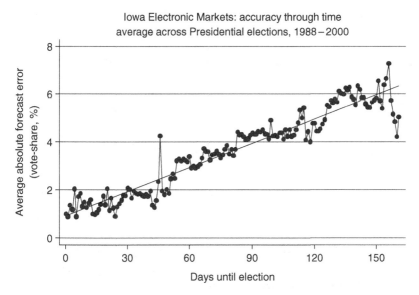

Figure 18.2 Information revelation through time
Source: Author's calculations based on data available at www.biz.uiowa.edu/iem/.

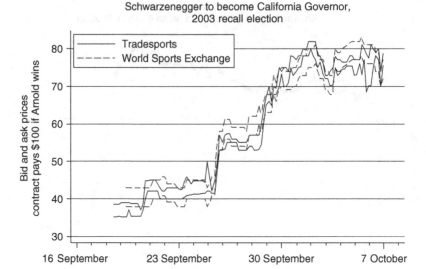

Figure 18.3 No arbitrage

Source: Prices collected electronically every four hours by David Pennock.

A third characterisation is that these markets, when well capitalised, appear to be robust to certain forms of manipulation. There are several case studies that emphasise this point. Rhode and Strumpf (2004) report that there were largely unsuccessful attempts by the big party bosses at manipulating the betting on early twentieth-century political markets. Strumpf (2004) placed random $500 bets on the IEM and traced their effects, while Leigh and Wolfers (2002) provide examples of candidates betting on themselves in order to create a 'buzz'. Camerer (1998) placed and cancelled large bets in parimutuel horse-racing markets. While all of these attempts at manipulation met with failure (except for brief, transitory effects) we obviously cannot draw any conclusions about the prevalence of the types of manipulation that have escaped the attention of analysts.

Finally, in most cases these markets seem to satisfy at least the weak form of the efficient markets hypothesis. There appear to be no profit opportunities from using simple strategies based on past prices. Leigh, Wolfers and Zitzewitz (2003) demonstrate this for the TradeSports 'Saddam Security', a contract that paid $1 if Saddam Hussein was ousted by a particular date. Rhode and Strumpf provide evidence for early twentieth-century political markets. Tetlock (2004) reports that in general the financial and political contracts that trade on TradeSports are efficiently priced. We provide more evidence on the accuracy of these markets in section 18.5.

18.4 When will prediction markets yield accurate predictions?

There are three main facets to prediction markets. First, the market structure is essentially an algorithm for aggregating (and sharing) opinions. Secondly, the financial and other incentives inherent in the market mechanism provide for truthful revelation. Finally, potential winnings provide robust incentives for information discovery. These features provide the power of prediction markets, and when one or more are missing the market's ability to predict will be undermined (Wolfers and Zitzewitz, 2004). We will address the problems in each category in turn.

18.4.1 Information aggregation

As the old saying goes, in the short-run markets are a voting machine, and in the long-run a weighing machine. Much of the power of markets derives from the fact that they provide an algorithm for aggregating diverse opinions: weighting the votes of market participants according to their willingness to back them with money.

However any algorithm will fail if it is deployed on an unclear task. Thus, contracts in prediction markets must be clear, easily understood and enforceable. A contract such as 'Howard Dean will win the presidential election' appears to satisfy the first two conditions, but could easily be challenged by a sore loser on the grounds that although Dean was clearly out of the running in the 2004 election, he may win in 2008. Adding a date, – i.e. 'Howard Dean will win the 2004 presidential election' – may not be enough as 'win' could refer to either the popular vote or the Electoral College. The requirement of clarity can be harder to satisfy than it appears at first glance. For instance, the day after the 1994 US Senate elections Senator Richard Shelby (Democrat Alabama) switched parties, throwing what seemed like a well-written contract on how many seats each party would take into confusion. Sometimes there is a trade-off between contractibility and capturing the event of interest. In 2003, TradeSports ran markets in 'Will there be a UN Resolution on Iraq (beyond #1441)?' and 'Will Saddam be out of office by June 30?' The former is clearly more contractible, but the latter is what traders wanted to bet on.

The key information aggregator is the market mechanism, and most prediction markets are run as a continuous double auction. Buyers and sellers submit bids and asking prices, respectively, and trade occurs when they reach a mutually agreeable price. Other markets, such as those used to predict announcements of economic statistics, are run according to a parimutuel system. There is not enough data at this point to determine which market designs work best in which situations, particularly when markets are thin.

Since prediction markets have designs similar to many gambling markets, we can learn a lot about potential problems from studies of gambling. The longest-standing stylised fact regarding horse-race betting is the favourite-longshot bias, which is depicted in figure 18.4. Close examination of this phenomenon suggests that the behaviour it embodies is of concern in prediction markets, a point emphasised by Manski (2004).

On average, gamblers lose about 18 cents of every dollar wagered, and this ratio approximately holds for most horses – those with a 5 per cent to 50 per cent chance of winning. At the extremes, however, there are substantial deviations. Wagers on longshots produce much lower returns, offset by somewhat higher (albeit still negative) returns for betting on favourites. The overbetting of longshots ties in with a range of experimental evidence suggesting that people tend to overvalue small

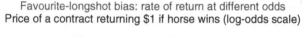

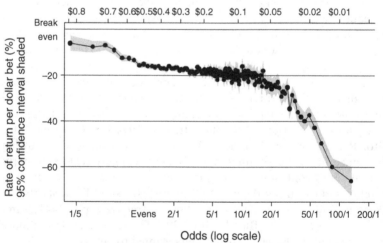

Figure 18.4 Miscalibration of small probabilities

Note: Sample is all horse races in the US, 1992–2002. $n = 5,067,832$ starts in 611,807 races.

Source: Trackmaster, Inc.

probabilities and undervalue near-certainties. We see that these errors persist beyond the psychology lab in equilibrium even in large and extremely active markets (Snowberg and Wolfers, 2004).

A related phenomenon is the 'volatility smile' found in options. This refers to overpricing of strongly out-of-the-money options, and underpricing of strongly in-the-money options relative to Black–Scholes benchmarks; thus the 'smile' refers to the shape of the relationship between implied volatility and strike price. Aït-Sahalia, Wang and Yared (2001) argue that the conclusion of miscalibration is less clear-cut in this context, because these prices may be driven by small likelihoods of extreme price changes. Additionally, when dealing with the pricing of options, one must take into account non-probabilistic factors such as wealth-dependent risk aversion, margin requirements and time to maturity. The effects of these constraints are more likely to be felt in small, poorly capitalised and long-horizon markets, so one should be especially careful when interpreting prices in such markets.

The miscalibration that causes the favourite-longshot bias and the 'volatility smile' appears in the pricing of certain securities related to financial variables on TradeSports. Table 18.1 reports the price of securities that paid off if the S&P finished 2003 in certain ranges. These securities can be approximated using December Chicago Mercantile Exchange (CME) S&P options. Comparing TradeSports prices with the state prices implied by CME option prices suggests that deep-out-of-the-money options are relatively overpriced on TradeSports. In the case of the most bearish securities, the price differences created a (small) arbitrage opportunity, one which persisted for most of the summer of 2003. Similar patterns existed for TradeSports' state securities on other financial variables (e.g. crude oil and gold prices, exchange rates, other indices). This is consistent with the favourite-longshot bias being more pronounced on smaller-scale exchanges.

While these behavioural biases may affect pricing in prediction markets, to the extent that they are systematic it remains possible to de-bias market prices so as to yield efficient forecasts.

18.4.2 Truthful revelation

Prediction markets must provide incentives for truthful revelation of information. However, these incentives do not necessarily need to be monetary. Indeed, the thrill of placing bets and the bragging rights of correct predictions may be enough to motivate traders. Some sites, such as NewsFutures.com use play money, where those who amass the largest play fortunes may be eligible for prizes. There is not enough evidence to

Table 18.1. *Price of S&P state securities[a] on TradeSports versus CME market close, 23 July 2003*

S&P level at end of 2003	Price on TradeSports		Estimated state price[b] from CME S&P options
	Bid	Ask	
1200 and over	2	6	2.5
1100 to 1199	11	16	13.2
1000 to 1099	28	33	33.3
900 to 999	25	30	30.5
800 to 899	14	19	13
700 to 799	3	8	5
600 to 699	4	7	2
Under 600	5	8	1
S&P level on 23 July 2003		985	

Note:
[a] Prices given are the price of a security that pays $100 if S&P finishes 2003 in given range
[b] State prices are estimated from CME option settlement prices using the method in Leigh, Wolfers and Zitzewitz (2003), adjusting for the thirteen-day difference in expiry date.

ascertain whether the use of real money makes an economically significant difference, although Servan-Schreiber, Wolfers, Pennock and Galebach (2004) provide suggestive evidence that play-money markets predicted NFL results as well as real-money markets. Since the only way to amass play-money is through a history of accurate prediction, it may even be that play-money outperform real-money exchanges. Since real- and play-money exchanges are not arbitrage linked there exist differences in the prices on the different types of exchanges. For example, in August 2003, Bush was a 2 to 1 favourite to win re-election on real-money exchanges, but was even-money on NewsFutures. By exploiting these differences in sufficiently large samples, it should eventually be possible to determine the factors driving the relative accuracy of real- and play-money exchanges.

Trading in prediction markets is much less attractive when the person you are betting against has control over the event in question, or if a relatively small group possesses most information on an event. Indeed, attempts to set up markets on topics where there are insiders with substantial information advantages have typically failed. For instance, market-makers withdrew liquidity from markets on the winner of the pre-recorded reality show *Survivor* after CBS employees were accused of insider trading. Perhaps for the same reason, the TradeSports contracts on the next Supreme Court retirement have generated very little trade, despite the inherent interest in the question.

Finally, there is some evidence that the smaller-scale prediction markets are slower to incorporate information than deeper related financial markets. For example, Leigh, Wolfers and Zitzewitz (2003) found that changes in the 'Saddam Security' lagged war-related changes in the S&P or oil prices by 1–2 days. This is to be expected given that deeper financial markets have more traders investing larger sums of money, so there is more attention to buying and selling quickly when news breaks.

18.4.3 Information discovery and sharing

The incentives provided by a prediction market must be large enough to motivate the collection and sharing of information through the market mechanism. It is important to note here that although the vast amount of money in prediction markets may be uninformed, it is the marginal, not average dollar that sets prices. Thus, the presence of a few informed traders can still lead to very accurate predictions. It is because of this distinction between the average and marginal dollar driving prices that one cannot simply earn a profit betting against the New York Yankees (although one may derive some pleasure from doing so).

Figure 18.5 shows the price of a contract on whether or not weapons of mass destruction (WMD) will be found in Iraq. Note that at some points the value of the contract exceeded 80 per cent, yet weapons were never found. It is likely that this market performed poorly since the cost of gaining new information was quite high. Since WMD can be non-existent almost everywhere, but still exist somewhere, it was difficult to bet against the strong case made by the White House, at least initially.

Even if the market designer can avoid the above pitfalls a market will fail unless there is a motivation for trade. Trade in these markets can be motivated by a desire to hedge against risk, the thrill of pitting one's judgement against others, or a perceived profit opportunity on both sides because of divergent opinions over outcomes.

None of the prediction markets run on the websites we surveyed are large enough to truly hedge against significant risk. George W. Bush could not take a large enough stake against himself in order to ensure a win–win in the upcoming election. By providing contracts that are better linked to the underlying source of risk in individual portfolios, it seems likely that prediction markets will become more liquid, yielding more accurate pricing.

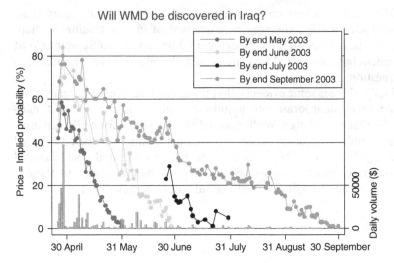

Figure 18.5 Inefficiencies in prediction markets
Source: Average daily price data provided by www.tradesports.com.

That said, as risk aversion becomes an increasingly important driver of trade, it may become necessary for researchers to adjust market prices for the risk premium, rather than interpreting them directly as probabilities.

These factors suggest that prediction markets are most likely to succeed when events are widely discussed with diverse interpretations of the available public information. The general interest creates both a larger pool of potential traders, as well as a greater thrill of being right. The public nature of the information makes it unlikely that there will be a perception of manipulation or corruption.

18.5 Performance of prediction markets

As troubling as some of the theoretical and practical problems with prediction markets may be, they generally – but not always – perform well. The evidence on this comes from a range of fields as diverse as the imaginations of the experimenters who use them. In the political domain, Berg, Forsythe, Nelson and Rietz (2001) summarise the evidence from the IEM, documenting that the market has both yielded very accurate predictions and also outperformed large-scale polling organisations. Figure 18.6 shows the aggregate forecast performance of all these experimental markets (or at least those for which data is publicly available). Each point represents the proportion of contracts trading at a given price that won. If

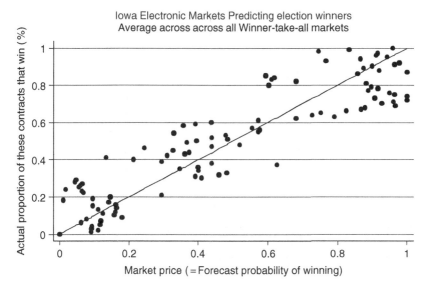

Figure 18.6 Accuracy of predictions
Note:
$n = 23{,}941$ daily price observations in 100 split-adjusted winner-take-all contracts over twenty-five elections.
Source: Author's calculations based on data available at: www.biz.uiowa.edu/iem/.

markets were perfectly accurate, then we would expect the data to lie along the 45 degree line. Not only are these markets typically quite accurate, but previous research has documented that they are better predictors than the Gallup poll.

In spite of the concerns we raise above about the amount of interest and liquidity necessary for a functioning prediction market, there are examples of smaller markets that work well. At the level of individual political districts there is often little interest in, or money for, local polling. Yet when Australian bookmakers started opening contracts on district-level races, Wolfers and Leigh (2002) show that they were extremely accurate.

Politicians and pundits use more than just polls when evaluating election chances and policy choices. They also rely on expert opinion. Figure 18.7 shows that the 'Saddam Security' co-moved tightly with both expert opinion (Will Saletan's 'Saddameter' – his estimate of the probability of the US going to war with Iraq) and oil prices (which respond to turmoil in the Middle East).

In a business context, Chen and Plott (2002) report that a well-designed internal market produced more accurate forecasts of printer sales than the

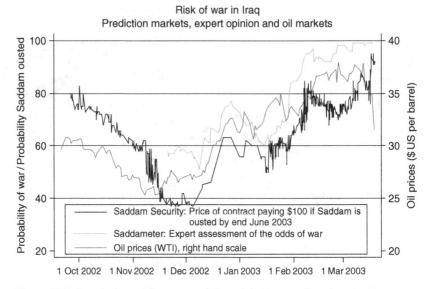

Figure 18.7 Correlation with expert opinion and other markets
Source: Trade-by-trade Saddam security data provided by Tradesports.com; Saddameter from Will Saletan's daily column in State.com.

firm's standard processes. Project planning has also been subjected to the judgement of prediction markets. Ortner (1998) launched an experimental market that predicted that a firm would definitely not meet its delivery target even when traditional planning tools suggested that it may have been on track. The market prediction proved correct. In the world of entertainment, Pennock, Lawrence, Giles and Nielsen (2001) show that the Hollywood Stock Exchange can usefully predict box office takes of films on their opening weekend and is about as accurate in picking Oscar winners as a panel of experts.

New markets in 'economic derivatives' also provide a useful contrast with expert opinion. Typically, in the run-up to the release of economic numbers such as inflation surveys, non-farm payrolls, retail trade and the Institute for Supply Management (ISM) purchasing managers' index, experts offer their opinions about what the numbers will be. These numbers are aggregated into a 'consensus forecast' and the market's reaction to the release of the economic numbers is often tied to whether, and by how much, the actual number differs from the consensus forecast. In table 18.2, we compare the performance of the consensus estimate with the results of the economic derivatives auctions, from their first year of operation.

Table 18.2. *Predicting economic outcomes comparing market-aggregated forecasts with consensus surveys, mean absolute error of forecasts*

	Non-farm payrolls (monthly change, 000)	Retail trade (ex-autos) (monthly change, %)	ISM manufacturing purchasing managers' index
Consensus estimate	71.1	0.45	1.10
Economic derivatives	72.2	0.46	1.07
Prediction market sample size	16	12	11

The consensus and market-based estimates of these economic indicators are extremely close – so close that there is no statistically (or economically) meaningful difference in forecast performance. This is true if one examines either correlations with actual outcomes or average forecast errors. That is, in this case the consensus estimate appears to aggregate expert opinion about as well as the prediction market. Even so, this early sample is sufficiently small that precise conclusions are difficult to draw.

18.6 Using prediction markets in decision making

We know we can use prediction markets to make accurate assessments about uncertain future events. We now turn to how to use these predictions to better inform decision making.

The simplest approach is to just use the predictions directly. For instance, in their experiments at Hewlett Packard, Chen and Plott (2002) elicited expectations of future printer sales through a market in which employees bet against each other. These expectations are likely of direct interest for internal planning purposes.

Researchers have also tried to link the time series progression of prediction markets with other variables in order to find the correlation between the two. For instance, prior to the 2004 election, several analysts tried to find a link between the probability of George W. Bush's re-election and the price of the S&P 500. The result is a strong positive correlation between an increase in Bush's chance of re-election and the health of the stock market. While this has been trumpeted as evidence that Bush would be better for the economy than Kerry, this provides a very clear case where correlation does not imply causation. It is just as likely that a strong economy would increase the chances of Bush's re-election as the other way around.

Two further elements are required for a regression analysis to be feasible: (1) time series variation in event probabilities, and (2) a sufficiently strong correlation to allow one to distinguish the relationship from other events affecting the probabilities. By using a slightly different set of contracts, however, it is possible to estimate correlations even when these conditions are not satisfied. For example, we could sell two securities, one which pays $P a year from now if Bush is re-elected (where $P is the price of the S&P 500 a year from now) and the purchase price is refunded if Kerry is elected, and a second that pays $P if Kerry is elected, with the purchase price is refunded if he is not. The difference would be the market's expectation of the relationship between the election of Bush or Kerry and the S&P 500. Of course, while these securities form a contingent market – one that allows us to gauge the market's expectation of one event contingent on another event occurring – they do not resolve the issue of whether this correlation reflects a causal relationship.

Very few contingent markets have been constructed, but they are growing in popularity. In 2004 the IEM offered securities linked both to the two-party vote share of each Democratic candidate and the vote share of Bush if he were to face that particular candidate. These contracts pay nothing if that particular match-up does not occur. These securities can be used to infer the probability that a given Democrat wins the primary, as well as the expected two-party vote share if s/he were to win the nomination. The prices and calculations from two days before the Iowa Caucus appear in table 18.3.

Column (A) shows the price of a contract that pays the Democratic vote share in the general election; the bettor must also pick the Democratic nominee, or the security pays nothing. Column (B) shows the price of a contract that pays Bush's vote share, if the bettor also correctly picks the Democratic nominee and nothing otherwise. The prices thus reflect the market's assessment of both the chance of the candidate winning the Democratic nomination and the share of the vote he would take against Bush.

No matter who the candidate is, the expected Democratic and Republican shares of the two-party vote must sum to one. Thus, adding the prices of the securities shown in columns (A) and (B) yields the probability that each candidate wins the Democratic nomination (shown in column (C)).

A more interesting statistic would be the market's expectation of how each candidate would fare versus Bush if they win the nomination. As suggested by Robin Hanson (1999), this number could then be used to inform the nomination decision of the Democrats, as they presumably would like to nominate someone with a good chance of winning the general election. The calculation is done in column (D). This logic suggests that

Table 18.3. *Contingent markets*

Candidate	Candidate vote-share (A) ($)	Bush vote-share given this candidate (B) ($)	Prob. this candidate wins nomination (C) = (A) ÷ (B) (%)	Expected vote-share if nominated (D) = (A)/(C) (%)
Howard Dean	0.289	0.245	53.4	45.9
Wesley Clark	0.101	0.102	20.3	50.2
Richard Gephardt	0.017	0.019	3.6	52.8
John Kerry	0.062	0.067	12.9	51.9
Other Democrats[a]	0.042	0.049	9.1	53.8

Note:
[a] By this date, 'Other Democrats' was more or less the same as John Edwards. Edwards did not have a security tied to him until four days after the Iowa caucuses.
Source: Closing prices, 17 January 2004, IEM.

they should choose Edwards or Kerry as the nominees (Gephardt was already largely out of the running). This implication has led these contingent contracts to sometimes be called 'decision markets'.

We are optimistic that contingent contracts can be used to inform decision making; however, some care must be taken when doing so. There are many plausible stories one could come up with for the reason why the Kerry security is trading higher than Bush|Kerry. For instance, the markets may believe that Kerry won't win the nomination unless the country makes a dramatic shift to the left, but that if this does happen it is likely that Kerry will win both the nomination and the election. Simply nominating Kerry based on these contingent contracts would then be a mistake, since it will not make the country swing to the left, and Kerry would thus be more likely to lose the general election than, say, Edwards.

Irrespective of such issues, the predictions based on these contingent contracts seem to be consistent with subsequent events. On 19 January 2004, Howard Dean lost the Iowa Caucus in spectacular fashion, and that evening self-destructed as he uttered the now infamous 'Dean Scream'. His likelihood of winning the Democratic nomination tumbled from 53.4 per cent to 24.5 per cent by the end of that night. John Kerry, who won that day, saw his probability rise from 12.9 per cent to 25.8 per cent while John

Edwards, who came second, saw his rise from 9.1 per cent to 22 per cent. These candidates were predicted to fare much better against Bush, and accordingly, Bush's expected share of the two-party vote fell – from 52.1 per cent the night before the Iowa caucuses to 48.5 per cent the night after. (In an analogous example, Berg and Rietz, 2003, found that as it became clear in 1996 that Bob Dole would win the Republican primary, Bill Clinton's re-election chances soared.)

We also have preliminary results from an experimental contingent contract we ran on TradeSports. This experimental security paid $1 if both Bush were re-elected and Osama bin Laden were captured by the election. It seems likely that bin Laden's capture would have a positive effect on Bush's re-election chances, and the markets agree. In mid-June a contract on Bush's re-election was trading at $57 and an implicit contract on bin Laden being captured by 2 November was trading at around $27. The joint contract requiring both events to occur was trading for approximately $21. Using the prices and method above, this tells us that the market assessed the probability of Bush winning if bin Laden were captured at 77 per cent. It also tells us that the market thought that the chance of Bush being re-elected if bin Laden were not captured was 50 per cent.[4]

A cleaner example of the difficulty of untangling correlation and causality comes from a second contract we ran on TradeSports. This contract paid $1 if Bush won the 2004 election and the terror alert on election day was at its peak level of 'red'. The market put the probability of this occurring at 8.0 per cent, and the probability of red alert on 1 November (the day before the election) at 8.2 per cent. Using these two numbers, we infer that the market believes if the terror alert level is at 'red' then Bush has a 97 per cent chance of winning the election. This estimate seems rather high. There is probably some imprecision due to the problem of miscalibration of small-probability events and the small amount of trading in this market.

If we take this estimate at face value, however, we are confronted with another problem. One explanation might be that the increased threat of terrorism would cause Americans to rally around Bush and re-elect him. However, recall that in Spain in early 2004 a terrorist attack caused the incumbent party to lose the election. If terrorists think a similar thing might happen in the US, we might be tempted to infer that the market believes that if Bush looks strong in the election, this may increase the threat of a terror attack, raising the alert level.

If we were to pass an econometrician data on the likelihood of Bush winning the election and the terror alert level in many states of the world, the econometrician would note a strong correlation between Bush winning and an elevated terror alert level. However, she would not declare a causal relationship between the two. Instead, she would note that there are 'selection effects' – that is, the states of the world in which the country is on red alert are not random.

Just as an econometrician uses a selection model to correct for selection bias (Heckman, 1979) one can simply add another security or contingency tied to a variable that is driving the terror alert level (such as reports of terrorist activity overseas). If the probability of a certain contingency is high, then only stories that include it are plausible explanations of what will cause a 'red' alert. However, this eliminates scenarios only in a piecemeal fashion, and to the extent that there are an infinite number of possible scenarios involving an infinite number of variables, not all of which are observable, it will never be possible to absolutely pin down causation.

The preceding paragraphs may make it sound as if there are extreme difficulties with prediction markets that make their use in this domain hopeless. However, the difficulties here are no different than those in any other econometric situation. These issues should be the topic of further research and application. In the meantime, simple prediction markets continue to be extremely useful for estimating the market's expectation of moments or distributions – even multivariate ones.

18.7 Looking forward

This chapter has focused jointly on the promise and the limitations of prediction markets. While these markets manifest the pathologies of all financial markets more deeply, it is important to keep in mind that they also outperform many other prediction tools, often at lower cost. One's optimism about the further use of prediction markets in business, government and finance depends a lot on what sorts of mechanisms for prediction one is comparing the market-generated prices with.

Furthermore, there is a broad pool of research into more common financial markets that has not yet been applied to these markets. Currently the level of sophistication of prediction markets in practice is such that they can be understood using very basic financial tools and rules of thumb. As these markets prove themselves and become better capitalised there will be an incentive to apply more advanced methodologies to their execution. This in turn will lead to more effective and efficient markets that will embody fewer of the problems we have outlined and allow for true hedging against geopolitical and other risks.

We have also focused on an emerging, more complex form of markets that try to predict the probability of multiple events happening simultaneously. These contingent contracts, or 'decision markets', can be used in conjunction with simpler securities to tease out the market's perception of factors important to public decisions. As we note, there are difficulties in separating correlation from causality but, carefully applied, we believe that there are domains in which these markets will be useful public policy inputs.

Prediction markets are, at their core, a tool for deriving consensus estimates and assessments from a diverse body of people and opinions. To the extent that there exist questions that are important enough to generate interest, and thus liquidity, prediction markets may be used to replace or augment more primitive technologies such as frequent meetings or arbitrary algorithms.

Notes

The authors would like to thank David Pennock, Emile Servan-Schreiber of NewsFutures, David Dempsey and John Delaney of TradeSports, David Siegel and Scott Hereld of Trackmaster and George Neumann of IEM for help with data. Thanks to Kay-Yut Chen, Andrew Leigh, Rohan Wolfers, Betsey Stevenson, Tim Taylor, Hal Varian and Craig Yee for stimulating discussions. Brett Danaher, Doug Geyser, Chris Lion, Paul Reist and Ravi Pillai provided outstanding research assistance. Justin Wolfers would like to acknowledge the financial support of the Hirtle, Callaghan & Co. – Arthur D. Miltenberger Research Fellowship.

1 The price of a winner-take-all security is essentially a state price, which will equal an estimate of the event's probability under the assumption of risk-neutrality. The sums wagered in prediction markets are typically small enough that assuming that investors are not averse to the idiosyncratic risk involved seems reasonable. But if the event in question is correlated with investors' marginal utility of wealth, then probabilities and state prices can differ. In what follows, we leave this issue aside and use the term 'probability' to refer to risk-neutral probability. For more on this topic, see Wolfers and Zitzewitz (2005).

2 There is a subtle, an almost metaphysical question here: What is the 'market's' expectation anyway? Throughout, we will speak as though the market is itself a representative person, and that 'person' has a set of expectations. Consequently there are important but subtle differences between parameters such as the market's median expectation and the median expectation of market participants.

3 Rhode and Strumpf (2004) investigate turn-of-the-twentieth-century markets that were used to predict the outcomes of presidential elections. If you see sports gambling as a rudimentary form of prediction markets, then obviously prediction markets are quite a bit older.

4 This last figure can be calculated by Bayes' Rule: $(57-21)/(100-27) \approx 50$ per cent.

References

Aït-Sahalia, Yacine, Wang, Yubo and Yared, Francis (2001) 'Do Options Markets Correctly Price the Probabilities of Movement of the Underlying Asset?', *Journal of Econometrics*, 102, pp. 67–110

Athanasoulis, Stefano, Shiller, Robert and van Wincoop, Eric (1999) 'Macro Markets and Financial Security', *Economic Policy Review*, 5, pp. 21–39

Berg, Joyce, Forsythe, Robert, Nelson, Forrest and Rietz, Thomas (2001) 'Results from a Dozen Years of Election Futures Markets Research', in Charles Plott and Vernon Smith (eds.), *Handbook of Experimental Economic Results*, New York: Elsevier Science

Berg, Joyce and Rietz, Thomas (2003) 'Prediction Markets as Decision Support Systems', *Information Systems Frontiers*, 5(1), pp. 79–93

Camerer, Colin (1998) 'Can Asset Markets be Manipulated? A Field Experiment with Racetrack Betting', *Journal of Political Economy*, 106(3), pp. 457–82

Chen, Kay-Yut and Plott, Charles (2002) 'Information Aggregation Mechanisms: Concept, Design and Field Implementation for a Sales Forecasting Problem', Social Science Working paper, 1131, Pasadena: California Institute of Technology

Hanson, Robin (1999) 'Decision Markets', *IEEE Intelligent Systems*, 14(3), pp. 16–19

Heckman, James J. (1979) 'Sample Selection Bias as a Specification Error', *Econometrica*, 47(1), pp. 153–61

Leigh, Andrew, Wolfers, Justin and Zitzewitz, Eric (2003) 'What do Financial Markets Think of War in Iraq?', NBER Working Paper, 9587

Manski, Charles (2004) 'Interpreting the Predictions of Prediction Markets', NBER Working Paper, 10359, March

Ortner, Gerhard (1998) 'Forecasting Markets – An Industrial Application', Technical University of Vienna, mimeo

Pennock, David, Lawrence, Steve, Giles, C. Lee and Nielsen, Finn Arup (2001) 'The Real Power of Artificial Markets', *Science*, 291, pp. 987–8

Rhode, Paul and Strumpf, Koleman (2004) 'Historical Prediction Markets: Wagering on Presidential Elections', *Journal of Economic Perspectives*, 18(2), pp. 127–42

Servan-Schreiber, Emile, Wolfers, Justin, Pennock, David and Galebach, Brian (2004) 'Prediction Markets: Does Money Matter?', *Electronic Markets*, 14(3), pp. 243–51

Shiller, Robert (2003) *The New Financial Order: Risk in the Twenty-First Century*, Princeton: Princeton University Press

Snowberg, Erik and Wolfers, Justin (2004) 'Understanding the Favorite-Longshot Bias: Risk Preferences versus Misperceptions', University of Pennsylvania, mimeo

Strumpf, Koleman (2004) 'Manipulating the Iowa Political Stock Market', University of North Carolina, mimeo

Tetlock, Paul (2004) 'How Efficient are Information Markets? Evidence from an Online Exchange', University of Texas at Austin, mimeo

Wolfers, Justin and Andrew, Leigh (2002) 'Three Tools for Forecasting Federal Elections: Lessons from 2001', *Australian Journal of Political Science*, 37(2), pp. 223–40

Wolfers, Justin and Zitzewitz, Eric (2004) 'Prediction Markets', *Journal of Economic Perspectives*, 18(2), pp. 107–26

(2005) 'Interpreting Prediction Market Prices as Probabilities', University of Pennsylvania, mimeo

Index